THE
Minor Arts
OF
Daily Life

Map of Taiwan

THE Minor Arts OF Daily Life

POPULAR CULTURE IN TAIWAN

EDITED BY
**David K. Jordan,
Andrew D. Morris,**
AND
Marc L. Moskowitz

University of Hawai'i Press
HONOLULU

5. Taiwan's Mass-Mediated Crisis Discourse   89
Pop Politics in an Era of Political TV Call-in Shows
ALICE R. CHU

PART IV   **Economic Life**
           MONEY AND MEANING

6. The Other Woman in Your Home   111
Social and Racial Discourses
on "Foreign Maids" in Taiwan
CHIN-JU LIN

7. Hot and Noisy   129
Taiwan's Night Market Culture
SHUENN-DER YU

8. Disciplined Bodies in Direct Selling   150
Amway and Alternative Economic Culture in Taiwan
CHIEN-JUH GU

PART V   **Entertainment and the Audience**
           LIVING FOR THE MOMENT AND MOMENTS FOR THE LIVING

**9. Baseball, History,
the Local and the Global in Taiwan**   175
ANDREW D. MORRIS

10. Yang-Sucking She-Demons   204
Penetration, Fear of Castration, and
Other Freudian Angst in Modern Chinese Cinema
MARC L. MOSKOWITZ

Notes   219

Glossary of Terms and Abbreviations   237

Glossary of Characters   241

References   247

Contributors   269

Index   271

THE Minor Arts OF Daily Life

POPULAR CULTURE IN TAIWAN

EDITED BY
**David K. Jordan,
Andrew D. Morris,**
AND
Marc L. Moskowitz

University of Hawai'i Press
HONOLULU

© 2004 University of Hawai'i Press
All rights reserved
Printed in the United States of America
09 08 07 06 05 04   6 5 4 3 2 1

Library of Congress Cataloging-in-Publication Data
The minor arts of daily life : popular culture in Taiwan /
edited by David K. Jordan, Andrew D. Morris,
and Marc L. Moskowitz.
    p. cm.
Includes bibliographical references and index.
ISBN 0-8248-2737-6 (alk. paper)—
ISBN 0-8248-2800-3 (pbk. : alk. paper)
    1. Taiwan—Social conditions—1988– 2. Popular culture—Taiwan.
I. Jordan, David K. II. Morris, Andrew D. III. Moskowitz, Marc L.
HN747.5 .M56 2004
306'.095124'9—dc22
                            2003015330

University of Hawai'i Press books are printed on acid-free
paper and meet the guidelines for permanence and durability
of the Council on Library Resources.

Designed by Kaelin Chappell

Printed by The Maple-Vail Book Manufacturing Group

Contents

Preface ... vii

PART I **Background**
A HISTORY TROUBLED AND GLORIOUS

1. **Taiwan's History** ... 3
   An Introduction
   ANDREW D. MORRIS

PART II **Religion and Ritual**
THE CELEBRATION OF BELIEF AND DOUBT

2. **Fowl Play** ... 35
   Chicken-Beheading Rituals and
   Dispute Resolution in Taiwan
   PAUL R. KATZ

3. **Pop in Hell** ... 50
   Chinese Representations of Purgatory in Taiwan
   DAVID K. JORDAN

PART III **An Emerging Public Sphere**
SAYING NOW WHAT COULD NOT BE SAID BEFORE

4. **From Hidden Kingdom to Rainbow Community** ... 67
   The Making of Gay and Lesbian Identity in Taiwan
   SCOTT SIMON

5. Taiwan's Mass-Mediated Crisis Discourse   89
Pop Politics in an Era of Political TV Call-in Shows
ALICE R. CHU

PART IV **Economic Life**
MONEY AND MEANING

6. The Other Woman in Your Home   111
Social and Racial Discourses
on "Foreign Maids" in Taiwan
CHIN-JU LIN

7. Hot and Noisy   129
Taiwan's Night Market Culture
SHUENN-DER YU

8. Disciplined Bodies in Direct Selling   150
Amway and Alternative Economic Culture in Taiwan
CHIEN-JUH GU

PART V **Entertainment and the Audience**
LIVING FOR THE MOMENT AND MOMENTS FOR THE LIVING

9. Baseball, History, the Local and the Global in Taiwan   175
ANDREW D. MORRIS

10. Yang-Sucking She-Demons   204
Penetration, Fear of Castration, and
Other Freudian Angst in Modern Chinese Cinema
MARC L. MOSKOWITZ

Notes   219

Glossary of Terms and Abbreviations   237

Glossary of Characters   241

References   247

Contributors   269

Index   271

Preface

Taiwan is often described as a Chinese island. In many ways this is a fair enough description; the population of Taiwan is made up overwhelmingly of speakers of Chinese, and Taiwan's culture is intimately related in many ways to the culture of the mainland's southeastern Fujian Province. However, it is important to note one major way in which it is not "Chinese": during the last 109 years, Taiwan has been ruled by the ruling government of China for a total of four years. For the remaining 105 years, it has been ruled by regimes Japanese, Chinese, and Taiwanese that have not controlled the Chinese mainland. This century-plus of independent development has not made Taiwan "non-Chinese" so much as "culturally Chinese, but with a difference."

For these reasons, the scholar or student who wants to study China must also understand Taiwan. And while the Chinese mainland has been closed to free research by foreign scholars for much of the past half century, Taiwan has provided an open environment for research and has generated an enormous body of English-language literature on topics for which there is no comparable research for mainland China.

Clearly, despite the fact that it is often overshadowed by its giant neighbor, the People's Republic of China, Taiwan is worthy of a study on its own account. One of the twentieth century's most startling examples of economic success—and of the triumph of democracy over totalitarianism—Taiwan is also a shining example of intellectual productivity and artistic creativity.

This book is an account of some of the many ways that people in modern Taiwan approach daily life. It is, of course, not exhaustive. That would not be possible. Our goal has been to touch a wide range of different aspects of everyday life and to convey something of the world as people in Taiwan experience it. What is happiness? Who matters? What does it mean to be Taiwanese?

The intended audience is North American college students, and for this reason we have deliberately tended to avoid technical jargon and have taken pains to outline our theoretical points in a clear way that should be easy to understand. Our authors are from a range of disciplines and approach their topics in many ways, including, in some cases, open advocacy and direct condemnation. We hope that this will keep the readings interesting, but also that it will facilitate different kinds of classroom discussions—not just about Taiwan, but also about how to study broad cultural themes in a large population. Recognizing that many American college students study Chinese, we have included Chinese characters in a table at the end for many of the terms mentioned in the text.

The book begins with a history of Taiwan and then moves directly to essays on highly specific topics, each with brief introductory remarks by the volume editors, which are intended to summarize some of the main points. We recommend that instructors assign the historical chapter first, since it provides useful background for the rest. Other chapters can be assigned according to the instructor's preference.

We wish to express our deepest appreciation to Hsin-yi Lu and Murray Rubinstein for their thoughtful comments on an earlier version of this work. They provided us with valuable insights that greatly improved the book overall. Thanks also to Patricia Crosby of the University of Hawai'i Press, who, as always, was a model of efficiency and good cheer. We also wish to express our appreciation to our students for their helpful reactions and comments on material in this volume.

PART I
Background
A HISTORY TROUBLED
AND GLORIOUS

1

Taiwan's History
An Introduction
Andrew D. Morris

EDITORS' INTRODUCTION

Nothing happens that is not at least in part a result of what has gone before, and so we start this volume with a brief account of Taiwan by historian Andrew D. Morris.

This chapter is not the whole story. That would take many volumes. It is not the only perspective. There are many voices that deserve to be heard. It is not final. Much is yet to be discovered about the past just as about the present. But it can serve as an orientation to the subject and as a background to the other chapters in this volume.

Briefly, Taiwan is located off the coast of southeastern China, between the Philippines and Japan. Taiwan has the highest mountains east of Tibet, with a water runoff that could power all of Asia if it were used to power generators on a rainy day. Most people live in the small areas that are comparatively flat—principally the western plain formed over the millennia by mud washed down from the mountains.

The island's aboriginal Austronesian population is closely related to the peoples of the Philippines. About four hundred years ago, increasing numbers of Chinese began moving across the Taiwan Strait from Fujian Province and settling in Taiwan. Their origins varied slightly, and their squabbling over land rights and other issues in Taiwan often led them to seek alliances with people from the same places of origin to conduct petty local wars with other settlers, as the earlier non-Chinese population took refuge in ever-higher mountainous areas.

The dawn of centralized Qing administration of the island came in 1683, and in 1885 it was granted provincial status under the Qing dynasty. The two centuries between those dates were characterized by increasing population, settled farming, frequent plagues, occasional uprisings, and almost constant feuding and petty wars among ethnic groups and local interests. The whole island was a wild and woolly frontier, and no magistrate was enthusiastic about representing the imperial government in this remote and unruly region. Today every part of the island can produce accounts—not always true but always interesting—of the tragedy of its plagues or the nobility of its local militia or the intervention of its local gods during the imperial period.

In 1895, less than ten years after it was made a province, Taiwan was abruptly ceded by the Qing emperor to Meiji Japan. For the Japanese, this introduced the sudden responsibility to administer a subject population. For the Taiwanese, it was more than a change of government. It meant subjugation to a new and inexperienced colonial administration, speaking a foreign language, the imposition of foreign ways, and Japan's determination to convert the whole populace from being Chinese to Japanese.

The colonial record of Japan in Taiwan is mixed. In retrospect, and with our current distaste for colonialism, it is easy to be critical. It is also easy to forget that the political situation in Japan between 1895 and the end of World War II was rapidly evolving, and so colonial policy toward Taiwan also varied. Quite possibly, no two Japanese ever agreed on what the empire's "steady-state" relationship with Taiwan should be. But for better and for worse, Japanese possession of Taiwan—for an even fifty years—comprises part of the island's history and part of its identity. Industrial and commercial development during this period clearly provided the basis for the prosperity that was to follow.

Events in the rest of China were not static during those fifty years. Rebels threatened the imperial government at the end of the nineteenth century in the famous and bloody Boxer Rebellion, suppressed only with the help of European powers in 1900. Taiwan was untouched by this uprising because it was under Japanese administration.

In 1911 the dynasty was overthrown and in 1912 a new Republic of China was established, headed by the Nationalist Party, also known as the KMT (Kuomintang) or GMD (Guomindang). But the KMT government was so weak that some areas it claimed to control never in fact passed under its effective administration. The revolution was not without bloodshed, and local warlords ravaged the countryside in some areas. Taiwan again escaped the turmoil, for it was part of Japan.

In 1937, Japan—increasingly falling under the control of extremist military factions—invaded China, seizing much of the Eastern part of the country and imposing a brutal administration that lasted until the end of World War II in 1945. Taiwan, already long under Japanese administration, was once again sheltered from the suffering inflicted upon the mainland. In 1945, with the defeat of Japan by the allied forces, Taiwan was turned over to the Republic of China, a government unknown to the people of Taiwan—and one scornful and suspicious of them as "Japanese collaborators."

From 1945 to 1949, the government of the republic was engaged in a vicious civil war with forces of the Communist Party. The Communists prevailed and established a new People's Republic of China. The government of the Republic of China lost control of all of China—all, that is, except Taiwan, the island it had so recently acquired and so scorned. The organs of government were hastily moved to Taibei, in northern Taiwan, which was identified as the "provisional capital" of the Republic of China during the "temporary period" of Communist rebellion.

With the chaos and change of regime on the mainland, there arrived in Taiwan about a million refugees: soldiers, teachers, merchants, bureaucrats, policemen, the good, the bad, the vicious, and the innocent, thrown in confusion upon the unwilling hospitality of a population that had not long before been briefly granted Japanese citizenship.

In this chapter, Morris recounts all these events and the remarkable challenges, contradictions, tribulations, heroism, and sometimes comic ironies that were involved.

In the midst of the civil war on the mainland, on February 28, 1947, tensions in Taiwan boiled over in a riot which, within days, led to a government-sponsored massacre. The die was now cast for an enduring Taiwanese hostility to mainland immigrants and "their" KMT government. The date 2/28, or "228," was destined to live forever in the Taiwanese imagination as the formative moment in the emergence of a post-Japanese identity of Taiwanese as not really being Chinese after all. For if Chinese could do what the KMT did on 228, Taiwan wanted no part of it.

A state of martial law prevailed on the island until 1987. It is easy to imagine the period of martial law as darker than it was. Babies still giggled, children still laughed, and the sun continued to shine. Economic progress was so rapid that even severe critics conceded that it was almost a miracle. But criticism of the KMT or of the goal of retaking the mainland for the Republic of China was not tolerated. When martial law was lifted, a new era of openness and of open criticism of KMT abuses dawned. Taiwan, with a population now over 22 million—more than three times what it was in 1945—had at last became a democratic state.

Today the distinction between "Taiwanese" and "mainland immigrants" has been much muted with the passing of half a century since the fall of the KMT on the mainland. But many aspects of life are affected by the history of mainlander-Taiwanese relations. Meanwhile, the Communist government on the mainland has continued to insist that, as the successor to the Republic of China on the mainland, it is the only legal and legitimate government of Taiwan. The mainland, with nearly sixty times the population of Taiwan, has easily persuaded nearly all the nations of the world to conform, at least nominally, to this view. Recognition of the government of the Republic of China—Taiwan's current democratic government—brings the withdrawal of diplomatic relations from China. Few countries support Taiwan's claims to its legitimate independence under that threat.

Thus Taiwan today faces two dominant and inescapable dilemmas that are reflected through its cultural institutions. One is the question of how united its population is. Are the people of Taiwan all really Taiwanese, or are they all different, as history would seem to indicate? The other is the question of whether in the future (perhaps next week) Taiwan will abruptly become a province of the Communist state across the straits—once again a part of China. Within these ambiguities and under this threat, the people of the island go about their daily affairs, making themselves a remarkable font of creativity and cultural innovation.

The essays in this volume all relate in one way or another to this anxious situation, for it is the overwhelming reality of life in Taiwan today. In this introductory chapter, Morris provides the critical background that is so ready and real in all that Taiwanese do in daily life. ∎

> Long, long ago
> For generations on this piece of land
> Where no wealth or prosperity grows
> Where no miracles are ever produced
> My ancestors wiped away their sweat
> And brought forth their fated children.
>
> Wu Sheng, preface to *Vignettes of My Village*

Land of the Eastern Barbarians[1] (Yizhou), Little Ryukyu (Lequeo Pequeno, Xiao Liuqiu), Little Eastern Island (Xiao dong dao), Beautiful Island (Ilha Formosa), Land of the High Mountain People (Gaoshanguo), gateway to Chinese commerce, place of banishment, solitary island, stone pointing at the south, first Asian republic, colonial laboratory, the Orphan of Asia, rebel province, Free China, unsinkable aircraft carrier, "Chinese Taipei," Republic of China on Taiwan, Austronesian homeland, and green silicon island—these are just some of the terms that have been used to describe Taiwan over the last several centuries.[2]

Clearly, the nationalist slogan of the 1980s and 1990s that Taiwan is "just Taiwan" is far too simplistic to be true. At the same time, its absolute converse—that Taiwan "has always been an inseparable part of the Chinese mainland"—is several dimensions farther removed from reality. Over the last several centuries, Taiwan has been home to or served as the subject of expansionist desires of far too many peoples and nations—native Austronesian, Chinese, Dutch, Spanish, Manchu, British, German, French, American, Japanese, and Taiwanese—for its history to be summed up in either of these naïve fashions. This introductory essay on the history of Taiwan is meant to provide perspective on the diverse and eventful history that the people of this island state have inherited and made.

THE SETTING

Taiwan is a mountainous island 245 miles (394 km) long by 90 miles (144 km) at its widest. It is shaped from north to south, depending on the taste of the beholder, like a tobacco leaf or a sweet potato—or even a whale. The island, the southern third of which is below the Tropic of Cancer, is separated from the coast of southeastern China by the deadly, rough, and shallow waters of the Taiwan Straits, some 81 to 137 miles (130–220 km) wide. About 70 miles (113 km) east of Taiwan lies Yonaguni-jima, the southwesternmost of the Sakishima Islands of Japan, and some 50 miles (80 km) to the south across the Bashi Channel lie the Batan Islands, the northernmost of the Philippine Islands. While Taiwan shares the continental shelf with China, it is part of the same island system as Japan.

With a total area of some 13,836 square miles (35,834 km^2), Taiwan is slightly larger than Belgium or Maryland, half the size of Panama or West Virginia, or about one-twelfth the size of California. Its present population of 22.3 million makes Taiwan one of the most densely populated nations on earth.

EARLIEST INHABITANTS

Taiwan's original inhabitants—thought by some to have migrated from the Indonesian and Philippine archipelagos and by others to have come from southeastern China—have been divided into fourteen groups of lowland peoples and nine groups of mountain peoples (Stainton 1999b, 29–41; Wang 1980, 32). The first settlements of these groups, speakers of the earliest known Austronesian languages, date back at least fifteen thousand years. Their descendants today number some four hundred thousand, about 2 percent of Taiwan's population. They are known as aborigines *(yuanzhumin),* and they have suffered repeated discrimination by various colonizing powers in Taiwan.

The date of the earliest Chinese travel and migration to Taiwan is also the subject of great political debate. For decades, Chinese Nationalists have used vague references to the Land of Eastern Barbarians or the Ryukyu Islands in the *History of the Later Han dynasty* (25–220 C.E.) or the *History of the Three Kingdoms* (mid-third century C.E.) in an effort to prove that Taiwan has always been part of a timeless Chinese "motherland" (Fang 1994, 13–20). To assume, however, some intimate China-Taiwan relationship through the millennia would be wrong. Jack Wills has more accurately shown that even in 1600, Taiwan still "was on the outer edge of Chinese consciousness and activity" (Wills 1999, 85). Four centuries ago there was no permanent Chinese settlement on (or name for) Taiwan, although by that time there were Chinese and Japanese traders, fishermen, and pirates willing to brave the malarial fever that claimed the lives of so many visitors there. In 1603, the scholar Chen Di spent twenty-two days in Taiwan before publishing his *Record of the Eastern Savages (Dongfan ji),* marveling at their backward ways: "To this day they have no calendrical system, nor any writing system and they do not feel the lack. Is that not strange?"[3] (Teng 1999, 445–450)

As would become a pattern in the island's history, Chinese interest and settlement in Taiwan picked up only with the presence of other foreign powers in the Taiwan Straits—in this case, the Dutch. Hoping to obtain a foothold in the lucrative China trade, the Dutch failed to gain trading posts in southeastern China. Ming dynasty officials pushed these pesky and dangerous traders farther east to an island not considered imperial territory but known to early seventeenth-century Chinese officials as Taiyuan, Dayuan, Taiwan, or Dawan (Nakamura 1954, 114).[4] The Dutch knew this island as Ilha Formosa, as it had been named by passing Portuguese sailors in the 1540s, and they set up their China trading operations there.

When they arrived in southern Taiwan in 1622, Dutch East India Company agents estimated populations of a thousand Chinese sojourners and traders and some seventy thousand plains aborigines on the western Taiwan coast (Wills 1999, 87–88; Hauptman and Knapp 1977, 175). After several tough years fighting Chinese and Japanese pirates and competitors, native and Chinese revolts on Taiwan, and Spanish forces from Manila colonizing the northern tip of Taiwan, in 1636 the Dutch colonial administration began farming land out to Chinese sojourners in order to acquire a more consistent food supply and regular tax revenue. By 1650, some twenty-five thousand Chinese had come to the Dutch colony to grow and sell rice, vegetables, sugarcane, and indigo, as well as to fish and hunt, during the three years that Chinese law allowed them to reside abroad. While some fled to Taiwan to escape the destruction of the Ming-Qing dynastic transition, others set sail on Dutch ships to Taiwan, attracted by Dutch promises of oxen, tools, and seeds for Chinese pioneer farm labor (van Veen 1996, 65–67).

At its largest, the Dutch population in Taiwan was a mere twenty-eight hundred, of whom some twenty-two hundred were soldiers. These vulnerable numbers required colonial forces to spend most of their income on fortifications, and their worst fears were realized in 1652. In an event later immortalized as the first Chinese "anti-Western uprising" in history, some fifteen thousand Chinese settlers armed with sharpened bamboo set out to "kill the Dutch dogs" at Fort Zeelandia. The Dutch recruited some two thousand Austronesian natives to aid in suppressing the revolt (Hsu 1980a, 15; van Veen 1996, 65–67, 71).

But the Dutch days on the Beautiful Island were numbered. Their presence on Taiwan forced the outgoing Ming dynasty and the new Manchu Qing to pay more attention to the island. Only under the Qing in the mid-seventeenth century was the name "Taiwan" officially adopted to refer to the whole island (Nakamura 1954, 114). It was in the context of this new Chinese consciousness of Taiwan that Zheng Chenggong (Koxinga) sought to make the island the base of his movement to overthrow the newly founded Qing dynasty in the name of restoring the vanquished Ming.

THE CHINESE/MANCHU PRESENCE ON TAIWAN

In 1661, after fighting Manchu Qing forces for more than a decade, Zheng's fleet of two hundred ships and twenty-five thousand men set sail from the southeastern Chinese coast for Taiwan. By this time, the number of Chinese settled in Taiwan had reached some fifty thousand. This large fifth column was twenty times larger than the entire Dutch occupation force, and it made Zheng's conquest easy. Zheng thus established the first Chinese administration of Taiwan—ironically, a regime formed in rebellion against China's ruling Qing. Zheng died four months later, but the easily appropriated elements of the story of this son of a Chinese pirate and a Japanese mother now dwarf the import of the twenty-one-year rule of his descendants on Taiwan. Diverse modern political forces in China and even Japan have sanctified Zheng for delivering Taiwan into Chinese hands for the first time—notwithstanding the myth that Taiwan had "always" been part of China. (Also ironic is the fact that before his sudden death, Zheng schemed to capture Luzon and the Philippines, suggesting a different goal than some consecrated mission of capturing Taiwan for Chinese posterity.)

The state administered by Zheng's son and grandson sought to expand land cultivation and transform the culture, economy, polity, and agriculture of Taiwan according to Chinese models. The regime provided thousands of soldiers with land and supplies, encouraged thousands more Chinese migrant farmers to open up new farmland, and established Chinese schools and Confucian temples in settler and native areas. These new migrants quickly made themselves at home, naming their new settlements after their hometowns in Fujian and Guangdong Provinces (Lin 1975, 5). Taiwan's position as a commercial center in maritime East Asia continued, as the Zheng regime pursued foreign policy according to trading needs. Formal relations were established with Japan, the Ryukyuan Kingdom, Vietnam, Thailand, the Philippines, and even England. The government was staffed largely with merchants from Fujian Province in China, another reason why one Taiwanese historian defines Zheng-era Taiwan simply as a "merchant nation" *(shangren guojia)* (Hsu 1980a, 25–27; Weng 1995).

During the Zheng period, the Chinese population, concentrated in the southwestern coastal plain, began to rival the numbers of Austronesian natives on Taiwan, doubling to roughly a hundred thousand after twenty-one years. Yet these numbers were of no aid when forces of the Manchu Qing dynasty, taking advantage of a famine on Taiwan, attacked in 1683. Koxinga's son Zheng Jing had hoped to negotiate independence from the Qing, promising to remain a loyal tributary state like Korea (Ren 1996, 85, 154). The Kangxi emperor, ruling that no ethnic Chinese state could exist separately from the dynasty, rejected this offer. This Kangxi Doctrine was formalized when the Qing navy took Taiwan by force. Qing conquest seems to have been inspired more by Manchu annoyance at this defiant Chinese island than by practical considerations. Immediately after taking this peripheral territory, Qing naval commander Shi Lang attempted to sell the island back to the Dutch, and other high Qing officials planned to abandon and evacuate it altogether (Wills 1999, 102; Shepherd 1999, 108). Finally—for reasons not of Chinese historical destiny but of the very practical wish to keep the island out of the hands of pesky foreigners—Taiwan was integrated into the empire in 1684 as a prefecture of Fujian Province.

Once the Qing made the decision to undertake formal administration of Taiwan, Shi's forces moved quickly to consolidate rule and assure Chinese and native populations of the new government's benevolent intentions. Yet Qing officials were perhaps more nervous about this new frontier possession than were its inhabitants; they feared that rebellions could erupt on this far-off island, led by Chinese immigrant farmers incited by pirates and Ming remnants or by native Austronesians frustrated and displaced by growing Chinese immigration. These concerns guided the first century of Qing administration in Taiwan, marked by regulation of Chinese immigration to the island and cautious respect for the natives' positions in the mountainous eastern half of the island.

Admiral Shi Lang quickly moved to send back to the mainland any sojourners in Taiwan with neither wife nor property (and thus seen as less accountable), and it is estimated that as much as half of the Chinese population departed by the end of 1684 (Shepherd 1993, 106). The Qing soon prohibited family migration to Taiwan, hoping that any population there would consist of seasonal migrant laborers only. This "agricultural colony" of Fujian Province (DeGlopper 1980, 143) had to be maintained by someone. Yet the promise that this "island frontier" (Shepherd 1999) offered Chinese pioneer farmers, combined with the growing population pressures in southeastern China, made it hard for the Qing to maintain tight immigration controls for long. Immigration continued, and in a few decades Taiwan became the rugged, disordered frontier that the Qing so feared. For the next 150 years, these young rootless men would make up as much as 30 percent of the Chinese population in Taiwan (Chen 1990, 111).

There was a popular pioneer proverb that expressed the unlikely hopes of fulfilling the domestic Taiwan dream: "Having a wife is better than having a god."[5] Far away from their homes and without family ties, these Chinese men turned to other forms of mutual support in religious societies and sworn brotherhoods among men of the same ancestral places and dialects (Hsu 1980b, 88–90). Yet, as was true throughout so much of Chinese history, there was an infinitesimally thin line between these societies' functions of mutual support and the mutual competition that emerged between these same groups. Disputes between these organizations on the rough frontier could easily erupt into violent communal strife *(fenlei xiedou)*—often between the three main settler groups, Hoklos from Quanzhou and Zhangzhou Prefectures in Fujian and the Hakkas from northeastern Guangdong—or into popular uprisings against the Qing state.

Qing officials annoyed by this malarial frontier joked, with black humor, that Taiwan produced "a minor revolt every three years, a major one every five years." This was no exaggeration. During the 212 years of Qing rule in Taiwan, 171 "disturbances among the people" *(minbian)* were recorded—including 68 anti-Qing revolts and 38 battles fought between migrants from rival home prefectures on the mainland (Chen 1987, 11–12; Hsu 1980b, 94; Lamley 1981).[6]

Maintenance of a peaceful frontier became one of the dynasty's main objectives. For lack of an imperial military presence to handle such matters properly, rebellions were typically put down by hiring Austronesian natives or rival settler groups to fight the rebels. During the 1721 Zhu Yigui Revolt, led by a precocious duck breeder committed to restoring the Ming dynasty, the Qing military paid native Austronesian warriors a piece rate for every rebel they could kill (Shepherd 1993, 147). The Qing also took more Confucian long-term measures to prevent the rebellions in the first place, providing generous scholarships to encourage more Taiwan residents to seek advancement via the imperial exam system rather than through rebellion and forgiving farmers their land taxes during droughts (209–213, 289).

Qing officials were also concerned about the Austronesian native population, which they divided into two groups: the plains "cooked savages" (*shufan*, literally "cooked," meaning matured by their exposure to the radiance of Chinese/Manchu culture), who were seen as more trustworthy than the exotic "raw savages" (*shengfan*) of the mountains. Qing officials feared, justifiably, an aboriginal "blowback"—that Chinese settlement in Taiwan could, by destroying Austronesian ways of life, force these aboriginal people to strike back against the settlers and the state. Accordingly, the first century of Qing rule in Taiwan was marked by coherent policies of protecting Austronesian land rights in the eastern half of Taiwan while hoping to acculturate these aboriginal peoples through the Confucian exam system and the spread of Chinese farming techniques (Shepherd 1993).

This level of attention to the remote Taiwan frontier was not maintained indefinitely, however. When the pressures of great population growth,[7] official corruption, and domestic unrest began to plague the proud Qing dynasty in the late 1700s, the administration of Taiwan was downgraded from an annoying but necessary responsibility to a nonpriority. For nearly a century, from the 1780s until the 1870s, Qing officials seemed in many ways to shut their eyes, hold their noses, cross their fingers, and hope that the officials judged to be "unfitted for responsible and administrative work" and corrupt troops stationed on this far-off island would be sufficient to maintain peace and regular rice shipments to Fujian (Davidson 1903, 100; Goddard 1966, 129).

This proved not to be the case, but this failure is not what revived the Qing commitment to Taiwan. As was true with the faltering Ming court more than two centuries before, it took a germinating imperialist interest—this time Japanese, British, French, American, and German—in the island to convince the Qing dynasty to renew its imperial title. In the 1850s–1870s, Qing sovereignty over Taiwan was openly challenged by American, British, Japanese, and German merchants and governments in several humiliating incidents, especially with respect to the Austronesian-populated eastern half of the island that the Qing admitted was "not yet entered in the maps" *(wei ji shouru bantu)* (Carrington 1977, 55–106; Chan 1973, 135–163; Gardella 1999, 167; Gordon 1976, 550–554; Huang 1986,

240–244; LeGendre 1874, 5). Domestic rebellions every few years were one thing, but repeated foreign incursions in Taiwan were another. In 1874 the Qing began considering how to strengthen their own claims to the island in order to halt these imperialist plans.

For the next two decades, and especially after a French invasion of Taiwan in 1884, the Qing sought to integrate Taiwan back into the empire after nearly a century of utter neglect (and to teach the foreigners a thing or two) by turning the island into a "foundation of national wealth and power" (Kuo 1973, 237). Upgraded in 1885 from a prefecture of Fujian Province to a province in its own right, Taiwan became the object of several modernizing reforms in military, industrial, educational, commercial, political, communications, and administrative spheres, particularly in the north. These reforms were as progressive as any in the empire, but the sudden influx of scholars and businessmen from the well-to-do central coast of China into the new capital at Taibei alienated many of the settlers who had done so much of the grunt work in recently reclaiming this northern part of the frontier (Chen 1956, 7; Lamley 1977, 201; Morris 2002, 5–8). This period also saw the abrupt reintegration of Taiwan into the world marketplace, as Taiwan's economy and society were quickly reordered to provide for the efficient export of tea (Taiwan's "green gold"), camphor and sugar, accompanied by the import of foreign cotton, wool, and opium (Gardella 1999, 171–176).

Yet even this work to establish a Qing dynasty presence over every inch of Taiwan could not prevent the interest of the eager imperialists of the Japanese military, who hoped to protect their nation from European and American expansion in Asia by expanding their influence in the same fashion as these Western powers. Many in China sensed this looming threat and made attempts to keep Taiwan out of Japanese hands. In 1894, Yung Wing, famed as the first Chinese graduate of an American university (Yale, 1854), proposed instead leasing Taiwan to a Western power at the price of $400 million for ninety-nine years (Yung 1909, 244).

The reckoning finally came in 1895, when Japan defeated the Qing in the Sino-Japanese War, started by the Japanese in 1894 over the weighty Chinese influence in Korea. In the Treaty of Shimonoseki, Japan demanded possession of Taiwan, along with an indemnity of 200 million ounces of silver and various industrial privileges in China. Li Hongzhang, the unfortunate Qing envoy entrusted with the Japanese negotiations, sought to save the island by trying to convince the Japanese of just how troublesome Taiwan could be, what with the malaria, the British opium pushers, and the dangerous rebels who rose up from time to time to kill officials. The strategy failed, however; his counterpart Itō Hirobumi merely answered, "We have not swallowed [Taiwan] yet and we are very hungry" (*NCH* 1895).

Eventually, the decision to trade Taiwan for an end to the war became an easy one for the Qing. The governor of Taiwan, Tang Jingsong, learned of the cession two days later in a simple telegram, in which the imperial court reminded him that "Taiwan is certainly important to us, but obviously not as important as Beijing . . . since Taiwan is all by itself out there in the ocean, we would not be able to help defend Taiwan anyway" (Lishi Jiaoxue 1954, 51). Forsaken by Beijing, the scholarly elite of Taibei formulated another strategy of avoiding colonization by the Japanese: an independent Taiwan, which could not be ceded legally by the Qing. These elites, with the reluctant cooperation of Governor Tang, founded the Taiwan Republic (with Tang as president) and issued the following statement: "The Qing court has not heard the mandate of the people; in ceding Taiwan they totally ignored our anger. . . . The public is full of grief and fury; a call for autonomy *[zizhu]* will arouse the people. . . . We must unite the people and gentry of Taiwan and establish a Taiwan Republic [Taiwan minzhuguo]. Together we will push forward a draft of a constitution, taking the good points of the American and French models. . . . This will be Asia's first republic" (Zheng 1981, 81).

In terms of international law, the Taiwan Republic's advent rendered meaningless the Treaty of Shimonoseki, which ceded the island (Chen and Reisman 1972, 633). Yet the legal status of Asia's first republic was no match for the military might of Asia's first modern imperialist power. By the end of 1895, any large-scale organized resistance was squashed, and the Japanese were able to purchase with special privileges and honors the cooperation of gentry leaders up and down the island in helping to suppress the local anti-Japanese guerrilla activities that would plague the new government for years (Lamley 1964, 215–225).

Many in Japan had supported the war with China as a way of proving Japan's new imperialist mettle, in order that "Japan could no longer be regarded as a mere Far Eastern park . . . [but] should now be reckoned with as a definite world power," but they had not seriously considered taking on any colonies in the process. After Taiwan fell into their laps, some Japanese officials even suggested the by now very unoriginal idea of selling the island to France for 100 million yen—an amount that would have been more than Japan's annual government expenditure (Chen 1977, 62, 71; Halliday 1975, 85). But for others in Japan, the conquest of this "stone pointing toward the south" was a first step in the "southern strategy" *(nanshin)* of establishing a Japanese presence throughout Southeast Asia—and their view won out. Another deciding factor was the "living space" argument. Many Japanese were overjoyed that their population, constrained for so many centuries by Japan's mountainous terrain, could now look to colonies like Taiwan (and soon Korea and Manchuria) as extra living space for a surplus Japanese population, which could then exploit the resources of the colonies to help feed the healthy, growing homeland (Peattie 1984, 89). It was for these reasons that, in just days, Taiwan went from being a model province of the Qing dynasty to Asia's first republic and then to the first colony of Asia's newest imperialist power.

JAPANESE COLONY

After taking command of Taiwan, the Japanese lost no time in transforming it and its people. This newest symbol of Japan's imperial power could not continue to look the way it had under what the Japanese saw as the obsolescence and decay of Chinese culture. This "laboratory," as Civil Administrator Gotō Shimpei saw Taiwan, would be the perfect site to test the most modern theories of colonialism and showcase the brilliance of Japanese modernity. Two official doctrines of Japanese colonialism—"assimilation" *(dōka)* and "equal treatment under one [imperial] view" *(isshi dōjin)*—were representative of the enlightened, humanitarian ethos promised under Japanese rule. Not everyone in Taiwan took these pronouncements to heart, however. Over the next several years until 1902, the Japanese killed some twenty thousand "bandits" and "rebels" leading attacks on occupying Japanese forces (Lamley 1999, 207).[8]

Besides force, the Japanese also used more constructive colonialist justifications to pacify Taiwanese hard feelings. The colonial administration portrayed itself as a strong, strict, but benevolent force working for the betterment of Taiwan's people, even if the natives could not appreciate it. Under Gotō's civil administration, the Japanese continued the modernization projects begun under the Qing dynasty, building modern roads and railroads, establishing intensive and invasive police institutions, expanding postal and telegraph networks, introducing modern banking and currency measures, founding modern hospitals and public health services, standardizing weights and measures, entering Taiwan in the Greenwich time system, and even publicizing these advances through the use of propagandist motion pictures. The Japanese undertook the modernization of every aspect of agriculture in Taiwan, systematizing and expanding production of sugar, rice, and camphor, developing improved breeds of poultry and pigs, fruits and vegetables, and tea (Li 1995, 123–124; Williams 1980, 229; Wu 1995).

Yet this colonialist modernization program was a mixed bag. Improving the lives of Taiwanese farmers was clearly secondary to the obvious colonial goal of ensuring richer and richer exports back to Japan. Nitobe Inazō, a Quaker in charge of these agricultural modernizations, put it plainly: "Merely being kind to [colonial subjects] is insufficient. Primitive peoples are motivated by awe" (Peattie 1984, 88).[9] Chief among Japan's "primitives" were Taiwan's Austronesian aboriginal population; Gotō and Nitobe in fact used many American policies of "civilizing," policing, and destroying Native Americans as a model for their own aboriginal policies in Taiwan (Knapp and Hauptman 1980).[10]

Japan's fifty-year administration of Taiwan came to be defined by this model of the strict colonial overlord working in mysterious ways for the betterment of his native subjects. (Indeed, one important source of income used to pay for these agricultural modernizations was the 12,420,000 yen that the Japanese were able to earn from their official monopoly on opium sales in Taiwan from 1898 to 1907 [Ka 1995, 54–55]). The Japanese education system was extended to Taiwan, but Taiwanese youth were rarely able to complete education past the elementary level. Taiwanese were promised fair treatment as good Japanese imperial subjects, but Tokyo's extraordinary (and unconstitutional) "Law No. 63" gave the ordinances of the Japanese governor-general of Taiwan the same status as the law of Japan, making him an independent lawmaker unto himself until 1921 (Chen 1984, 251–252).

Taiwanese "natives" could be only second-class imperial subjects under Japanese colonial rule—no surprise, given the government's attempts to master the policies first employed by the British in India, the French in Algeria, or the Germans in Alsace-Lorraine (Fraser 1988, 95; Peattie 1984, 88).[11] But second-class imperial subjects were still imperial subjects, and early in this colonial era the Japanese set out to teach the Taiwanese people how to act as such. In 1903, it became official policy to expand Japanese language use to Taiwanese subjects, for the purpose of "assimilating" them into Japanese colonial society (Wu 1987, 7). Elementary schools, founded in 1896 for Taiwanese boys and girls (You 1988, 272), became ground zero for this experiment, as the new administration sought to attract students away from the Chinese-style *shufang* private schools by merely hiring their tutors to teach in Japanese schools. But this schooling was typically available for children of the upper classes only; in 1915, only 9.6 percent of elementary-age children were enrolled in schools. As late as 1919, after twenty-four years of colonial administration, only some 1.51 percent of the Taiwanese population of 3.54 million had been acculturated in Japanese schools. Where the education system could not do the job, Taiwanese elites, eager to demonstrate their Japanese imperial morality, founded public societies such as the Acculturation Society (Tongfeng Hui) or the Native Language Prohibition Society (Tuyu Jinzhi Hui) in the decade before 1920 to extend Japanese language education in their home cities (Tsurumi 1977, 13–44; Wu 1987, 8, 12).

The first decade of the 1900s saw the launch of several other movements to transform Taiwanese into good (if second-class) imperial subjects by eradicating what the Japanese saw as two of the "lowest customs" (Japanese *rōshū*; Chinese *louxi*) of Taiwan's ethnic Chinese population: the binding of women's feet and men's wearing of the Manchu-style queue (or pigtail). In 1897, Japanese newspapers in Taiwan reported, perhaps apocryphally, that several foot-bound Taiwanese women were killed in a typhoon because they were not able to leave their homes (Wu 1995). A colonywide anti-footbinding movement had begun in earnest by 1900, with elites all over Taiwan transforming their community leadership along Japanese lines by forming local Natural Feet Societies (Tianranzu Hui) and newspapers holding public speaking contests on the topic of anti-footbinding (Wu 1986, 73–80; Wu 1995).

In 1911 the colonial government publicly started pressuring men to modernize their image, opining that the modern West would continue to laugh at Taiwanese if their men were still wearing queues and scholars' robes in the twentieth century (Wang 1960, 14). Taiwanese community leaders, in organizations such as the Society for the Improvement of Folk Customs (Fengsu Gailiang Hui), called the queue unnatural, inconvenient, uneconomical, and unhygienic, and declared victory in 1915 when it estimated that only eighty thousand queue wearers (or just 5.7 percent of the male population) still remained in Taiwan (Wang 1960, 21–22).[12]

This acculturation campaign, part of what many Japanese saw as their "civilizing mission" *(bunmei kaika)* in Taiwan, also was the keystone of Japanese imperial rhetoric that separated their benevolent colonial project from the proven violence of Western colonialism (Ching 2001, 103; Ka 1995, 59). An important side effect of such an ideology, however, was the production of Taiwanese colonial subjects who demanded to be treated as equal subjects under the gaze of the emperor. President Woodrow Wilson's thoughts on self-determination for all the peoples of the world, voiced at the end of World War I, became a guiding light for Taiwanese political activists, as well as for young thinkers in China, Korea, India, Vietnam, and the Philippines. In 1918, Taiwanese students and intellectuals in Tokyo founded an Enlightenment Society (Keihatsukai) in order to work for Taiwanese equality within the Japanese Empire. Groups such as the New People's Society (Shinminkai), the Taiwanese Cultural Association (Taiwan Bunka Kyōkai), and a journal called *Taiwan Youth (Taiwan seinen)* soon followed. These Taiwanese elites in Tokyo fought for a "self-determination" defined not by Taiwanese independence but by the right to vote for their own representatives to Japan's National Diet—and for the abolition of the hated Law No. 63, which institutionalized discrimination in Taiwan (Kerr 1974, 119–125). The League for the Establishment of a Formosan Parliament (Taiwan Gikai Kisei Dōmei) even submitted fifteen official petitions between 1921 and 1934, requesting formal self-governance on the island (Fulda 2002, 366). The colonial government by no means appreciated this literal but creative use of the Japanese authorities' official ideology of "equal treatment." Movement leaders were threatened and harassed, had business licenses revoked and loans recalled, and, during the crackdown following the 1923 Tokyo earthquake, were arrested and imprisoned as "agitators."

The issue of Taiwanese status within the empire was a compelling one in a maturing Japanese Empire, as the 1920s saw a growing Japanese understanding of Taiwan as a genuine part of their nation. During this era of the "extension of the homeland" *(naichi enchō),* more and more Japanese were educated, officially registered, and even buried in Taiwan. These developments worked to give more gravity to the growing intellectual movement for "local autonomy" (or "home rule," *chihō jitsu*) (Kerr 1974, 122). Furthermore, Japanese once opposed to these notions also came to see this "reformist" movement calling for equality under the emperor as infinitely preferable to more radical forms of anticolonialism led by socialist study groups. An example of the latter was the Taiwanese Communist Party, founded in 1928 and dedicated to overthrowing Japanese imperialism altogether and establishing an independent Taiwan Republic (Taiwan Gong-hueguo) (Hsiau 2000, 30–34; Hsiao and Sullivan 1983; Lu 1992, 55–62).[13]

By the 1930s, Taiwan had been transformed into a relatively stable, peaceful, and prosperous Japanese colony.[14] Thousands of college-educated Taiwanese, as one scholar described, "entered the ranks of Japanese [intellectuals], becoming almost indistinguishable from them."[15] Taiwan had become a reliable "sugar bowl" and "rice basket," providing foodstuffs and light industrial products for Japan's home islands; one proud example of this transformation was the 81 percent increase in land productivity achieved over the period 1901–1938 (Ka 1995, 61). The calm could be disrupted, as with the 1930 Musha (Chinese: Wushe) Rebellion, when Taroko tribesmen killed 197 Japanese as revenge for the repeated sexual assaults carried out on local women by Japanese police. Yet the official system of "local autonomy," ensuring more low-level official control by Japanese colonists and Taiwanese elites, continued to evolve and was extended gradually to more cities and administrative districts during the 1920s and 1930s. In 1935, local elections were held, with suffrage extended to the 3.3 percent of the population (Japanese or Taiwanese) who had paid taxes of 5 yen or over and who could write the name of their candidate (Wu 1996).

These expanded rights for Taiwanese as Japanese subjects would soon be accompanied by additional responsibilities as Japanese as well, with the beginning of Japan's "total war" against China in 1937. The colonial regime began to forcibly desinicize Taiwan's ethnic Chinese majority, to be replaced by pure imperial Japanese culture in an intense Movement to Create Imperial Subjects (Kōminka Undō). During wartime, in order to mobilize true Japanese sentiments, use of the national language was pushed even harder. Chinese-language sections of newspapers were eliminated, Taiwanese public servants were ordered to speak only Japanese, and Taiwanese language was forbidden on public buses (Chou 1995, 126; Wu 1987, 69). Japanese-speaking Taiwanese families became eligible for a 50 percent raise in salary (Wu 1995). In 1940, the government even unveiled a public campaign to "sweep away non-Japanese speakers" *(kokugo hukaisha o issōsu)* (Chou 1995, 134).

That same year the colonial regime announced a name-changing *(kaiseimei)* campaign, encouraging Taiwanese (not forcing, as in Korea) who spoke Japanese and had the stuff of a good imperial subject to take Japanese names. One applied through the local government for this privilege, and those whose requests were approved had to follow several guidelines in choosing their new name; for example, the use of Chinese place names was forbidden. Eventually some 7 percent of Taiwanese people made this change—an especially significant step, given the Chinese importance of the surname in connecting to one's ancestors (Lamley 1999, 240; Wu 1995).

Any "un-Japanese" cultural institution could be suppressed during the Kōminka Movement. Taiwanese Buddhist temples were transformed into official Shinto shrines, and traditional puppet theater was banned, as was the wearing of traditional Chinese clothing in public (Lamley 1999, 241–242). The colonial school system played a crucial role in this movement, and by 1944, 71.31 percent of Taiwan's school-age population was enrolled in elementary schools learning Japanese ways (Hsiau 2000, 46). Yet the supreme measure of equality as Japanese subjects was delivered in 1941 with the encouragement that Taiwanese men volunteer to serve—and "die beautifully," if need be—in the Imperial Japanese military. Indeed, Li Qiao, in his epic novel *Wintry Night,* describes members of the Taiwan Youth Labor Corps in Miaoli in 1943, singing (2001, 185):

> For Heaven we fight the unrighteous;
> Soldiers loyal and true are we.
> In glory we depart,

> Leaving the motherland,
> Never to return unless victorious.
> Bravely, we vow to fight to the death.
> Banzai! Banzai!

For years, Taiwan elites had been requesting this "privilege" as part of their appeal for equal treatment (Kondō 1996, 34–36). Between 1941 and 1945, some two hundred thousand Taiwanese volunteered or were drafted into the armed services, with more than thirty thousand of these young men making the supreme sacrifice for their emperor (Lin 1996, 217–227).[16]

Pressures to conform and desires to be accepted aside, however, Japan's war against China, the land of their ancestors, was clearly a difficult war for most Taiwanese to support.[17] Taiwanese subjects learned their position in the imperial order the hard way. Even though rice shipments to Japan decreased during wartime because of the lack of available ships, the rice not sent to Japan was stored rather than being distributed back to the Taiwanese population. The adult rice ration in 1943 was 414 cc (less than a cup and a half) a day—an amount justified by wartime pseudoscientists' "findings" on just how little caloric intake humans actually needed to survive (Kerr 1965, 38; Wu 1996). The men who gloriously volunteered for the military were also accompanied by at least twelve hundred young Taiwanese women who were deceived or taken by force to war fronts in China, Indonesia, the Philippines, Burma, Singapore, Borneo, or Okinawa to serve as sex slaves that the Japanese military grotesquely called "comfort women" (Wang and Chian 1997). This suffering and overall hypocrisy, characterized by Japanese novelist Ozaki Hotsuki as bestowing the honor "not to live as Japanese, but to die as Japanese" (Ching 2000, 252), brought most Taiwanese to anticipate the defeat of the Japanese military and a return of the island to Chinese rule after five decades of colonialism.

Yet the question that remained for the Taiwanese was: *Which* Chinese rule? Would Taiwan be restored to independence? Would it be incorporated into the Republic of China (ROC) government on the mainland, the successor regime to the Qing dynasty that ceded Taiwan fifty years earlier? No such questions troubled the minds of the American, British, and Chinese Allied Powers, however, which had resolved at Cairo (without consulting any actual Taiwanese people) to award Taiwan to the ROC government led by Chiang Kai-shek (Jiang Jieshi).[18]

In 1945, at war's end, Taiwan had been heavily bombed in American air strikes but largely spared from the hell of invasion suffered on other Japanese islands, such as Okinawa. General Douglas MacArthur, supreme commander of the Allied Command in the Pacific, authorized Taiwan's surrender to Generalissimo Chiang Kai-shek and his ROC government as a trustee on behalf of the Allied Powers (Chen and Reisman 1972, 611). This surrender itself implied nothing about whether the ROC was the rightful "owner" of Taiwan. At the same time, Vietnam was also surrendered to Chiang as a trustee on behalf of the Allied

Powers; Manchuria and North Korea to Joseph Stalin as another such trustee; South Korea to U.S. General John Hodge as another, and so on (Taiwan Documents Project 1945). It did begin decades of debate over the legal status of Taiwan—namely, over the right of the ROC to accept command in 1945 over an island ceded to Japan by the defunct Qing dynasty in 1895.[19] Yet these debates could not change the fact that as of October 1945, Taiwan's half-century as "the Orphan of Asia" was over, and now the island's people had a new master—the government of the Republic of China.

RETROCESSION: 1945–1949

Elation was the typical Taiwanese reaction to the news that the Japanese colonial authorities would be leaving their island. During the two months between Japanese defeat and the arrival of ROC forces, Taiwanese elites worked to ensure a smooth transition to Chinese rule. Several Taiwanese intellectuals approached the Japanese about possible support for an independent Taiwan regime, but they met with the stern opposition of the last Japanese governor of Taiwan, Andō Likichi (Kondō 1996, 666; Itō 1993, 133).[20] Meanwhile, most elites turned their attention to the imminent arrival of Chinese forces, founding Preparatory Committees to Welcome the National Government and fervently organizing basic propaganda projects on behalf of their new Chinese rulers (Phillips 1999, 280).

This sense of appreciation would not last long, however, as Taiwanese people soon learned their place under the ROC government, which was wholly dominated by the Chinese Nationalist Party (Guomindang, also commonly called KMT for Kuomintang). Due to the island's unique status as a former Japanese colony, Chinese leaders decided to govern the new Taiwan Province in quite a different way than the rest of the ROC. Taiwan came under joint party-government-military administration, with Governor-General Chen Yi enjoying a very broad mixture of civilian and military powers shockingly reminiscent of the early Japanese governors (Phillips 1999, 282). For having lived in relative peace under the modernizing Japanese colonial regime for fifty years, Taiwanese people were dismissed as brainwashed "slaves" who did not deserve the relatively modern conditions that they enjoyed (especially in comparison to conditions in China after eight years of war against Japan).

Perhaps not understanding the excitement most islanders felt about being annexed by the ROC, the conquering regime immediately began working in Taiwan toward two main goals that had little to do with the hopes of the recently liberated Taiwanese. First was the project of replacing any Japanese or unorthodox customs with Chinese, in order to make the island safe for ROC rule. Nothing bothered the Nationalists more than the fact, after eight years of awful war against Japan, that their newest and richest province looked, acted, and sounded Japanese![21] The new regime's second goal was to use Taiwan's relative wealth—in 1939, Taiwan's per capita value of foreign trade was thirty-nine times that of China (Chen and Reisman 1972, 611)—to win their new civil war on the mainland against the Chinese Communist Party (CCP).

The implementation of these measures served quickly to erase the goodwill that the new government had won just for being Chinese. As Taiwan was officially and forcibly resinicized, unemployment lines became distinctly Taiwanized. Some 37,000 Taiwanese government workers lost their jobs in the transition, a trend made the more galling by the fact that only 22 percent of the posts in the Guomindang official bureaucracy were held by Taiwanese, as opposed to 56 percent of the posts under the Japanese (Lai et al. 1991, 65). A program of de-Taiwanization, designed to "eradicate the slave mentality" among Taiwanese, meant the banning of Japanese newspaper pages, rendering voiceless an entire generation of intellectuals educated under the Japanese and propagating an official cult of the benevolent and sagely dictator Chiang Kai-shek, honored as "Savior of the People" and "Grand Family Head" (Hsiau 2000, 53–54; Chang 1993, 141).

The ROC's takeover of Taiwan also involved the establishment of control over all aspects of the economy for the public (but far too often, the private) good. The official "Taiwan Provincial Japanese Property Managing Committee" enriched the ROC state and its officials by relieving governmental organizations, enterprises, and individuals of 50,856 pieces of property worth 10,990,900,000 yen, or some 17 percent of Taiwan's 1946 net domestic product (Itō 1993, 141; Lai et al. 1991, 71). Since Taiwan now belonged to the ROC, what belonged to Taiwan would belong to the ROC as well; organized carpetbagging units descended on Chinese Taiwan, stripping the island of everything from railway wiring and signal equipment to luggage on random rail baggage cars, industrial machinery, plumbing equipment, and entire factories—all to be sent back to Shanghai, Xiamen, or other coastal mainland cities (Kerr 1965, 132–135; Peng 1972, 49). This was in addition to the great amounts of raw materials—sugar, coal, salt, and cement—appropriated and shipped to the mainland in official fashion. Inflation quickly set in, reaching a rate of 350 percent during the first eight months of Guomindang rule (Lai et al. 1991, 73, 81). Official neglect also reached staggeringly dangerous levels. It was probably no coincidence that the first cholera epidemic to strike Taiwan in twenty-seven years came in the summer of 1946, after just several months of Nationalist rule, killing some 1,460 Taiwanese. Others were diagnosed with the bubonic plague, totally eradicated by the Japanese thirty years before the arrival of Chinese forces. The government had other worries, however; as the director of Public Health explained, "after all, only the poor people are contracting the disease" (Kerr 1965, 179–180).

Tensions were only exacerbated by the condescension with which so many Taiwanese viewed these arrivals from a very poor China. The following passage vividly expresses the shock that so many self-consciously modern Taiwanese felt in 1945 upon their first contact with "China" in fifty years:

> The ship docked, the gangways were lowered, and off came the troops of China, the victors. The first man to appear was a bedraggled fellow who

looked and behaved more like a coolie than a soldier, walking off with a carrying pole across his shoulder, from which was suspended his umbrella, sleeping mat, cooking pot, and cup. Others like him followed, some with shoes, some without. Few had guns. With no attempt to maintain order or discipline, they pushed off the ship, glad to be on firm land, but hesitant to face the Japanese lined up and saluting smartly on both sides. My father wondered what the Japanese could possibly think. He had never felt so ashamed in his life. Using a Japanese expression, he said, "If there had been a hole nearby, I would have crawled in!" (Peng 1972, 51–52)

Taiwanese resentment of the corruption and waste that plagued the island under the Nationalists often was voiced in class terms; stories circulated about the military forces that the Taiwanese derided as "blanket soldiers" washing their rice in toilet bowls, mistaking hair dryers for fantastic pistols, and stealing bicycles but not being able to ride them. Taiwanese protests against the Guomindang began to take the shape of direct (and unanimously unfavorable) comparisons with the Japanese colonial regime. Voicing such concerns loudly was not wise, however, and was treated as the work of "disloyal subversives" who could only be planning Communist rebellion against the ROC. The government gave lip service to their promises of democracy; in 1946 public elections were held for village and town councils, who then elected county and city council representatives, who then elected a Provincial Consultative Assembly. These organs were very heavily represented by Taiwanese citizens, but they were given only "consultative" or advisory powers and thus could do little to relieve the frustration that was growing so rapidly (Phillips 1999, 286).

Disaster struck on the evening of February 27, 1947, when several Guomindang agents beat a forty-year-old widow for the offense of selling black market cigarettes. When word spread of the incident, pent-up Taiwanese anger at the Nationalist regime erupted in forms ranging from organized protests to premeditated violence against random mainland officials and soldiers. Protesters removed the characters for "China" from official and commercial signs, others put up Japanese-language banners screaming "Down with Military Tyranny," while others chanted Taiwanese-language slogans such as "The Taiwanese want revenge now!" "Beat the mainlanders!" "Kill the pigs!" "Let Taiwan rule itself!" and "Let's have a new democracy!" Even angrier Taibei residents began interrogating any mainlanders they could find and beating the unlucky ones who could not answer in Japanese or Taiwanese languages (Lai et al. 1991, 105–107). Over the next four days, through March 4, violence erupted throughout all of Taiwan's cities as the retribution for one original act of violence grew into a full-fledged urban uprising against Guomindang rule (121–134).

As this raw Taiwanese rage boiled over in the streets, elites in Taibei and other cities quickly founded Resolution Committees (Chuli Weiyuanhui) in order to negotiate between the Taiwanese majority and the Nationalist military government. These committees were in fact dominated by pro-Guomindang Taiwanese elites who should have been able to formulate demands amenable to the government. Negotiations between these committees and the state stalled for days, but the commander of the Fourth Gendarme Regiment called on the Taibei Resolution Committee on March 8 to promise: "The Central Government will not dispatch troops to Taiwan" (Kerr 1965, 291). He was lying. Beginning that same day, two entire divisions of ROC troops were transferred to Taiwan from the mainland, and a reign of state terror against its opponents began. The Resolution Committees were abolished, and some outspoken members were tortured and executed (Lai et al. 1991, 138–150; Peng 1972, 70). Chinese troops landing on Taiwan began random killings of Taiwanese as soon as they came ashore, many shooting guns loaded with soft-nosed dum-dum bullets designed to wound even more painfully (Kerr 1965, 260). As Peng Ming-min (Peng Mingmin) remembered: "As the Nationalist troops came ashore they moved out quickly through Keelung [Jilong] streets, shooting and bayoneting men and boys, raping women, and looting homes and shops. Some Formosans were seized and stuffed alive into burlap bags found piled up at the sugar warehouse doors, and were then simply tossed into the harbor. Others were merely tied up or chained before being thrown from the piers" (Peng 1972, 69–70).

For the next several months, thousands of Taiwanese elites who were seen as posing a threat to the regime—professors, doctors, lawyers, professionals, college and even high school students—were systematically arrested and executed in cold blood (Vecchione 1998). As George Kerr, a U.S. State Department official stationed in Taiwan at the time, described: "By March 17 the pattern of terror and revenge had emerged very clearly. First to be destroyed were all established critics of the Government. Then in their turn came Settlement Committee members and their principal aides, all youths who had taken part in the interim policing of Taipei, middle school students, middle school teachers, lawyers, economic leaders and members of influential families, and at last, anyone who in the preceding eighteen months had given offense to a mainland Chinese, causing him to 'lose face'" (Kerr 1965, 299–300).

Anyone highly educated or accomplished in the Japanese language and/or culture could be targeted, as the "poisonous" Japanese influence on Taiwan was blamed for the uprising (especially since so many of the protests and insurrectionary radio broadcasts had been in Japanese). Taiwan was cleansed of any Japanese items—records, publications, flags, and so on, which were confiscated—at the same time as it was being cleansed over the next several months of its Japanese-educated elites, dual processes of finally "sinicizing" Taiwan for good (Hsiau 2000, 57–58). It was this kind of violence that led Taiwanese such as dissident Peng Ming-min's father, a prominent Presbyterian doctor in Gaoxiong, to abandon totally their "Chinese" identity: "He went so far as to cry out that he was ashamed of his Chinese blood and wished that his children after him would always marry foreigners until his descendants could no longer claim to be Chinese" (Peng 1972, 69).

Final numerical estimates of the massacres of the spring and summer of 1947 vary widely, from an official government report estimating sixty-three hundred total casualties to anti-Guomindang activists' own estimates that more than twenty thousand Taiwanese were killed in the suppression (Lai et al. 1991, 158–159). And what was called the "white terror" *(baise kongbu)* did not end in 1947; by the mid-1950s, the government had some fourteen thousand political prisoners (both Taiwanese and mainlander) in custody and had executed probably one or two thousand more (Taylor 2000, 211–212).

In 1949, the Republic of China government was chased out of mainland China by a victorious Chinese Communist Party after more than three years of civil war. In what can only be called a cruel irony, this newest Chinese province of Taiwan, the province in which the ROC government had the least legitimacy, became home to the entire regime. At the time of the 1947 uprising, Chiang Kai-shek, author of that year's brutal measures, could hardly have imagined that in just two years, this most despised and "poisoned" province of Taiwan would be all that he and his party would ever control again. Considering that even in the early 1990s, some anti-Nationalist activists would still be screaming that "KMT" really stood for "Kill Many Taiwanese" (*Xu Rongshu* 1991), the title of one book on the 1947 uprising—*A Tragic Beginning*—is thus all too accurate in describing early Nationalist rule of Taiwan (Lai et al. 1991).

FREE CHINA: 1950–PRESENT

By 1949, the fundamentally brutal nature of Guomindang rule in Taiwan, and the loss of all hope of avoiding a Communist victory in China, convinced the Truman Administration to give up on Chiang's "ChiNats," to swear off publicly aiding Chiang, and to allow the island to be "liberated" by the CCP. Yet the assumptions of the Cold War quickly led General Douglas MacArthur and other policy makers to question this decision, as a worldwide struggle against Soviet and Chinese Communism could not allow the surrender of any possible anti-Communist allies, no matter how brutal or unpopular. When North Korean forces invaded South Korea in June 1950, launching the first hot war of the Cold War era, the importance of keeping Taiwan—this potential "unsinkable aircraft carrier"—out of Communist Chinese hands became crucial. Thus, the U.S. military command was ordered to defend Taiwan as a base of operations against China, renewing the ROC's status as a loyal client state and giving tacit American approval to the harsh regime for more than two decades to come (Garver 1997, 16–31).

Only in 1979 did the United States recognize the Communist People's Republic of China (PRC) regime as the government of China. Thus, for thirty years, the American government mouthed the inane fiction that Chiang's ROC regime on Taiwan was the rightful government of China. During the 1950s and 1960s, Americans referred to the ROC on Taiwan as "Free China" with a straight face, a notion made possible only in comparison to the uncannily low standards set by three decades of Maoist rule in the PRC. This "Free China" myth was not attractive because it was cheap either: Chiang's regime was funded by American taxpayers to the tune of U.S. $4 billion over the period 1951–1965 (Jacoby 1966, 38, 118).

Guomindang rule in Taiwan after 1950 was of a different sort than the awful late 1940s, as the party began a long transformation into a "soft authoritarian" regime. The civil war in China and the Nationalists' landing on Taiwan were disastrous enough that Chiang Kai-shek led his party through a period of serious, reflective reorganization from 1950 to 1952. One of the most important reforms was the transformation of the Guomindang into a party that, while still not democratic, was much more representative of the general population than it had been in China. Serious efforts were made to recruit peasant Taiwanese farmers, workers, and intellectuals, although a glass ceiling that favored mainlanders over Taiwanese was in place well into the 1970s (Dickson 1993, 79–81). The ROC government's insistence that it should be governing all of China meant that Taiwanese people were represented in the government only "proportional to their percentage of the 500 million people of China, giving them three per cent representation in their own homeland" (Chen and Reisman 1972, 614–615).

For the next two decades, Chiang and his ruling Guomindang were dedicated to this goal of retaking the Chinese motherland, often with explicit American aid. Tactics ranged from the quaint (sending care packages of chocolate, shoes, and pistols to Chinese "compatriots" by balloon) to the daring (landing hundreds of agents on PRC territory to set up rebel radio stations in hopes of sparking a counterrevolution), the sleazy (growing opium in northern Burma to fund pro–ROC forces in that border region), and the purely terrorist (blowing up a PRC–chartered Air India jet in 1955 in an attempt to assassinate Premier Zhou Enlai). (And Chiang was not done with Zhou, either; in 1971 his spies planned again to kill Zhou, this time with a trained "kamikaze dog" wearing a remote-controlled bomb [Minnick 1995, 55].)[22]

There was more to life in Taiwan than these cross-straits intrigues, however. Chiang's authoritarian rule was coterminous with—and in many ways related to—an incredible economic transformation that brought to "the Orphan of Asia" a major role in the world economy. The Guomindang was determined to assure that the economic collapse that spelled its doom in China would not be repeated in Taiwan. Land reform was instituted fairly, peacefully, and effectively during the early 1950s. Rents were reduced to a maximum of 37.5 percent of annual yields, and great expanses of public land were sold to tenant farmers (Wang 1999, 324). One of the most foresighted elements of this land reform was to use stocks and bonds to purchase excess lands from wealthy landholders and then sell these lands to more than 194,000 tenant farming families (Yang 1970, 82).

Of the billions of American taxpayers' dollars flowing into Taiwan during the 1950s, the minority not earmarked for the military was funneled into communications, transportation, and agricultural and industrial development. The American government, hoping to prove that capitalism was a superior form of development, encouraged and subsidized heavy export production in Taiwan, hollowing out American postwar industry but providing an invaluable boost to Taiwan's economy (Johnson 2000, 195; Wang 1999, 328–332). Oakland and Cleveland's loss was Taiwanese industry's gain: By the 1980s, almost half of Taiwan's exports were purchased by Americans (Rubinstein 1999a, 375). An important characteristic of Taiwan's industrial development—and one that led to the uncommon equality of income distribution on the island—was the importance of small-scale factories that could be set up and run by members of the rural lower middle classes (Ho 1979; Wang 1999, 333). These government strategies and American aid programs, when combined with high household savings rates (13 percent in 1963) and a highly successful education system, produced an economic boom so dramatic and comprehensive that outsiders could only describe it as the "Taiwan miracle." The Guomindang was fortunate, for it took an economic program this miraculous to sustain the Taiwanese people's faith in the ROC government after the "tragic beginning" of the late 1940s.

The economic transformation under Chiang did not imply or account for an equally miraculous political liberalization. "Retaking the mainland" was the only acceptable political orientation; any institution or practice that did not reflect this goal could be suppressed. The 1950s literary world was dominated by the semiofficial genre of "combat literature" *(zhandou wenyi)* (Hsiau 2000, 66). For the purposes of "unity," only Mandarin Chinese was technically acceptable in government offices, courts, and schools. As the most stubborn and persistent reminder of a unique Taiwanese identity, Taiwanese language was targeted brutally as an inferior "dialect." Even young students speaking Taiwanese were routinely beaten, humiliated, or fined (even into the 1990s) as the Guomindang and its supporters continued to work to "sinicize" this complicated island. In 1994, President Lee Teng-hui (Li Denghui) stirred painful memories of this Nationalist legacy when he spoke to reporters about how his children had been made to wear "a dunce board around their necks in school as punishment for speaking Taiwanese" (Hsiau 2000, 125).

Signs of civil society were slow to develop under Guomindang rule. On the one hand, dissidents such as Peng Ming-min, chairman of the National Taiwan University Political Science Department and advisor to the ROC United Nations delegation, were still imprisoned for public, high-profile acts of defiance.[23] On the other, everyday Taiwanese found more room for free expression in the thousands of civic organizations, such as Rotary and Lions Clubs, founded in an era of very slow but sure political liberalization. Opponents of the Chiang regime who pounced on signs of weakness in the ROC's international standing were punished mercilessly, at the same time that the government worked to inculcate in the Taiwanese public a sense of nationalism and loyalty to the government as their own.

One such crisis in the early 1970s was the gradual erosion of the ROC's claim to represent "Free China" on the international stage. Though the United States had championed this regime as the rightful Chinese government for more than two decades (and would continue to do so until 1979)—and pressured many of its allies to do the same—the PRC had been successful in convincing more and more First, Second, and Third World nations to recognize it as the true government of China. Richard Nixon and Henry Kissinger's strategic shift toward "serious dialogue" with Communist China as a way to isolate the Soviet Union doomed the Chiang regime's international position. In 1971, the ROC delegation walked out of the United Nations General Assembly immediately before the assembly voted to award China's UN seat to the PRC and to "expel forthwith the representatives of Chiang Kai-shek from the place which they unlawfully occupy at the United Nations" (Appleton 1972). It was a tellingly strong rebuke to Chiang's ROC, one of the founders of the UN and a Security Council member, and one that could only wound Chiang's legitimacy in Taiwan as well.

Opponents of the Chiang regime who favored Taiwan's independence from any Chinese rule took advantage of this development with coordinated protests all over the world, chaining themselves together in public places to call for recognition of Taiwan as an independent nation seated in the UN (Peng 1972, 259). A final indignity for the ROC government came the next year, with Nixon's 1972 visit to China. There, hoping to garner PRC help in ending the war in Vietnam, Nixon ended the ROC's special relationship with the United States by signing the Shanghai Communiqué, which "acknowledge[d] . . . there is but one China and that Taiwan is a part of China" (*Joint Communiqué*, 1972).

This was the sorry state of the island nation when Generalissimo Chiang Kai-shek died in 1975. Long incapacitated, Chiang had already left government affairs to his son Chiang Ching-kuo (Jiang Jingguo) for several years. The young Chiang, who had lived in Taiwan longer than he had lived in China, had a much more tolerant view of Taiwanese culture and political activity, and almost immediately set out to increase Taiwanese participation at the highest levels of ROC governance (Taylor 2000, 326). This new tolerance was in some ways an answer to persistent demands for a government that reflected the true population of Taiwan. A "native" *(xiangtu)* literature movement was inaugurated in the 1970s as cultural elites sought to rediscover the beauty of Taiwanese culture, suppressed for so long under the Guomindang (Hsiau 2000, 68). While many mainlander officials saw this kind of pro-Taiwan stance as a threat, Chiang Ching-kuo welcomed it, even going so far as to say that after four decades of living in Taiwan, he was "Taiwanese," too.[24]

This liberalization under the young Chiang came in fits and starts. His government still used force to suppress dissidents, sometimes acting through ultra-nationalist secret societies that visited violent wrath upon opponents of the minority Guomindang regime. One famous case was that of the Gaoxiong Eight, dissidents associated with *Formosa* magazine who were given long sentences for their provocative roles in a World Human Rights Day rally in 1979. The Iron Blood Patriots, a radical gang associated with one of Chiang Ching-kuo's sons, added their own kind of justice, murdering the twin daughters and mother of one of the defendants, Lin Yixiong. This same Chiang son was also found to be behind the Bamboo Gang's murder in Daly City, California, of Henry Liu, author of an unflattering biography of President Chiang (Taylor 2000, 357, 386).

Simultaneously, however, Chiang was taking steps to guarantee that he would be succeeded by Taiwanese leaders who could carry on a pro-Taiwan Guomindang legacy, not by mainlanders with more loyalty to the long-lost mainland than to the Nationalists' Taiwan base. This mission eventually led Chiang to make three decisions in 1986–1987 that flew in the face of Guomindang orthodoxy: ending martial law, ending mainland "representation" in the ROC's elected bodies, and choosing as his personal successor Lee Teng-hui, a Japanese- and American-educated agricultural economist (Taylor 2000, 408, 418). When Chiang died suddenly in 1988, Lee was named president and Guomindang chairman, and the "Taiwanization" of the Chinese Nationalist Party had truly begun.

TAIWAN FOR THE TAIWANESE?

Lee's twelve-year presidential reign, the second longest in the history of the ROC, saw Taiwan irreversibly transformed from Chiang's "soft authoritarian" regime to a free democratic society. By 1989 a viable opposition, the Democratic Progressive Party (DPP; Minzhu Jinbu Dang), arisen from Taiwan independence forces persecuted so violently under the Chiangs, was seriously challenging the Guomindang in county and provincial elections. In 1991, the government terminated the "Period of National Mobilization for Suppression of the Communist Rebellion"—the formal name for martial law—and the limitations on constitutional freedoms it mandated for four decades under the Chiangs. This

A 1991 pro–DPP handbill urging Taiwanese not to go along with the Guomindang (KMT) in their project of reunifying with mainland China. (Literally, "Please do not board this [KMT] flight.")

Taiwanese phone cards from the mid-1990s commemorating both (top) the modern elements of the Japanese occupation period and (bottom) Liao Tianding, a Robin Hood figure who supposedly bedeviled Japanese police with his thievery and bravado.

gesture signaled finally that administering Taiwan—not recovering mainland China—was the real goal of the Guomindang. Since then, Taiwan has held two direct presidential elections. Those held in 1996 and captured by Lee Teng-hui were billed as the first in the five thousand years of Chinese history. In 2000, the Taiwanese DPP candidate, Chen Shui-bian (Chen Shuibian), captured victory for his once-illegal pro-independence party.[25]

This "quiet revolution" *(ningjing geming)* and the Taiwan population's conspicuous reveling in their new political freedoms (as demonstrated in the essays by Alice Chu and Scott Simon in this volume) have also resulted in a new dialogue on ethnicity and the notion of Taiwan as a multiethnic, multicultural nation. The new native leadership of the DPP and Guomindang often portrayed their struggles as those of "the Taiwanese" vs. "the mainlanders." However, two culturally and linguistically distinct minority groups—the Hakkas (approximately 12 percent of Taiwan's population) and Taiwan's several aboriginal tribes (2 percent)—were ignored in this formulation, in much the same way that they had been ignored by Japanese and Guomindang regimes describing a monolithic and inferior "Taiwanese" native population. As a result, both of these groups have taken advantage of this new political era to state their own claims to cultural and political significance (and even self-government) and to challenge a new Hoklo chauvinism often present in the new "Taiwanese" politics.[26]

Taiwan's economic boom also continued during this astounding political liberalization of the 1990s. Taiwan's export strategy led to huge trade surpluses that, although angering trading partners—including the United States—allowed the ROC to amass mammoth foreign exchange reserves ranking first or second in the world through most of the 1990s.[27] Since the 1980s, the electronics and information technology industries have headed this export strategy, a fact made possible by the government's unusually high expenditures in education (Woo 1991, 1039). This "green silicon island" *(lüse xi dao)* has been the world's third most important supplier of computer hardware (after the United States and Japan) since 1995 (*Republic of China Yearbook* 2001). In 1999, Taiwan's gross national product was U.S. $290.5 billion, the seventeenth largest in the world.[28] Unfortunately, however, in many cases the people of this tiny island achieved such great wealth by devastating their own environment, destroying wildlife, agricultural land, and freshwater sources, while saturating the air and soil with the chemical and metallic by-products of industry (Williams and Chang 1994, 242–244).

Perhaps the most important tension in Taiwan at the turn of the millennium is the presence of the People's Republic of China right across the Taiwan Straits. Abandoning its original position that Taiwan was a separate nation, distinguished culturally from the rest of China (Hsiao and Sullivan 1979, 447–458), the Chinese Communist Party during the 1990s stepped up its campaign to "reunify" the entire Chinese nation by extending its control to Taiwan. Relying, often very successfully, on the brute force of nationalism to distract its citizens from political repression and the volatility of market transformations, the CCP has convinced not only their own people but most of the rest of the world that the PRC has legal title to Taiwan—an island that has never been under its control. Without realizing the possible boon that such an argument could be to diehard loyalists of the Ryukyuan, Dutch, Spanish, and Japanese empires, the PRC's argument is based on the fact that since Taiwan was once part of the Manchu Qing empire, it should be part of China in perpetuity. The great majority of people in Taiwan look at the immense changes that have occurred in Taiwan and China in the century plus since Taiwan's cession by the Qing, and they prefer the autonomy that has existed under more than fifty years of ROC rule.[29]

The PRC's main strategy has been to isolate Taiwan diplomatically on the international stage, most successfully by blocking any attempts by Taiwan to reenter the United Nations after three decades of exclusion from that body. The PRC also is able to use its almost superpower status and economic clout to prevent virtually any international recognition of Taiwan as a sovereign state. The pettiness of these measures can be mind-boggling, such as the PRC's unconditional demand that any international organization recognize Taiwan's diplomatic representatives, Little League and Olympic teams, or even Miss Universe contestants (*CND* 2000) only as representatives of "Chinese Taipei." But they can also be deadly. In 1999, Beijing used its pull in the World Health Organization (WHO) to keep Taiwan out of the international body and its citizens ineligible to benefit from or contribute to advancements made by WHO (AFP 1999). In September 1999, after a disastrous earthquake struck in central Taiwan, killing over two thousand people, the PRC government prevented UN and Russian rescue teams from reaching Taiwan for more than two days, explaining that "as Taiwan is not a member of the UN, then aid must be channeled through Beijing" (AFP 1999; *CND* 1999).[30]

As one China watcher puts it, for the PRC's leaders, "Taiwan is an obsession, one that creates a hideous spectacle of a large dictatorship trying to intimidate a small democracy" (Chang 2001, 37). Yet this forceful approach to resolving the "Taiwan question" is exactly what many people inside mainland China have learned to welcome. In July 1999, a rare public opinion poll conducted in Chinese cities found that 86.9 percent of those surveyed favored an invasion of Taiwan "if necessary" (Reuters 1999).[31]

These actions have earned the PRC great enmity among many Taiwanese, yet many businessmen from Taiwan have found the profits to be made in China more significant than the threats to their nation's sovereignty. Taiwan businesses, large and small, see China as an endless supply of cheap exploitable labor and loose environmental regulations. As a key to maintaining a "competitive edge," these enterprises have invested more than U.S. $100 billion in China, even as this has hollowed out Taiwan's own industrial base (Hsing 1998; Studwell 2002, 280). As one Taiwan journalist writes, "Beyond the fact that the water, power, and environmental protection costs [in China] are all low, land can be acquired for next to nothing. Every Taiwanese businessman who comes here feels like a prince—complete with his own fiefdom" (Li 2001, 9). Consequently, a huge trade (U.S. $25.84 billion in 1999) links Taiwan and China, a fact that many observers feel makes some form of reunification inevitable in the near future (*Republic of China Yearbook* 2001). Even in Taiwan itself, the struggling tourism industry is looking to well-heeled mainland Chinese tourists as a new source of income; as one business leader said in 2001, "Taiwan can become China's Hawaii" (AP 2001). The PRC government also wisely uses these growing ties in order to sell Taiwan officials, academics, and businessmen on the financial benefits of reunification and has succeeded in pushing figures such as President Chen Shui-bian onto the defensive, calling for "economic war" against China (*The Economist* 2000, 48; *TTO* 2001).

Taiwan's unique status at the turn of the twenty-first century is reflected best in one recent series of events. Liberal International, a London-based coalition of eighty-four liberal political parties from sixty-seven countries, selected President Chen Shui-bian to receive its 2001 Prize for Freedom, hailing his "solid record as a human rights activist" (Taipei Government Information Office 2001). Liberal International was scheduled to present the award in Copenhagen, Denmark. Yet because of political pressure from China—which forbids its diplomatic allies to allow visits by Taiwanese leaders—the Danish government refused to grant Chen a visa so he could receive the Freedom prize. And when Liberal International offered to present the award to Chen at a later European Parliament meeting in Strasbourg, the French government also refused to issue Chen a visa.[32]

Though it is Asia's most vibrant democracy, Taiwan's leaders must beg for visas to visit the United States or other countries that supposedly stand for principles of freedom and liberty. With the admission of Tuvalu into the UN in 2000, the Republic of China on Taiwan is the last nation in the world to be excluded from the world body. The world's seventeenth largest economy, Taiwan is recognized by less than two dozen tiny African and Caribbean nations. A sovereign nation in every way, Taiwan has to justify continually why it should *not* be swallowed up by the PRC, a regime that has never administered an inch of Taiwan's territory. And, intimately tied culturally and economically to China, Taiwan's future as a sovereign nation depends on its ability to convince the world of its historical independence from the mainland. Yet somehow these singular conditions seem fitting for Taiwan, an island whose history, as the following chapters describe, has been nothing if not complicated and extraordinary.

PART II
Religion and Ritual
THE CELEBRATION OF
BELIEF AND DOUBT

2

Fowl Play

Chicken-Beheading Rituals and Dispute Resolution in Taiwan

Paul R. Katz

EDITORS' INTRODUCTION

It is in the nature of human life that people do not all agree all of the time, and dispute settlement, formal and informal, is a necessary part of living together. It is often said of Chinese society that mediation and dispute settlement are among its greatest accomplishments. In imperial times, the famous civil service system sent magistrates to all corners of the empire, charging them to oversee tax collection, road repair, civil service exams, police administration, and local ritual. But also—and of central importance—they were charged to settle disputes.

Most dispute settlement, of course, takes place outside of courts through the intervention of friends, the "final word" from parents or bosses, an occasional fistfight, or the agreement to disagree. In Taiwan all of this happens, but in this chapter, Paul Katz describes an extremely unusual mode of dispute settlement in cases involving accusations of lying: swearing an oath that one is right, and dramatizing the event by slaughtering a chicken. The oath, furthermore, is linked to the world of popular religion.

This custom was never particularly frequent and has not been practiced for most of a century, so far as we know, but Katz shows us that it has a very long history and that it still has a firm hold on the popular imagination in Taiwan. Why should slaughtering an animal prove that one is telling the truth? Why should the animal be a chicken? Why is the ritual conducted in a temple dedicated to gods concerned with death? Why do Taiwanese today still find this a vibrant symbol of truth telling?

Katz treats us to a number of specific and rather colorful cases in Taiwan and then traces the history of chicken beheading back to Fujian Province, where much of Taiwan's modern population originated. Temples associated with death traditionally played a role in dispute mediation in Fujian, as in Taiwan, and there too chickens were beheaded. And there are more colorful cases available for examination.

But why use chickens? In fact, chickens are not the only animals whose blood had ritual uses in earlier times, and the use of animals to identify wrongdoers did not always involve sacrificing the animals. But the symbolism, Katz points out, would have been very appropriate in an earlier world when justice was often associated with the shedding of blood. Several very old traditions are probably intertwined in the chicken-beheading oaths of Taiwan.

Mediation and dispute resolution is no longer undertaken by slaughtering chickens. But through the careful study of this unusual custom, we can appreciate the tight integration of religion, politics, moral behavior, and the seriousness of physical symbols, and we can understand the cultural knowledge that allows something as "simple" as a political cartoon of a headless chicken to be complexly meaningful in Taiwan today. ∎

One important element of conventional wisdom about Chinese culture involves its emphasis on harmony. Many scholars, especially those who specialize in the study of Chinese thought, cite ideas of harmony in ancient Chinese cosmology—specifically the blending of yin and yang, and the interaction between the Five Phases (*wuxing*, traditionally known as the Five Elements). They also cite passages from the Chinese classics, including so-called Confucian writings such as the *Book of Rites (Liji)* and the *Mencius (Mengzi)*, which stress the importance of harmony at the cosmic, social, and individual levels. Above all, such texts were concerned with the attainment of social harmony, stating that people were meant to interact both ritually and socially according to their status, with relationships between family members as well as rulers and the ruled considered to be of prime importance (Li Yih-yuan 1995; Overmyer 1989–1990). Despite the prevalence of such lofty ideals, however, local communities throughout both urban and rural China were torn by familial disputes and conflicts among neighbors and coworkers, not to mention tension between the officials and elites who attempted to maintain some degree of control.[1]

Taiwan was no exception. Local gazetteers, archival materials, newspaper articles, and ethnographic accounts dating from the seventeenth century to the present day contain numerous instances of state attempts to contain tensions, quarrels, and feuds, many of which turned violent.[2] Such data provide gripping images of those tensions and disputes that so often disrupt Taiwanese society and that have persisted despite the island's rapid modernization and democratization.[3]

People in Taiwan who are embroiled in disputes have generally chosen to pursue three courses of action: private mediation, the legal system, and judicial (some would prefer to call them quasi-judicial) rituals. Depending on the nature of the dispute and the status of those parties involved, people could choose one or a combination of these options. But while considerable efforts have been devoted to the study of Chinese law and while a growing number of scholars have begun to undertake research on private mediation,[4] relatively little work has been done on what I term "judicial rituals"—that is, ritual remedies for disputes similar to actual judicial proceedings. This is a pity, as historical and ethnographic data indicate that people were often more likely to perform judicial rites at a temple than pursue formal legal action.

Widely ranging judicial rites have been performed in China and Taiwan for many centuries, the most common of which include the formal making of an oath *(lishi)* or filing an indictment *(fanggao, gao yinzhuang)* at a temple dedicated to a deity belonging to the judicial bureaucracy of the under-world.[5] In this essay, I explore one judicial ritual that has been performed in Taiwan for over two centuries: the making of an oath accompanied by the ritual beheading of a cockerel *(zhan jitou)*, or young male chicken. Declaring one's innocence, especially in the presence of incriminating circumstantial evidence or widespread disbelief, is a challenge in any society. In Taiwan, beheading a chicken in appropriate ritual circumstances could help increase one's credibility while also providing an opportunity for parties involved in a dispute to release pent-up tensions. Our first question, of course, is "Why a chicken?" Or, for that matter, "Why a beheading?" But as we think about these issues, we shall find that we also want to know when and why such a ritual brought credibility and who could and could not expect to be believed in such a context. I will also argue that chicken-beheading rituals share some similarities with Balinese cockfights (see Geertz 1973) in that both present public commentaries on key social issues.

CASE STUDIES

Case studies of chicken-beheading rites in colonial Taiwan may be found in the work of Masuda Fukutaro, a graduate of the Law Faculty of Tokyo Imperial University who possessed a profound interest in the relationship between religion and the law. Masuda went to Taiwan in 1929 as chief researcher for religious affairs for the Taiwan Governor-General's Office and became a professor of law at Taihoku (Taibei) Imperial University (today's National Taiwan University) in 1930 (Tsu 1998, 41–42,47–50). His many essays and books contain two summaries of newspaper accounts and two lengthier field studies of chicken-beheading rites performed in Taiwan during the 1930s.

Case 1

One chicken-beheading ritual took place in the town of Douliu (then in Tainan Prefecture; now in Yunlin County) during May of 1934. Some chickens and a pig belonging to one of the town's leading families were poisoned, and suspicions soon focused on thirty-two households that had been entangled in a land dispute with this family. In order to put an end to these suspicions, the heads of these thirty-two households gathered together in a local hall, knelt down, proclaimed their innocence, and beheaded chickens in front of an image of the City God (Chenghuang) from a nearby temple. A Japanese policeman from the local precinct office was also invited to serve as a witness to the proceedings, which were open to the public. The dispute seems to have been resolved shortly thereafter (Masuda 1942, 97). This example demonstrates the important role of public ritual as a means of attempting to resolve long-standing social tensions.

Case 2

The second example of a chicken-beheading ritual took place in Taizhong's City God temple at 2:00 P.M. on September 30, 1933. The events preceding this ritual had to do with a tangled web of connections and interests involving an inheritance case. Following the deaths of the head of the city's wealthy Lin family and his wife, their adopted and natural descendents as well as other relatives engaged in a bitter struggle for control of their assets, which ended up in the local courts. When the father of one of the parties suddenly died of "pneumonia" on September 3 and was promptly buried the next day, suspicions of foul play arose. Eventually, the relatives gathered in Taizhong's City God temple and beheaded three squawking chickens, again in the presence of a crowd of curious onlookers and nervous representatives of the colonial government (this time also including a prosecutor, a clerk, a native interpreter, and numerous policemen) (Masuda 1942, 97–100). I have yet to determine how the case was eventually resolved, but it provides a fascinating example of how Taiwanese practices of marriage and adoption studied by Arthur Wolf and other scholars could occasionally spark tensions that spilled into the realm of local religious traditions (see Wolf and Huang 1980; Wolf 1995). Moreover, we again see ritual serving as a public means of dispute resolution, as well as the presence of local officials at an event one might consider to be outside the bureaucratic realm.

Case 3

The remaining two cases of chicken-beheading rituals were actually witnessed by Masuda and his colleagues. The first took place in Dongshan Township (in today's Yilan County). Masuda and an individual named Kimura Teijiro transcribed a running dialogue in Southern Min purporting to be the actual remarks of the people involved. According to this account, Wang Buren borrowed 50 yen from his friend Chen Youyi (the names appear to be fictitious) but refused to return the money to Chen's widow after Chen's untimely death, claiming that he had already repaid it. The distraught woman and her only son immediately sought assistance from the ward chief, but he stated that he was powerless to do anything because Chen had failed to keep a receipt proving he had lent Wang the money. At that point, Chen's widow suggested going to Dongshan's City God temple and performing a chicken-beheading ritual to determine who was telling the truth. The next morning, Wang, Chen's widow, and the ward chief went to the temple. After kneeling down and worshipping the City God, Wang proceeded to make his oath: "Lord City God, I live at number 20 in Dongshan and my name is Wang Buren. I'm currently 53 years old. Last year I borrowed 50 yen from my elder brother Chen Youyi,[6] which I returned to him last month. If [in fact] I didn't return the money, may I fail to live out the year, and not even regret the deaths of all my children and grandchildren, just like this chicken [beheads the chicken]" (Masuda 1942, 79–80).

Chen's widow went next: "Lord City God, I live at number 15 in Dongshan and I am Chen Youyi's wife. I am 51 years old. If my husband had indeed received 50 yen from Buren may I have no descendents and die this year, just like this chicken [beheads the chicken]" (Masuda 1942, 80).

Just twenty days later the ward chief spotted Wang madly running through the streets, babbling that he had lied and would now be willing to give 100 yen to Chen's widow to put the matter to rest (Masuda 1942, 58–83). Regardless of the overall veracity of this story—which in its emphasis on madness as a form of divine punishment resembles an account recorded in Amoy by the British missionary John Macgowan (see Case 5)—we can again see the tendency for people to rely on judicial rituals when all other means had failed or were perceived as ineffective. This story also reveals that people did not take cursing literally. Therefore, despite the fact that neither Chen nor Wang actually perished within a year, the entire custom of making contingent curses in the presence of judicial deities did not suffer a loss of credibility. Moreover, Wang's confession of guilt, albeit in madness, solves the problem of the reliability of the ritual being at risk; it does not solve the problem of what would have happened if Wang had *not* confessed.

Case 4

The final example, which is also the one for which we have the best data, involved members of the elite from northern Taiwan. The plaintiff was the head of the Zhang family (originally from Xinzhuang, a city slightly south of Taibei, and later moved to Taibei), while the defendant was the head of the Ye family of Taibei. Between 1913 and 1914, Zhang's grandfather had failed in a business venture and, in order to hide his remaining assets from creditors, listed them under the name of his son-in-law Ye. After the grandfather's death, however, Ye refused to return control of these assets to the Zhangs. The Zhangs filed a lawsuit, but Ye proved a formidable adversary, having made a fortune in the canning industry and amassed assets of well over 100,000 yen. The suit languished in the courts for years until finally Zhang and Ye agreed to participate in two chicken-

Images on the altar of the Xiahai Chenghuang Temple, Taibei. (Photo by David K. Jordan)

beheading rituals to be held on the morning of May 10, 1933. The first was near the Zhangs' original home at Xinzhuang's Abbey of Ksitigarbha (Dizang An) and the second was near the Ye home at Taibei's famous City God temple (Xiahai Chenghuang Miao).

At 8:00 A.M. on the morning of May 10, four cars carrying Zhang, his lawyer, and Japanese officials (including a judge, a clerk, and an interpreter) pulled up in front of the Abbey of Ksitigarbha. Two white chickens were trussed up along the sides of Zhang's car. In an impressive display of support, two thousand locals had gathered outside the abbey, and the police had to deploy in force to maintain order and keep traffic moving. But Ye failed to show up, and by 10:30 the Japanese judge phoned him and instructed him to appear. By 11:00 it had become obvious that Ye was not planning to come, and so, after taking a photo to record the scene, Zhang and the officials set out for Taibei's City God temple at 11:30. By the time they reached the site, they found that an unruly crowd of over three thousand people had gathered, whistling and yelling as soon as Zhang stepped out of the car. After the police had restored order, Zhang and Ye finally strode inside the temple, made oaths of innocence, and beheaded the two chickens. Masuda's account reproduces a series of charges written in Chinese that the Zhangs had filed against Ye in 1927, followed by this declaration:

> If the above facts are true, and the defendant [Ye] refuses to admit this may his entire family—male and female, young and old—perish and may his ancestors be demoted to hungry ghosts.[7]
>
> If the above facts are false, and the plaintiff has filed a false plaint, may his entire family suffer the same fate, and his ancestors be demoted to hungry ghosts. (Masuda 1942, 94)

Shortly after the completion of this rite, which appears to have turned out unfavorably for Ye, his wife, son, and daughter-in-law filed a document with the Taihoku District Court declaring their refusal to recognize the rite's efficacy due to the fact that it was "superstitious" *(mixin)* as well as a "debased custom" *(louxi)*. The impact (if any) that the above chicken-beheading ritual had on actual legal proceedings is as yet unknown, but in August of 1934 the Zhangs won their case in court.

In considering the overall significance of the four chicken-beheading rituals described above, a number of important issues come to mind. We should begin by recognizing that all four cases involve conflicts that the parties were unable to resolve by mediation, two of which had entered the legal system. Secondly, in terms of their geographic scope, these cases cover the entire island of Taiwan, while in terms of social class they extend from farmers and workers to members of Taiwan's urban elites. Thirdly, while the chickens were beheaded in front of the gods, they were not sacrificial items. After the ritual had concluded, their bodies were not cooked, offered to the gods, and then eaten, but rather, they were thrown away. In other words, the chickens resembled scapegoats rather than offerings.[8] Finally, all four rituals were staged in front of Taiwan's underworld gods. In three examples, these deities simply witnessed the rite, but in Case 3 the City God was thought to have acted as judge and executioner as well.

Chicken-beheading rituals were also performed in postwar Taiwan, but they differed from their colonial era predecessors in being performed during elections as well as disputes. Little systematic research has been done on this topic, but as Li Yih-yuan once noted, some politicians or candidates who had been accused of wrongdoing would not hesitate to publicly behead live chickens in order to demonstrate their innocence (Li Yih-yuan 1983). Chicken-beheading rites are performed only rarely in Taiwan today, apparently due to a growing sense of discomfort with their bloody nature. Still, such rituals occasionally serve as metaphors in political campaigns. For example, during the 2000 presidential campaign, when James Soong (Song Chuyu) was accused of having embezzled funds from his own Nationalist Party (KMT), a local cartoonist published a picture of him performing a chicken-beheading ritual in order to emphasize his innocence (*Liberty Times* 1999, 15). This cartoon proved particularly amusing because Soong, a thoroughly westernized member of the elite, would be unlikely to even contemplate performing such a rite, and because most people assumed he was in fact guilty as charged. Other politicians continue to make oaths without choosing to behead chickens. In one example that took place in the spring of 2001, when Yan Qingbiao, the former Taizhong County Council speaker and current member of the Legislative Yuan, was accused of extortion and attempted murder, he made an oath in one of Taiwan's most renowned temples (the Zhenlan Gong, dedicated to the goddess Mazu) proclaiming his innocence. Candidates embroiled in tight political races will not hesitate to make oaths in leading local temples.

"Presidential Candidate James Soong Beheads a Chicken." Presidential candidate James Soong (Song Chuyu), wearing a butcher's apron emblazoned with his surname, beheads a squawking fowl in an unidentified temple, exclaiming: "I am honest! I am honest!" In the background, then-president Lee Teng-hui (Li Denghui) is shown asking KMT presidential candidate Lien Chan (Lian Zhan): "Is this his last trick?" The placard in the lower right corner reads: "Oath-Making; Chicken-Beheading." (Cartoon by Yü Fu from Liberty Times [Ziyou shibao], December 18, 1999)

ON THE NATURE OF CHICKEN-BEHEADING RITES

Until recently, people in Taiwan usually chose to perform chicken-beheading rituals after other attempts at dispute mediation had failed, with the exception of politicians who did so in order to prove their innocence in the face of charges of corruption or vote buying. The Chinese term for oath making, *"duzhou"* (literally, "to gamble on an oath"), and the Southern Min *"zhouzu"* (literally, "an oath and an imprecation") clearly express the elements of risk and danger involved in submitting to the rigors of this ritual process. As the folklorist Wu Ying-t'ao noted in his description of Taiwanese customs:

> In most cases, so-called "gambling on an oath" is accomplished by facing the heavens and making a vow *(duitian lishi)*. In more serious cases, when a simple oral expression [of innocence] proves unable to satisfy the other party or fully resolve the matter, additional steps are taken, which involve the parties making a vow in the presence of the City God . . . or other judicial deities. This expresses the solemnity of the occasion.
>
> The contents of these vows generally involve the expression of the willingness of the party who speaks falsely to accept any punishment the gods may choose to inflict, including the death of his/her entire family, death while on a trip away from home,[9] or a bad death before one's time. The parties also formulate promises to be fulfilled, and those who actually make oaths dare not break them.
>
> The most serious form of "gambling on an oath" is to make a vow and slaughter a chicken in the presence of the gods, which is called "killing a

chicken while making oaths and imprecations." The meaning of this rite is to express one's willingness to be killed should his/her oath prove false. In the past, local officials used these forms of oath-making in adjudicating cases, something which could be termed psychological trials. Because the people have always felt fear and reverence for their gods, they rarely dare make a false oath in their presence due to their deep fear of divine punishment. Even in those rare cases when someone makes false statements, they soon become faint of heart and often make fools of themselves. People often end up quaking with fear, or suffering other inexplicable occurrences. (Wu Ying-t'ao 1987, 167–168)[10]

Wu's account is highly significant because it indicates that the deities worshipped during chicken-beheading rituals frequently included members of the underworld bureaucracy responsible for helping to administer justice there. Wu's account identifies the City God, while other sources also list the Emperor of the Eastern Peak (Dongyue Dadi) and the Bodhisattva Ksitigarbha (Dizangwang Pusa). These gods are generally associated with judgment and punishment in the underworld. Thus, people making an oath would not invoke a deity such as the Guanyin, the Bodhisattva of Compassion. Similarly, Yan Qingbiao's oath to Mazu caused some amusement among his critics, who remarked that if he had really been innocent he would have dared to make his oath in front of an underworld deity. Other instances can be more complicated. Gods of loyalty and integrity such as Guan Di are usually not invoked during disputes, yet some secret society initiation rituals feature the making of an oath of loyalty in the presence of Guan Di (ter Haar 1998, 192). When it comes to disputes between two individuals, however, the issue of divine judgment and the imagery of punishing courts seem central.

In terms of their ritual structure, chicken beheadings appear to have consisted of two main components: the making of an oath and the slaughter of the cockerel. While some disputes could be settled by oath making alone, more complex or potentially explosive cases clearly required the sacrifice of an animal victim (Wu Ying-t'ao 1987, 167–168). The fact that a white cockerel was usually the bird of choice may be because it has long symbolized the sun and yang forces of life and vitality, but on a more practical level, cockerels were cheaper to purchase than other animals (de Groot 1892–1910, 1: 200–218, 6: 965–970; ter Haar 1998, 157, 183). One scholar has even suggested that cockerels were never eaten because of their potential use in oaths (Williams 1941, 199–200). As for the gods invoked during these rituals, they served as impartial witnesses that also had the power to judge the guilt or innocence of the participants and enforce the grim punishments cited in the oath's maledictions (ter Haar 1998, 163, 178). People believed that wrongdoers who made false oaths were doomed to suffer a wide range of divine punishments, including illness and even death.

If we consider the overall purpose of judicial rites such as chicken beheadings, as well as their structure, it soon becomes clear that they represent a key component of a process whereby individuals entangled in a dispute convince themselves to go to a temple and publicly make contingent curses listing horrific consequences for the party who dares commit perjury. Contingent curses appear to be an interesting generic subcategory of cursing, with potentially provocative contrasts to other forms of cursing. For example, such curses differ from the simple act of wishing misfortune to befall someone else (for example, "Damn you!" or "Drop dead!") in that they feature a greater degree of self-restraint by not seeking immediate harm. Indeed, while verbal abuse sometimes substitutes for physical abuse, a contingent curse cannot necessarily do so, since it is to be triggered by future events that may occur when the abuser is not around to deliver the blow. Contingent curses can also be attached to a wide range of circumstances, only some of which need be in the control of the person who will be the recipient of the curse. Finally, contingent curses are frequently used to wish misfortune on oneself, which also stands in contrast to the usual characteristics of cursing.

Regardless of the circumstances underlying their performance and the nature of the curse, judicial rituals such as chicken beheadings are clearly marked by a window of peril for the guilty party. While the gods invoked during such rites are not necessarily obliged to pass and execute their grim judgments immediately after the ritual's conclusion, people scrutinize what happens to the participants in the hours and days thereafter. In some instances people suffer divine retribution shortly after a rite has been performed, but in others the results remain unclear. Moreover, it appears that people are not always literalistic about cursing: The retribution suffered by the guilty party does not necessarily have to match the contents of the curse, and perjurers who in theory are supposed to die only suffer illness or other forms of misfortune. Perhaps more importantly, however, the performance of a judicial ritual and the period of waiting for divine judgment that follow may allow for tempers to cool and the entire matter to be brought to a peaceful resolution before disputes turn violent (see, for example, Case 4 above).[11]

HISTORICAL ANTECEDENTS

Any attempt to trace the history of Taiwan's chicken-beheading rites would logically begin in the areas along China's southeastern coast, from which many Han Chinese migrated to Taiwan. It should thus come as no surprise that the data from this region—especially the province of Fujian—indicate that temples there were frequently sites for both making oaths and doing so as part of a chicken-beheading ritual. Yao Han-ch'iu's research reveals that in southern Fujian, individuals suspected of theft were often hauled before images of judges (*panguan*) and instructed to make oaths proclaiming their innocence. Then, someone hiding behind the image would move its right arm to point at the defendant, who if guilty would supposedly break down and confess (Yao 1981,

120). The effectiveness of such rites in actually catching thieves is unclear. In addition, Michael Szonyi's groundbreaking research on late imperial Fuzhou also shows that villagers there occasionally staged trials in the presence of the Earth God or other tutelary deities, and that the managers of their temples often served as judges (Szonyi 2002, 190).[12]

Detailed accounts of chicken-beheading rituals in Amoy can be found in the writings of the British Presbyterian missionary John Macgowan. A member of the London Missionary Society, Macgowan journeyed to Amoy in 1863 and preached the gospel there, while also traveling to other parts of China for over fifty years. In two books, published in 1910 and 1912, he provides gripping accounts of oaths and chicken-beheading rites he witnessed at Amoy's City God temple. The data Macgowan presents largely conform to what we know about chicken-beheading rituals in Taiwan—particularly their links to irresolvable social conflicts, the fearful imprecations accompanying the rite, the grim consequences that could be visited upon the guilty, and the potential for local officials to become involved.

Case 5

Macgowan's first account describes what happened when a shop owner accused one of his two apprentices of stealing one hundred dollars. The suspect promptly decided to file an indictment against the other apprentice, whom he suspected of having stolen the money, and so, with a large white cockerel in his left hand and the newly accused in tow, he led a throng of people to the City God temple. There, in the presence of the god, he hurled imprecations against the as yet unknown individual who had actually stolen the money. Macgowan records his words as follows: "Let his life be one long torture. . . . May every enterprise in which he engages end in disaster; may his mother and father die and let him be left desolate . . . may he become a beggar with ulcered legs . . . may he never have a son . . . may madness seize upon him so that his reason shall fly and he shall be a source of terror to this fellow-man; and finally, may a tragic and horrible death bring his life to a sudden end, even as I bring to an end the life of this white cock that I have brought with me [he beheads the cockerel]" (Macgowan 1910, 140).

The young man then took a previously prepared written indictment and burned it. The other apprentice remained silent during the rite, perhaps due to his own guilty feelings, for just two weeks after the conclusion of the rite his sister drowned and his family's fields were washed away in a flood. Eventually, the poor fellow went insane, and like Wang Buren in Case 3 aimlessly wandered the streets muttering about ghosts chasing him. His madness soon turned violent, and he had to be restrained with ropes to prevent him from hurting himself or others. Finally, his distraught father somehow located or produced the stolen amount, and the assistant who had performed the chicken-beheading rite submitted a written petition to the City God in which he dropped the charges. The guilty party recovered shortly after the completion of this rite (Macgowan 1910, 140–145).

Case 6

The second chicken-beheading rite Macgowan witnessed involved a wealthy man who had a considerable sum of money stolen from his home. When he blamed his assistant, the latter denied all knowledge of the crime and volunteered to bring a white cockerel to the temple of the City God and make an oath in the deity's presence in order to prove his innocence. This ritual differed from the one described above in that while the plaintiff also read aloud and burned a written indictment, this time the defendant solemnly proclaimed his innocence and declared his willingness to submit to any punishment the gods saw fit to inflict should he in fact be lying. After concluding by stating his willingness to suffer sudden death, the defendant beheaded the white cockerel he had brought with him. A few days after the ritual, the real culprit became so terrified at the thought of his impending doom that he found a way to return the wealthy man's money without revealing his identity. At this point, the plaintiff had to take the rather embarrassing action of appearing in public before the City God and withdrawing his indictment of the original defendant (Macgowan 1912, 137–140). One interesting aspect of this case is the vagueness of the punishment the plaintiff proposed to suffer, as this could protect the gods from suspicion of being ineffective while subjecting him to the risk of being judged guilty should any ill fortune befall him.

Case 7

Macgowan also provides an example of reckless oath making that almost culminated in a chicken-beheading ritual. A wealthy individual had assumed possession of someone else's ancestral land when the family had gone through hard times, and he refused to resell it to a family member who had earned enough money to buy it back. When this man filed a complaint with the local officials, the magistrate, who clearly sympathized with the family, decided to try the case in the City God temple. Once the trial had begun, the magistrate declared his inability to determine the rightful owner's identity and suggested asking the god to decide. Messengers were sent out to purchase a white cockerel, and the ritual began. But when the rich man began to list the imprecations to afflict him and his family should he be caught lying, a scream was heard and one of his sons fell to the ground in a faint. At this point, the magistrate stepped forward and awarded the house to the family (Macgowan 1912, 140–142). This is akin to the man going mad in Case 3 and again suggests how seriously these oaths were sometimes taken. But also of great interest here is that the making of an oath enters into the procedure of a regular law court, suggesting that judicial rituals were not always conceived of as being distinct from actual legal practice.[13]

Fujianese and other Chinese who migrated overseas also practiced chicken-beheading rituals. For example, one account about Chinese communities in Singapore states that the beheading of a cockerel "is a procedure which the Chinese only resort to in cases of the greatest importance, for many of them intensely dislike thus killing the cockerel. . . . I have seen men turn livid and perspire when they have had to cut off a cock's head on such occasions" (Ward and Stirling 1925, 1:71; ter Haar 1998, 164–165).

While the long-term historical development of chicken-beheading rituals is too complex to treat in detail here, the following items of information might serve to whet the appetite of interested readers.[14] The earliest possible antecedents to Taiwan's chicken-beheading rituals are the oaths and blood covenants of ancient China, as well as ancient judicial rituals involving the sacrifice of a goat (Ch'ü 1961, 210; Huang Zhanyue 1986, 16–17; Lewis 1990, 67–96, 195–205; Liu 1998, 147–172). Oaths and blood covenants were frequently performed throughout Chinese communities during the early modern era, particularly among soldiers, militiamen, gangsters, and members of secret societies (Chin 1996; Faure 1990; Niida 1964; ter Haar 1995, 31; ter Haar 1998, 152–164, 181–189). Daoist priests and ritual masters who resided in Fujian and other parts of south China during the Song and Yuan dynasties also beheaded chickens in the course of cementing alliances with the deities that protected them during exorcistic rituals (Katz 2000, 179–180; ter Haar 1998: 153–156). If we cast our nets even wider in search of evidence about the history of chicken-beheading rituals, we soon discover that numerous minority peoples of southwestern China also practiced similar rituals well into the twentieth century (Xia 1990; Zhang 2000).

CONCLUSION

The historical and field data presented in this essay clearly indicate the importance of judicial rituals such as chicken beheadings in the social and cultural history of China and Taiwan. It is no easy task to interpret the significance of such an ancient rite with so many variants. In reading the accounts presented above, however, one is soon struck by the fact that such rituals frequently contain threats of violence against the accuser and the accused, as well as occasional acts of violence involving a blood sacrifice. The ritual slaughter of animals appears significant because such victims may have served as scapegoats for the parties involved in disputes—and perhaps even the entire community. In a stimulating treatment of ritual violence, Rene Girard maintains that violent tendencies with the potential to disrupt communal life are frequently redirected onto defenseless surrogate victims during rituals (Girard 1979; see also Henninger 1987a, 1987b). Practices such as chicken-beheading rituals feature the violent deaths of animals as part of an attempt to prevent outbreaks of violence between plaintiffs and defendants and thus may fit Girard's ideas. It is also important not to forget the very real threat of violence that could occur if disputes were not resolved quickly and effectively. Late imperial courts were infamous for torturing defendants and, on occasion, even plaintiffs, while other cases that never made it to local courts ended up degenerating into vigilante justice, euphemistically referred to in Chinese as "private punishments" *(sixing)*. In Fujian and Taiwan, for example, people accused of stealing, who never had their cases heard by human magistrates, could have their tendons cut, be hung by ropes and beaten, or be force-fed excrement, while accused rapists were buried up to the neck and left to die (Kataoka 1921, 61–68; Macgowan 1912, 167–168). Philip Kuhn's research on soul-stealing *(jiaohun)* panics during the eighteenth century also cites numerous examples of wrongly accused sorcerers being brutally lynched by angry mobs before officials had a chance to try their cases (Kuhn 1991).[15]

It also seems clear that chicken-beheading rituals and their historical antecedents centered on one central theme: the pursuit of fair and impartial justice, an ideal that appears not only in judicial rituals but also numerous works of fiction and drama.[16] The recent popularity in Taiwan of the television series *Bao Qingtian,* about the renowned Song dynasty judge known as Lord Bao (Bao Gong), may be due to this factor. Even in contemporary China and Taiwan, the combination of fear felt toward underworld deities combined with faith in their judgments remains real and profound. Numerous temples for such deities contain murals or sculptures vividly portraying the tortures wrongdoers can expect to face in the underworld, as well as gripping images of the judges and lictors responsible for the administration of divine justice.[17] Some temples that are dedicated to China's underworld deities even display large abacuses in order to represent the accuracy with which the gods could calculate one's good and evil deeds.[18] Others have placards bearing the words, "So, you [too] have come [to be judged]!" *(Ni/er [ye] laile)* (Duara 1988, 12; Lü 1992, 23). One moving inscription composed in 1847 and carved on a pair of wooden placards in Tainan's City God temple vividly expresses both the fear and awe people felt for these deities. A portion of it reads: "I ask you, what have you done during your lifetime? Grasped at other peoples' wealth, ruined their lives, fornicated with their women, destroyed their ethics. . . . When you come here, all injustice will be requited. Reduce your lifespan! Destroy your possessions! Annihilate your descendents! Punish your licentiousness! Open your eyes, fear ye not? Of all those violent and vicious [souls who have come here], how many can escape [their fate]?" (Lü 1992, 24).

Despite the fact that some works of literature portray the underworld bureaucracy as being capricious or even corrupt (for example, see Campany 1996; Dudbridge 1995; Teiser 1988, 1993, 1994), the rituals described above were clearly predicated on the notion that this system provided better justice than its earthly counterpart. Chen Youyi's widow in Dongshan, the Zhangs of Xinzhuang, the shop assistant in Amoy, and many others placed their faith in judicial rites and the underworld bureaucracy they invoked.

This thirst for justice, combined with the need to confront the causes of injustice and disharmony, suggests that chicken-beheading rituals may be somewhat similar to the Balinese cockfights studied by Clifford Geertz (1973). Apart from involving fowls that are the objects of a blood sacrifice, both events appear to feature forms of "deep play," in the sense of addressing moral and social issues of keen interest to the men and women who participated in or observed them. Chicken beheadings center on the issue of justice, while Balinese cockfights tend to address issues of social status, yet both are public performances that attempt to render experience comprehensible by focusing attention on acts and objects that have had their consequences removed. In both performances, the only real victims are the unfortunate fowls. For the people who witness a chicken-beheading ritual or a cockfight, the goal of the performance appears not to be the immediate determination of guilt or a change in social status but to publicly consider the very nature of justice or hierarchy. In effect, then, both chicken-beheading rituals and cockfights are reflexive events that provide a public commentary about social structure and cultural values that all can see and feel. As a result, these performances may allow the Taiwanese or Balinese to better come to grips with a particular facet of their own society.

3
Pop in Hell
Representations of Purgatory in Taiwan
David K. Jordan

EDITORS' INTRODUCTION

Like Paul Katz in his chapter on chicken-beading rituals, David Jordan is interested in long-lasting Chinese cultural traditions and their contribution to the concepts that people in Taiwan use in approaching the world today. Even when these traditions are not believed or followed, Jordan argues, they constitute part of the "mental furniture" with which people in Taiwan approach daily life.

In this chapter, Jordan describes two ancient sets of Chinese ideas. The first is the understanding that after death we are all subjected to a close examination by a supernatural court (usually called "hell" by English writers about China) that punishes us for our evil deeds and assigns us a reincarnation appropriate to our merit. Ideas about reincarnation and a divine accounting of our earthly deeds were prominent in the Buddhism that entered China from India. The "Chinese twist" is a purgatory modeled on traditional Chinese magistrates and their courts.

Hell has been represented in gruesome detail in Chinese popular art and texts for many centuries. Jordan briefly describes some of the most common popular representations of hell in modern Taiwan—paintings, movies, children's books—making the point that, whether people believe in hell or not, they cannot help knowing something about it. But Jordan goes one step further: He tries to explain why the idea of hell, unlike many other ideas that have appeared in the course of history, has remained so popular.

He then moves on to quite a different tradition: honoring and obeying one's parents—filial piety, a concept so fundamental in China that some English writers borrow the Chinese term *(xiao)* rather than even attempting to translate it. Filial piety is a core value of mainstream Confucianism and has been central to Chinese morality (and Chinese law) for over two thousand years. As with the courts of hell, Jordan reviews some of the modern sources by which people in Taiwan are inevitably exposed to filial piety. Once again, he argues that even people who disagree cannot avoid knowing about it, and he explores some of the psychological implications of this moral principle.

Then he poses a puzzle: What sort of society maintains that parents must be honored but also represents them as going to gruesome torments in hell after death? Indeed, lurid pictures of hell are even hung around a parent's coffin. Doesn't that suggest a good deal of hostility toward one's parents?

Far from being conflicting traditions, hell and filial piety are complementary, mutually reinforcing ones, Jordan argues. In the following discussion, he explains how this can be. ■

This essay is about two pervasive and enduring bodies of Chinese popular tradition found in Taiwan: ideas about hell, which represent the human soul after death as subject to hideous tortures, and understandings about filial piety, which stereotypically involve nearly unquestioning love for and obedience to parents.

Both hell and filial piety have clearly been interesting and salient ideas for centuries. And yet there would seem, on the face of it, to be something contradictory about them, since it seems potentially unfilial to contemplate parents being subjected to the tortures of hell. The title is intentionally a triple pun: father ("Pop") in hell, pop culture about hell, and representations of hell available to be "popped into."

The first section discusses some of the representations of hell that both create and reflect its continuing importance in popular imagination. The second section very briefly discusses the role of filial piety as seen through popular representations, which I have discussed in more detail elsewhere (Jordan 1986). The third section presents an argument about how these potentially link to each other.

HELL

We don't know exactly what prehistoric Chinese believed would happen to them after death, although the presence of grave goods is usually taken by archaeologists as suggesting a belief in an afterlife. By early historic times, we know that ancestor worship had come to play an important role in Chinese life and had become one of the most important behavioral symbols of filial piety.

Filial piety, in turn, had come to be seen as a prime human virtue, a central human emotion, and a critical code of behavior (Jordan 1998). When Confucius and his school consolidated the established wisdom concerning morality about 500–400 B.C., filial piety and ancestral worship had central roles to play.

The arrival of Buddhism from India beginning in about the first century brought with it the notion of postmortal accountability for one's deeds during life, and almost immediately there are references to a kind of postmortal system of courts and prisons in which the dead are made to stand trial and suffer punishment. These courts are usually referred to as "hell" by English writers. In Chinese they are called the "earth prison" *(diyu)* or sometimes "dark regions" *(mingjian)* or "the realm of the dead" *(yinjian)*.[1]

In its developed form, the belief in a place of postmortal judgment inspired elaborate descriptions of the courts of hell, as well as paintings and sculptures of them, stressing fortified gates, frightened prisoners, frowning officials, and monstrous lictors and beadles gruesomely torturing prisoners to extract confessions or punishing them for their sins. Long lists were compiled of human failings and their otherworldly punishments,[2] and different schemes existed as to how these courts were organized, culminating with one's assignment to a new incarnation by the judge of the last court of the system.

In the ninth or tenth court, just before one is reincarnated, one is asked to mount the "Terrace of Exorcism and Forgetfulness" (Quwang Tai) and sip the "tea of five flavors" *(wuwei cha)* offered by a figure known as Grandmother Meng (Meng Po). This beverage obliterates all memory of previous lives or of the punishments just suffered, preparing the soul for the innocence of childhood in a new incarnation.

Some of the crimes for which one might be punished in the courts of hell were traditionally associated with Buddhism—most conspicuously, drinking alcohol or killing animals—and nearly all depictions show butchers suffering in hell because of their profession.[3] Despite the Buddhist origins of the idea of a postmortal system of courts, however, the crimes for which Chinese believed one might be punished were not necessarily very Buddhist. On the contrary, any violation of general public morality might be represented as likely to attract the sanction of the courts—above all, any lapse in filial piety.

In some ways, tales of hell even represent the triumph of Chinese popular "Confucian" morality over Buddhist excess; that is, the person who is an exemplar of filial piety does better in hell than one who tries to be a Buddhist and slips up even a little bit. One popular tale, repeated especially in theatricals and films, tells of a monk named Mulian, one of the disciples of the Buddha, whose mother is sent to the nethermost parts of hell because she has callously butchered a cow. Mulian, overcome with filial grief at his mother's suffering and determined to share his Buddhist merit with her to bring about her rescue, visits hell against all obstacles. In the end, the infernal Powers That Be—in large part moved by Mulian's self-sacrifice on behalf of his mother—release her back to life. Thus the exaggerated punishment for a symbolic Buddhist sin is exonerated by an extravagant, symbolic Confucian gesture.[4]

Texts about Hell

People learn about hell in a variety of ways, ranging from proverbs to paintings and from theatrical productions and films to small printed tracts, usually with vivid illustrations. A century ago the tracts featured woodcut illustrations. Today they often have brightly colored cartoons.

There is no single, standard description of hell. Texts describing hell have been generated at various periods right up to the present, sometimes by spirit mediums writing in trance[5] and sometimes by authors self-consciously creating morality tracts. In recent centuries, hell has been divided into ten courts *(dian)*, each presided over by a king *(wang)*.[6]

In recent centuries, many of the texts describing hell have had the name "Jade Almanac" (Yuli), and for several centuries one text in particular has been reproduced more often than the others that provides us a reasonable view of what most people have been told happens in hell.[7] The text is called the "Precious Manuscript of the Jade Almanac" (Yuli baochao), although it too has slight variants.[8] It circulates widely in Taiwan and can readily be found among the religious pamphlets and tracts left in temples for free distribution to anyone who wants them.

In elaborate versions of the "Jade Almanac," each court may be divided into several subhalls.[9] In simpler presentations each court may be presented as more or less unitary. The text usually consists of a list of the sins identified in that court and of the punishments associated with them. The soul of a person who has slandered another may have its tongue cut out, for example, or one who failed to respect a parent-in-law may be burned by lightning. A large proportion of the number of the sins have to do with failing to respect people in authority, particularly parents. Most of the punishments involve stabbing, chopping, disemboweling, flaying, mincing, or burning the offending soul.

To suggest the flavor of this text, here is the portion devoted to the Third Hell, as rendered by Herbert Giles (1916, 472–473):

The Third Court
His Infernal Majesty Sung Ti reigns at the bottom of the great Ocean, away to the south-east, below the Wu-chiao rock, in the Gehenna of Black Ropes. This Hall is many leagues wide, and is subdivided into sixteen wards, as follows:

In the first everything is Salt; above, below, and all round, the eye rests upon Salt alone. The shades feed upon it, and suffer horrid torments in consequence. When the fit has passed away they return to it once again, and suffer agonies more unutterable than before. In the second, the erring shades are bound with cords and carry heavily-weighted *cangues*. In the third, they are perpetually pierced through the ribs. In the fourth, their faces are scraped with iron and copper knives. In the fifth, their fat is scraped away from their bodies. In the sixth, their hearts and livers are squeezed with pincers. In the seventh, their eyes are gouged. In the eighth, they are flayed. In the ninth, their feet are cut off. In the tenth, their fingernails and toe-nails are pulled out. In the eleventh, their blood is sucked. In the twelfth, they are hung up head downwards. In the thirteenth, their shoulder-bones are split. In the fourteenth, they are tormented by insects and reptiles. In the fifteenth, they are beaten on the thighs. In the sixteenth, their hearts are scratched.

Those who enjoy the light of day without reflecting on the Imperial bounty; officers of State who revel in large emoluments without reciprocating their sovereign's goodness; private individuals who do not repay the debt of water and earth; wives and concubines who slight their marital lords; those who fail in their duties as acting sons, or such as reap what advantages there are and then go off to their own homes; slaves who disregard their masters; official underlings who are ungrateful to their superiors; working partners who behave badly to the moneyed partner; culprits who escape from prison or abscond from their place of banishment; those who break their bail and get others into trouble; and those infatuated ones who have long omitted to pray and repent—all these, even though they have a set-off of good deeds, must pass through the misery of every ward. Those who interfere with another man's Feng-Shui; those who obstruct funeral obsequies or the completion of graves; those who in digging come on a coffin and do not immediately cover it up, but injure the bones; those who steal or avoid paying up their quota of grain; those who lose all record of the site of their family burying-place; those who incite others to commit crimes; those who promote litigation; those who write anonymous placards; those who repudiate a betrothal; those who forge deeds and other documents; those who receive payment of a debt without signing a receipt or giving up the IOU; those who counterfeit signatures and seals; those who alter bills; those who injure posterity in any way—all these and similar offenders, shall be punished according to the gravity of each offence. Devils with big knives will seize the erring ones and thrust them into the great Gehenna; besides which they shall expiate their sins in the proper number of wards, and shall then be forwarded to the Fourth Court, where they shall be tortured and dismissed to the general Gehenna.

O ye sons of men, on the 8th day of the 2nd moon, register an oath that ye will do no evil. Thus you may escape the bitterness of these hells.

The details change with different authors or, in paintings, with different artists. A version circulating in Taiwan starting about 1920 or so has a woodcut of what appears to be a tractor with industrial cogs for wheels chopping up the bodies of sinners. A tract published in Taiwan in the 1980s describes the torments of such newly salient sins as taxi dancing and homosexuality and features a waiting room for those killed by others through abortion or who have been hit by cars, who must wait until their appointed time of natural death before being allowed to proceed. A new hall has been set up, according to this tract, for the punishment of drunk and careless drivers (Jiang 1984a).

In the last court of hell, the soul is assigned to a new life. Here is Giles' rendition of the beginning of the description of the Tenth Hell (1916, 482):

The Tenth Court
His Infernal Majesty Chuan Lun reigns in the Dark Land, due east, away below the Wu-chiao rock, just opposite the Wu-cho of this world. There he has six bridges, of gold, silver, jade, stone, wood, and planks, over which all souls must pass. He examines the shades that are sent from the other courts, and, according to their deserts, sends them back to earth as men, women, old, young, high, low, rich, or poor, forwarding monthly a list of their names to the judge of the First Court for transmission to Feng-tu [the capital city of the Infernal Regions].

The imagery of bridges of reincarnation is vivid enough that for years, visitors to the Tiger Balm Gardens in Hong Kong could pass over a gold bridge set among the many dioramas of Chinese myth and story.

Not all literary works that discuss hell make its punishments the central point. In some cases, the torturers and jailers are merely the background to a concern with reincarnation. Divination societies produce a genre of text in which the present life situation of a society member is explained as the natural result of two previous lives, with the kings of hell being the decision makers about what each life is to be (see Jordan 1981; Jordan and Overmyer 1986, 112–114). Stories of this type are not limited to divination texts. In 1995 a series of comic books on this theme was being distributed free in the temples of central Taiwan, apparently aimed principally at children.[10]

Chinese films also make frequent reference to hell, for it is inevitably involved in the ghost stories that are a continuing feature of the Greater China cinematic world.[11] An example was released in 1984 under the title *The Reincarnation of Golden Lotus (Pan Jinlian zhi Qianshi Jinsheng)* (Luo 1989). Golden Lotus is a figure from an anonymous novel, *Jin Ping Mei,* of the Ming dynasty (1368–1644), in which the action is set about five centuries earlier. Golden Lotus is the fifth wife of a lascivious official who has a total of six wives but also conducts numerous amorous affairs, all described in great detail. (Chinese have been describing this popular book as obscene for several centuries.) For Golden Lotus, it is a second marriage, for it is revealed that she murdered her first husband and tried to seduce his brother. The 1985 film about her reincarnation plays upon this tradition, of which it is assumed the audience is aware, at least in broad outline. The reincarnated Lotus lives in our own period and has a career similar to that of her Song dynasty namesake. (Pictures of a manuscript version of the old book are interspersed throughout the film, lest there be any question about the audience catching the reference.)

What about hell? In the first few minutes of the film, we meet Lotus as a soul in hell, lined up to drink the tea of five flavors. Grandmother Meng, represented in the garb of a Buddhist nun, tells her she must drink three cups, despite the bitterness of the brew. As she drinks, Lotus has flashbacks of the many men she has loved or who have abused her. Suddenly, as she is about to drink the third cup, she remembers an outrageous murder, throws down the cup, and shouts, "I want revenge!" This sets the stage for flashbacks throughout the rest of the movie that underline the parallels between her troubled modern life and faintly remembered images from her life in the Song dynasty.

The film can be understood in many ways and has been interpreted as an allegory of the vices of materialism and floundering values in modern Hong Kong. What is of interest here is that the film depends critically on Grandmother Meng in its opening scene and on the viewer's understanding that Lotus' failure to drink the third cup and "forget the past and start anew," as she is advised to do, leads to her undoing in the present.

In chapter 10, Marc Moskowitz discusses one of the most popular films in recent years, *A Chinese Ghost Story (Qiannü Youhun)* and its similarly named sequels, based on a collection composed by author Pu Songling (1640–1715).[12] The action focuses on a ghost who has been enslaved by a demon, and this has prevented her timely reincarnation. Reincarnation, of course, is a process that takes place in the last court of hell. Despite the danger that the ghost of the film poses to him, the protagonist, out of nobility of character, undertakes to rescue her from the demon so that she can be properly reincarnated. Although hell is not directly represented in any detail, it is a background presence in these films. And the representation of the reincarnation wheel of hell shown in a cartoon version could just as well be taken from an old woodcut of the tenth court of hell.[13]

An important genre of Chinese film is comic horror. Comic horror films play with what is frightening by introducing bumbling and stupid characters often trying to make their way in a world that entangles them with ghosts. Though few of these films directly portray hell and its courts, it is clear in film after film that hell is part of the reality with which the ghostly characters must deal. The point is that, even for people who do not look at temple tracts or morbid paintings, some knowledge of hell is part of everyday life.

The most important of the underworld kings is Yanluo. In the modern Chinese scheme, Yanluo usually presides over the fifth court of hell.[14] His is a name most people are likely to know, and it is he who appears in proverbs about death and hell. Mao Zedong was only one among many millions of old people who spoke of his impending death as an appointment with King Yanluo. That is also how one can describe the actions of a careless driver or of someone who constantly courts danger. Any native speaker of Chinese sooner or later knows something about Yanluo.

Hell in Art

Hell was been represented in paintings, woodblock prints, and sculpture for many centuries. Beijing's Temple of Eighteen Hells (Shiba Diyu Miao) was fa-

A life-sized diorama at Bagua Shan in Zhanghua portrays a sinner being fried in a wok by torturers in hell. (Photo by David K. Jordan)

mous for its "life-sized" sculptures (Goodrich 1981), and other temples also sometimes devoted whole galleries to such sculpture. Herbert Giles (1916, 467) reports that many a Daoist temple in particular would contain such a "Chamber of Horrors," as he tells us foreigners called them. Such displays are not entirely a thing of the past. Near Zhanghua's Eight Trigrams Mountain (Bagua Shan) in Taiwan, a private association has erected an unnerving, partially animated walk-through display occupying several stories of an apartment building. And galleries of waxworks in Tianjin, Qingdao, and other mainland cities often contain selected items or scenes from hell, as do the famed Tiger Balm Gardens of Hong Kong and Singapore.

Temples that could not afford large sculpture or had no space for it might make use of smaller sculptures or mural paintings. In Taiwan, mural paintings have been the norm. One particularly expects them in temples devoted to the

Emperor of the Eastern Peak (Dongyue Dadi), who is specifically associated with the admission of new souls into hell and in whose temples memorials to the dead are performed; or in temples devoted to the City God (Chenghuang), associated with leading the souls of the newly deceased to the underworld. But murals showing the courts of hell are also found in countless other temples, including temples devoted to the goddess Mazu and other figures who have no particularly close connection themselves to memorializing the dead.[15]

Perhaps most important are paintings (and in recent decades, prints) mounted as scrolls and hung on the sidewalls of tent temples erected by Daoist liturgists for the conduct of funerals.[16] In the most common arrangement, a tent is erected in the courtyard of a house or in the street out in front. Temporary altars are erected at one end where liturgy will be performed, and the other is left open, with the coffin positioned more or less in the center. The scrolls representing hell are hung along the side walls, where they are visible to all and are often an object of great curiosity to small children. The finer and more expensive a funeral is, the more elaborate the equipment that is used, and the better quality and more detailed the paintings are.

Hell is clearly a referent for much funerary and memorial ritual. Although many paper models of houses, clothes, automobiles, and other comforts of life are burned for the service of the dead, imitation money ("mock money" or "hell banknotes") is particularly prominent, and informants over the years have been unanimous in telling me that it is at least in part to be used to bribe the judges and other functionaries in hell.

Yet specific rites in the course of a "traditional" funeral also remind mourners that the newly dead and many of the long departed still languish in infernal regions and can benefit by liberating ritual performed by the living. Among the most vivid of these acts is the physical destruction of paper models of individual prisons in which ancestors are thought to be trapped (Huang Wenbo 1992, 103–114, 197–214).

Popular religious processions are another opportunity to be reminded of the justice and torments of hell. Processional troupes of various kinds, collectively called *zhentou* or *zaji*, include stilt walkers, martial arts troupes, lion dancers, and musical troupes. Importantly, they also include young men dressed as lictors and beadles from the courts of hell who come to frighten away wandering demons and to seek the souls of the damned and lead them to judgment (Huang Wenbo 1989, 230–242; Jordan 1983). The players who make up such a group—normally referred to as an "Eight Generals Troupe" (Bajiajiang)—are considered to be in constant danger of possession by the presences that they imitate, whose immanence is therefore particularly salient as the members of the group process in a swaggering gait from place to place and perform martial arts routines at temples and other religiously significant points along their route. Unlike other processional troupes, the Eight Generals do not eat, drink, or urinate along the way, and they seek to remain "in character" with severe faces during the rest stops cheerfully taken by other performers.[17]

Why Hell?

The point I wish to establish in all of this is that hell is part of the mental furniture of everyone in Taiwan. Whether or not a person actually believes in hell, either vaguely or in detail, it is impossible to be unaware of hell as a place full of law courts to which all people go at death, where they are subjected to gruesome tortures, and from which they are subsequently reincarnated. Further, for all the sport made of the idea in comic books and films—and despite the doubts that people express if asked to take it seriously—the idea of hell remains salient and interesting to people in Taiwan today. For many people, such as the producers of the hortatory comic books about karma, it is taken very seriously indeed. And finally, there is considerably greater explicitness and detail in the image of hell than is found in most other societies.[18] Hell in Taiwan is a place where, in the words of my title, one can "pop in" and have a look around very easily.

What keeps this idea prominent century after century? In an earlier paper (Jordan 1983), I opined that the continuing everyday salience of hell could reasonably be interpreted as a culturally constituted adaptive mechanism for the sanctioned expression of resentment in a society with many constraints on individual behavior. That was a highfalutin way of saying that people who get tired of being pushed around enjoy imagining the pushy people in hell. Hell, described as a place where gossips have their tongues cut out and thieves have their hands cut off, is a satisfying idea to people who are their victims.

I did not argue that Taiwan had more annoying people to put up with than other places—only that it had a folkloric tradition that provided ideas that were psychologically useful in doing so. Such a tradition is not strictly necessary to a population, but once it is in place it is *available* to them and *comforting* to them, I argued, and that is what keeps it alive. I still believe that this is probably the case. But it is not the whole story.

Returning to the words of my title, hell is a place where one may find "Pop," one's own father—or mother, or other immediate intimates. What are we to make of a custom in which people hang pictures of the torments of the damned over the coffins of the dearly beloved?

FILIAL PIETY

In a society dominated by generational hierarchy, the subordination of the young to the old necessarily requires cultural supports, and anthropologists have long taken their Chinese informants quite seriously when the latter emphasize the central role of filial piety—*xiao*—in Chinese life. Although there is continuing public discussion of the nature, importance, and desirability of filial piety in Taiwan, signs abound of the continuing vibrancy of the idea in popular thinking.

The tales of the *Twenty-Four Filial Exemplars* are widely distributed in book form but also occur as edifying artwork in temple murals and on graves. The retaining walls beside this gravestone are covered with ceramic tiles of these stories. (Photo by David K. Jordan)

One of the most visible and explicit manifestations is a continually reprinted Yuan dynasty (1279–1368) set of stories for children called the *Twenty-Four Filial Exemplars (Ershisi Xiao)*. Modern editors have created countless latter-day compendia with slightly different selections of stories, but the Yuan edition remains the most popular. An analysis of children's editions of such stories and of the use of the stories in films, temple murals, and gravestone decoration suggests that modern Taiwanese continue to understand filial piety to be a central moral principle, rooted not so much in mutable human convention as in nature itself (Jordan 1986).[19] Here are three examples:

1. The Feeling of Filial Piety Moved Heaven
Emperor Shun of the Yu dynasty was the son of Gu Shou (=Blind Old-Man). His nature was most filial. But his father was obstinate and his mother was boorish. His younger brother Xiang was proud and overbearing. Shun ploughed on Mount Li [in Shandong Province], where the elephants ploughed for him and the birds weeded for him, for his feelings of filial piety were so great [that even the beasts were moved]. Emperor Yao [of Tang] heard of this; he sent nine of his sons to wait on him and two of his daughters to be his wives and later abdicated the throne in his favor. Verses praise him saying:

> Herds of elephants plough in the spring;
> Flocks of birds pull the weeds;
> He is the heir of Yao and mounts his throne;
> The spirit of filial piety moves the heart of Heaven.

Emperor Shun is one of China's earliest culture heroes, and this story has been told since the time of Confucius, so Shun's inclusion among the Twenty-Four Exemplars is not surprising. The message in the tale is clear: Little Shun was filial despite the unworthiness of his parents. But nature itself was responsive to his virtue, as the animals came to help him in his labors. And in the end he was rewarded by none other than the "emperor" himself, the famous culture hero Yao. The story is reminiscent of Cinderella for Western readers, and the motifs are universal. The distinctive twist here, however, is that the focal issue is not patience or modesty or stepmothers, but filial piety. The picture of Shun plowing the fields assisted by elephants and birds is one of the most common motifs painted on the walls of temples in Taiwan.

23. He Wept until the Bamboo Sprouted
Meng Zong of the Three Kingdoms period was also called Gongwu. His father died when he was small, and his mother was very ill. One winter she longed to eat a soup made with boiled bamboo shoots. Zong had no means to give her such a thing, and he went out to the bamboo grove where, seizing a bamboo stalk, he wept. His filial piety moved heaven and earth. In a moment, the earth cracked open and many stalks of bamboo shoots appeared. He gathered them and returned home to make soup for his mother. When she had eaten it, she recovered. Verses praise him, saying:
Tears drop; the north wind is cold
And moans through a stand of bamboo;
But winter bamboo shoots come forth!
The wish of Heaven is to bring harmony.

Once again, the clear message in this story is that nature itself is responsive to filial piety and supportive of it. Filial piety is not an arbitrary cultural convention, the story tells us; it is an inevitable part of the way the universe is built. The visitor to Taiwan will sooner or later come upon a picture of a boy (or sometimes a teenager or even a grown man) weeping in a bamboo grove, with young bamboo shoots sprouting below him. The figure is Meng Zong, and the message is that the cosmos resonates to filial piety.

11. He Let Mosquitoes Consume His Blood
When Wu Meng of the Jin dynasty was eight years old, he was very filial towards his parents. The family was poor, and the bed had no mosquito net. Every night in summer mosquitoes in droves nibbled at their skin and sucked their blood without restraint. Although there were many, Meng did not drive them away, lest in leaving him they bite his parents. So great was his love of his parents! A poem praises him:
On summer nights without a mosquito net,
When mosquitoes are many he dares not wave them off;
They gorge themselves on his flesh and blood,
And thus he avoids their bothering his parents.

This third story has several important messages: In the first place, no child is too small or too weak or too poor to be filial. Filial piety is a virtue that can be practiced by everyone. Secondly, filial piety, even exemplary filial piety, although it moves heaven, should not be expected to bring rewards; one is filial because that is the moral thing to do. Wu Meng presumably suffered in silence, even if later generations praised him.

The original compiler of the *Twenty-Four Filial Exemplars* no doubt hoped that recounting these tales would have the effect of making children (and adults) more filial. That may or may not happen. In Taiwan at least, the stories and their various representations, despite their didactic intent, are probably better interpreted as a sign of the importance of filial piety than as a cause of it. But their continuing hold on the public imagination forces us to ask: What makes young Taiwanese want to feel filial? In a separate analysis, I wrote: "We have seen that the psychological challenge of trying to feel nurturant toward individuals for whom one must also make sacrifices may be accomplished in part through identification with the recipient's status, in part through a culturally supported sense of self-righteousness, and in part through the use of filial piety as a rationalization for advancing family interests that include one's own" (Jordan 1998, 278). In other words, by being supportive toward a parent and at the same time identifying with the parent, one is symbolically supporting oneself. And to the extent that parental interest is family interest, filial piety is a moral banner under which to advance family interests (including one's own).

This analysis is probably accurate, but it doesn't seem to fit well with the display of the torments of hell beside the coffin of one's parent. If one imagines that weeping in the bamboo grove will produce soup to heal one's mother, why does one also imagine that she will be tormented in hell? That is the problem we turn to now.

WHY IS POP IN HELL?

Let me now try to link these two traditions of popular culture together. On the one hand, filial piety, defined principally as filial subordination, is regarded as a cornerstone of individual morality. One honors one's father and mother. On the other hand, there is great interest in the prospect that after death all go to judgment—a judgment inevitably portrayed as involving painful and long-lasting torture, reduced only slightly by the efforts of those left behind among the living. One believes one's father and mother are up for severe torture for their sins.[20]

One link, of course, is that funerary ritual provides ample opportunity for the public performance of acts symbolizing filial piety as an emotion and illustrating it as a behavior. But I submit that there is another psychological mechanism at work. Filial piety, in its Chinese form of subordinating the desires of an individual to the desires of his or her parent (or parent-in-law), not only involves acknowledgment of the parent's superior status but also acknowledgment of the parent's dependency, a point I missed in my earlier discussions of the subject.

Further, the more attention the parent requires and the more dependent the parent is, the greater the superiority of the child in all but jural status. While it is tempting to see filial subordination as potentially masochistic, we must also see it as carrying the confirmation of superior competence—and hence the roots of its own transcendence.

The need for filial subordination to a parent may easily create resentment, but the resentment cannot be directly expressed in the context of a moral system that celebrates the cosmic desirability of filial behavior and filial emotion. We can therefore imagine the appearance of Pop in hell to be psychologically satisfying as a kind of vengeance against the suppressed resentment of years of subordination. This would indeed seem to explain why scenes of hell continue to be "appropriate" to portable funeral chapels and temples devoted to memorial services.

But there is more to it than that. Pop in hell continues to be Pop in trouble, Pop in need, Pop dependent. Folkloric representations of the world of the dead dwell not only on their judgment and suffering but also on their dependency on the living for assistance. We recall that the film *A Chinese Ghost Story* hangs exactly on this point, with the deceased girl dependent upon the virtuous living hero for her chance at reincarnation. It is by no means the only film (or tale) that represents ghosts in need of assistance. The view of ghosts as pathetic and dependent is quite ancient and widespread.

In popular culture, no tale illustrates the dependency of the dead upon the living better than that of Mulian, the Buddhist monk whom we met earlier, who saved his mother from the deepest bowels of hell, and whose adventures came to be celebrated in theatricals, popular tales, and occasionally films, often with dramatic martial arts routines. The story was incorporated into funeral ritual centuries ago and is occasionally enacted by Daoist priests in old-style funerals in Taiwan even today (Ch'iu 1989; Seaman 1989). I noted earlier that the story of Mulian links Buddhism and Confucianism. But it also links filial piety to parental dependency. Mulian's mother, having sinned, is helpless against her severe punishment without the intervention of her virtuous son.

Pop in hell, then, may be getting his just deserts: deserved punishment for a lifetime of slights, great and small, against others—human and divine. But Pop has also moved from the demanding dependency of the living senior to the utter helplessness of the suffering and imprisoned deceased. He has become a potential object for the continued expression of filial rectitude, but now largely at the discretion of the living.[21] Filial subordination, a core value vividly celebrated in popular culture, is transformed into filial superiority without losing any of its moral credibility.

It should not surprise us, then, that Pop is in hell, or that we can pop into hell—or that these motifs continue to be stimulating to the actors involved. It is more useful and more bearable to be filial when filial subservience can be reversed into filial superiority. Fashions in funerals are changing, and many are now Western in style, without the hell scrolls hung around the coffin; but the image of these old-fashioned funerals will probably be preserved in popular media long after the practice itself disappears, if it ever does. But why would it? These are ancient symbols that fit together well. If asked to predict, I would anticipate that Pop will stay in hell for a long time to come.

PART III
An Emerging Public Sphere
SAYING NOW WHAT COULD NOT
BE SAID BEFORE

4

From Hidden Kingdom to Rainbow Community

The Making of Gay and Lesbian Identity in Taiwan

Scott Simon

EDITORS' INTRODUCTION

Same-sex sexual attraction is part of the human biological heritage. But different societies have quite different reactions to same-sex attraction on the part of their members. Since the birth and filiation of children are involved, the study of sexual attraction inevitably links to the study of marriage.

Traditional China saw marriage as a system of social obligations. These included sexual relations between the marriage partners but did not place sexual attraction as such at the center of the relationship. Although women were expected to be sexual partners only to their husbands and to bear them children, there was a wide acceptance of men having other partners in addition to their wives. Concubinage and prostitution were widely accepted through most of Chinese history, and casual sexual affairs by men were condemned more for their potential to disrupt marriage obligations than because they involved sex.

Sex itself was considered to deplete the energy of the male partner, and it was discouraged outside of marriage for that reason. But, like the consumption of alcohol, the long-term health effects were usually considered the business of the person involved. Morality was not the issue.

Marriage was effectively compulsory in traditional China, usually arranged by children's parents, often early in their lives. Although single people did exist and although there were celibate religious orders, the overwhelming reality was that single people were rarely either trusted or honored. Indeed, failure to marry and bear offspring was considered a prime offense against filial piety, a cornerstone of Confucian morality. No parent could happily contemplate a child remaining unmarried, and the failure to find a mate for one's child made a parent a target for the clucking tongues of neighbors and relatives alike.

Homosexual liaisons, which of course did not produce children, were socially irrelevant so long as they were not permitted to disrupt family affairs or squander family resources; they were merely a minority taste in extramarital sex. But being gay was simply not a reason to remain single, and it would be misleading to speak of anything like a "gay lifestyle" as a stable part of Chinese tradition.

Scott Simon's work chronicles how gay people and gay issues have come out of the closet in Taiwan. He begins by distinguishing homosexuality (homosexual acts) from gay identity (of an individual person) and from gay community (living among many gay people). Today gay identity nearly always involves rejection of heterosexual marriage, and therefore it can be argued that gay identity as we know it could hardly have existed when men had to be married whether they wanted to or not. Gay identity is therefore something new in Taiwan. Since a gay community involves the support institutions of gay identity, it too is largely new.

Relieved at last of many of the earlier pressures toward social conformity, gay people have suddenly become both visible and respectable in Taiwan, and gay identity and gay community are blossoming rapidly. Indeed, the process is impressive for its rapidity and for the lack of a backlash of negative public opinion.

Simon presents coming out and the abandonment of traditional marriage and childbearing as meeting a degree of acceptance one could not have predicted on the basis of earlier tradition. To some extent this can be seen as part of a worldwide evolution or as inspired perhaps by the slightly earlier emergence of gay respectability in the United States. But Simon points out that earlier tradition did in fact leave space for male gay sex. It was the particular historical circumstance of the world scene and evolving Taiwan politics, in interaction with the background of family values, that provided space for the emergence of gay identity and gay community. The lesson is that neither of the two factors alone—international influence or an understanding of Taiwan's past—enables an observer to predict what cultural form lies ahead. There is always interaction.

Despite the sudden openness of the gay community in Taiwan, relations between gay youth and the parents and siblings from whom a gay identity potentially estranges them are often still difficult, and the future evolution of the Taiwan gay community will be fascinating to observe. ■

> There are no days in our kingdom, only nights. As soon as the sun comes up, our kingdom goes into hiding, for it is an unlawful nation; we have no government and no constitution, we are neither recognized nor respected by anyone, our citizenry is little more than rabble. . . . The area between our borders is pitifully small, no more than two or three hundred meters long

by a hundred meters wide—that narrow strip of land surrounding the oval lotus pond in Taibei's New Park, on Guanqian Street. . . . But we are always keenly aware of the constant threat to our existence by the boundless world on the other side of the fence. (Bai 1995, 17)

When Bai Xianyong first published *Crystal Boys* in 1978, Taiwan was still under martial law. His novel depicts the gloomy and hopeless lives of Taibei homosexuals living on the dark edges of urban marginality. The characters in his book are largely outcasts from society: an "unfilial" son chased out of his family by a pistol-toting father, "immoral" boys thrown out of school, an epileptic aborigine, an aging mainlander, "sex fiends" on the search for eternal youth by the lotus pond in New Park. Their world was a hidden kingdom of darkness, social life in the park being the only escape from the oppression of the closet. Under martial law, it was difficult to organize political groups of any kind, let alone a gay rights organization. There was little room for gay identity in Taiwan.

Twenty-two years later, Taiwan was a different place. Martial law was lifted in 1987, and the opposition Democratic Progressive Party (DPP) even gained the presidency in 2000. Gay and lesbian life, too, changed from night to day. Taibei gays were no longer limited to cruising or seeking the solace of friends at night in New Park. Gays and lesbians were free to join gay groups, lobby for marriage rights, discuss their lifestyles openly in the media, and look for partners in a range of social spaces. Some gays and lesbians even married in public ceremonies. Instead of a hidden kingdom, they were establishing a rainbow community. In the ten years from 1990 to 2000, a gay and lesbian community was created and gained tolerance—though not full acceptance—in Taiwanese society. How have Taibei gays and lesbians passed from darkness to the other side of the rainbow, building a community of their own?

This essay is based on five years of research and residence in Taiwan: two years in Tainan, one year in Gaoxiong, and two years in Taibei. While living in southern Taiwan, I joined both a gay reading group at Gaoxiong's "Living with Hope" and the underground gay student society at National Chenggong University in Tainan. I also participated in two self-development retreats held at Kending and Sun Moon Lake by Haojiao, a gay publishing house in Taibei. After moving to Taibei, I continued to participate in the gay community through events at Gin Gin Bookstore, as well as through social events and continual readership of the gay press. Participation in gay groups provided me with good opportunities to discuss issues of concern to Taiwanese gay men (e.g., coming out, family pressure to marry, homophobia, etc.) and to learn from them in a process similar to focus groups.

OUT IN THE FIELD:
AN ANTHROPOLOGIST ENCOUNTERS GAY TAIWAN

In August 1996, when I first arrived in Taibei, the first issue of *G&L* magazine—promoted as the world's first Chinese gay magazine[1]—had just arrived on the newsstands. Reading *G&L*, as well as weekly gay/lesbian columns in the *Independence Morning News* and the *China Times*, I started learning a gay vocabulary in Chinese. Gays and lesbians, for example, were called *tongzhi,* ironically taken from the political term for "comrade," a term used not only by the Chinese Communist Party but also by the KMT and DPP (see Chou 1995). The first issue of *G&L* included a full-page advertisement of the opposition Democratic Progressive Party promising to be "comrade of comrades."

1996 was an important year in Taiwan's gay and lesbian history. In November, Taiwanese novelist Xu Yousheng and his Uruguayan partner married in a public wedding ceremony. Taiwan's first gay church, the Tongguang Jiaohui, was also established in Taibei and affiliated with the generally progressive Presbyterian Church. National Taiwan University's gay and lesbian club also attracted media attention for its open meetings on campus. Yet the gay men I met were still mostly "closeted," expecting to marry women, and hesitant to openly join gay organizations or affirm gay identity. It seemed as if "gay community" was just a remote ideal of the Western-educated intellectuals in Taibei.

Gay Pride Demonstration, Taibei, 2002. The characters on the man's chest read "Raging Blue," a gay pride motto, homonymous with the common expression, "raging waves." (Photo by Scott Simon)

A young participant masquerades as the goddess Mazu during his performance at a gay consciousness-raising retreat in Pingdong. (Photo by Scott Simon)

Nearly five years later, I attended a gay pride celebration sponsored by the Taibei Municipal Government. Both President Chen Shui-bian (Chen Shuibian) and Taibei Mayor Ma Yingjiu were meeting with gay/lesbian activists. In 2000, *G&L* published its last issue as a magazine for gay culture and politics, the publishers shifting their efforts to gay erotica as soon as Republic of China (ROC) publishing laws were amended to permit frontal nudity. In the mainstream media, being gay had gone from fashionably alternative to everyday passé, and newspapers no longer bothered to publish gay columns. Yet scholars at National Taiwan University and Academia Sinica were publicly lobbying for gay marriage rights. The Legislative Yuan was considering a human rights bill with a clause giving gays and lesbians the rights to form partnerships and adopt children. And local businesses had discovered the gay marketplace, eagerly signing up as part of a citywide "rainbow community."

A wide network of counseling and support groups had been established, including groups for married gays and parents of gays and lesbians, and they seem to be effective. Only one of my male gay acquaintances (among over a hundred) actually married a woman, to be divorced a year later; and the others had abandoned that idea entirely. Some have announced to their families that they are gay and have been accepted. The dream of a gay community seems to have reached deeper into Taiwanese society. The speed of the cultural change deserves explanation, as well as the fact that it has so far occurred without the strong public backlash that the gay movement has experienced in the United States. There has been, for example, no equivalent of the American Defense of Marriage Act signed by President Clinton in 1997.[2] These changes were probably facilitated by a specific cultural context that gives men a great deal of sexual freedom, largely by "turning a blind eye" to actual sexual behavior.

From Hidden Kingdom to Rainbow Community

CONTEXTUALIZING MALE SEXUAL CULTURE IN TAIWAN

Since same-sex eroticism has always been a part of Chinese societies (Chou 1995), it is important to distinguish here between homosexuality, gay identity, and gay community. Homosexuality refers simply to sexual relations between members of the same sex. Gay identity occurs when individuals embrace those sexual acts as part of their identity and construct their lives around it, usually by rejecting heterosexual marriage and seeking emotional fulfillment through relationships with the same sex. Gay community refers to the institutional framework that builds up around this identity when a critical mass of gay-identified individuals has been reached—as well as to group identification with that set of institutions. One of the most exciting parts of my five years of residence and research in Taiwan from 1996 to 2001 has been the opportunity to observe the growth of a gay community and the solidification of gay identity in this small island nation.

Cultural expectations about marriage have shaped male sexual culture in Taiwan, leaving men with a certain degree of sexual freedom as long as they fulfill their filial duties. Although there are clear trends toward conjugality everywhere from urban Taibei to rural mainland China (Yan 1997), the cultural norm in Chinese societies has been a patriarchal family structure focused on "continuity" of the family line. Anthropologist Francis Hsu (1983) thus contrasted the Chinese model of family continuity to the husband-wife domain of Western society. Men are strongly expected to marry and provide their parents with grandsons, norms that gay men experience as cultural pressure. Gay men, in fact, often quote the Confucian scholar Mencius as they deal with family guilt: "There are three kinds of unfilial behavior, the greatest of which is not providing descendents" *(Buxiao you san, wuhou weida).* These cultural expectations are so strong that some gay men often receive the greatest pressure to marry after "coming out" to their parents. One man in Tainan told me that his mother insists that he marry: "She tells me I have to get married even if I am gay. She says that I can have as many male lovers as I want on the side, but I have to get married and have a family. It's a question of 'face.' Chinese people are expected to get married. My parents would lose face if their families and friends knew I was gay."

The type of relationship she suggested remains fully in accord with the continuity principle of Chinese kinship. According to that cultural ideal, a man could have many wives, but women were expected to have only one man in a lifetime. Even as polygamous traditions have been replaced by legally enforced monogamy, many Taiwanese women are still expected to tolerate their husbands' extramarital affairs (Hsu 1998, 531). It is only a small step from tolerating mistresses to turning a blind eye to occasional homosexual behavior. Some heterosexual women have even told me that they would prefer to marry gay men. Their extramarital liaisons are less likely than those of heterosexual men to lead to unexpected pregnancies, claims on property, or possible divorce in order to satisfy a jealous mistress.

Although not all Taiwanese men are so inclined, there are ample opportunities for men to seek erotic pleasure outside of marriage in Taiwan. For mere visual pleasure, female strippers are sometimes part of the entertainment at rural temple fairs and even funerals, and scantily clad young women selling betel nuts adorn the highways from Taibei County to Pingdong. Men can drink and flirt with hostesses in piano bars, KTV parlors, and "teahouses," and relationships with such women can potentially develop into sexual relations. Such establishments are frequently attended by groups of men, and taking clients to these places has actually become part of business practices in some circles. Prostitution is often thinly veiled behind the smoky windows of barber shops, massage parlors, and saunas that are open all night (Skoggard 1996, 143–144). Set against this background of relative sexual freedom for men, occasional homosexual behavior can easily be interpreted as an eccentric habit or as a temporary measure when no woman is available, and it is tolerated as long as no gay identity forms that precludes marriage and continuity of the family line. Tolerance is not the same as acceptance; it has, however, made gay sex easier for individuals in Taiwan than in contexts where there are explicit legal and moral restrictions against such behavior.

Set against this cultural background, homophobia in Taiwan is qualitatively different than in the United States. In America, the sex act itself is problematic owing to interpretations of the Judeo-Christian textual tradition of gay sex as a sin punishable by death. Antigay violence is not uncommon; I grew up in Indiana seeing young men in both high school and college beaten by strangers or classmates because they were suspected of being gay. In one incident, a group of young gays gathering in an urban park were beaten by a group of "rednecks." When the police came to investigate, they found that it was a gay-bashing incident and beat the young gays a second time. American state laws are also often antigay; sodomy laws still forbid homosexual sex in over twenty American states. Taiwan has neither a subculture of antigay violence nor a legal tradition of forbidding gay sex acts. When I share these stories with Taiwanese gays, they are shocked at the possibility of hate and public violence in a country—the United States—that they often imagine to be a gay and lesbian paradise.

In Taiwan, the major tension regarding homosexuality revolves around the questions of marriage and childbirth. Both gay men and lesbians feel strong social pressure to marry and have children, as only married people with children are viewed as full adults. Although helpful offers from colleagues to introduce prospective spouses is also perceived as social pressure, the main pressure comes from family members. It must be remembered, however, that even strongly rooted cultural concepts like filial piety are subject to reinterpretation. Buddhist monks and nuns stress that their Buddhist cultivation is filial, even when they refuse to marry and have children. Reinterpreting the concept of filial piety, they stake the claim that chanting and other practices help their dead ancestors enter the Pure Land. The point is not that gays and monks face exactly the same pressures (although there are many gay monks), but rather that cultural ideologies such as filial piety can be reinterpreted by individuals. A gay man in Tainan defends his refusal to marry a woman, for example, by saying: "If I get married to a woman, I will be unhappy. It's unfair to my wife because she will sense that I don't love her and she will be unhappy too. Our children will sense that our relationship is not good, and they will be unhappy too. If my parents see me in an unhappy marriage, they will be unhappy too. So if I want to be filial, the best thing I can do is just be my gay self." The development of this new gay identity merits further analysis.

THE "HAPPENING" OF GAY IDENTITY

Some scholars have looked to economic change for the preconditions of collective gay identity. Stephen Murray (1992), for example, argued that the "familialism" of poverty—especially the crowded living conditions endured by most Third World families—inhibited the "development" of homosexuality in Thailand and Latin America. John D'Emilio (1993) similarly contended that gay identity in the United States was made possible only by capitalism, as identity was formed in gay bars and other commercial establishments. Stevan Harrell argues that industrial capitalist societies tend to develop an increased tolerance of alternative family forms such as homosexuality (Harrell 1995, 475). Taiwan, as a developed nation with an unabashedly capitalist economy, lends credibility to such arguments. Capitalism alone, however, cannot explain such a rapid growth in institutionalized gay identity.

Globalization has also been an important influence on the formation of a gay community in Taiwan. The rainbow flag, obviously an American import, is visible in many gay commercial venues. One famous sauna in Taibei has used the name of a Tokyo sauna for well over a decade. Gay bars often have English names, and gays often directly use English words to describe their own experiences, using words such as "gay," "lesbian," "bi," and "straight." Some gay men flee family pressure by studying abroad, or they take vacations in places like San Francisco and Bangkok, where they encounter an international gay community. Activists in the gay movement keep a careful eye on developments outside of Taiwan and use gains elsewhere to pressure the Taiwanese state on such issues as antidiscrimination laws. In June 2001, a new human rights bill, including a clause granting gays and lesbians the rights to form civil unions and adopt children, was first proposed by the Ministry of Justice. Taiwanese gays and lesbians now live in the "imagined world" (Appadurai 1996, 33) of an international gay community. As one man told me about his memories watching the 1993 Gay March on Washington on TV: "We were having sex all along. We had the desire, but we didn't know what it meant until we saw the demonstrations on TV. Suddenly we saw men kissing men on TV, and we knew we were like them. For the first time, we knew we were something that is called gay, and that there are other people like us. When we saw that on TV, it woke us up. It was as if we were awakened from a dream."

The idea that gay rights are part of modernity and progress has already become a part of "political correctness" in Taiwan. That understanding also helps parents accept their children's new gay identities as merely a generation gap to be tolerated. The creation of a gay and lesbian community, however, was in no way an automatic reaction to capitalist development, modernity, or even globalization. The fact that this occurred only after martial law was lifted demonstrates that it was also made possible by democratic reforms allowing gays and lesbians to form associations of their own. The formation of gay identity involved committed political struggle as well as the dedication of a critical mass of courageous individuals and political interest groups. Taiwan's gay/lesbian community progressed in roughly four historical stages: (1) the appropriation of public space, (2) the establishment of gay/lesbian commercial venues, (3) entry into the political sphere, and (4) the creation of a publicly recognized gay/lesbian community. The events that happened along the way were often inspired, or at least understood, in reference to developments outside of Taiwan. Gay community did not evolve naturally in Taiwan; it "happened" in the context of specific economic and political changes, first of all in new forms of public space brought to Taiwan when the island was under Japanese administration (1895–1945).

THE APPROPRIATION OF PUBLIC SPACE

Public space has long played an important role in the lives of gay people in Taiwan, as men with homosexual desire need meeting space beyond the confines of their families and social communities. Urbanization and the growth of modern institutions such as parks and railways made such use of public space possible. Even in small towns such as Hualian and Gangshan, the park nearest the train station (usually called the Sun Zhongshan Park) is frequented by gay men at night. New Park, built by the Japanese, is the best-known example. Every night after dusk, men start appearing in the park. They stand as individuals around the Chinese-style pagoda and goldfish pond, waiting for others to approach them for conversation. Or they meet in small groups of friends in the tree-lined paths near the west entrance, the park providing a free social venue for students and younger gays without the disposable income needed to enter bars and coffee shops. Informal groups of homosexual men, based on friendships made in the park, have played a role in the development of a gay community.

Lai Zhengzhe (2000) has interviewed men of three generations who frequent New Park. He learned that New Park has been a homosexual gathering place for decades, primarily because its proximity to the train station, the central bus station, and the shopping district of Ximending made it a convenient place for anonymous contacts. Although Lai documented homosexual activity in the park only since the 1950s, one of his older informants claimed that the park was already a meeting place for homosexuals in the later years of Japanese rule. Considering the descriptions by Yukio Mishima (1951) of Japanese homosexual life at the time, it is not improbable that New Park was already a place for homosexual encounters shortly after the park, train station, and Ximending's commercial areas were built.

After Chiang Kai-shek (Jiang Jieshi) and the KMT took over Taiwan in 1945, New Park became popular as a gathering place for lonely mainlander soldiers, many of whom sought lovers among local Taiwanese men. Bai Xianyong's literary depictions of former mainland soldiers taking pictures of young men and seeking to gain their affection reflect this part of New Park history. Southern Taiwanese youth seeking jobs in Taibei could often earn money as hustlers in the park, a scene later to be repeated by rural hustlers working urban parks in the People's Republic of China (PRC) of the 1980s (An 1997). The use of public space was especially important in the early years after World War II, when the Taiwanese economy was still underdeveloped and many people could not afford to consume in bars or coffee shops. As the economy developed, homosexual activity gradually spread out into nearby commercial areas and laid the foundations of a commercial gay scene.

BEYOND THE PARK:
SELLING SEX IN THE TAIWAN MIRACLE

As early as the 1950s and 1960s, some wealthier patrons of New Park were already frequenting nearby coffee shops, bars, and hotels, mixing in subtly with heterosexual patrons. The "New Southern Sea" (Xin Nanyang) cinema became well known during that time as another place for men to meet one another. In the 1970s, the first self-consciously "gay" bars opened in basement rooms near New Park. The first gay sauna opened in the 1980s (Lai 2000, 147).

By the late 1990s, local entrepreneurs in even small towns like Jiayi and Taidong were creating commercial meeting spaces for gays and lesbians. Whereas gay public space had previously been a male domain, a lesbian scene also developed (Zheng 1997; Simon 1998). The ethnographic description I provided in my study of lesbian entrepreneurs, originally published in Chinese, presents a glimpse into that part of the emerging lesbian and gay community:

> One Saturday night in April 1998, a group of women invited me to go with them to Women's Space, a lesbian bar in Gaoxiong. The bar was dimly-lit, with art deco lamps hanging from the walls and supporting pillars. Old movie pictures of such American stars as Rita Hayworth and Katherine Hepburn hung on the walls. In the front was a stage set up for karaoke, and a small dance floor. Tonight was unique, however, as women came from all over southern Taiwan to drink, socialize, and watch a special performance. There was an entry fee of NT$500 (US$15).
>
> The bar was crowded with people, mostly women but a few men. The cigarette smoke was so thick it irritated my eyes. One of my lesbian friends said that lesbians smoke even more than men, and I could certainly believe it that night. The room was so long and narrow that only those fortunate

enough to be seated at the tables up front could see the performance clearly. Having arrived late, we were seated in the back of the bar in a semi-enclosed karaoke room. The waitress, a mannish young woman with glasses and short-cropped hair, seated us and took our orders.[3] She distributed empty red envelopes to the women, instructing them to put money in the envelopes and give them to their favorite performers.

The performance began at midnight. It started out with a transvestite show, men dressed in extravagant female dress and lip-syncing to Mandarin pop music and American songs such as Whitney Houston's "I Will Always Love You." When women liked the performance, they rushed out and tucked a red envelope into the performer's clothes. But the most popular part of the performance was yet to come. A woman in a black dress came out on the stage. Like the female impersonators who had preceded her, she lip-synced a Madonna tune and danced. The next woman did her performance in yet a sexier dress. The first one returned to the stage and sang a song wearing revealing lingerie. She was followed by a woman wearing even less. These performances were very popular with the women, some of whom rushed out and tucked red envelopes into the performers' bras or panties. At around 2:00, the crowd up front screamed in excitement, as the women emerged on stage almost completely naked for the final performance. One woman wore only a string of feathers around her neck. A second woman started out in see-through lingerie which she quickly discarded as she danced her way naked from the front to the back of the bar. This time, the fans put the red envelopes in their mouths and offered them to the performers, who accepted the envelopes in their mouths and collected them in their hands. When the show was over, the crowd began to thin, and we went home.

The emergence of commercial LesbiGay establishments was a major change in Taiwanese consumer society. From the beginning of the evening when we bought tickets to enter the bar, to the end when women offered red envelopes stuffed with money to strippers, sex—or the possibility of finding it—was the main commodity for sale. Capitalism in Taiwan has thus deepened the commodification of human relations that was already happening in public space, especially if one accepts Bryan Turner's argument (1996, 220) that casual homosexual contacts constitute a commodification of sexuality. As capitalism deepens, women also become consumers of sex and men, too, can become objects of consumption. Such particular cases, however, do not merit a reconsideration of feminist emphases on male commodification of women (e.g., Bishop and Robinson 1998; Rubin 1975), especially because sexual venues for male consumers exponentially outnumber the available venues for female consumers.

Commercial venues for gay men include gay bars and saunas; both types of establishments are located in cities and towns across Taiwan. Gay bars are similar to the lesbian bar described above, ranging from small pubs and karaoke bars to large disco pubs. Saunas, however, are the most overt type of sexual commodification. Men pay NT$350 (US$10) for admission into saunas. As the name implies, they generally offer shower facilities, steam rooms, and sauna baths of hot, cold, and tepid water. Some saunas, however, offer extra facilities ranging from exercise rooms to internet access. Gay porn films are often shown, and private rooms are available for more intimate contact. These saunas are sometimes an extension of Taiwan's family economy. At one centrally located Gaoxiong sauna, for example, husband and wife work together at the front counter. The elderly mother treats the nearly naked men like customers in any other establishment, serving up tantalizing Hakka dishes to towel-clad men who need a rest between erotic encounters.

Saunas, however, have not contributed directly to the development of a gay community, any more than brothels have led to a community of brothel patrons. In fact, the commodification of homosexuality renders such a community unnecessary to many people, in that they can fulfill their desires on the market and do not need an arena for long-term relations with members of the same sex. For homosexual men married to women, in fact, saunas have the advantage of providing anonymous encounters unlikely to disrupt family life. One married man I interviewed said: "It's a bad thing to go to a sauna. I know that. But I have sexual desires, like everyone else who goes to a sauna. I can go there, have sex with men, and get rid of that desire. I know I like men, but at the end of the day I always go back to women."

Another man justified his decision to marry a woman, saying that: "Heterosexual men 'play' around outside of marriage. They are married, but they still go to heterosexual saunas, or go to prostitutes. When I get married, I can do the same thing. The only difference is that they 'play' with women and I play with men. Americans don't understand that mentality, but Taiwanese people can accept it. It's part of our culture."[4]

According to Ke Naiying, a medical anthropologist who has studied gay saunas in southern Taiwan, this attitude is not uncommon among sauna patrons (personal communication). The main victims of this "culture" are women married to homosexual men. Psychologically, they come to feel sexually alienated and ignored by their husbands, often failing to understand the reasons behind their husbands' apparent lack of interest in sex.

Because these men do not identify themselves as "gay," even when they admit to enjoying sex with men, they often reject information on "gay" topics, including safe-sex education. The result is that men who have low degrees of gay identity have higher risks of AIDS than those men who self-identify as gay. They then risk transmission of the AIDS virus to their wives. These men have fulfilled their duties as filial sons but at the expense of becoming fatally unfaithful husbands.

Lai (2000) argues that an "imagined community" began in New Park and later commercial establishments. Since male visitors to saunas and other places tend to have varying degrees of gay identity, however, it is difficult to make the case that such establishments have directly led to gay identity and the formation of a gay community. Gay men, moreover, gathered at New Park for decades before establishing a gay community in the contemporary sense of the term.

The seeds were certainly present in Bai Xianyong's evocative "hidden kingdom," but the homosexual use of public space and private commercial venues were only the preconditions for gay community building.

The formation of gay identity is thus similar to that of class identity in that it is formed in specific historical circumstances. In a remarkable similarity to the development of class consciousness in England (Thompson 1965), it also traces at least some of its roots to "public houses," or pubs. Political oppression and resistance, moreover, were also important factors in crystallizing that identity. It is only when gay establishments become politicized through state oppression and gay resistance, as happened at Stonewall in 1969,[5] that they become sites of community building. Sexual identities are thus like other forms of group identity—they are "happenings" rather than "things."

GAYS VS. THE STATE:
OPPRESSION, RESISTANCE, AND IDENTITY FORMATION

Gays have never been legally oppressed in Taiwan to the extent that they were in the United States and former British colonies, all of which had sodomy laws inspired by biblical precedents.[6] Unlike the former British colonies of Singapore and Hong Kong, Taiwanese law has never prohibited homosexual acts between consenting adults. Moreover, there is no prohibition against gays serving in the military.[7] Many gays, as I discovered in the support groups organized by Haojiao Publishing Company, began exploring homosexuality while in the military. Legal blindness toward homosexuality, however, also prevented Taiwan from passing laws to legalize gay/lesbian marriage or from protecting individuals from discrimination based on sexual orientation—until 2001, when such a bill was presented to the Legislative Yuan, which I will return to later.

Although sodomy in the privacy of one's own home has never been illegal in Taiwan, gays have been harassed by police during the forty years of martial law and even afterward. Until recently, identity card searches were frequently conducted in New Park, as well as in gay bars and saunas. Gay men have been taken into police custody for short periods of time and have had their photographs taken for police files. Police have also informed the families of gay men about their whereabouts during such searches.[8] The contours of a gay community in Taiwan have thus been shaped by state power, much as they were in the West. While government and police have played a smaller role in the formulation of gay community in Taiwan than in some places, three incidents in particular have contributed to the formation of a gay community in Taibei: (1) controversy over the historical designation of New Park, (2) police harassment of gay men on Changde Street, and (3) a police raid on the AG Gym.

The New Park/228 Memorial Controversy

In 1995, the administration of DPP mayor Chen Shui-bian decided to convert New Park into the 228 Memorial Park in memory of the people who had died there and elsewhere during the tragic February 28 ("228") events of 1947. A student from the National Taiwan University Graduate Institute of Building and Planning, concerned that the park might no longer be used as a gay meeting place, started the "Front for Gay/Lesbian Space" (Tongzhi Kongjian Zhenxian) in November 1995 to bring the issue out into public discussion. Approximately thirty to forty students and community members joined that group to promote the gay history of New Park and educate the public about gay and lesbian issues in Taiwan. Their activities became known as the New Park Movement.

The New Park Movement did not succeed in preventing the renaming of the park, nor did they succeed in getting it officially recognized as gay space. Nonetheless, neither the construction of a monument and museum for 228 victims nor the building of a subway stop in New Park had the anticipated impact of driving gays away from the park. What is important about the group is that it mobilized activists and encouraged public discourse on homosexuality.

In 1996, gay activists affiliated with the New Park Movement launched a collective "coming-out" campaign in Taibei, to demonstrate how common homosexuality is and to make it a topic of public discourse. Rather than outing prominent community members or trying to encourage individuals to come out at home and in the workplace, common strategies of gay activism in the United States, they held a widely publicized vote for the ten most-wanted gay and lesbian sex symbols. Gays and lesbians were encouraged to cast ballots for their sex idols at "voting booths" set up in gay and lesbian commercial establishments. The roster included prominent politicians Chen Shui-bian, Ma Yingjiu, and James Soong, as well as musicians and movie stars. Singapore pop singer Tracy Huang won the prize for lesbian sex idol and Taiwanese-Japanese pop star Jin Chengwu was elected gay sex star. The sexual identities of the people voted for was unimportant, even though Tracy Huang would come out publicly as a lesbian in 2001. The point was that the large number of votes demonstrated that "gays are everywhere." Police action, however, drove that lesson in even more forcefully.

Police Raids on Changde Street

Under martial law, Taiwanese gays had already become accustomed to identity checks at New Park and in the vicinity. In 1997—ten years after martial law had been lifted—this practice was finally challenged. On July 28, a Taiwanese man who uses the pseudonym "Bruce" in public discourse was subject to an identity check on Changde Street outside of New Park. He responded by publishing an editorial two days later in the *China Times* arguing that gay people have the same rights as heterosexual people to use Taibei streets and should not be the subject of police discrimination.

On the night of July 30, the very day Bruce's editorial appeared, ten armed policemen sealed off the two ends of Changde Street and rounded up the forty to fifty gay men who had congregated there. They confiscated their identity cards and took them to the police station in a police van. The police took photos of two men but stopped after other men protested that they had done nothing wrong and that the action was a human rights violation. After thirty minutes, the police returned the identity cards and released the men. One of the men arrested that evening said: "A lot of people who were seized by the police are like me. I wanted to protest, but I chose silence, because I am under pressure of being outed. I know that when police behave like that, they also seize the mind-set of gays who don't dare to come out. When they treat me like that, I keep my anger in my heart."[9]

Taiwan's gay and human rights activists responded immediately. Bruce and Ke Fei, another activist, set up a "Changde Street Committee" in order to document the incident, protest police harassment of gays, and promote public discussion of human rights. On August 19 they held a public discussion of the event that was attended by journalists, scholars, and human rights activists. Through BBS discussion lists, national newspapers, and local radio talk shows in cities from Taibei to Gaoxiong, news of the incident quickly spread throughout the entire island, becoming a focus of public concern. In spite of public protest, however, it was not the last time that police acted against gays in Taibei. A year later, police actions once again became the center of public discourse as a result of a raid on AG Gym.

Police Raid on the AG Gym

The AG Gym was more than a gym. Located on the fourth to sixth floors of a downtown Taibei building and just above a branch of the American chain restaurant TGI Friday's, it was one of the most popular gay establishments in Taibei, drawing a clientele from all over Taiwan and beyond. The fourth floor was a gym, with free weights, treadmills, and exercise equipment. On the fifth floor were lockers, shower facilities, an unlit maze-like steam room, jacuzzi, and sauna. The sixth floor comprised private rooms, where men who met elsewhere in the establishment could go for greater intimacy. Knowing that some men would have sexual conduct on the premises and wanting to encourage safer sex, the management distributed free condoms to clients.

On December 20, 1998, in an incident similar to the Changde Street Incident, the Taibei police raided AG and inspected the identity cards of all men present. Two men, a Taiwanese university student and a tourist from Macau, were found together in one of the rooms on the sixth floor. The police demanded that they drop their towels and pose for a photograph simulating anal sex. The two young men, including the tourist who could not understand Mandarin, complied out of fright. The two were then arrested and charged with public obscenity, and the photo was used as evidence against them.[10] Acheng, the trainer present in the gym at the time, had tried to stop the police from conducting the raid and was charged with "harming public morals." The police used over three hundred new and used condoms as evidence in their case that AG was a homosexual sex club. Gay activists noted the hypocrisy of raiding a gay "sex club," yet leaving untouched hundreds of illegal brothels all over the island.

From Hidden Kingdom to Rainbow Community

Having already set up a network after the Changde Street Incident, gay activists including Xu Yousheng, Wang Ping, Ke Fei, and staff from *G&L* magazine immediately rushed to the scene in order to support the three men who had been arrested. Once again, they brought the issue into public discourse through BBS, print, and broadcast media. They also coordinated an international protest through the International Gay and Lesbian Human Rights Commission, including a letter-writing campaign directed toward the Taibei municipal government. On February 10, 2000, the three men came to trial and were declared innocent, partly because the court judged that the police had improperly gathered evidence. Much to the disappointment of gay activists, however, subsequent charges against the police were refused a court hearing. Nonetheless, this series of events had already contributed to a greater sense of gay identity across the island.

GAYS AND CIVIL SOCIETY:
THE SUN RISES ON THE HIDDEN KINGDOM

By the year 2000, gay/lesbian groups had been started in most Taiwanese cities. Many were primarily social, but some were designed for particular segments of the population, such as gay Christians, gay Buddhists, or the students at particular universities, junior colleges, and high schools. The Gender/Sexuality Rights Association Taiwan (Taiwan Xingbie Renquan Xiehui), formerly a working-class lesbian group called "Queer & Class," was one of the more political. A gay hotline was set up in 1998 as an information clearinghouse about groups and activities. A number of new developments suggested that dawn had risen on Taiwan's "hidden kingdom," especially because of (1) the development of a "Rainbow Community" in Taibei, (2) the official sponsorship of a gay pride event in Taibei in 2000, and (3) the birth of a movement for gay marriage rights.

Taibei's Commercial "Rainbow Community"

The Changde Street and AG Incidents inspired entrepreneur Lai Zhengzhe to create new gay space in Taibei. Like many gays, this young man from Jilong immediately went to New Park after moving to Taibei, exploring the lotus pond and museum described so poetically in Bai Xianyong's novel. He even wrote his M.A. thesis on New Park as part of his training in community planning and historical preservation at the National Taiwan University Graduate Institute of Building and Planning.

In 1998, he accompanied his elder sister, already a long-time American immigrant, to New York. He stayed with his sister for two months and then spent several months in San Francisco with a grade school classmate who also turned out to be gay. He spent his time in New York and San Francisco exploring gay communities in those cities. Noting Taiwan's recent past of human rights violations, including the Changde Street Incident, he decided to return to Taibei and promote a "rainbow community" like the ones he had observed in the United States. "The media also writes that gays live in darkness," he said. "That's because society doesn't give them space. Nobody sees the marginal places like bars and saunas. That's why I decided to open a gay bookstore."

On January 1, 1999, Lai Zhengzhe opened Taiwan's first exclusively gay bookstore in an alley near National Taiwan University. With bright lights, big glass windows, and a large rainbow flag hanging from the ceiling, Gin Gin Bookstore is unabashedly visible. The bookstore was successful enough that Lai could open up a gay coffee shop across the street. In 2001, he opened an art gallery and meeting space in the neighboring house, rented from the elderly neighbors when they moved to a smaller flat. Lai proudly notes that his businesses have been well accepted by his neighbors.

Trained as he is in community planning, however, Lai has not been content to concentrate on his own business projects. He was impressed by the gay guides of North America and decided to launch a similar project in Taibei. The owners of several gay bars, coffee shops, saunas, and other establishments collectively published a small "rainbow map" of Taibei. Taibei's "rainbow community" of gay-friendly businesses now has over forty members all over the city. They all affix rainbow stickers on their store windows and place rainbow maps near the cash register for clients to pick up. Under this initiative, gay life has left the dark corners of New Park and become a part of daytime shopping in all parts of Taibei.

Gay Pride 2000: Mayor Ma Yingjiu "Comes Out"

Political change was clearly in the air in April 2000, when heterosexual Taibei mayor Ma Yingjiu appeared on the front page of *G&L*. Surrounded by a group of gay/lesbian activists, he publicly congratulated *G&L* on its fourth anniversary. Under his administration, moreover, the Taibei City Bureau of Civil Affairs, primarily responsible for household registration, sponsored a Gay and Lesbian Pride Festival on the first weekend of September 2000. In a turn of events scarcely imaginable in the United States, politicians have started competing to demonstrate that they are "gay friendly" and progressive and slandering others for not adequately protecting gay rights.

The main event was an open-air festival held at the shopping center and movie cinema complex Warner Village, near the Taibei City Hall. Taiwan's major gay and lesbian organizations, including gay teachers, gay Buddhists, gay Christians, gay students from Taibei universities, and Between Us set up booths promoting their activities. Visitors to the festival were encouraged to play games at the booths to learn about the groups' activities and gay life. Some games were playful, such as the contest of throwing hoops over phallic objects (carrots, cucumbers, etc.) to win condoms as prizes. Others were overtly political, such as "marriage photos" and registration offered by Between Us to show support for legalization of gay/lesbian marriage. Those who played six games and collected stamps from sponsoring organizations to prove it could collect a rainbow-colored mobile phone holder as their prize.

The Taibei municipal government published a "Getting to Know Comrades Handbook," with the subtitle "Your family, your friends." The booklet included articles on homophobia, the history of Taiwan's gay movement, and a glossary of Chinese language gay and lesbian terminology from "comrade" to "t" and *"po."* Mayor Ma Yingjiu himself wrote the introduction, apologizing for past human rights violations against gays, including the Changde Street and AG Incidents, which occurred when Chen Shui-bian was mayor. Mayor Ma wrote: "I believe that all groups have equal rights to exist and to share social space. That is a basic condition of all progressive cities. . . . In the future, the gay and lesbian civil rights movement will grow with the city of Taibei."[11]

The festival at Warner Village was so crowded that it was difficult to walk from booth to booth. Stage performances highlighting drag queens attracted a large audience, as well as most of the event's media coverage. A number of parents brought their children to the spectacle, as if it were just another festival in the park, and even older people were in attendance.

In a minor event that illustrates latent tensions in Taiwanese society about homosexuality, some Christian groups protested the event with letters to the mayor. The U.S.–based Exodus Prayer and Ministry Center also distributed their brochures inside the Warner Village shopping complex and claimed that they could cure homosexuality. "They don't dare distribute it at the festival," said one friend I met at the festival. "Those Christian groups will protest, but they don't have the same influence in Taiwan as they do in the States. Most people in Taiwan are not Christian. That's why I think that Taiwan will legalize gay marriage before the United States."

The second day of the event was more overtly political. Michael Bronski and Nan Hunter, gay rights activists from the United States, were invited to give speeches at the Taibei City Council. Other speeches were given by Taiwanese activists such as Wang Ping of the Gender/Sexuality Rights Association Taiwan and feminist scholars, including Josephine Ho of National Central University. In the discussions held that day, they announced the legalization of gay marriage as their next political goal.

The Marriage Rights Movement

The first publicly celebrated gay/lesbian wedding in the gay rights era was a lesbian marriage in 1991. Gay author Xu Yousheng also made a media event of his 1996 wedding to his Uruguayan lover Grey Harriman. Those events brought the possibility of gay marriage into public discourse. When Xu and Harriman took their honeymoon trip at the southern resort of Kending, they found that they had become media celebrities. "Nobody said anything negative," said Yousheng. "Everyone we met wished us well."

By the year 2000, gay marriage had become an item of pressing concern to Taiwan's nascent gay and lesbian community. On October 22, 2000, four Christian lesbian couples and one gay couple married publicly at Taibei's Tongguang Christian Church and demanded that the state recognize gay and lesbian marriage rights. The lesbian group Between Us even made marriage the main theme of their booth at the 2000 Gay and Lesbian Pride Festival. Their demands were soon picked up by sympathic scholars. When President Chen Shui-bian presided over a "human rights marriage" in December 2000, National Taiwan University professors Zhang Xiaohong and Zhu Weicheng, as well as the Academia Sinica Institute of Sociology's Fan Yun, protested that the exclusion of gays and lesbians from the event was itself a violation of human rights. The Gender/Sexuality Rights Association has put marriage rights at the front of their agenda.

By mid-2001, prospects for gay marriage seemed good. On June 26, the Ministry of Justice submitted a draft of the Basic Law on the Guarantee of Human Rights to the Legislative Yuan for approval. On the recommendation of the Minister of Justice Chen Dingnan, Clause 6 stated, "The government shall protect the rights of homosexuals, and homosexuals shall be allowed, in accordance with the law, to establish families and adopt children." Taiwan seems poised to surpass the United States on this issue by adopting a European model of gay rights as human rights. Some critics of Chen say this is only because Taiwan in the 1990s defined progressive reforms on such issues as a way of demonstrating that they are separate from the PRC and a good citizen in the global community. I think, however, that such critics are reductionist. Gay people in Taiwan have worked hard to build their community, and it is crucial to recognize their efforts to put such issues on the agenda in the first place.

COMING OUT AT HOME: THE FINAL FRONTIER

In spite of the many similarities between the Taiwanese and Western gay rights movements, there have also been important differences—the most important having to do with family. Since many Taiwanese gays and lesbians have not come out to their families and strongly value the family harmony that such tactics would threaten, the local gay rights movement has generally avoided the aggressive activism of flamboyant gay rights parades and a coming-out movement based on individual sexual identity. On the issue of coming out, activists are divided roughly into two camps: those who advocate coming out (*xianshen*: literally, "to reveal one's self") as the only effective way to achieve gay rights, and those who oppose unconditional coming out as incompatible with Chinese culture (Chu 1998, 40). As Hong Kong sociologist Chou Wah Shan has also argued, the identity politics of coming out are the product of a specific Western logic and material conditions of the postwar era; it is not necessarily applicable to Chinese societies (Chou 1997, 370–371).

In Taiwan, the main problem faced by gays and lesbians continues to be family pressure (Chu 1998, 44). Chou Wah Shan thus advocates a soft and harmonious process of "coming out" to family members (1997, 53). He suggests that gays and lesbians introduce their partners to their families, demonstrate that they love and care for one another like spouses, and give their parents time to accept them as "good friends." In accordance with this logic, Taibei's Gay/Lesbian Hotline established a support group for parents of gays and lesbians. At the hotline's 2001 fundraising party at the Taibei City Council, supportive parents thus received an especially warm welcome from the young people in the crowd. I myself have witnessed the effectiveness of this strategy in dozens of Taiwanese families, the most notable being one man who even attended a gay reading group with his mother in Gaoxiong. When one man came out to his family, his primary school–educated mother in Tainan said, "It is better to be gay and happy than heterosexual and unhappy." His father and two unmarried aunts have also been very supportive of his long-term relationship with a foreign man.

Not all gays and lesbians are lucky enough to have such understanding families. Many intentionally move to Taibei or even abroad to escape what they perceive as oppressive family pressure. The most difficult case I witnessed was a young man from Gaoxiong whose parents told him to choose between staying in the family or staying with his male partner. He chose his partner and moved to Taibei, after which his parents refused telephone calls from him for a short period of time. A few weeks later, however, he wrote a letter to them explaining that he did not choose to be gay, that his homosexuality had nothing to do with them, and that he still loved them. His mother called him to reconcile, and they have been close ever since. He lives with his younger sister, who has even helped him find gay partners.

These private family events will eventually determine the future of Taiwan's gay community. Even gay-friendly laws such as the Human Rights Bill will have little impact on real lives of individual people if Taiwanese gays and lesbians do not successfully deal with the problem of family pressure.

CODA

A study of the making of Taiwan's gay community reveals several dimensions of modernity as experienced in the island nation. First, new arenas of public space and capitalist development created the physical space and social preconditions for new social identities and forms of civil society (Weller 1999). For the first time in Taiwanese history, it was possible for men and women to form a civil society of sorts as gay and lesbian individuals. They did so by forming a sense of community as a group.

As Marx pointed out in reference to class, however, there is a difference between the objective existence of a group (e.g., class-in-itself) and the subjective identification of its members with that group (e.g., class-for-itself) (Marx 1847).

If gay/lesbian existence had remained only at the level of sexual encounters, that subjective identity might not have happened among gays and lesbians any more than it has among brothel patrons. State repression against gays—and resistance organized against that in reference to American models—contributed to the crystallization of gay identity. This was possible only in the context of Taiwan's democratization. By no means, however, did it arise spontaneously. It has always been pushed along by core groups of dedicated and usually unpaid activists. Their contributions should not be forgotten.

The forms that Taiwan's gay community have taken were strongly influenced by globalization. The institutions of bars and saunas, the symbol of the rainbow flag, and popular discourse about homosexuality have all been inspired and adapted from Western precedents. Many important actors in the gay rights community, including Xu Yousheng and Lai Zhengzhe, were educated in the United States or had formative experiences there. Mayor Ma Yingjiu, who has been generally supportive of gay rights, had his first encounter with the gay/lesbian movement while studying at Harvard Law School. The Taiwanese gay/lesbian movement is thus part of what Appadurai calls a "global ethnoscape" (1996, 33). Opposition to the movement is also embedded in a global ethnoscape that includes ties to American Christian organizations. New media, including the Internet, have brought these global forces into the homes of most Taiwanese people. The gay and lesbian movement in Taiwan is, however, different from its North American and European counterparts in important ways, especially in the way it downplays "coming out" and emphasizes harmonious communication with family members.

It is important to note that men and women have experienced these social processes differently. Whereas gay men have claimed public space in Taiwan for decades, lesbians have had no equivalent to New Park. Since single women in general have lower incomes and thus less spending money than single men, lesbian commercial establishments came into existence much later than their gay counterparts, are much fewer in number, and tend to have shorter life spans. Women, however, have been on the political front lines of the movement, probably because they have suffered more in Taiwan's patriarchal social system and can also draw on the activist experience of feminist groups. Without the radical activism of lesbian groups such as Between Us and Queer & Class, Taiwan's gay and lesbian community would be very different than it is today.

There can be no conclusion to this essay, as the making of a gay/lesbian community in Taiwan is a construction in progress. Its future will depend on the progress of human rights in general in Taiwan. Yet a vibrant gay and lesbian identity is rapidly becoming part of social life in Taiwan, and the contours of its community are clearly visible as an imagined "Queer Nation" (Bi 2001; Chu 2000). Moreover, Taiwan is one of the most rational and secular states in the world and is not restricted by the habitus of a Judeo-Christian inheritance or the political might of its more fundamentalist adherents. Some Taiwanese people even declare that Taiwan should become a model of human rights and an example to the world.

As President Chen Shui-bian said, "Taiwan's gay rights movement began in 1990, 21 years later than the Stonewall Riots in New York, but is developing with full steam. We believe it will succeed" (DPA 2000). If his prediction is correct, the inhabitants of Taiwan's "Hidden Kingdom" may soon arrive at the other end of the rainbow.

5

Taiwan's Mass-Mediated Crisis Discourse
Pop Politics in an Era of Political TV Call-in Shows
Alice R. Chu

EDITORS' INTRODUCTION

The role of television and radio in forming public opinion and in responding to it is a fundamental feature of the world we live in. This plays out differently in different countries and is subject to fads and fashions. Taiwan television produces a mix of sitcoms and children's shows, evening news and cooking shows, talking heads and nature specials. If there is a foreign model inspiring all this, it is certainly American; but at the same time, certain kinds of programs seem to have an especially strong appeal in Taiwan—notably, politically tinged celebrity interviews and call-in shows.

In the following chapter, Alice Chu describes the culture of the Taiwanese call-in shows and analyzes the underlining tone of "crisis" that is found in them as they take on significant problems of public policy. On the one hand, the sense of crisis contributes to the perception of importance that such shows generate, raising audience size and revenues. On the other hand, engaging "crisis" issues allows participants and audiences to enjoy a freedom of public expression that became available only gradually after the end of martial law in 1987. Before that time, the government and the ruling party (the KMT) actively suppressed dissent on most political topics, so open political discussion today still has a slightly daring quality that makes it doubly enjoyable.

A pervasive issue is the relationship between Taiwan and mainland China. As noted in the discussion of Taiwan's history in chapter 1, China claims Taiwan as a province that was never properly reintegrated with the motherland after the establishment of the People's Republic of China (PRC)

Election posters in Tainan, 1992. With the end of martial law, election campaigns at all levels took on a new excitement for the Taiwanese. (Photo by David K. Jordan)

in 1949, while the Republic of China (ROC) government in Taiwan is the same one that formerly governed all of China, lost the civil war in 1949, and took refuge in Taiwan, vowing to reconquer the mainland. The mainland has declined to forswear the use of force and a direct military conquest of its "breakaway" province.

For many years, the ROC claimed to be biding its time to retake the mainland eventually. Obviously the dream of tiny Taiwan reconquering mighty China has not materialized, and today few people in Taiwan imagine that it ever will. But what choice is left, in that case? Taiwan cannot unilaterally declare itself separate from China because China threatens invasion in that case and because China would cut off diplomatic ties with any nation that recognized an independent Taiwan. This leaves two unpalatable choices: reunion with the much poorer mainland under authoritarian Communist government or continuing the present implausible position of being a rival government of all of China. The wide range of opinions, proposals, and carefully nuanced positions on how Taiwan should deal with this issue colors everything, and now that it can be openly discussed on television, it is not surprising that people want to discuss it.

Chu's article shows how call-in shows and their hosts reflect and manipulate these issues, how they use them to keep and build audiences, and how they profit by them. ∎

Turn on the TV in Taiwan and the viewer will find Japanese culinary contests à la the *Iron Chef,* HBO *Sex and the City* reruns, Star TV selections such as *Ally McBeal* or *The X-Files,* Mando Pop top-ten MTV countdowns hosted by Mandarin-English bilingual VJs, and Japanese anime from *Pokemon* to *Slam Dunk.* What does this eclectic fare reveal about Taiwan's pop TV culture? A cursory assessment suggests a predilection for American and Japanese programs. Taiwan-based distributors and consumers, however, have repackaged "foreign" TV shows into recognizably "Made in Taiwan" products. A prime example of an imported programming genre that has become "Taiwanized" can be found in the politically oriented TV call-in show. Loosely resembling U.S. talk shows such as *Larry King Live,* local versions in the form of *2100: All People Open Talk (Quanmin kaijiang)* and *8 o'clock Loud and Soft Voices (Badian da xiao sheng)* have been modified to reflect Taiwan's distinct sociopolitical environment.[1] In a society where *Survivor* and *Big Brother* have yet to arrive,[2] Taiwan's call-in shows represent the local equivalent of "reality TV" in which participants blithely judge the staying power of political parties and their candidates.[3]

This essay explores the part-reality, part-drama makeup of Taiwan's political TV call-in shows—and specifically, the "crisis discourses" surrounding each program topic. In other words, call-in shows promote and their participants enact a discourse of crisis through their topic selection, participant roles, and language practices. The call-in program's crisis orientation privileges in equal measure the sensationalism of popular sentiment and the recycling of sociopolitical ideologies. Due to political tensions with China, a prevailing state of crisis hangs over the island nation, and this offers enterprising call-in shows ample newsworthy events to generate—and profit from—anxiety-laden topics.

In revisiting this theme episode after episode, call-in programs promote the ritualization of crisis issues that not only plays into the hands of party politics but also caters to the public's appetite for pop political or "infotainment" programming. Mr. Xi Shenglin, producer of the political TV call-in show *Face-to-Face Debate (Xiang dui lun),* told me in 2000 that compared "to the rest of the world [Taiwan's viewers] like to watch news and news programs the most. A broad audience has been developed that is willing to watch it." Whether Mr. Xi's claim can be substantiated is not important; the important fact is that this impression exists.

"CALL-IN MANIA":
MEDIA HYPE OR POST–MARTIAL LAW DISCOURSE?

Participants of call-in shows, however, are doing more than just talking or watching. As the neologism "call-in mania" *(kouying rechao)* suggests, a mass-mediated fanaticism has swept Taiwan that is characterized by participants who are obsessed with the production, deliberation, and contestation of sociopolitical issues and events. Inviting viewers to address these topics also represents a key component of call-in programs.

In the following passage, Mr. Li Tao, the moderator of *2100,* demonstrates the call-in show's dramatic undertone in his opening remarks for an episode on ethnopolitical relations *(shengji qingjie),* also known as Taiwanese-mainlander relations (*benshengren/waishengren,* literally, "people of this province" vs. "people from outside the province"): "Hello everyone. Welcome to *2100: All People Open Talk!* Right now we are going to discuss a problem. It is possible that this problem has always existed in our society, but seldom do people talk about it because this issue is quite . . . sensitive. So today we are going to deliberate . . . what has thus far been avoided. A forbidden topic. That is, so-called Taiwanese-mainlander relations." By strategically using words such as "problem" *(wenti),* "sensitive" *(mingan),* "avoided" *(bu yuanyi),* and "forbidden" *(jinji),* Li Tao lends the featured topic a feeling of urgency and significance. His words exhort viewers to engage in its deliberation, implying that participation is a privilege that should not be wasted. Such persuasive overtures resonate with audiences in Taiwan's post–martial law society, as substantiated by their viewing and calling habits that place *2100* among Taiwan's top-ranked cable TV programs and the number-one political TV call-in show.[4]

Coupled with Taiwan's democratic development, TV call-in shows offer political figures—including politicians, media personalities, and scholars—and the viewing public a novel outlet for venting frustrations and voicing concerns. Currently, these discursive practices are redefining the style and substance of sociopolitical discussions in Taiwan. The country's call-in mania for "open talk" *(kaijiang)* increasingly replaces closed-door party congresses as the medium of choice for disclosing and debating political agendas. The melding of newsmaker pols on studio sets with couch-potato political junkies phoning in from living rooms thus creates a generation of new sociopolitical voices in the mass-mediated space of Taiwan's TV call-in shows.

Call-in programs contribute to demystifying backroom politics by packaging it as a televised "show," or *xiu.*[5] The programs present a hip interpretation of politics by featuring sexy topics, such as confrontations between pop stars and PRC government censors, as well as downplaying scholarly theorizing in favor of off-the-cuff quips and verbal sparring, otherwise known as "saliva wars" *(koushui zhan)* in Taiwan.[6] Ms. Jin Xiuli, moderator of ETTV's *Always Speak Your Mind (You hua laoshi jiang),* finds the preference for indiscriminate jibes over reasoned argument a sign of the times: "In the past when speaking with reason, they [the scholars] would say, 'Confucius says this. So we must endeavor to do that.' Today, [if you said this] no one would pay attention to you, right? So my point is, viewers of the 8 to 9 o'clock [call-in show] time slot . . . they like to watch this kind of boisterous [program]."

According to *2100* moderator Li Tao, increased boisterousness can have a positive influence on viewers—and even on Taiwan's sociopolitical environment. Specifically, Li Tao claimed to me that call-in programs promote public participation and social stability by advancing an "I represent myself" attitude. This interpretation proves revealing, as it suggests that call-in shows inspire greater appreciation of and increased emphasis on individual expression. With its infotainment and participatory approach to the presentation of sociopolitical events and issues, the political TV call-in show thus serves as a key barometer of Taiwan's democratizing society.

As programming products, call-in shows are nonetheless concerned with A. C. Nielsen ratings, profit margins, and commercial income. To a certain extent, the programs draw high ratings and earn revenue.[7] When I asked him what a call-in show's primary goal should be, *Face-to-Face Debate* producer Mr. Xi

Shenglin unhesitatingly stated that both "ratings, making money" and aiding viewers "in reaching a consensus on existing opinions" are important. Rowdy, morally conscientious, and fiscally ambitious, call-in shows strive for the ultimate validation—namely, achieving commercial success and wielding sociopolitical clout in Taiwan's new mass-media environment.

To better understand Taiwan's TV call-in show phenomenon, a brief survey of U.S. talk shows—including their diversity, format, topic orientation, and target audience—helps situate the unique circumstances that contributed to the emergence and form of Taiwan's political TV call-in shows.

DEFINING THE TALK SHOW: FROM OPRAH TO LARRY KING

Describing a talk show by its most basic elements—format (talk) and participants (speakers)—seems rather redundant, for what else can a talk show be other than a cast of talking heads, well . . . talking? This pithy summation, however, merely scratches the surface of a diverse television genre. In the United States, the term "talk show" might elicit references to daytime varieties such as *Donahue*, *The Oprah Winfrey Show,* and *Rosie O'Donnell.* But the program genre also captures the more sensationalistic versions, including those hosted by Jerry Springer, Montel Williams, Ricki Lake, and Maury Povich. Politically oriented talk shows can also be incorporated in the mix. *Meet the Press, The Beltway Boys,* and *Face the Nation* represent the more serious "Sunday morning talk" variety, while *Hardball* and *Crossfire* comprise their hard-hitting but politics-lite cable TV weeknight counterparts. A growing array of hybrid talk shows diversifies the range of audience participation programs even further. These include the personal interview-oriented programs that are supplemented by call-in opportunities, such as on *Larry King Live* and *Imus in the Morning.* Meanwhile, *The Spin Room* epitomizes the new high-tech talk show with its triumvirate format that amalgamizes talk, call-in, and electronic chatroom features into a single program. In the United States, the talk show genre has thus evolved in step with each advancement in communication, broadcasting, and technology, but it has shown no sign of exhausting viewers' desire to watch and, more importantly, participate in their deliberations.

Since appearing on U.S. televisions in the late 1940s, the standard talk show format has remained largely unchanged. This encompasses one or two hosts who moderate a panel of invited speakers who themselves embody or are well-versed in the selected topic. Among the more participatory programs, a live studio audience and/or phone-in callers are incorporated to counterbalance the guest panel.[8] Question-and-answer interactions between panelists and home/studio audiences represent the crux of daytime talk shows, while a roundtable of political experts exchanging witty commentary epitomizes the Washington D.C. "beltway-insider" culture of politically oriented programs. Daytime and political talk show audiences also differ, with the former drawing more female viewers (Shattuc 1997, 8)[9] and the latter attracting elite power brokers such as politicians and mass-media personalities (Hirsch 1991, 64).[10]

Despite—or because of—the diversity of public discussion forums, detractors argue that talk shows promote "toxic talk" (Abt and Mustazza 1997, 2) and script mudslinging worthy of the drama of professional wrestling (Hirsch 1991, 57). Several factors contribute to these impressions, including limited speaking time per participant, target-audience marketing, and narrow topic agendas. Talk show admirers, however, counterargue that the programs offer a valuable verbal space for marginalized groups (Gamson 1998, 45–47) and promote a civil religion of recovery (Lowrey 1999, 23) that reflects and recreates sociopolitical trends (Shattuc 1997, 3). From this perspective, talk shows facilitate the exploration and exploitation of identity politics in all its messy glory.

This chapter's investigation of Taiwan's political call-in shows explores both of these readings. Central to this examination, however, is the premise that call-in shows foreground common sense and everyday experience as alternative interpretations of the "truth" (Shattuc 1997, 93), including Taiwan's sociopolitical crisis discourses.

FROM UNDERGROUND TO OPEN TALK: THE RISE OF THE POLITICAL TV CALL-IN SHOW

Originally inspired by U.S. talk shows, Taiwan's political TV call-in shows have crafted a style and format that reflects Taiwan's unique mass-media development and sociopolitical landscape. This difference can be distinguished through the terminology used to reference this television genre. Rather than using the term "talk show," such programs are known as "call-in shows" *(kouying jiemu)* in Taiwan. While talk remains at the crux of call-in shows, this slight yet revealing distinction alludes to the program's focus on the viewer—and specifically the caller—rather than on the talking heads or guest panelists. Playing on the English pronunciation of "call-in," the Mandarin transliteration—*kouying*—literally means to "knock and respond" (Shen 2000, 146). This double entendre wittingly demarcates the genre's interactive format as well as its appreciation for the subtleties of language.

Taiwan's call-in shows also follow a different developmental trajectory than their U.S. counterparts. While the United States enjoys a strong 227-year democracy coupled with more than sixty-two years of television broadcasting, a post–martial law Taiwan continues to develop its sixteen-year-old democracy and liberalize its ten-year old mass-media environment. Political TV call-in shows appear at an opportune moment in Taiwan's democratization process as they tap into a well of suppressed frustrations built over half a century of one-party rule under the Nationalist Party (Guomindang).

During Taiwan's forty-year martial law era (1947–1987), call-in shows could be found only in nonmainstream venues, as the Guomindang regime controlled and operated the country's print and broadcasting media (Chen 1998, 16–18). Appearing on underground radio stations in the late 1970s, the opposition or *dangwai* movement used these programs to advocate and forward a "Taiwanese consciousness" *(bentu yishi)* among a local populace comprised mostly of "local Taiwanese" *(benshengren)*, which sought to counter a Chinese worldview promulgated by the China-derived Nationalists.[11] Call-in programs also attracted a public that used this anonymous, interactive forum to share their viewpoints with reduced risk of state retribution.

Underground radio transcended standard journalistic practices in Taiwan in other critical ways. Most visibly, this medium broadcasts its programs in Taiwanese (Taiyu) or Hoklo rather than in the officially decreed "national language" *(guoyu)* or Mandarin, which is a northern Chinese dialect. In March 1990, the underground media made a breakthrough in promoting democratic and ethnic awareness when the opposition party, the Democratic Progressive Party (DPP), established an islandwide network of radio and television stations dubbed "The Voice of Democracy" (Chen 1998, 26).

In the late 1960s, underground cable TV stations also began broadcasting in Taiwan (Rawnsley and Rawnsley 2001, 73).[12] This illegal television service became locally dubbed "the fourth channel" *(disitai)* in a facetious nod to the island's three terrestrial, Guomindang-owned TV stations (Chen 1998, 26). The 1993 Cable TV Law subsequently legalized private ownership of cable TV stations (Rampal 1994, 73), opening the door to foreign and local investment in Taiwan's nascent mass-media market. Later that same year, a Hong Kong–based news enterprise (TVB) launched Taiwan's first all-news channel, TVBS.[13] Since the mid-1990s, five twenty-four-hour TV news channels have competed on Taiwan's airways in a nation of 23 million residents. This news broadcasting-to-population ratio is even more impressive when compared with that of the United States, which has five national all-news TV channels for a population twelve times larger than that of Taiwan.[14]

SITUATING CALL-IN SHOWS IN TAIWAN

Given the call-in show's underground radio beginnings in Taiwan, its role and agenda have evolved into a more popularized and personalized orientation in its legal, televised incarnation. In 1994, the country's first political TV call-in show aired in the form of TVBS' *2100: All People Open Talk*.[15] TVBS thus introduced the infotainment news program to Taiwan, educating its viewers that deliberating sociopolitical events can be more informative and entertaining than covering them.

Taiwan's political TV call-in programs differ most from their U.S. counterparts in striving to present a nonideological, nonpartisan image. The reasons for this approach are twofold: to appeal to a diverse audience, thereby receiving higher ratings, and to avoid the biased, censored coverage reminiscent of newscasts during the martial law period (Chiu and Chan-Olmstead 1999, 495).

Despite these aspirations, viewers criticize call-in programs for favoring a certain political party or candidate. Nevertheless, TVBS vice president and *2100* moderator Li Tao credits his call-in show's rapid and sustained success to its ability to earn acceptability and credibility in the eyes of the public. This feat requires the call-in program—and particularly its moderator—to project a "neutral" *(zhongli)* image, which includes avoiding leaning openly toward any particular candidate, political party, or stance on Taiwan's sovereignty issue.[16] As Jin Xiuli of *Always Speak Your Mind* explains: "If [a call-in program] already [has] a preconceived standpoint, the people that you attract are the small masses *[xiaozhong]*. So I feel that Li Tao, the reason why he is successful, is understandable; that is, he definitely does not only attract a [niche] market." Jin's perspective reveals that a moderator with both political acumen and broad appeal is central to a successful political call-in show in a country whose populace remains leery of state intervention and media manipulation.

Of course, not all political TV call-in hosts in Taiwan subscribe to Li Tao's middle-of-the-road philosophy. Yu Fu of *8 o'clock* regards call-in shows as primarily performative and consequently eschews the moderate and conciliatory demeanor that Li Tao espouses and displays.[17] As a political cartoonist whose other "day jobs" include hosting a weekday radio call-in show and running an Internet animation company, Yu Fu's eclectic professional life emerges in his interjecting speaking style and tongue-in-cheek delivery. While Yu Fu agrees that a moderator figuratively and literally serves as a call-in show's anchor, he describes his primary responsiblity as provoking guest panelists and promoting the program's entertainment value. This requires catering to the viewer's short attention span rather than appealing to his or her reasoning skills. Yu Fu explained to me how he saw this as a futile endeavor:

> A lot of moderators say that they educate people. What are they educating? Basically what have you taught? The entertainment that I talk about is not the type, the immoral type of entertainment. It's taking politicians [and] playing with them for you to watch. . . . You take their formal side, and play it up for [viewers] to see. Because if you make them [the politicians] mad, their emotions will come out. Their real . . . face is then exposed. Otherwise on TV you normally pretend to be very . . . profound. Right? . . . They all say that kind of *bullshit*.[18] That kind of dog shit. . . . So . . . what's my job? I tease out their real faces for you to see.

Yu Fu justifies his goading approach as a means to provide viewers with glimpses of each guest panelist's true personality, which can be interpreted as manipulative at best, Machiavellian at worst. To him, this underscores the call-in show game of testing each panelist's performative mettle and linguistic dexterity.

Yu Fu's perspective vividly captures the call-in show as an infotainment product that ambitiously—and awkwardly—occupies the intersection of news coverage and popular performance. As a hybrid entity, such programs have the dual task of appealing to both seasoned political heavyweights and garden-variety armchair pundits. This eclectic participation pool manifests itself through a diversity of language use—ranging from insider politik talk to lowbrow mudslinging—which exists side by side, sound bite for sound bite on Taiwan's political call-in shows. Mr. Zhou Jinsheng (Jonathan Chou), coproducer of ETTV's *Always Speak Your Mind,* attempts to reconcile these seemingly disparate aspects in his explanation of why call-in shows descend into verbal sparring or "saliva wars": "Of course saliva wars will exist. This cannot be denied, because the populace is at an average level . . . not all of them are the elite. So I would hope that . . . by attracting viewers through saliva wars [we can] create some *interactive*[19] development to their general knowledge or political knowledge, or at least an alternate perspective or some diversity [in their thinking]." At once apologetic and optimistic, Zhou's comments expose the political call-in show as an oxymoron that features both the best and worst of Taiwan's sociopolitical arena and its participants' dramatic linguistic practices.

PERFORMING CRISIS DISCOURSES ON POLITICAL CALL-IN SHOWS

The call-in show's semiscripted format privileges certain ideologies and participants—namely, those that contribute to the program's overarching crisis ambiance. A dictionary definition describes "crisis" as an "unstable or crucial time or state of affairs in which a decisive change is impending" or "a situation that has reached a critical phase" (*Merriam-Webster's Collegiate Dictionary* 1995, 275). Thus the call-in show's framing of Taiwan's sociopolitical sphere as locked in a "perpetual crisis" represents a conceptual oxymoron (Rollins 1996). The construct nonetheless captures the ritualized format of Taiwan's political TV call-in shows whereby participants produce and recreate crisis discourses through strategic language use. The use of urgent-sounding terminology represents a common tactic, as epitomized in an earlier excerpt where *2100* moderator Li Tao used hot-button terms to frame the issue of Taiwanese-mainlander relations. This linguistic practice encourages the recycling of Taiwan's crisis discourses on each subsequent episode, reinforcing the observation that "a crisis, like all news developments, is a creation of the language used to depict it" (Edelman 1988, 31).

Yet the crisis discourses that Taiwan's political TV call-in shows promote and their participants perform assume a different, even realistic aura given the existence of actual crisis events and issues in the sociopolitical realm. This unique sociopolitical backdrop proves important, as it differentiates the crisis orientation of Taiwan's political call-in shows from their U.S. counterparts. On Taiwan's politically oriented call-in shows, the program revolves around the crisis topic, whereas on political talk shows in the United States, the personalities of its participants overwhelm the featured issues (Hirsch 1991,70). The call-in show's crisis orientation also maintains a longstanding discursive practice that defines Taiwan, given its tumultuous sociohistorical past as well as its geopolitically unstable present and uncertain future. Taiwan's call-in shows thus represent the latest evolution of a well-established verbal custom—namely, the discussion of politics within traditional spaces such as in village temples, teahouses, and public parks—that now extends to mass-mediated venues.

Consequently, what call-in programs offer speakers that these other sites do not is the potential to disseminate their political perspectives to a broader audience and in a variety of mediated forms that face-to-face verbal interactions preclude. Similarly, call-in shows instantly create an imagined community (Anderson 1991) of political consumers and producers that connects in-studio guest panelists and home viewers with participants in "on-site" *(xianchang)* broadcasts. These are transmitted from domestic locales, including the disaster area surrounding Jiji (Chi-chi) following the 1999 earthquake, and even abroad, such as U.S. metropolitan areas with high concentrations of Taiwan residents (i.e., San Francisco, Los Angeles, and New York).[20] In short, Taiwan's call-in shows serve as a conduit for the country's sociopolitical crisis discourses while unifying a disparate and dispersed community around a shared worldview.

GROUNDING TAIWAN'S CRISIS DISCOURSE: SOCIOPOLITICAL BACKGROUND

A primary crisis discourse that continues to preoccupy Taiwan's leaders and populace since the mid-twentieth century revolves around the issue of Taiwan's sovereignty: Is it a nation-state or is it a part of an envisioned "China"? To the Chinese Communist Party (CCP) that rules the People's Republic of China regime, Taiwan remains a province of China. In Taiwan, however, this question is answered very differently, depending on whom (DPP, Guomindang) one asks. In the early twenty-first century, these groups' dueling interpretations (independence vs. part of a single "China") continue to vie for supremacy in cross-straits relations as well as in domestic political struggles within Taiwan itself. The combined facts of a "mainlander" or *waishengren* party that ruled Taiwan for fifty-five years and its suppression of the local (predominantly *benshengren*) population during that period contributes to lingering ideological tensions between these two ethnopolitical groups (Wachman 1994, 30–33).

Since the implementation of direct national elections in the late 1980s, "Taiwanese-mainlander" distinctions figure as an even more salient issue, as political parties and candidates use these identifiers and their assumed pro-Taiwan independence and pro-China unification worldviews to categorize, divide, and attract voters (Rigger 1999, 141). For instance, Taiwan's first locally derived political party, the Democratic Progressive Party (DPP or Minjindang), advocates Taiwanization *(bentuhua)* and Taiwan independence *(taidu)* in an effort to mobilize *benshengren* voters (Arrigo 1994, 147–149).[21] In contrast, the Guomindang and its splinter party, the New Party (NP or Xindang), are generally regarded as having a *waishengren* following given their pro-China reunification stances.[22]

But these dichotomized "Taiwanese-mainlander" demarcations no longer suffice within Taiwan's present multiparty system.[23] For instance, the gradual splintering of the Guomindang over the last decade into the New Party in 1993, the People First Party (PFP or Qinmindang) in 2000, and most recently the Taiwan Solidarity Union (TSU or Taiwan Tuanjie Lianmeng) in mid-2001, has complicated the voter portrait of these political parties.[24] The Guomindang itself now embraces a predominantly *benshengren* membership, an evolution that began with former chairman Lee Teng-hui (Li Denghui) and his "Taiwanese Guomindang" agenda (Rigger 1999, 182).

Moreover, while the DPP previously represented the lone party that promoted Taiwan independence, it has now moderated its independence rhetoric since becoming Taiwan's ruling party in May 2000. ROC President Chen Shuibian (Chen Shuibian), himself a former independence advocate, currently promotes a cross-straits policy that maintains the status quo by neither pursuing official Taiwan independence nor conceding to a "one China" perspective.[25] As a result, the recently formed Taiwan Solidarity Union now represents the most avid advocate for an independent Taiwan among the major political parties.

"MEDIA-TING" A CRISIS DISCOURSE

A survey of Taiwan's political TV call-in program topics creates a Gestalt-like impression that appears to be pieced together by disparate issues and interests. Yet these topics nonetheless paint a crisis-themed portrait of Taiwan's sociopolitical landscape that revolves around "what ifs" and "could happens." Call-in show participants have subsequently deliberated on the police's dramatic pursuit and capture of the kidnapper-murderers of singer Bai Bingbing's daughter; the central government's inadequate monetary reparations to victims of the September 1999 earthquake that claimed over 2,300 lives; whether a Clintonesque presidency—Lewinsky, Travelgate, and all—might befall an ROC president; how to resolve the impasse in cross-straits relations; the confusion over Taiwan's national identity as being either "Chinese" (Zhongguoren), "Taiwanese" (Taiwanren), or both; and the constitutionality of impeaching Vice President Annette Lu (Lü Xiulian) for undermining President Chen's administration and his cross-straits policies through a string of verbal blunders.[26] Ranging from serious reflection to mock consideration of sociopolitical events and issues, these topics illustrate the odd coupling of sensationalism and news coverage in this infotainment massmedia venue.

Distinguishing real from imagined crisis discourses represents in many respects a futile endeavor. Yet the exercise foregrounds how frequently call-in topics straddle this arbitrary and fuzzy line. For instance, is it just call-in show spin that Vice President Annette Lu's criticism of President Chen Shui-bian's mainland policy jeopardizes cross-straits relations? Similarly, should viewers credit or dismiss a call-in show's claim that the people of Taiwan face an identity crisis when high-ranking officials stumble in answering questions regarding their national identity, such as whether they consider themselves "Chinese," "Taiwanese," or both?[27]

Unfortunately, in crafting a crisis ambiance for their programs, call-in shows demonstrate a predilection for oversimplifying topics as either/or, pro/con, and right/wrong scenarios. This is most vividly captured in the program's restricted twenty-second caller commentaries and questionable polling practices conducted through phone-in voting and program-sponsored opinion polls. As program participants alternately reify and contest the call-in show's dichotomized crisis interpretations of Taiwan's sociopolitical environment, they perpetuate and expose the fallacy that Taiwan and its people only face bifurcated choices regarding the country's problematic issues.

WHITHER A CRISIS DISCOURSE: HOT AIR OR OPEN TALK?

The format of Taiwan's political TV call-in shows—including *2100* and other similar programs such as *8 o'clock Loud and Soft Voices, Face-to-Face Debate (Xiang dui lun), Always Speak Your Mind (You hua laoshi jiang), Everyone Let's Deliberate (Dajia lai shenpan),* among others—blends the roundtable discussion of U.S. political talk shows such as *Insider Washington* or *Meet the Press* with the populist call-in format of *Larry King Live.* Most of Taiwan's call-in shows have a single moderator, invite a three-to-five-member guest panel,[28] solicit viewer call-ins, and conduct phone-in polls pertaining to that episode's topic(s).[29] Broadcast between the weeknight "primetime" hours of 8 to 10 P.M., the hourlong programs compete against an array of serial dramas and variety programs.[30] Although viewer profiles vary slightly for each call-in show, these programs generally attract a high school–educated male audience over forty years of age.[31]

The guest panel selection also contributes to a discursively constructed crisis format. Panelists featured on call-in programs represent a range of sociopolitical figures, including politicians, academics, and mass-media personalities. Yet panelists can easily be identified by their political affiliations and ideological stance. Speaking time allocation further highlights the call-in shows' disproportionate orientation. Depending on the program and the context (introductory/concluding remarks vs. general discussion), a panelist's average turn to talk ranges from fifteen seconds to three minutes.[32] In contrast, callers are restricted to twenty seconds, although on some programs they are provided a more flexible one to two minutes per call.[33] The number of calls a program accepts also influences the length of time each caller is allowed to speak. While most call-in shows feature an average of six callers, *2100* receives twenty to thirty callers spaced throughout its program.[34]

Speaking time thus represents a valuable commodity on these programs. Participants often devise ways to increase their verbal presence by introducing provocative and witty remarks, yet doing so within the parameters of the program's topic(s). The following excerpts demonstrate how speakers strategically address the featured issues while contributing to—and maneuvering within—the program's crisis frame.

CREATING THE CALL-IN SHOW SPECTACLE: MODERATORS

Among political TV call-in show moderators, Li Tao of *2100* is recognized for his dramatic, elaborate delivery that tends to wax poetic about the topic, as well as his lengthy summations of panelist remarks.[35] The following excerpt illustrates his emotive style. Taken from an episode entitled, "Big Reconciliation: Who Are We?" (Da hejie: Women shi shenme ren?), Li Tao expresses the country's struggling identification as a "Chinese" versus "Taiwanese" society, which is linked to latent ethnopolitical tensions between *waishengren* and *benshengren*.[36]

> Currently, if we talk about—if anyone wants to know . . . what my [national] identity is, I can say it aloud. A teacher should be able to safely teach [this issue], including not needing to confront a parent after class who immediately runs over and states, "You say that you have [purposely garbled nonsense speech] a national identity!" Any teacher who is criticized this way would go insane. When I am hosting a call-in program even I am asked [in falsetto],[37] "Where are you from? What is your national identity?" [Normal speaking voice] Ah—each government official who goes to the Legislative Yuan,[38] he also faces the question [falsetto], "So, who are you [what is your identity]?" [Normal voice] Uh-uh-uh—in such cases the official needs to consult his notes for guidance. [Muttering] "Which identity do I claim?"

Li Tao's choppy transitions from one performed voice to another—including himself as moderator, an irate parent, a demanding caller, and finally a pressured government official—lead his audience through various locally recognizable figures, vividly animating the individuals and discursive stances Taiwan's national identity crisis indexes and incorporates. Furthermore, his tonal shifts from falsetto to a normal speaking voice and from lucid to nonsense speech increasingly escalate the topic's stridency. Selective word choice, such as the terms "criticized" and "insane," likewise contributes to creating a sense of urgency. By performing an eclectic range of personas through the use of constructed dialogue (e.g., "Which identity do I claim?"), Li Tao personalizes the national identity issue as one that "real" people face in everyday interactions.[39] His verbal dexterity succeeds in dramatizing the topic at an emotional level while downplaying its theoretical and rational dimensions.

In contrast to Li Tao, *8 o'clock* moderator Yu Fu favors a speaking style characterized by rapid and persistent questioning along one line of inquiry. This moderating technique attempts to catch panelists off guard, thus leaving them less time for reflection and increasing the possibility for slips of the tongue. Yu Fu's pointed questioning demands simple yes or no responses and preempts long-winded responses. He also uses a broken-record approach that reiterates a query until the preferred answer is given, which invariably involves validating Yu Fu's crisis interpretation of the featured topic. Another tactic Yu Fu frequently uses includes reiterating a previous panelist's words and turning it into a follow-up question for another guest.

The following excerpt vividly demonstrates Yu Fu's unique moderating tactics. It is drawn from an episode that deliberates whether Vice President Annette Lu's comparison of herself as the "black face" *(heilian),* or bad cop, to President Chen Shui-bian's "white face" *(bailian),* or good cop, reveals tensions between Lu and Chen. The verbal interaction captures Yu Fu attempting to present Vice President Lu's controversial remarks as endangering cross-straits relations and Taiwan's national security:[40]

Yu Fu:	Right—it's not—the main point is [unintelligible]. . . .
DPP:[41]	The main point is that Vice President Lu . . . and the President's office basically are not quite on the same page. This is what the public feels.
Yu Fu:	Has it endangered national security?
DPP:	Actually it—up to now it has not endangered national security.
Yu Fu:	It hasn't endangered national security.
NP:[42]	Ah—that's not quite grasping the sensitivity between the two sides [Taiwan and China].
Yu Fu:	Yes.
NP:	It's also not quite grasping the complex relationship between the two sides. Because even though there originally wasn't this, eh, black-white face [bad-good cop] remark, uh, there were possibly already some aggressive factions in mainland China . . .
Yu Fu:	Yes.
NP:	First of all, I want to particularly emphasize one point, okay? We[43] do not have any gender bias . . .
Yu Fu:	Gender bias. Has it endangered national security?

In this passage, Yu Fu maintains the panelists' focus on the issue of national security by repeatedly including the phrase in his line of questioning (e.g., "Has it endangered national security?") as well as when summarizing a previous speaker's comments ("It hasn't endangered national security"). Even when the discussion shifts directions—namely, from Vice President Lu's "black face, white face" comment to gender bias—Yu Fu stays on topic by incorporating the issue of gender bias within his national security line of questioning ("Gender bias. Has it endangered national security?"). Consequently, Yu Fu succeeds in linking this particular verbal action to the featured crisis topic—namely, have Lu's recent verbal gaffes undermined relations between the ROC president and vice president, as well as increased cross-straits tensions between

Taiwan and China. Yu Fu's repetitive, almost unimaginative moderating tactics strategically leave panelists little opportunity to diverge from his preoccupation with Taiwan's national security or even the space to introduce a new direction for discussion.

THE CALL-IN SHOW CIRCUIT/CIRCUS: GUEST PANELISTS

Selected for their embodiment of institutional voices from politics, academia, and print and mass media, call-in producers interview potential panelists for their perspectives toward the selected topic before inviting them for that evening's broadcast. An ideal panel is rife with dissenting perspectives to generate discord between guests and heighten dissention regarding the featured issue. While guests are free to express their personal perspectives, the subtitles floating beneath their televised visages nevertheless label each panelist by name, occupational title, and, in most cases, affiliation to a political party, organization, or profession.[44] Given that call-in shows often recycle and share the same guests, panelists become familiar with each other's speaking styles and arguments as they tread the call-in show circuit. The fact that viewers expect panelists to consistently represent a given ideological stance from program to program also entrenches a guest panelist's linguistic behavior. Furthermore, panelists and moderators develop a feeling of camaraderie over time from frequent interaction, which diminishes the likelihood of "hardball" questions from hosts in the attempt to discomfit and catch the panelists off guard.[45]

Recognized as a Taiwan independence advocate, DPP legislator Li Yingyuan frequently appears as a guest panelist on *2100* to argue this ideological perspective. In the following excerpt, which is taken from an episode on ethnopolitical relations,[46] legislator Li's comments include symbolically marked words that readily identify his party affiliation and political stance. Generally, the guest panelists and television viewers already have the sociopolitical knowledge to "decode" such ideologically laden arguments: "Like I just said, presently the cultural situation [in Taiwan] is not that serious. Culturally speaking, however, language still represents the crux of the problem ... one day we should be able to say that Taiwan's Hakka language, Taiwan's Formosan language [Fo'er hua], Taiwan's Beijing language [Beijingyu], and Taiwan's Chinese language [Huayu][47] are all equal."

To grasp the import of Li's remarks requires being familiar with the former Nationalist regime's language policies, including establishing Mandarin Chinese, which is based on the Beijing dialect, as Taiwan's official "national language" *(guoyu)* (Phillips 1999, 285).[48] Pro-Taiwan independence supporters, and particularly the DPP, protest this hegemonic assignation by using alternative terms to identify the Mandarin language. As uttered by legislator Li, these subversive identifiers include the "Beijing language" or the "Chinese language." Through the deliberate and combined use of "Formosan language,"[49] "Beijing language," and "Chinese language," legislator Li articulates an alternative multilingual perspective that replaces the Chinese-centric worldview promoted by the Guomindang. Legislator Li begins this passage by stating that Taiwan's "cultural situation is not that serious." By introducing the aforementioned key words, however, he reminds his fellow panelists and call-in show viewers that discriminatory language ideologies continue to exist in Taiwan and must be addressed.

Although guest panelists often fall into stock roles on call-in shows, other panelists prefer to play with ideological panelist casting. Variable, whimsical guests appeal to both producers and viewers alike, as they insert moments of unpredictability in an otherwise orchestrated format. The following excerpt comes from a *2100* episode that considers the PRC government's total ban on all commercial endorsements, CDs, and future concert appearances by Taiwan pop singer Zhang Huimei (popularly known as Amei), following her participation in President Chen Shui-bian's 2000 inauguration. With his witty observations and surprising interpretations, Professor Xie Zhiwei injects humor into a discussion that had thus far merely regurgitated the standard "the PRC just doesn't understand Taiwan" line. Xie begins his remarks by summarizing previous panelist comments, including the general perspective that the PRC's Amei ban[50] interpreted her performance of the ROC national anthem as an expression of support for Taiwan independence.[51] But Xie gives the "misunderstanding" interpretation a new twist when he links Amei's national anthem performance with President Chen Shui-bian's cross-straits policy:[52]

> I feel that this issue is basically a misunderstanding . . . [and] should be the responsibility of both the Democratic Progressive Party and [President] Chen Shui-bian. Why? Because this national anthem is [written] in a very high key. To want Amei to sing in a high key, [and] with Chen Shui-bian's initial declaration that he wanted a low-key resolution to the cross-straits issue, are completely at odds. To say that [cross-straits relations] should eventually have a low-key resolution [and] to find [someone] to sing the national anthem in a high-key is the first, the first misunderstanding. The second point I want to clarify is just to say that [those who are]—dissatisfied with the national anthem do not [only] include the DPP. . . . [They] definitely exceed the DPP's 200,000 members. *I am not a DPP member,* [but] I also am not satisfied with the [ROC] national anthem.

In this passage, Xie demonstrates his adeptness as both amusing entertainer and insightful analyst by interweaving puns and policy in a refreshing explanation that challenges listeners to comprehend his part-serious, part-facetious reading of pop culture and politicking. The professor also succeeds in concealing his own stance toward the Amei/national anthem incident until the very end, at which point he admits that although he is "not a DPP member," he too is dissatisfied with the ROC national anthem.[53] His skillful reinterpretation of the PRC/Amei controversy performs a discursively circuitous yet logically coherent argument that delays immediate interpretative gratification and builds audience anticipation with his every word.

Although these excerpts focus upon two guest panelists who use distinct linguistic styles in addressing two different issues, the examples nonetheless capture them simultaneously contributing to and critiquing the featured crisis topic. Even as the panelists recycle tried and true arguments, they reexamine such popularized understandings through their personal readings of crisis scenarios. Moreover, the two panelists demonstrate their ability to identify subtle ironies within Taiwan's sociopolitical crisis discourses and rearticulate them in a creative manner that is uniquely cultivated and appreciated within the call-in show context.

ENTER THE ARMCHAIR PUNDITS: CALLERS

Positioned as the voice of the private citizen, call-in show callers are generally regarded by producers and television viewers as being more "authentic" than their guest panelist counterparts. Their perspectives are also considered to be representative of the "truth," at least in the world of call-in shows. Featured as so-called nonexperts, callers' commentaries are valued for their grounding in personal life experiences and their noninstitutional viewpoints. While call-in programs identify each guest panelist by name, title, and affiliation, callers remain anonymous save for a generic introduction by the host that includes the caller's surname, gender, and calling location.[54] A caller's voice thus literally represents her primary identity, which stands in sharp contrast to guest panelists and moderators, who are both visible and audible to television audiences.

Yet the image of the caller as a private citizen who phones in from home takes a unique turn in Taiwan's politically intense call-in show arena. Inspired by increasingly competitive local and national elections, "call-in teams" *(kouying budui)* have emerged on the political call-in show scene.[55] Comprised of paid or volunteer workers from a given political party or candidate, these teams dial the programs en masse during live call-in show broadcasts.[56] Some call-in teams are even equipped with computer-dialed phone lines that can flood a program's switchboards, significantly increasing that team's chances of being selected for broadcast.[57] Once on air, these callers frequently read prepared text that the campaign staff of a political party or candidate has written. These scripted lines are filled with campaign slogans or denigrating diatribes against opposition candidates and parties, a practice that is locally referred to as "black-facing" *(mohei)*. The advent of call-in teams reflects the intimate and interactive relationship between politics and mass media in Taiwan (Rawnsley and Rawnsley 2001), a phenomenon that also augments the generation of crisis discourses on call-in shows.

As discussed above, call-in programs allocate less speaking time to callers than guest panelists. This proves particularly apparent on *2100*, which restricts each caller to twenty seconds. As a result, callers produce dense remarks filled with pithy proverbs or concise narratives that still manage to address the complexity of the crisis topic and personalize its everyday realizations. In the following excerpt, Mr. Yao demonstrates the individualized character of caller comments in his remarks on Taiwanese/mainlander identities: "Ah, I—I want um, to ask you [something], okay? About my two children, one was born in 1950, the other was born in 1951. But, he is—I—I am a Shanghairen [a person from Shanghai]. But my two children were both born in Taiwan. That is to say, are they to be considered Taiwanren or *waishengren?*"

Mr. Yao's comments provide chronological and geographic references that both personalize his narrative as well as illustrate the arbitrary and ideological nature of "Taiwanese"/"mainlander" identifiers. By introducing his children by the year they were born (e.g., in 1950 and 1951), Mr. Yao tactfully establishes them as being born after 1949, thus situating his children's ethnopolitical identities vis-à-vis Taiwan's sociopolitical environment at the time. Next, Mr. Yao identifies himself as a Shanghairen, a word choice that deliberately avoids the political connotations associated with the term *"waishengren."* In concluding, he calculatedly refers to his children as being "born in Taiwan," again sidestepping the ideologically loaded terms "Taiwanren" or *"benshengren."* Mr. Yao juxtaposes this carefully phrased descriptor with a parting query that pointedly questions whether his children can be categorically identified—namely, "are they to be considered Taiwanren or *waishengren?*" By positing this deceptively simple question, Mr. Yao foregrounds these two ethnopolitical labels as outdated and, moreover, inadequate descriptors for capturing his and his children's identities.

By blending narratives and commentary in their call-ins, callers illustrate that the boundary between lived experience and sociohistorical "fact" is not only porous but also arbitrary. The following caller, Mr. Wang, provides a personalized reading of history when he challenges dominant discourses by reassessing past and current sociopolitical incidents in Taiwan: "I am a second generation mainlander. I don't have any fear of the future. But I feel that there is often inequality as well as injustice [in Taiwan]. The DPP has been elected [as the ruling party and] used [ethnopolitical] sentiments to get—what they wanted. But mainlanders have been thoroughly tricked by them. . . . Let me ask [you], what does 228 have to do with us? We arrived [in Taiwan] in 1949. Let me ask, did mainlanders profit from 228? Didn't—didn't mainlanders also die?"

Wang begins his remarks by introducing himself as a "second-generation mainlander" *(waishengren di'er dai)* who is not afraid of the future—namely, one in which the Guomindang no longer represents the ruling party.[58] In introducing the constructs of inequality, injustice, and trickery, notions commonly associated with the Guomindang, Wang situates the DPP as the present-day perpetrators of these political devices. In a calculated coup de grace, Wang next turns the February 28 Incident on its head by inverting the oppressor-victim relationship. He argues that mainlanders who arrived in Taiwan after 1947—including his family who came from the Mainland in 1949—had nothing to do with the incident. Moreover, Wang challenges the prevailing view that only native Taiwanese suffered in the violent confrontation and points out that mainlanders perished as well. His comments not only highlight Taiwan's changing sociopolitical landscape by referring to recent political power shifts but also illustrate the personalization of Taiwan politics. Through a rereading of sociohistorical events and Taiwanese-mainlander relations, Wang succeeds in debunking several long-standing ethnopolitical ideologies in the process.

CONCLUSION

As a mass-mediated forum that showcases a range of voices, Taiwan's political TV call-in shows offer a unique space to reconfirm, reevaluate, and reshape mainstream discourses, including ethnopolitical ideologies and identities, national identity formation, and cross-straits tensions. Central to this chapter's discussion has been the exploration of how call-in show participants negotiate crisis issues and events through their linguistic practices. The program excerpts reveal a rebalancing in Taiwan's sociopolitical arena between dominant ideologies and personal experiences on the one hand and historical mythologizing (or reification) and popular sentiment on the other. Yet these passages also depict a more complex composite where the personal and the popular are layered over symbolically rich texts in sometimes transparent but oftentimes opaque ways.

At first glance, the crisis discourses that participants promote and perform on Taiwan's political TV call-in shows confirm the general critique that talk/call-in programs suspend reality, skimp on specifics, and avoid resolution (Shattuc 1997, 95–96). This reading assumes that "reality" must be discerned from performance and fact from sensationalism. What critics overlook, however, is the interplay between self-effacing facetiousness and self-conscious neutrality, ideological stereotyping and individual case studies, as well as self-serving propaganda and social consciousness. The call-in show participants presented in this chapter utilize linguistic ingenuity to dismantle and reconfigure dichotomizing schemas of "staged" show versus "real" events and issues. Traditional boundaries between information and entertainment, senders and receivers, and spectators and performers dissolve before participants' and viewers' eyes, making such distinctions increasingly irrelevant in new mass-mediated forums. Consequently, media and popular culture cannot be viewed as social activities separated from the political (Livingstone and Lunt 1994, 30).

While the passages presented in this chapter may not diminish the talk/call-in show's soundbite-prone image, they do exhibit a range of perspectives and voices that stock news broadcasts and legislative debates neglect, if not exclude completely. Most importantly, Taiwan's call-in programs restructure a previously censored and restricted mass-media environment that is most vividly captured in the transformation of passive, TV remote-wielding viewers into phone-calling, "I represent myself" vocal participants.[59] Presented as purveyors of higher ratings, consensus builders, and hawkers of a twenty-second version of Warholian fame, call-in shows provide a welcome space for "nonexpert" citizens to forthrightly share their personal stories alongside authoritative sociopolitical leaders.

Well positioned to accommodate and promote "open talk" discussions, call-in shows stand at the front lines of a new mass-mediated revolution in Taiwan that features increasingly popularized sociopolitical discussions, a practice unheard of merely two decades ago. Detractors of the call-in show's pop political treatment of news events disapprovingly point to its crisis-codifying format, raucous style of public deliberation, and its sensationalized presentation of controversial issues. What call-in shows lack in closure, however, they compensate for by offering Taiwan's nascent democracy rich narratives and stimulating verbal sparring in a largely uncensored public venue. This is reason enough to tune in or phone in every once in a while.

PART IV
Economic Life
MONEY AND MEANING

6

The Other Woman in Your Home

Social and Racial Discourses on "Foreign Maids" in Taiwan

Chin-ju Lin

EDITORS' INTRODUCTION

Hiring workers is not new in Taiwan. A century ago, tenant farming was one specialized way of hiring labor, but even tenant farmers themselves sometimes borrowed or hired extra farm workers during the busy agricultural season. In towns, hired shop assistants and assistant craftsmen of all kinds were common. With the commercial and industrial expansion of the twentieth century—and particularly of the last forty years or so—working in the family business gradually became a minority way of life, and a career working for others became the expectation and experience of most people in Taiwan.

But another change has also occurred. Taiwan today has more jobs than workers, and in particular there are more low-paying, menial jobs than there are people willing to accept them. As Taiwan has moved from being an "underdeveloped" nation with "cheap labor" to a "developed" one with a need for ever more unskilled workers, it has become an attractive destination for guest workers from other countries who visit to work a few years at higher wages than they can make at home.

Some jobs are essentially luxury labor—tasks that people would do for themselves or leave undone if they were not in a position to pay others to do them. As income has grown in Taiwan, increasingly affluent Taiwan households have discovered a new "need" for domestic servants, and domestic service in Taiwan provides a new opportunity for guest workers. Life without a maid has become "impossible" for some fashionable Taiwan families.

One of the nearby lands that is home to a fair number of Taiwan's guest workers is the Philippines. Many Filipinos travel to work temporarily in other countries around the world, including the United States. Spending some time overseas building up a nest egg or sending money home to one's family has come to be a normal part of life for many Filipinos, and there are many placement companies and much local lore about working conditions in different countries to which Filipinos travel.

In this chapter, Chin-ju Lin explores the world of women who travel from the Philippines to Taiwan to work for a time as housemaids. (In the mid-1990s, an overwhelming proportion of these maids were from the Philippines. Today an increasing number of Indonesians take these positions.) The expectations on both sides tend to be unrealistic at least some of the time, and the cultural differences seem almost predestined to lead to misunderstandings. Importantly, it is rare for the maid to speak more than a few words of Chinese, and it is nearly unknown for a Taiwan householder to speak Tagalog or any Philippine language, so communication is in broken English—hardly a formula for perfect understanding.

But the situation is more complicated than simply master-servant interaction across a language barrier. Lin believes that the ethnic difference becomes an additional tool by which people in Taiwan define their own identity in the world. Being Taiwanese, in other words, is partly defined as not being Filipino.

How can this be studied? As an entrée into the world of partially conflicting expectations and definitions of self and other, Lin examines the discourses or ways in which the Filipinas and their employers describe their respective expectations and situations. As she moves our perspective back and forth between the two sides, some regularities emerge about the tensions in this relationship. Lin is especially concerned about exploitation and abuses that emerge in this context, as the people in power, the Taiwanese, manipulate the people at the bottom, the Filipina maids. She proposes the concept of racism as an explanation of what comes to exist.

Discourses—the terms and statements used to discuss a topic—are not merely a way in which we can see how this relationship works. Lin argues that the discourses she discovers have been in fact an important influence on events in Taiwan, not just a window on them. She tells us that "'foreign maids' were gradually racialized into the category of 'ethnic other' through diverse discourses." The discourses are thus both our method of seeing what is going on and part of what we are looking at.

Lin describes the interplay between public discussion, official policy, and evolving popular stereotypes about the outsiders on the one hand and the pervasive underlying negative view of them and the possible "dangers" they might pose to Taiwan society on the other hand. The possible dangers include probably not fitting in, possibly never leaving, perhaps bearing dangerous diseases, and likely being ignorant, backward, and dirty in their habits. The Taiwanese view of the guest workers is not very positive, it develops.

Lin interprets these discourses as xenophobic and ethnocentric in this modern context, arguing that the combination produces a form of racism targeted very specifically against Filipina domestic servants. She argues that these discourses reflect the "racial identity" of Han-Taiwanese and proposes that this may prove to be important in the analysis of many other aspects of Taiwan society as well. ■

Race and ethnic relations in Han contexts are emerging areas of research. Since the 1990s, there has been an increasing amount of English-language anthropological investigation on Han racial identities in relation to other ethnic groups (Blum 2001; Chiu 2000; Dikötter 1992, 1997; Harrell 1995). In this research, all of the ethnic groups studied had a long history of interaction with the Han people (such as the Yi and Miao in southwest China or indigenous groups in Taiwan) and live within the territory of the nation-state where the PRC and ROC governments (both in pre-1945 China and post-1945 Taiwan) claim to hold sovereign power. In other words, they have been subject to the imperial expansion of the Han nation-states. Little has been addressed on ethnic relations between the Han and ethnic groups who are latecomers to their territory. How would the Han identify themselves in relation to foreign migrants? What interactions might occur between them? How shall we investigate the ways in which Han people discriminate against "ethnic others" in contemporary political and economic contexts?

This chapter investigates social and racial discourses in Taiwan that involve migrant workers in general and Filipina domestic workers in particular. Since the late 1980s, the comparatively higher level of economic growth has attracted migrant workers from other Asian countries to work as industrial workers, cooks, and domestics in Taiwan. A legal gateway for economic migrants was set up in 1992 when the Employment Service Act came into force. The implementation of this law followed a period during which the desirability of migrant workers was debated vigorously in Taiwan. The issue of "foreign maids" was part of the discussion.[1] Ordinary people, legislators, career women, academics, feminists, and government officials all had opinions about this group of women. Social actors of diverse interests produce different discourses in which concepts of gender, class, and ethnicity contest with each other. Through this specific case study, I will explore aspects of Han-Taiwanese racial identities in situated political and economical contexts. As opposed to the Taiwanese aborigines, who have interacted with and been exploited by Han-Taiwanese for centuries, migrant workers have been present in Taiwan for less than two decades. It thus provides an intriguing case to study the racialization processes of an ethnic group and the racial identities of Han-Taiwanese in relation to these latecomers, whom they regard as competing for scarce resources.

The time span in this research ranges from the late 1980s, when the "foreign maids" were still a distanced "ethnic other" to the majority of Taiwanese people, to the late 1990s, when their presence came to be recognized by the government as these women worked in many middle- and upper-class households. The source for analysis is the fieldwork data that I gathered in Taiwan in the summer of 1997. I collected related documents, including legal regulations, official publications, academic papers, newspapers, and publications from placement agencies. In addition, I also worked as a volunteer in an NGO—the Migrant Workers' Concern Desk—for one month and visited the foreigners' detention center on a weekly basis for six weeks. Moreover, I conducted twenty-six in-depth interviews with Filipina domestic workers, Taiwanese employers, Taiwanese domestic workers, brokers, activists in NGOs, and a governmental officer. My analysis of the social and racial discourses on "foreign maids" includes both texts and practices. I do not claim that the material presented here is exhaustive. It does, however, present a significant picture, and there are persistent racial tones in these texts and practices. There are limited counterdiscourses that foster the welfare and human rights of migrant workers. Nevertheless, as this essay aims to demonstrate the dominant discourses, I do not cite them.

I organize the diverse social discourses into five themes. First, I investigate the public opinions against the Foreign Maid Policy and explore the hidden presumptions in these discussions. In the second and third sections, I scrutinize the legal regulations and media representations of migrant workers and "foreign maids," while in the fourth and fifth sections, I examine the interactions between Taiwanese employers, brokers, Filipina maids, and the discourses produced in these processes. The first three sections focus on the discourses of xenophobia created by those who did not develop direct contacts with the "foreign maids" and regarded them as the distanced "ethnic other." The last two sections concentrate on ethnocentric discourses of employers and brokers, for whom interactions with "foreign maids" were part of their daily practices. In the conclusion, I elaborate on how these diverse discourses produced by social actors at different social locations constituted "foreign maids" as an "ethnic other." I further elaborate on how this specific case study of "foreign maids" contributes to our understanding of Han-Taiwanese racial identity in relation to the migrants who are latecomers to the Taiwanese society.

ANTIPATHY AND ESTRANGEMENT: PUBLIC OPINIONS AGAINST THE FOREIGN MAID POLICY

In 1992 there were already about 60,000 migrant workers in Taiwan (Wu 1992, 6). By 1997 it was estimated that this number had risen to approximately 250,000 (CLA 1997c). For the majority of Taiwanese, however, migrant workers and "foreign maids" were just a distanced group of people not present in their daily lives. The general public was either hostile or indifferent to the presence of "foreign maids" and "migrant workers" in Taiwan. A national-level survey conducted by the Council of Labor Affairs in 1991 reveals that 46.1 percent of the population disapproved of and 38.4 percent had no opinions about legitimizing "foreign maids." Only 15.5 percent of the people, mainly existing employers, were in favor of this policy (CLA 1991). Although there was a certain ignorance of or indifference to the presence of "foreign maids" in Taiwan, the wide-ranging xenophobic opinions in the public discourses cannot be dismissed. The following section addresses this issue.

In the Name of Social Costs

Public opinions against the Foreign Maid Policy that appeared in the newspapers were wide ranging. They included readers' comments on certain social events, scholarly articles, academic seminar papers, and government officials' opinions. Among these views, the "social costs" of legalizing migrant workers were often mentioned. Many scholars argued that the social costs of implementation were huge and contended that the government should reconsider these suggestions. Agriculture professor Cai Hongjin, on the faculty of the Department of Agricultural Extension of a well-known university, delivered a conference paper on "The Possible Negative Social Impacts that Foreign Workers Might Bring About," which was published in the *China Times* on the same day. He listed several negative effects—increase in crime, diseases, drugs, and so on—as if Taiwan didn't have these problems prior to the presence of migrant workers. He also suggested that migrant workers might complicate Taiwanese social structures because capital would flow to foreign countries and that Taiwan would become overcrowded and local workers would lose working opportunities. He argued that foreigners—be they from Southeast Asia or mainland China—would adversely affect living conditions in Taiwan. It was important, then, to limit foreign population strictly (Cai 1991, 3).[2]

Professor Zhan Huosheng, specializing in labor policy, worried about the difficulties of managing migrant domestic workers.[3] He argued that if foreign domestic workers were permitted to work legally, it would be easy for them to disappear without a trace, which would cause social problems. Therefore, he called for a multiperspective evaluation of the Foreign Maid Policy before implementation. Otherwise, he warned, the individual family and all members in Taiwanese society would have to face this "social difficulty" in the future (Zhan 1991, 3).

Both of these experts predicted that this policy would lead to a negative situation, offering no benefits for Taiwanese society. Migrant domestic workers raised greater fears than factory workers because they would be scattered in individual households and thus would be difficult to control. They were likely to "escape and blend into the Taiwanese labor market." Moreover, they were expected to have "adjustment difficulties" that could easily lead to social problems. Such authors perceived the existence of migrant workers as dangerous, causing problems and social disorder, and it was resolutely suggested that the government strictly limit the number of migrant workers. These fears permeated Taiwanese society. They also caused the president of the Council of Labor Affairs to have a "nightmare." President Zhao Shoubo, in a headline, was reported as "Waking up at Midnight, Sweating and Scared: How Do We Get Rid of Foreign Laborers in the Future?" (Huang and Yang 1993, 6). In this report, he said that he felt pressured when thinking of the racial conflicts in Germany and in France. He did not know how to "get rid of" the immigrants. Within these discourses, foreign workers and social disorder, unregulated foreign workers and social problems, and migrant workers and racial conflicts are articulated together. The interrelations of migrant workers and social disorder appear throughout government documents, research projects, and policy design. The fear, then, was carried into legal practice, which will be discussed later.

In the Name of Social Justice

In public opinion, class and racial justice were frequently mentioned as grounds to oppose the Foreign Maid Policy. One male veteran wrote to a female legislator who was pushing the policy to legislation that she was not representing the voice of "ordinary women." In his opinion, only rich and wealthy career women with great ambition would be likely to employ foreign domestic workers. The "ordinary women" who were not so ambitious at work and not wealthy enough to employ "foreign maids" did not need them. He continued to elaborate the negative effects of having "foreign maids" at home: It was difficult to get along with them because of different cultural backgrounds, and it was not easy to tolerate these "open and liberal" women. He asked, "Most importantly, how could you prevent your husband from having sexual relations with the maid?" He contended that it was against human rights to employ foreign domestic workers and exploit these maids' well-being. In conclusion, he asked the legislator, "If you are too busy to undertake your domestic work, why not go back to your previous job?" (Zhong 1991, 8).[4]

This writer's conclusion indicates that it was his conservative gender ideology that led him to protest the policy. He believed that domestic labor should be every woman's responsibility. Therefore, those capable working women who disobeyed the traditional gender division of labor and employed cheap foreign domestic workers to fulfill their domestic duty were not to be tolerated. In his article, both ethnic and class justice—such as oppressing women of another ethnicity and benefiting wealthy families—have been used to confirm his traditional idea that "women should undertake their domestic work." To advocate his gender ideology, the possible negative effects of employing foreign domestic workers were emphasized to frighten wealthy career women in the hope that they would go back home and become good housewives.

Ironically, both feminists and conservative men use social and racial justice as common grounds to resist the Foreign Maid Policy, although feminists challenge the idea that domestic work is women's work. The famous feminist scholar Li Yuanzhen wrote a newspaper article, "Women's Policies and Foreign Maids," arguing that only families with high incomes can afford to employ these workers. Cases of abuse from Singapore and Hong Kong were mentioned to elaborate on its exploitative nature. She contended that the policy would cause the exploitation of working-class women and foreign domestic workers. The former became unemployed and the latter were subjected to abuse. She urged the government to avoid implementing the Foreign Maid Policy. Eventually, she called for government attention to promote part-time work and a better child care system to solve working women's double burdens (Li 1991, 3). In her arguments, the exploitative side of this policy, which reinforced class and ethnic inequalities, was stressed to promote feminist demands for a state-oriented welfare system for Taiwanese women.

Feminist arguments on this issue appear to have been deepened and strengthened in 1997, five years after the implementation of the Foreign Maid Policy, when the Council of Labor Affairs held a conference on "Foreign Maid Policy and State Development." Many academic feminists were invited to give papers in which they formulated coherent feminist arguments. They argued that the Foreign Maid Policy benefited only a few rich women, reduced the working opportunities of Taiwanese domestic workers, and ignored the general needs of Taiwanese working women. Arguments that drew upon the negative effects of the racial division of domestic labor were integrated into their texts to protest this policy from a "feminist" perspective. Taiwanese feminists were opposed to the Foreign Maid Policy because first, it did not enhance levels of female employment (Cheng 1997; Hu 1997; L. R. Wang 1997; Yan 1997); and second, it did not free women from the responsibilities of domestic and caregiving work (Cheng 1997; Hu 1997; Yan 1997). In the course of examining the Foreign Maid Policy, these feminists shifted their focus from this policy to the women's employment scheme in place in Taiwan. It was argued that if the government wished to promote women's participation in the labor force, the Foreign Maid Policy was not adequate. They firmly advocated that since both the Foreign Maid Policy and women's policies took time to map out, it was better to make efforts on the latter. They concluded by suggesting sophisticated plans of flexible working time, state-funded child care systems, and an Equal Opportunity Employment Act for Men and Women to replace the Foreign Maid Policy.

This debate over the Foreign Maid Policy presents a disappointing example of the double standard in Taiwan's feminist discourse, which fails to cross ethnic and class lines in extending their concern to migrant domestic workers. In their discussions, the criticism of the ethnic and class injustices of the Foreign Maid Policy only serves to forge a consensus of "what are proper [Taiwanese] women's welfare policies." Foreign domestic workers are regarded as vulnerable and easily exploited, and the presence of foreign domestic workers is seen as a "residue of slavery." But in their papers, there was a surprising ignorance of the presence of at least fifty thousand legal and illegal migrant domestic workers in Taiwan in 1997. The feminists rarely demonstrated any concern about the living conditions of migrant domestic workers in Taiwan. They talked about the exploitation of "foreign maids" as something "out there," in other countries. Even if cases of abuse in Taiwan were mentioned, it did not lead to reflection on Taiwanese racist attitudes toward migrant workers. Nor did they pay attention to the design of the laws that caused the foreign domestic worker system to become in effect a "throwback to slavery," as they put it. If the discussion of ethnic justice stands, why is a consideration of the welfare and legal protection system absent from the debates? In other words, no one criticizes or challenges the position of foreign domestic workers as second-class residents in Taiwan.

By analyzing these social debates, I contend that these claims for social costs and social justice actually lose all of their meaning. Hidden in these claims was the fear and the antipathy of the Taiwanese public toward the presence of migrant domestic workers in Taiwan. Scholars worried about the negative "social costs," and men and women drew on rhetorics of social justice in both conservative and egalitarian ways, but no thought was ever really spared for migrant workers and the discrimination that they confronted. On the contrary—migrant domestic workers were merely associated with social problems and social disorder. Their presence was not welcomed by the general public and their attendance was not recognized by Taiwanese feminists, even though they had resided in Taiwan for more than ten years. These social opinions against "foreign maids," prevalent not only in academic scholars' writing but also in government officers' opinions, demonstrate the wide-ranging though unspoken xenophobia in Taiwan. The irrational fear of arousing social disorder was integrated into the law itself, which intends to control and regulate the undesirable presence of the "foreign maids" in Taiwan.

LEGAL SUBJUGATION: "FOREIGN MAIDS" AS THE "OTHER"

Taiwan, like the United States and other Western countries, has a strict legal gateway to regulate the stay of foreigners in the country. Before the 1992 Employment Service Act came into force, responsibilities for these regulations were scattered throughout several different departments. A foreign applicant obtained a work permit from the Ministry of Education, the Ministry of Economics, or the Council of Labor Affairs, depending on the nature of his or her stay. Most illegal migrant workers, white-collar and blue-collar workers alike, possessed visiting visas to Taiwan and overstayed to look for jobs (Y. K. Lee 1995, 1–3). The 1992 act makes no great distinction for "First World" foreigners who attempt to study or work in Taiwan. The way the bureaucracy deals with applications remains as idiosyncratic as it used to be. But the status of migrant workers from Southeast Asian countries changed significantly after the act came into force.

The Employment Service Act differentiates between blue-collar "Foreign Laborers" *(waiji laogong)* and white-collar foreign scholars, technicians, investors, and so on. Article 43 of the act singles out domestics and "other workers recruited in accordance with the needs of the country" to be regulated under Regulations Governing the Employment and Control of Foreigners (hereafter shortened to the Regulations). In fact, the Regulations only apply to blue-collar workers who do the work that is classified as "3D" (dirty, dangerous, and difficult) and domestics. This group of workers is referred to as *waiji laogong* both in government documents and in colloquialisms. Foreign domestics *(waiji nüyong)*, including domestic helpers and domestic caretakers, are subsumed under the general category of *waiji laogong* but with special regulations applying to them due to the nature of their work as domestics in individual households.

The public debates resolutely addressed the possible ways to prevent social problems and how to control *waiji laogong*. This was then implemented through legal practices. According to the Regulations, these foreign laborers are regulated very strictly in terms of length of working period, their residence, and changes of employer. In other words, they are not "free laborers." They do not have freedom with regard to mobility, choice of residence, work, or employers. Moreover, they are deprived of the rights to marry, to become pregnant, or to bring their children and family to Taiwan.[5] Furthermore, they are forced to undergo strict and humiliating health checks every six months.[6] None of these restrictions apply to foreigners other than *waiji laogong*.[7]

The maximum working period for migrant domestic workers is limited to three years,[8] after which they can no longer return to work in Taiwan. Other restrictions imposed upon domestic workers include limiting their working places to the registered address. Moreover, they are bound to one employer: They are not allowed to change employers[9] during this period, and 30 percent of their salary is deducted by employers.[10] The law also requires the employer to pay a "deposit" at the time of employing migrant workers, in addition to paying "stable employment funds" every month to the government during their employment. The deposit will be withdrawn if the migrant domestic worker "escapes" from the household. These measures incorporate employers into the surveillance system of the state to control and constrain the mobility of migrant domestic workers.

Under the 1992 act and the Regulations, the Taiwanese household is able to employ "foreign domestic helpers" to do household tasks or to employ "foreign domestic caretakers" to care for sick and disabled persons. A quota limitation and conditions for applicants are set up to control the number and the scope of "foreign maids," however.[11] These Regulations and their detailed application process are referred to as the Foreign Maid Policy throughout related discussions in Taiwan. The Foreign Maid Policy binds domestic workers to a private household and a single employer through the measures of the "deposit," "compulsory savings," and "stable employment funds." The design of the laws has placed migrant domestic workers in a vulnerable position and provides no labor protection for them.[12] It not only limits the rights of domestic workers, it also disciplines them. The resulting judicial power also supports the subjugating practices of Taiwanese brokers and employers in daily practices.

MEDIA STIGMATIZATION: CRIME, DISEASE, AND THE "BACKWARD"

Migrant domestic workers are represented in a very negative way in the media. As was also the case in public debates, the issue of "foreign laborers" is addressed in terms of "foreign labor problems" *(wailao wenti)* and reinforces the idea that foreign domestic workers and foreign laborers are inherently associated with a range of problems. Moreover, these foreign laborers are usually stigmatized and degraded as criminals and disease bearers. These racial tones have not changed much with the implementation of the 1992 act.

Long before the legalization of migrant workers, the editor of the *Economic Daily News* had tried to draw public attention in a headline warning people to "Face the Social Problems that Foreign Laborers Would Cause" (*Economic Daily News* 1989, 2). After the implementation of the Foreign Maid Policy, in another newspaper, the public was again asked to prepare itself for the coming social problems: "Foreign Maids Will Come, and Social Problems Should Be Prevented from Becoming Disasters" (Quan 1992, 3).

Because the public became so anxious about the social problems the "foreign maids" might bring, it seemed as if people were almost waiting for these troubles to appear. These problems included changes within the household, as well as crime and disease in society as a whole. A report entitled "Superb Filipina Managers May Bring Special Troubles" (Liang 1996, 3) discussed negative aspects of having "foreign maids" with regard to language training for Taiwanese children. This issue was taken up again three months later in another newspaper under the title "Filipina Maids at Home, Children Change Their Accents and Behavior" (Huang 1996, 11). Five academics were interviewed to support this argument.

There are repeated reports that connect foreign laborers with crime. Crimes committed by foreign workers were continually reported (Shi 1990, 3; Tan 1996, 6; Xu 1997, 6), so that the public was expecting serious social problems to occur. When Angelina, a domestic worker, killed her patient and then attempted suicide, the newspaper headline read, "The First Case of a Filipina Maid Killing Her Employer Breaks Out in Our Nation" (*China Times* 1995, 1). The phrase "breaks out" implies that there might be an epidemic of tribulations taking place; many seemed to be waiting for problems to plague the entire island. Since Angelina was suspected of having a mental disorder, the public soon worried about the "mental illness" of "foreign maids" as a whole. The necessity of checking the mental health of "foreign maids" immediately became a public issue.[13] The public collectively worried about these women's mental illnesses and wanted to excercise control by administering health checks. Counseling centers for foreign laborers were consequently set up in all major cities. Nevertheless, judging from the comments of the newspaper editors and readers, none of them questioned the legal structure that caused a stressful working situation and that might have contributed to Angelina's "mental illness."[14]

Disease is another aspect that worries the Taiwanese public. The legal system requires *waiji laogong* to take thorough health examinations before and after their arrival in Taiwan. After they start to work, they are required to have detailed examinations every six months. This measure is based on foreigners' socioeconomic status in Taiwan: Business managers and professionals are not to be examined at all, while foreign laborers are subjected to detailed and frequent health checks. This assumes that foreign laborers are potential virus bearers, bringing diseases to Taiwan. The assumption is further reinforced by the constant public reports of health check results, which claim that Filipino workers are "usually" found to have diseases: leprosy, parasitism, amoebic dysentery, and others (Li et al. 1996, 5; W. F. Wang 1995, 13; Xiu 1997, 5). When these cases were exposed, the Department of Health would warn employers to pay attention to the hygiene habits of their Filipina maids. One such headline read as follows: "Mind Filipina Maids' Hygiene Habits: The Number of Failed Health Checks Increased, Mainly in Parasite Tests" (Gong 1997). All of these reports serve to demarcate the boundary between the "infectious *waiji laogong*" and the "healthy Taiwanese."

The government boasts of Taiwan as a clean, healthy, and civilized country regardless of the fact that Filipino workers did get diseases when working in Taiwan (P. Y.Wang 1996, 5; L. W. Zhang 1996, 9). If foreign laborers were diagnosed as coming to Taiwan bearing the disease, the headline would state this point clearly. In contrast, if the reason for their infection in Taiwan was not clear, newspaper headlines usually claimed that foreign workers got "unknown diseases" while they worked in Taiwan. These headlines imply to the readers either that foreign laborers just "got" the diseases without any explainable reasons, or that the "strange diseases" were, for unknown reasons, exclusively caught by foreign laborers. All of these statements both create and perpetuate the myth that the diseases of migrant workers are either brought by them from their original countries or just happened by themselves. The suggestion, then, is that Taiwan has no responsibility for these "strange diseases" that *waiji laogong* are diagnosed as having. The hidden assumptions that *waiji laogong* are infectious beings are widely accepted.

The assumption that migrant domestic workers bring in diseases reinforces the image of *waiji laogong* as the "backward" ethnic other. In a placement agency's handbook for foreign workers—*The Foreign Domestic Helper Habit Guide* —basic sanitary habits are listed for workers to follow: They are told to brush their teeth, wash their hands with soap, take a shower every day, trim fingernails and toenails, and so on. The supposition is that the "backward" *waiji nüyong* might not have basic sanitary knowledge. This guide also teaches foreign domestics social etiquette at home and in public.[15] These efforts to "educate" Filipina maids reveal the fact that the Taiwanese people regarded Filipino workers as "backward" and "uneducated" foreign others.

SUBJUGATING "FOREIGN MAIDS": THE PRACTICES OF BROKERS AND EMPLOYERS

Brokers benefit a great deal from the "trade in maids" (Heyzer et al. 1994). Each of my Filipina interviewees paid around U.S. $3,500 to brokers for a placement in Taiwan,[16] while the Taiwanese employers paid only U.S. $750 to the broker to find them a "foreign maid." Even though the foreign domestic worker paid far more money than their employers did to make a placement, the broker was by no means on her side. The basic marketing rationale of Taiwanese brokers was to persuade their prospective customers that they could provide the best service from a "foreign maid" for the least amount of money. Very often, Filipina workers were promoted by brokers as fluent in English, which was seen as a strong point. English is a prestige language in Taiwan, and thus to employ a "maid" with English skills will symbolically enhance the employers' social status. In addition to this, to make employing "foreign maids" attractive to potential customers, brokers dehumanized the prospective workers and advertised the acceptability of poor working and living conditions for the workers. For example, brokers might tell their customers that it was not necessary for the maid to have a day off every week or that if a spare room was not available for the maid, she could sleep in the living room. In this discourse, the needs of the foreign domestic worker as a human being are ignored. It also creates the fantasy that the employer is going to have a "super-efficient maid" for very little cost.

Next came the problem of choosing a maid—a stranger who was going to work for her employer and his or her family for up to three years. To solve this difficulty, placement agencies provided catalogues, sometimes with videotapes, including personal details for employers' reference. What did Taiwanese employers want? The answer might be inferred from the most popular terms in advertisements to attract employers: honest, cheerful, and diligent. In addition to these characteristics, employers also wanted to make sure of the "quality" of the maid. They referred to her education, work experience, family background, and they wanted photographs of her. They also asked for skills that were much more inclusive than those normally expected from an ordinary maid. From the brokers' promotion of their business, they formulated the fantasy of a cheap but superefficient maid—something that could not be expected from a contemporary Taiwanese worker. The following quotations reveal the criteria from employers whom I interviewed:

> We need a maid who has experience of bringing up children. So, we wanted a *mother,* aged from 30 to 40. [My emphasis] (Mr. He)

> I chose those who were well educated. I had employed Taiwanese maids to do the housework . . . [but] I did not trust them to take care of my children. . . . Their standards were not very high. [If] the Filipino maid I employ can work together with me to *educate the children,* it would be very helpful. [My emphasis] (Mrs. Zhang)

> I looked at her picture at first, she was selling vegetables in a rural area, I thought she should be that kind of person who is *hard working and untiring.* [My emphasis] (Mrs. Wang)

Possessing a high level of education, being a good mother, being diligent, or, commonly, being an English speaker—these were the skills that Taiwanese employers demanded from foreign domestic workers. Experienced employers like Mrs. Zhang had recognized and appreciated the positive aspects of Filipina workers possessing high levels of education. But the majority of first-time employers chose maids not only on the basis of personal characteristics such as being young, attractive, and happy, as Tyne has suggested (1994, 603), but also for outstanding skills that could not be found for that price in the Taiwan market. They had very high expectations of these foreign domestics, taking for granted that a maid should do everything in the household, rather than limiting the work to what might be required of a Taiwanese maid. Broker A frankly told me: "Taiwanese employers want maids who are obedient, who need no holidays, who can work twenty-four hours a day and who are capable of doing everything.... [They want] 'Super Women.'"

Brokers' discourses serve to shape Taiwanese employers' unrealistic expectations of the "superb Filipina maid." In reality, however, employers were very often disappointed. Promotional images that were constructed by brokers about "Filipina maids"—as active and outspoken—were soon perceived by employers as being too autonomous and disobedient. Moreover, employers' disappointment was not directed to brokers who made these unrealistic recommendations. Rather, they condemned the Filipina workers as lazy and unqualified workers. Mr. He, for example, was quite disappointed with his maid's performance. He felt that she was not a diligent worker and he related it even further to the economic decline of the Philippines: "With citizens like this, no wonder that the Philippines's economy collapsed." As Mr. He looked down on his maid's country of origin, the privilege of being English speakers was also belittled: "We dare not expect very much from Filipino English."[17]

Brokers quickly learned that Taiwanese employers desired loyalty and obedience rather than independence in workers. Their marketing strategies were adjusted to the demands of the employers. In 1997, Indonesian workers, as latecomers in the market, were depicted in broker's advertisements as obedient, quiet, clever, and diligent. They were also described as innocent and faithful, which implied that they did not know how to argue for their own rights and would not deceive employers. Moreover, it was said that they required fewer holidays than Filipinos did. These competing images not only reflected employers' preferences, they also contributed to the growth of Indonesian workers in the market. When I was conducting research in 1997, ninety-seven out of a hundred foreign domestic workers were Filipinos (computed from CLA 1997c, 179). At that time, it was hard to believe that people would choose Indonesian workers instead of Filipinos because the former spoke no English and could hardly communicate with any family members. But by 2001, 63.5 percent of foreign domestics were Indonesian, while the Filipino's share in the market had been reduced to 28.8 percent (computed from CLA 2001). This claim of Indonesian passivity was not only presented to employers but also to Filipina domestic workers, who were facing competition from Indonesian workers.

Discourses requiring obedience from "foreign maids" were also practiced in mediation processes. By law, brokers are to mediate labor disputes between Taiwanese employers and foreign domestic workers. The proscribed negotiation was intended to settle the disputes, but it usually resulted in a pro-employer settlement. If brokers met employers who had very strict working standards for maids, they usually suggested that the maids obey the rule as far as they could.

Once, when an employer accused the maid of stealing, the foreign worker was asked to admit that she was wrong even though it was not true. In an interview, Broker A candidly summed up their unscrupulous principles: "It does not matter whether she was right or wrong. As long as she comes to Taiwan to work, she is a second-class citizen in Taiwan even though she spent lots of money to come here."

The discourses produced by brokers and Taiwanese employers are dynamic. Brokers dehumanized "foreign maids" to promote their business. Many Taiwanese employers accepted these ideas and looked for "superb maids." When their expectations could not be met, they blamed the "foreign maids" and stigmatized their nationality. In their daily interactions, both employers and brokers found that the obedience of maids was the most essential issue. In the process of mediating labor disputes, brokers exercised their power and reinforced these social discourses over "foreign maids." The whole process of requiring complete subordination serves to ensure obedience from these foreign domestic workers.

**TOTAL SUBORDINATION:
HUMILIATING METAPHORS**

The Taiwanese employers' desire to subordinate the "foreign maid" can be further read from the following instances. Lorna[18] was a qualified nurse from the Philippines who suffered degrading experiences in relation to cleaning up after her employer's dog in front of the guests: "It was *very terrible* what happened to me. When they had many friends, and the dog shitted, many, many. Before, they would be the one to clean it. [This time] they called me. Then, I would be the one to clean. Then, they laughed. I was embarrassed. . . . [Now,] when the dog shits on the second floor, 'Hello, go clean.' You must follow" [my emphasis].

In this event, which began as an unintentional slight but then seemed to become a vicious act, the employer exercised his power over the maid to do things against her wishes. This created a direct association between Lorna and dog feces and filth. In this instance, Lorna was simultaneously subordinated by her employer's power, forced to clean dog feces (a task she hated) in public, and laughed at; all of these factors added up to make this event a highly humiliating experience for her. This particular employer evidently felt that he could exercise his power over his maid by asking her to clean the dog feces. The metaphor of the "foreign maid" as the undesired was unexpectedly—but successfully—delivered to Lorna. Afterward, a task that was not supposed to be Lorna's responsibility became part of her job. The humiliation and the shame that resulted from the hierarchy and the metaphorical association of herself and defiled waste came to be reiterated in the daily working processes of the "foreign maid."

Regina was once a successful businesswoman in the Philippines. She also told me her degrading experiences when working:

But, in the market, you know, everybody knows us. You know why? Because people used to see us, she [the employer] is [like] having a dog with her. Even though you have a pet, you love it, right? She can't even treat me as a pet dog. [She shouts.]. . . . I don't know how to place myself. When I walk behind her, *"Zoula, zoula!"* [Go, go!]

She doesn't want to see my clothes hanging, just like this morning. Last night, I washed some underwear. I hung it of course. And this morning, I forgot to take it out. I was surprised she got up early because she used to get up late. She got up early and she saw it. Called me, "Regina!" I was scared. The daughter downstairs offers me sometime to hang up my clothes in her house.

In this narrative, Regina made the analogy of a dog and a maid to explain her shameful working experiences. She found herself being treated by her employer as if she were a dog. Her underwear was made to be equivalent to undesired shame and she was forced to hide her "dirt"—her underwear. In traditional Han culture, women were regarded as inferior and dirty, and thus their clothes were to be kept at a lower bamboo pole, differentiating it from men's clothes at a higher pole. The differentiation demarcates a symbolic hierarchy between genders; the superior to the inferior, and the dominant to the subordinate. By demanding that a "foreign maid" keep her underwear unseen (not at a lower pole, but unseen), the Taiwanese employer also creates and demarcates the hierarchy between them. By doing so, she demonstrates her power over the subordinated "foreign maid." In this situation, however, the hierarchy is no longer between genders. It is made possible on the basis of their unequal powers in different class and ethnic positions.

By analyzing the symbolic meanings and metaphors of the humiliating working experiences of "foreign maids," I argue that these seemingly naïve practices of Taiwanese employers contain prejudiced attitudes and the exaggerated power of Taiwanese employers over these foreign domestic workers. These instances of abuse are not new to Han families. Nevertheless, their meanings change with historical transformations. In traditional Han families, daughters-in-law and maidservants who were situated at the bottom of kinship and class hierarchies were also subject to such humiliations. In Taiwan's contemporary postindustrial society, abuses of this kind have been less likely to take place due to the increasing power of working daughters-in-law and paid domestic workers.[19] Nevertheless, since "foreign maids" entered Taiwanese families, similar patterns of abuse are now reenacted regularly. Because the unequal power relations between Taiwanese employers and Filipina workers are shaped by unequal economic powers between nation-states, such abuses are now tinted with racial implications. Through the intentional degradation and humiliation of these foreign workers, the racial hierarchy between Taiwanese and "foreign maids" has been symbolically established on the basis of their class relations.

SOCIAL DISCOURSES ON "FOREIGN MAIDS" AND HAN-TAIWANESE RACIAL IDENTITIES

My analyses of the public debates, media representation, and juridical subjugation have shown that "foreign maids" are perceived as the undesirable "ethnic other" in Taiwan. In the public imagination, they are stigmatized and associated with "social problems." Moreover, even those who have vested interests in "foreign maids"—brokers, employers, and the government—act to condemn the autonomy of these foreign domestic workers. In this set of discourses, "foreign maids" are also regarded as "backward" and bringing in disease, crime, and social problems. The sometimes unstated though often overtly declared message is that their presence in Taiwan should be constrained if not entirely prevented; their freedom should be limited; their mobility should be restricted, and their bodies should be controlled and constantly examined. Further, as "maids," foreign domestic workers should subordinate themselves to the orders and kinship hierarchies of the family of their Han-Taiwanese employers. The rough treatment of Filipina workers might duplicate the suffering of those powerless Han daughters-in-law or maidservants in the past. But this should not prevent Taiwanese employers from being accused of racial discrimination. On the contrary, it is precisely because of these unbalanced power relations between Taiwanese employers and "foreign maids"—which is supported by legal subjugation, social ignorance, media stigmatizing, and the practices of brokers—that Taiwanese employers are granted omnipotent power to practice racialized domination over the "foreign maids." These social discourses together constitute a specific form of racism in Taiwan in relation to "foreign maids" in particular and foreign migrant workers in general.

What can we learn from this specific case study about Han-Taiwanese racial identities? In terms of state intervention to control immigration and national borders and the panic of the general public over the "invasion" of "foreign others," these discourses are not very different from racist discourses on migration and asylum seekers in contemporary Western European countries. Yet Han Taiwanese have their distinctive racial identities owing to their culture as Han and their specific positioning in the world system as part of a developing country.

In Han culture, the family is identified by the anthropologist as the "key symbol." Not surprisingly, Han racial identity is also constructed on the normative model of the Han family institution, including courting, marriage, residence, inheritance, and sexuality (Blum 2001, 81–82; Dikötter 1997; Harrell 1995). In this case study of "foreign maids," I also demonstrate the ways in which foreign domestic workers were required to subordinate themselves to the kinship hierarchies of the Han-Taiwanese family. Moreover, in the public discussion, the sexuality of "foreign maids" was delineated as liberal and deviant from normative Han sexuality. Both the employer and the state felt the need to sanction the sexuality of the "foreign others." All these instances suggest that the Han family institution still plays an important role in shaping contemporary Han-Taiwanese racial identities.

This case study of "foreign maids" also shows that the discourses and metaphors of dirt, disease, and backwardness were constantly repeated. Blum (2001) also finds divisions of clean/dirty and advanced/backward significant in Han-Chinese racial identity. The point I want to pursue here is the ways in which the distinction between clean/dirty and advanced/backward could be linked to wider political and economic contexts. As a developing country, Taiwan is positioned in the middle of the world system. Accordingly, in the eyes of Han Taiwanese, westerners who are from "advanced" First World countries are seen as superior to Taiwanese. In contrast, Southeast Asians who are from "backward" countries are perceived of as inferior to Taiwanese. Foreigners from Southeast Asia are much more easily associated with dirt, disease, and backwardness than foreigners from the West.

This advanced/backward division also operates along the lines of class division. In Han culture, intellectuals are valued highly while laborers are degraded. In contemporary Taiwan, most westerners—with no regard to class or educational background—work as English teachers or in white-collar jobs and are always respected. In contrast, most Southeast Asians—including well-educated Filipina maids who are respectable teachers in their home country—can work only as blue-collar workers and are often despised. Race and national origins are judged prior to the actual educational qualifications of a specific individual. This racial stratification suggests that Han Taiwanese incorporate westernized worldviews into their social hierarchy that value intellectuals, despise laborers, and produce racial hierarchies between people of different nationalities. By so doing, Han Taiwanese have imported, internalized, and reproduced a form of "suborientalism" and "subimperialism" (Chiu 2000) that is simultaneously dominated by First World westerners and dominates other economically unprivileged Southeast Asians.

In this chapter, by investigating social discourses on "foreign maids," I have argued that Han-Taiwanese racial identities are centered on the Han family institution and are operated along the lines of the advanced/backward division. I believe these two concepts will be useful for future research. In the case of "foreign maids," further research could explore how these foreign domestics become subordinate to patriarchal kinship relations in the employers' family. Another interesting area for investigation is the contestation between Taiwanese employers and foreign domestic workers who receive higher education, speak English, and refuse to accept the subordinate status of "backward"—assumptions that Taiwanese employers impose upon them.

These two aspects of Han-Taiwanese racial identities can also be utilized to contrast and compare the experiences of different ethnic groups in Taiwan. For example, a "foreign bride" that comes from Indonesia and Vietnam might be simultaneously subjected to the assumptions of "dirty" and "backward" and to the ethnocentrism of the family institution as a daughter-in-law and a wife; thus they might have a comparatively tougher time even than a "foreign maid," who can only be a "maid" for the contracted three years. A white Anglo-Saxon man in Taiwan might be adored as a person from an "advanced" country, but his sexuality might be stigmatized according to Han-Taiwanese family morals and exaggerated notions of Western sexual liberation. In this way he might also confront the ethnocentrism of the Taiwanese family institution when he wishes to marry a Taiwanese woman.

Moreover, these two concepts can also be applied to study Han people in different political and historical contexts. This will avoid the danger of essentializing Han "culture" as a static entity and contribute to seeing "Han-ness" as changing within historical and political contexts. I believe that only by systematic analysis of diverse ethnic relations between the Han and other ethnic groups in different contexts can we deepen the knowledge of Han ethnic relations and Han racial identities, which is an area that urgently needs further exploration in the face of rapid globalization.

7
Hot and Noisy
Taiwan's Night Market Culture
Shuenn-Der Yu

EDITORS' INTRODUCTION

"Night markets" are periodic markets or fairs of a special kind held throughout the preindustrialized and early industrialized world, whether in France or Turkey, in Indonesia or Mexico. Night markets are in general more devoted to food and strolling with one's friends than are the more businesslike daytime markets. This is very much the case in Taiwan, and no town or city is to be found without one or more streets where people gather after dark to wander from food stall to food stall eating together. Among the food stalls, peddlers set out for sale miscellaneous goods of every description: clothing, kitchenware, antiques, books, DVDs, CDs, and small appliances.

Although established shops near a night market often sell their wares at the same time (sometimes outdoors), and although reputable small-scale merchants throng the crowded streets, there are also scams of every kind. Makers of sugar water tout its prowess in curing everything from indigestion to stupidity, and the public, knowing that there are no guarantees for night market merchandise, greet minor fraud with indulgence and continue to shop for bargains. Many night markets take place in squares and streets near temples, where some visitors like to stop to burn incense to the presiding deity along their way.

In Taiwan, the night market has always been a place of relaxation and social interaction, not merely a place to buy things. Taiwanese reflect on them with a certain nostalgia and memories of many happy hours strolling with friends in this ambience. For the merchants, however, the night market is hard work. It is potentially profitable, but it requires a good deal of astuteness in selecting items for sale and considerable hustle in promoting them to a rather casual public, there to look but not necessarily to buy.

In this chapter, Shuenn-Der Yu describes the world of Taiwan's night markets, beginning with a song affectionately mocking the unbridled greed that, according to the song, informs their eager merchants. He distinguishes them from other kinds of markets, throwing into relief their social functions. In the course of the discussion we learn about how time and space matter to night markets and about the critical Chinese notion of *renao*—an amiable, noisy confusion that marks a celebration of life. We also learn of the world of small snacks suitable to cooking and vending at pushcarts. No Taiwanese can speak unmoved of Yuanhuan oyster omelets, we are told, and night market food, like the context in which it is eaten, is part of what makes life worth living. ■

> Earn, earn, earn, more or less, earn, earn, earn! . . .
> Any new fad, come here and you will find it.
> Steak, *qieya* noodles, toys, cable TV decoders.
> Pikachu and Hello Kitty.
> Shoot the balloons and scoop up the goldfish.
> Pop music or nude albums.
> All made in nine-city. . . .
>
> Strolling back and forth in the night market, buy as much as you can
> So Taiwan will have a miracle.
>
> The police car has left, brother policeman has disappeared.
> Dear customer, what do you like? I'll give you a bargain.
> It's lag season, I'm just earning some more or less.
> What's popular abroad? Don't know? Come over here.
> Grandma, Issei Miyake, cosmetics and sexy lingerie,
> Cell phones and pagers. Diet teas and massage chairs.
> We sell generic brands and we sell Nikes.
> All made in nine-city. . . .
>
> —Shi Wenbin, "Made in Nine-City"

Shi Wenbin's song touches on many issues of importance to Taiwan's night market culture.[1] Sung in Taiwanese, it underscores the notion of night markets as a core part of Taiwanese popular culture. But Shi borrowed the melody from a famous Middle Eastern song, "Persian Market," and added his own interpretation of the context within which the Taiwanese cultural institution is situated. His opening phrase, "Earn! Earn! Earn!" may be viewed as a Taiwanese self-portrait; it bears an ideological resemblance to the title of another local song, "Strive to Win" (Aipin cai hui ying).[2] Shi's song praises the work ethic that has brought prosperity to this island, while simultaneously poking fun at the current generation of hard-working Taiwanese as only knowing how to make money without caring about cultural matters. Fair or not, it is a frequently heard criticism.

A strong work ethic is only one of many important aspects of night marketing. Long hours are accepted as part of the lifestyle, especially as the country endures its current phase of economic restructuring that is adversely affecting petty entrepreneurs, laborers, and other workers at the lower end of the economic spectrum. Thus night market vending, seen in the 1980s as a potentially profitable business, is going through a period of decline, and there is talk that the "good old days" are over. Police regulation has served to further marginalize street vending as a viable means of earning money in the face of Taiwan's increasing modernity. Night market vendors are therefore reduced to using moral arguments (as reflected in Shi's popular song) when facing the police, who act on behalf of the state. The state, meanwhile, attempts to mediate among the diverse interests wishing to promote or restrict night marketing.

According to Shi's lyrics, customers need the right attitude, dress, and bargaining skills, as well as adequate cash, to enjoy one of Taiwan's most important consumption environments. So when there is good weather, people should "Invite Each Other to Stroll the Night Market" (Xiangyao lai guang yeshi), as the title of yet another popular song on this topic suggests, and buy as much as possible so that Taiwan's economic miracle can continue to thrive.

Today, night markets serve as spaces in which global cultural flows meet: Shi's mix of Mandarin, English, and Japanese terms within his Taiwanese verses, combined with a Persian melody, accurately reflects this important aspect of night markets. Thus, to adequately describe such a mixture and to understand night markets as a form of popular culture requires a consideration of the dimensions of time and space, in addition to an analysis of its activities and content.

DEFINING NIGHT MARKETS

It is difficult to give a precise definition for conceptions of night markets because of the associated mix of activities, merchandise, and complex meanings. Night markets in Taiwan range from the large-scale nightly metropolitan kind located in larger cities (e.g., Taibei and Gaoxiong) to the small-scale ones in urban residential neighborhoods and to the periodic markets common in suburbs, townships, and villages. A cultural definition of a Chinese night market basically entails cooked-food vendors using pushcarts or stationed in stalls. Without prepared-food vendors, these clusters of retail vendors operating at night would not qualify to be named night markets. In recent years, a steadily increasing number of restaurants and established shops have set up business in or around once vendor-focused night markets and have become an important part of night markets. This has also moved in the other direction, with vendors "invading" some urban commercial districts and turning them into "marketlike" spheres. The selling of products manufactured by Taiwan's small-scale industries during the past quarter century has become an important vending business in night markets of all types and has given night markets a strong commercial image. But as Taiwan's traditional manufacturing sector has suffered from increasing labor costs and strong foreign competition, night market vendors and shops alike have increasingly become retailers for foreign imports. This is especially true for cheap imported goods (e.g., garments) from Korea and mainland China. Conceptually, night markets have a decidedly leisurely air, and they are distinctive from the morning or evening "vegetable" markets, which primarily sell groceries for daily necessities. Vendors in urban night markets normally begin setting up their businesses during the afternoon rush hour and work until midnight. Only a few remain open all night. Periodic markets generally open late, after normal dinnertime, and close one hour before midnight. The above features demonstrate that Chinese night markets are not merely any markets operating at night—they are specified forms with many complexities.

Strolling through night markets continues to be one of the most popular nighttime public leisure activities in Taiwan. Every evening, thousands of customers visit night markets to consume food, purchase merchandise, and try their hands at games of chance—or to simply enjoy the "hot and noisy" *(renao)* atmosphere that is a distinctive feature of Taiwanese night markets. Their popularity is such that they are found in medium-sized townships, rural villages, and even remote aboriginal settlements in the mountains. Regardless of location, their great popularity serves as proof that they exist as an important economic and social institution.

Chinese night markets made their first recorded appearance during the late Tang dynasty (in the eighth and ninth centuries) and quickly became a pervasive aspect of Chinese society. It was one of the earliest cultural institutions to reemerge in the People's Republic of China once the Communist Chinese government relaxed its strict societal controls in the 1970s. Night markets also spread to other countries with high concentrations of ethnic Chinese—Singapore, Indonesia, Thailand, and Malaysia. As might be expected, night markets reflect the economic and ethnic characteristics of the societies in which they exist: Singaporean night markets are highly gentrified and tightly controlled by the state, while major night markets in Hong Kong have been promoted for the international tourist trade.[3] Those found in Taiwan's major cities are cosmopolitan outlets attracting modern consumers, while those in smaller communities in Taiwan, Hong Kong, and throughout Southeast Asia are more parochial, consisting of a few food stalls that primarily serve crowds interested in socializing. All of these night markets share some common features: the cultural use of time and night markets' spatial meanings, food specialties cooked on the spot, and vendors selling products that link light industries with the popular cultures of their host societies. By examining some of these features in detail, it is possible to trace the evolution of night markets along specific cultural lines to their present form, as well as to understand their current status as a cornerstone of Taiwanese culture.

Despite their long existence in Chinese history, night markets have probably always been perceived as socially peripheral by the Chinese; unfortunately, there is a lack of evidence in favor of this argument from official historical documents. While county gazetteers have fully detailed descriptions of morning market activities, we find almost no record of night markets. Surprisingly, a similar situation exists today: Despite the recognition of night markets' economic significance, local and national government bureaucracies still fail to keep detailed records of their activities. At the same time, while most morning markets have been brought under the direct control of government agencies, the state has shown little interest in attempting similar efforts for night markets.

Yet from an economic viewpoint, only in recent years has vending (including night marketing) been strongly condemned as an activity sabotaging Taiwan's economic and social well-being. This scenario can be depicted as an economic informalization tied to the marginalization of night markets within both economic systems and societal values that relegates vending to an underground economy *(dixia jingji)*. The status of night marketing has been repeatedly recategorized in economic and legal terms, but each time it was situated at an even more disadvantaged position. Previously, vending was classified as "open-air stores" *(ludian)*. Although it was under tight Japanese colonial control, it was legal. In the 1960s, the Guomindang (KMT) government perceived it as a "self-help strategy" engaged by unemployed and handicapped citizens. Thus it embodied a form of social welfare. But it was also criticized as causing "vendor problems"—that is, traffic and sanitation problems.

As modernization occurred throughout Taiwan during the past two and a half decades, the value of vending has been debated within the confines of the island's capitalist economy. Because the vendors evaded taxes and had low overhead costs, a discourse arose that accused vendors of creating "unfair competition" with formal stores. This recategorized night markets as part of the underground economy. This informalization process began in the mid-1970s and was connected with the historical establishment of capitalist economic practices and their associated value systems as societal norms. In contrast, night market activities began to be criticized as anti-modern and backward. Although Taiwan's government has never made vending illegal, vendors' increasingly disadvantaged position has nonetheless legitimated a great deal of police regulation with regard to relocation practices.[4]

Nonetheless, as the position of the night market is pushed further toward the social periphery, its symbolic meaning as a cultural institution seems to increase in significance. There are increasing numbers of night markets that are singled out as important symbols of Taiwan's remaining folk culture. Thus, they have increasingly become a typical site—along with temples, older neighborhoods, and a handful of local museums—for Taiwanese people to give their foreign guests and relatives visiting from other parts of Taiwan an "authentic" experience of local culture. Discourses attempting to define night markets' legitimacy and meaning shed light on them as places of competing interests and values. The struggle over their legitimacy as pleasure sites, a cultural activity, and an economic form is intrinsically tied in with social power relations deriving from multiple sources. These contradictory messages embody complex meanings worthy of anthropological analysis.

HISTORICAL BACKGROUND

In A.D. 836, the Tang dynasty government imposed strict sanctions on night market operations, an indication that the markets had already achieved significant levels of organization and sophistication (Chi and Liu 1987, 106). Economic expansion during the late Tang forced a decline in state regulation, leading to the lifting of curfews and other restrictions on commercial activity. During the Song dynasty (960–1279), night markets became an established part of night life in all of China's major cities, where they were increasingly found in "remote and quiet" corners (Meng 1980, 21). These markets frequently operated past midnight and into the third watch (3:00–5:00 A.M.), with some core area markets occasionally staying open twenty-four hours a day. In the famous book, *Record of the Splendors of Hangzhou City (Menglianglu),* Wu Zimu gives a detailed description of goods and services found in Hangzhou's night markets during the Song, including fortune-telling, gambling, juggling performances, a wide range of arts and crafts, fruits and vegetables, clothing, Buddhist icons, tea, and prepared "snack foods" or *xiaochi* (Wu 1980, 242–243). Many prepared foods and fruits were sold throughout the day by vendors and shopkeepers, but Wu identified certain *xiaochi* items (along with specific fortune-telling services) as "night market special goods." Song period night markets were also associated with restaurants and brothels, since they were frequently located along main business streets and near red-light districts. In *The Eastern Capital: A Dream of Splendors Past (Dungjing menghualu),* Meng (1980) gives a description of the northern part of Kaifeng city, in the vicinity of Maxing Street, where many restaurants and a large night market were located. During the Song, it was reportedly the only area without mosquitoes, since it was so full of smoke from hundreds of candles and oil lamps.

When Taiwanese mention night markets, the first impression is always about *xiaochi* food. (Photo by Shuenn-Der Yu)

The similarity between Song dynasty night markets and those currently operating in Taiwan is striking. Today's markets also carry a diversity of goods and services, as well as providing a regular leisure activity for a society very interested in nighttime public activities. Though handicrafts have for the most part been replaced by the products of modern light industry and luxury art works have been replaced by cheap, mass-produced imitations, Taiwan's night markets continue to be noted for their snack food specialties and for their position as gathering places for a diverse population. This cultural form, it appears, has been rather stable over centuries.

Taiwanese night markets first appeared as small, local markets operating in popular urban gathering sites. The oldest and most famous night markets still operating today—such as Yuanhuan and Wanhua in Taibei and Sakariba and Xiaobei in Tainan—all started as small gatherings of food vendors on street corners, in temple plazas, or next to early morning vegetable markets during the period of Japanese occupation. They were quickly joined by a handful of retailers selling such items as traditional medicines and handicrafts and eventually established themselves as part of the street culture that had been so popular in Chinese society.

In Taiwan, Taibei exemplifies the development of night market networks. While small gatherings of night vendors were common in pre-1949 Taibei, they were not considered night markets because they did not attain the spatial meaning of the Chinese definition of "market" (to be explained in the next section). Prosperity for this particular generation of vendors did not occur until after Taiwan recovered from the destruction of World War II. The first wave of new night markets slowly emerged during the 1950s in Taibei's older urban core and during the early 1960s in a handful of settlements on the city's edges. They then rapidly spread into newly established suburbs and manufacturing centers in several satellite cities during the 1970s. Further into the marginal areas of the Taibei metropolis were traveling periodic night markets, similar to those found in more rural towns. These market networks became so efficient that by the mid-1980s, a full range of goods and services could be purchased in even the most remote areas of the island.

During the 1950s and 1960s, Taibei's night markets (especially Yuanhuan and Wanhua) reflected the tastes of urban migrant laborers who found temporary housing nearby and who formed an important segment of the night market customer base. To serve their needs, vendors created simplified versions of banquet dishes and catered *xiaochi* foods commonly found in southern Taiwan. The names of their originating towns were frequently appropriated for the names of the dishes (e.g., "Zhanghua meatballs"). The vendors used simpler cooking procedures, stronger flavors, and cheaper materials to serve those who could afford only inexpensive meals on a regular basis. But the special position of *xiaochi* in Chinese cuisine (discussed in a later section) meant that these night market specialties eventually attracted the attention of the local elite. Even today, as a means of attracting new customers, vendors tell stories of famous politicians and intellectuals visiting their night market stalls. Later, such stories became an important part of local nostalgic discourse, pitting modern images against older versions of night markets.

The mass-produced, inexpensive garments, shoes, ornaments, and toys for which Taiwan became famous and on which it built the foundation for its "economic miracle" were first sold in night markets in the early 1960s. The global recession of the 1970s actually improved opportunities for vendors to sell goods produced by Taiwan's family-based, small-scale light industries, since the number of canceled overseas orders made more products available to local markets. Vendors responded by promoting their merchandise as "returned export" and "export-cut," even for products that were in reality made for the domestic market. Taibei's Wufenpu area garment firms, which primarily produced inexpensive, low-quality clothing, used such slogans as "bankruptcy goods," "cut products," and "returned export goods" to capitalize on a market niche created by a new class of salaried urban office workers looking to buy readymade garments (Ka 1993). Vendors took advantage of this growing market to establish a night marketing network that continues to serve Taiwan's light industry today. These commodities replaced many traditional night market businesses, including Chinese medicines, handicrafts, and fortune-telling services. This in turn transformed night markets to embody the local as well as global modern popular culture that was created by commercial industries.

The increasing prosperity of night markets toward the end of the 1980s attracted higher quality garment and shoe stores to set up booths in night markets, leading to the further displacement of traditional businesses. During this period there was an increase in the use of neon signs, bright displays, and loud music by the stores to attract customers. This added to the overall energy of night markets. Cafeterias were replaced by restaurants, sundry stores by gift shops, and low-quality garment stores by sportswear outlets. Watch and clock shops became popular night market fixtures, as did optical stores. At the height of Taiwan's stock market surge in the late 1980s, various chains began to open franchises in or adjacent to night markets, including fast-food outlets such as McDonald's, twenty-four-hour convenience stores such as 7-Elevens, and many garment stores. The changeover continued into the 1990s, and many individually owned garment, shoe, and sportswear businesses were replaced by chains selling higher grade merchandise. Eventually, a few department stores opened branches nearby, as in the case of Taibei's Shilin and Tainan's Xiaobei night markets.

These changes transformed Taiwan's night markets from spaces that primarily sold traditional snack foods, handicrafts, and services into modern centers of popular culture. This led the way for postmodern juxtapositions of fads and temples, department stores and vendors, name-brand commodities and counterfeits, and convenience stores and traditional foods. Some markets are better known than others for rapidly responding to new trends, such as light manufacturing firms and their vendor outlets that try to capitalize on new fads by distributing their own embellished versions through night markets. This was especially true before the 1990s, with the lax enforcement of copyright and intellectual property protection laws. Markets were flooded with counterfeit merchandise, which attracted thousands of young customers willing to buy cheap copies of fashionable items at a price they could afford. With greater emphasis on enforcing these laws in recent years, counterfeit copies of name-brand fashions and CDs are more likely to be found in smaller neighborhoods or in traveling night markets. Younger customers with disposable income still flock to the larger markets, however, bent on finding reasonable copies of fashionable items even if they do not have name-brand labels. With McDonald's, Nets, and Tower Records neighboring *xiaochi* stalls and temples and with vendors pushing counterfeit CDs, this night market scene does not appear to be exotic to Taiwanese. One informant even points out that this nicely complements the night market's original disorderly and spatial characteristics.

The above description demonstrates the fact that night markets have, however, had significant changes. Perhaps the most important of these changes is their articulation with the modern capitalist economy. Yet as a cultural form, night markets have actually been rather stable for centuries. I will now elaborate on the basic cultural principles underlying night markets' cultural forms.

UNDERLYING CULTURAL PRINCIPLES

Time

Temporality—what Kellerman (1991) calls the conception and use of time—is a key factor in any description of night markets. They hold special meanings that are congruent with Chinese concepts tied to the same time slot during which these markets operate. For Chinese, the hours following the evening meal have always been oriented toward leisure and public interaction, in contrast to the tendency of westerners to use evening hours for private pursuits or intimate interactions (Zerubavel 1981, 145). In terms of what Schivelbusch (1988) called the "temporality of night time," the historical significance of modern technology in the form of street lighting (dating to the 1700s in the West) appears to be irrelevant to the Chinese situation. In Western countries, gas and electric lighting completely changed the way in which nighttime was viewed—from "chaos, the realm of dreams, teeming with ghosts and demons" (Schivelbusch 1988, 81) to a victory over nature. In contrast, evening hours have been an important part of Chinese urban life since at least the Song dynasty, during which some restaurants, shops, and other activities peaked at midnight or later. Today, many commercial activities in Taiwan also continue into the nighttime hours, although most areas are empty by midnight. Nighttime, it appears, has always been the right time for leisure in Chinese society—and strolling down urban night markets has been an important aspect of nighttime leisure for centuries.

Important cultural distinctions exist between night and morning markets, despite their substantial overlap in terms of goods and services. Obviously, night market visitors are less likely to find vegetables being sold from vendor carts or the backs of pickup trucks. Similarly, there are also prepared *xiaochi* foods, garments, toys, and small appliances sold in the morning markets. Morning markets, however, consistently emphasize practical functions in contrast to the night market's leisure orientation. In Taiwan, morning markets are called vegetable markets *(cai shichang)* and primarily sell raw food and daily necessities. Their clientele, consisting mostly of housewives, differs significantly from the diverse social groups who visit night markets to eat, play, shop, and entertain dates. Some night markets are located next to day markets, but the former certainly engender more energy, entertainment value, and social and economic mix than the markets that used to attract the attention of anthropologists. The initial impression of many Taiwanese and foreign visitors concerning night markets is that they have entered a *fair* rather than a *market,* in the conventional sense of the word. This is especially true when the medicine sellers stage their magic or martial arts shows and the bingo stalls begin to attract crowds. It is also evident in the name applied to periodic night markets in many rural areas: "commodity exhibitions" *(shangzhan).* Although it can be argued that this fairlike atmosphere is a part of morning markets too, shopping for daily necessities nonetheless appears to be drudgery rather than a pastime.

Space

The second principle focuses on the meaning of the term for market: "*shi.*" *Shi* has traditionally denoted a concentration of buyers and sellers in a confined space. Today it is used to describe a retail rather than a wholesale market. It also implies a degree of heterogeneity of businesses in one place. No minimum number of vendors is ever required to establish an "official" night market, but a dispersed distribution of traders over a wide area would not qualify for night market status even if there were a significant number of vendors involved.

Rather than using a specific ratio of vendors per square foot, a more important criterion for what constitutes a night market is the unquantifiable ambiance created by such an assemblage. In Taiwan, small storefront merchants and vendors use such terms as "compactness of a market" *(jieshi)* and "formation of a market" *(chengshi)* to describe whether or not business activity is sufficiently concentrated, noisy, and exciting to be considered a true market. A successful night market must be "hot and noisy," the best translation of the term *"renao."* Vendors alone do not a *shi* make; it is only after a good number of customers have gathered and a *renao* atmosphere has been formed that a true *shi* emerges.

To Chinese people, *renao* is a key concept and an important feature of any successful celebration. It is considered embarrassing or foreboding to hold a wedding, banquet, or in some cases, a funeral that lacks *renao*—the emotion that transforms formal occasions into warm and interactive events. *Renao* is also considered to be a manifestation of the "human flavor" *(renqing wei)* that is generated from enthusiastic human interactions. A *shi* that is completely devoid of *renao* is obvious to even the casual visitor, but informants use the term as a vaguely definable criterion for determining the degree to which a group of vendors have actually created a viable night market with acceptable levels of excitement and meaning. Dispersed businesses reduce the intensity of bargaining, which in turn reduces the sense of *renao*. Markets that fail to create this sense of excitement are said to be "chilly and desolate" *(lengqing)* or to have "dispersed *shi*" *(sanshi)*.

Marketers use various means to create *renao*, the most common being bright lighting, loud music, and exaggerated decorations. Vendors directly address nearby patrons to get their attention. Some owners or their employees will stand on chairs and give their sales pitches through portable public address systems, with the volume turned high to make sure that they are noticed. Vendors also have a tendency to place their carts or stalls very close together, forcing customers to pass through narrow spaces that are close to the merchandise as well as the sellers. Personal space is difficult to protect in such tight quarters, with customers jostling for position in front of the more popular food vendors. During the peak periods of market activity, Taiwanese people often have to share a table with complete strangers when eating *xiaochi*. Food vendors are especially deliberate in their presentation, leaving raw meat, stomach and other organs, seafood, and vegetables open for inspection. Merchandise vendors are more likely to scatter their wares haphazardly, believing that a neat and tidy presentation is incompatible with the vibrant crowds, smoke, music, and the shouting that come together in a *renao*-filled market.

The sense of chaos that is encouraged among vendors operating on sidewalks and along the streets of night markets also extends to the stores behind them. Most garment and shoe stores eliminate shop windows or walled-off entrances. Instead, they choose to operate in an open storefront style, an arrangement which signifies a desire to integrate with other night market activities. Store shelves are arranged to give a sense of overflowing stock, similar to the preferred presentation of street vendors. The exceptions to this open-air storefront style are a few middle- and high-end restaurants and top-of-the-line garment stores whose owners want a purposeful separation from vendor activity.[5] These business owners, focusing on the apparent lack of regulations and planning in the market's spatial arrangement, would probably use the negative term for chaos—*"luan"*—to describe the same activities that most Taiwanese people refer to positively as *renao*. Attempts to make night markets conform to modern marketing concepts can actually work against them; those with formal rules, standardized stalls, and uniform appearances are in danger of alienating customers, some of whom complain about the loss of a market's character.

Spatial arrangements significantly influence behavioral patterns and human interaction. While customers remain strangers—even when sharing the same table—they are nevertheless attracted to the market by its crowds and the promise of safe participation in a shared event. This fits with Tuan's (1982) contention that individuals constantly seek a balance between communal life and isolation. He argues that as the consciousness of self has intensified in tandem with the development of modern society, people have tended to create spaces for withdrawal while simultaneously creating spaces for the reintegration of communal life. The latter effort is evident in Taiwan's night markets. Customers enter temporary social relationships with clearly defined boundaries and ending points. Thus, night market *renao* is considered to be neither noise nor chaos. Instead, patrons caught in the energy and disorder of a market feel a sense of communal life through sharing a common space.

Night market patrons typically attend night markets in groups, within which interactions occur among people with established relationships. That, in addition to the anonymity of being in a crowded space, creates a feeling of safety that allows them to ignore the gazes of other customers and to act outside of their "normal" characters. A physical and emotional sense of relaxation leads to what many informants believe is undisciplined behavior, the thrill of which encourages return visits. Dressing down is perhaps mentioned more frequently than any other aspect of relaxed behavior—wearing slippers instead of shoes and shorts instead of pants is part of what night market strolling is all about.

While these points may seem trivial, they were repeatedly emphasized during interviews. Other frequently cited examples of relaxed behavior raised during interviews include eating while walking along a street, eating food in an inappropriate manner, talking and laughing freely in a public place, bargaining without considering one's own status, rummaging through merchandise without upsetting the vendor, and littering carelessly. All of these are commonly considered to be the actions of people from lower social and economic classes—except when they are done in night markets. In Babcock's (1978) words, such acts are "marked by an instability wherein the normative order is both presented and withdrawn at the same time." Such surroundings may be described as "ordered disorder" or "controlled decontrol." The transgressions are both minor and specific, but because they provide a sense of refreshment and renewal, the night markets in which they occur serve as significant sources of pleasure in daily Taiwanese life.

Food

Xiaochi foods have been a distinctive and indispensable feature of night markets ever since the Song dynasty. Descriptions of Song markets in Kaifeng and Hangzhou by Meng (1980), Wu (1980), and Zhou (1983) all focus on the surprising variety of *xiaochi* items that were available. Today they still constitute a significant portion of night market business. Providing the context and space for local gatherings, vendors offering local *xiaochi* specialties often become the focus and selling point of specific night markets. The special meanings attached to certain dishes are incentives for many Taiwanese to travel long distances in order to experience their flavors.

Understanding the important role of night market *xiaochi* dishes requires an explanation of their overall place in the hierarchy of Chinese cuisine. A loosely defined category, *xiaochi* includes all items that are not considered "rice or other staples" *(fan)* or "vegetable and meat dishes" *(cai)*. The Cantonese dim sum items, familiar to many westerners, are considered *xiaochi*, as are "steamed buns with fillings" *(baozi),* "Chinese dumplings" *(jiaozi),* "rice cakes" *(gao),* pork and fish congee, noodles, soups, dried foods such as nuts, and pickled fruits. Less traditional items include Western-style crackers, breads, cakes, candies, cookies, and ice cream. Flavored shaved ice is also part of this list, while soda pop and juices are considered *xiaochi* by some Chinese.

Central to the *xiaochi* concept is unity between *fan* and *cai*. In a typical Chinese meal, *cai* dishes are meant to *pei*—"match," "complement," or "supplement"—*fan*. In other words, *fan* is considered a basic, while *cai* is thought to be a supplement. The characteristics of *xiaochi* can be described in terms of *zhufu heyi*—a word that connotes the unification of "major food" *(zhushi)* and "supplemental dishes" *(fushi)*. *Xiaochi* is considered to be a separate category from "formal, regular meals" *(zhengcan)* because it is normally consumed as "snacks" *(dianxin)* between meals. *Xiaochi* items stand apart from this basic structure because they combine *fan* and *cai* ingredients. Western breads and desserts are generally considered *xiaochi* because they mix flour with flavorings; toast becomes *xiaochi* as soon as jam is added. In Taiwan, Western-style bakeries produce a variety of breads with such fillings as taro, red beans, or even powdered pork and fish. The northern Chinese custom of preparing "noodles without ingredients and flavoring" *(baimian)* to be eaten with the *cai* is seldom practiced among Taiwanese families. Noodles are normally—if not always—prepared and cooked with ingredients and flavoring and presented as a form of *xiaochi*, especially in restaurants and food stalls.

Another interesting example of how a foreign food is incorporated into a form of night market *xiaochi* is steak. Steak was at one time considered to be an expensive, exotic food sold only in Western luxury restaurants and represented to Taiwanese people a Western way of eating a meal. This consisted of soup as the first course, to be followed by salad, the main course (i.e., steak), coffee, and dessert. In the mid-1970s, a number of vendors began selling cheap steak meals, soon creating a major fad in Taiwan's major cities. Similar to Western restaurants, additional courses include soup, salad, bread, and tea (hot or iced), but not dessert. There is a notable absence of potatoes, and the steaks are served in one-eighth-inch slices. Unlike the Western steak dinner, in Taiwan vendor steak meals come with pasta and a raw egg cooked on a sizzling steak platter at the very last moment. The raw egg symbolically transforms the steak, vegetable, and pasta combination into something that can be considered Chinese *xiaochi*. In this process, starch (pasta) and supplements (steak and vegetables) are mixed together to reach a cultural definition of night market food. Like other night market foods, this vendor version of steak dinner is considered to be—and consumed as—a *xiaochi* instead of as a full meal. This became very popular in the 1980s and has become a regular food item in most night markets around the island.

Unlike the English term "snack," which refers to anything that can be eaten quickly and informally, Chinese *xiaochi* is loaded with cultural meanings. Most families make their own *xiaochi* only during major holidays—for example, sticky-rice dumplings wrapped in bamboo leaves *(zongzi)* are eaten by Chinese around the world during the Dragon Boat Festival; moon cakes accompany the

Mid-Autumn Festival, and rice cakes are eaten during Chinese New Year celebrations. On the other hand, *xiaochi* items are also commonly served at formal banquets, with Taiwanese hosts serving fried noodles or fried rice mixed with *cai* ingredients instead of plain rice as a special act of hospitality. A typical twelve-course banquet generally includes two or three *xiaochi* courses. Deluxe dishes remain the central focus of these occasions, but the addition of *xiaochi* items marks them as special events such as birthday parties and wedding dinners. *Xiaochi* dishes are also used to indicate the various stages of a banquet.

The informal aspects of making or eating *xiaochi* foods with friends or relatives are equally important. Many Chinese have experienced the intimacy associated with sitting around a table while making dumplings. In some ways, *xiaochi* foods serve the same function as barbecued foods in Western countries: Instead of preparing elaborate, formal meals for informal occasions, a host may substitute *xiaochi* dishes. In this way, they signify closeness in relationships. Eating *xiaochi* foods in cramped night market spaces is also indicative of intimate friendship.

These *xiaochi* foods were often created by people who were unfamiliar with the elaborate culinary knowledge held by the elite, which gave night market *xiaochi* a strong sense of being representative of local folk culture. It must be remembered, however, that night market *xiaochi* is not an exclusive product of market vendors or the middle and lower classes of society. As mentioned earlier, some deluxe banquet dishes were transformed into less delicate and affordable forms to be served in night markets. Unlike the many famous dishes representative of China's regional culinary styles, whose recipes are widely shared through popular cookbooks, night market *xiaochi* specialties are more restrictive in terms of locale and origin. Many foods are labeled with the names of the places where they were created as trademarks: Zhanghua meatballs, Tainan noodles, and Jilong fish cakes are all considered to be specialty *xiaochi* foods with authentic meaning. As such, they are depicted as special folk culture foods *(xiangtu xiaochi)* with their own distinctive flavors associated with their origins. Great gatherings of *xiaochi* foods also represent the exotic features of nonlocal cultures and ethnic groups. When Beijing reopened its night market in the late 1980s, it advertised the *xiaochi* foods of China's different provinces and various ethnic regions as its major attraction. In Taiwan, vendors constantly experiment with foreign foods from Japan, America, and even Middle Eastern countries in the hope of finding a lucrative *xiaochi* fad.

A detailed list of Taiwan's night market *xiaochi* is hence a representation of Taiwan's history, including traces of indigenous and successive foreign—particularly Japanese, mainland Chinese, and American—cultural influences. Japanese Udon noodles, mainlanders' dumplings, and American steak have all become typical food items in Taiwan's night markets, telling stories of Taiwan's colonial heritage, KMT rule, and a predominance of American and Japanese cultural influences. The localization of some of these transnational foods, like tempura (fried Japanese fish cakes),[6] are so profound that nowadays Taiwanese people often consider the food's authenticity in terms of *xiaochi* having originated at a particular night market vendor. These foods have been very much incorporated into Taiwanese society—to the extent that we can scarcely tell which is "local" and which is "foreign."

Despite its diverse nature, however, night market *xiaochi* has always been illustrated as the representation of a Taiwanese indigenous culture by Taiwanese people. The story of oyster omelets is a typical example of how such a discourse is constructed. Oyster omelets were said to have been created by a famous stall in Taibei's oldest night market, Yuanhuan. The great success of oyster omelets has made this stall virtually emblematic of Taibei's night market *xiaochi*. Its locality name, "Yuanhuan," has become a brand name for oyster omelet stalls throughout Taiwan despite the fact that this snack food is also served in other night markets. Many of the food stalls use "Yuanhuan Oyster Omelets" as their title in a clear attempt to link their connection with the original. The oyster omelet was actually a famous dish in Xiamen (a port city of Fujian Province, the ancestral land of many Taiwanese). One stall owner claimed that it was his ancestor who transformed it into the current form by adding two new ingredients, a starch base and greens, to the original oyster and eggs. This Taiwanese version was a huge success and provided great income to the stall owners. Today the authentic oyster omelet served at this particular stall has become the object of nostalgia for many generations of customers. Because of this, they continue to pay special visits to the stall despite the fact that the prosperity of Yuanhuan has greatly declined in recent years.

A detailed examination reveals this simple change in preparing the oyster omelet to be surprisingly significant. The addition of a starch base that mixed the *fan* and *cai* components together structurally transformed a dish into *xiaochi*, making it a suitable food item for night markets. But the significance of this transformation was much more than a change in cultural categorization to adapt to a particular Chinese consumptive habitus—it opened the potential for profit. This slight change allowed a claim to be formed: an emergence of a *xiaochi* tradition that is indigenously developed in Taiwan. In other words, what we see is that the claim originated from an economic interest—their attempt to make distinctions for a commodity that was later to be utilized to designate a break from its Chinese heritage. In this way, the construction of an indigenous Taiwanese popular culture could be made.

The oyster omelet story is not a singular case. Stories of how stall owners strive to maintain authentic flavors have become an important aspect of the discourse linking night markets to indigenous folk culture. One example of this is the famous story of how one southern Taiwanese vendor has simply added ingredients to the same wok for over forty years instead of emptying out its meat sauce contents for cleaning. This nonstop simmering is said to give his Tainan noodles a special flavor found nowhere else. Such stories are abundant in tourist books, night market guides, magazine articles, and web sites, which often use night market (or *xiaochi*) "tales of marvel" as the subtitle. In the context of Taiwan's strong connection to Chinese cultural heritage, night market *xiaochi* is one of the few raw materials for which a discourse of indigenous Taiwanese tradition could be well grounded. As Taiwanese consciousness began to compete with the orthodox Chinese identity represented by mainlanders and the KMT regime, night market *xiaochi* was naturally adopted as the source for raw materials upon which a Taiwanese identity could be constructed. This is most clearly demonstrated by Taiwan's new president, Chen Shui-bian (Chen Shuibian), who defeated the pro-unification KMT and PFP candidates in the year 2000 election. He used a few Tainan *xiaochi*—including three commonly found items from night markets—to mark his Taiwanese identity in representing a new political stance of government during the national banquet celebrating his inauguration.

Vending

Vendors are called *tanfan* or "small traders" *(xiaofan)* in Taiwan, which refers to small-scale traders using simple equipment to sell merchandise or services in streets or markets. When used as a verb, the Chinese character *"tan"* means "spreading out." Used as a noun, *tan* means "stalls" or "stands." However, *tan* can also mean having no fixed structure; spreading out merchandise on the ground also makes it a *tan*. Thus, the category *tanfan* refers to both stall owners and street vendors who use a stand, a pushing cart, or simply a piece of cloth for displaying merchandise. Being a vendor is an age-old profession in Chinese society. Many of them were engaged in many different businesses. Today, most night marketers are either retailers of modern commodities or vendors of cooked food; only a few traditional services, like fortune-telling and massage services, still remain.

Without vending, night markets could never achieve *chengshi*—the state in which a market is formed—and would therefore remain ordinary business districts. Vending embodies a form of commerce that is an important part of Chinese street culture. In those places where vending has not been absorbed by more formal business operations, one still finds spaces that contain special meanings in terms of informal business transactions, personal interactions, street performances, and leisure activities. At the same time, they are home to an efficient retailing network of distribution centers for goods produced by Taiwan's labor-intensive light industrial sector. The variety of goods and *xiaochi* foods sold by vendors in certain night markets has given them the reputation of "having almost everything." Even though vending has played an increasingly important role in Taiwan's modern economy, its legitimacy as an economic practice has suffered. Nevertheless, as vendors are pushed further toward the periphery, their symbolic significance grows.

As a long-established feature of Chinese culture, vending has always been viewed as an easy, flexible means of starting a small-scale business. Because they used public spaces, the first vendors adopted many of the professions common to Chinese street life such as fortune-telling, traditional medicine, and the selling of religious objects. Many of these can still be found in modern night markets. In rural areas, it is easy to find vestiges of the "itinerant peddler" *(pao jianghu)* tradition. Like medicine show operators in nineteenth- and twentieth-century America, these traders travel from town to town, staging dramatic performances, martial arts, magic shows, and an occasional striptease performance to attract potential customers for medicines or traditional massage. The current versions of *pao jianghu* are used to promote such new products as multipurpose car wax or "miracle" toothpaste marketed by little-known manufacturers or trading companies that can be commonly found in urban markets.

Certain night markets are closely associated with local festivals, during which large numbers of vendors congregate to capitalize on their customers' high spirits. During the most important holiday, Chinese New Year, the police customarily relax their regulations and allow vendors to take over certain intersections and neighborhoods. The presence of vendors at festivals adds a strong sense of tradition in a country that is increasingly dominated by modern forms of popular culture. Whereas organized capitalism has tended to transform road space to accord with its own values, street vendors are often viewed as reclaiming public space for traditional street culture, rendering night markets a more distinctive place in Taiwan's contemporary economy.

Retail vendors, who are predominant in night markets, serve as channels for the flow of global products and culture. Popular forms of international fashion are normally marketed on a level far above the average Taiwanese night market. Yet vendors are quick to offer local versions of emerging fashion trends and fads produced by small-scale manufacturers looking to make a quick profit. While most of these products are direct copies (some even bearing brand name logos), many have slight variations in style, color, or material that match local tastes. This is a reflection of the ability of indigenous light industries to respond quickly to market demands and to take full advantage of the informal economic practices of night market vendors. Hence, night markets have a strong sense of being a culture created by commoners—that is, *xiaochi* vendors and small manufacturing firm owners—and are important consumption centers for the country's middle and labor classes.

Perhaps because of these counterfeit practices, night market vendors are frequently associated with the "low-culture" side of modern consumerism and are looked down upon as purveyors of low-quality merchandise and as symbols of a "greedy Taiwan." Even today, the simple act of strolling through a night market is seen by some as a marker indicating the low cultural standing of those involved. The selling of pornography, the existence of striptease shows, the promotion of gambling, and even the practice of bargaining at night markets are all viewed by elites and the government as vulgar pursuits that contradict the elegance of Chinese culture.

Societal perceptions of vending add another aspect to night markets. Vending is seen by many as a means for people to make the switch from laborer to "boss" or "business owner" *(laoban)*. Researchers who have studied Taiwanese and Hong Kong vendors (Smart 1988; Tai 1994; Yu 1995) have all noted that most vendors voluntarily leave their formal jobs to enter night market vending, believing that the economic prospects are better. The ability of night markets to attract crowds also makes them natural starting points for vendor success stories of near-mythical status. The mass media is quick to pounce on stories, regardless of their truth, of vendors making million-dollar incomes and driving imported cars.[7] A closer look reveals that these stories apply only to a handful of vendors in a few famous night markets. Night marketing has nevertheless gained a reputation as a way of life that has great economic potential, especially for those interested in climbing the ladder of social mobility. Thus, at a time when Taiwan was suffering from labor shortages (the 1970s to 2000),[8] instead of facing unemployment, a handful of extremely hardworking vendors dramatically demonstrated the potential of Taiwan's family-based entrepreneurship.

The idea of vending as a profitable business presents conflicting images. On the one hand, it strengthens the portrait of hardworking Taiwanese and the strength of family-based enterprises that underlie the discourse of the "Taiwan miracle." On the other hand, the result of this portrait provides the source of attack that vendors compete unfairly with more formal businesses. Despite the fact that the legitimacy of working in the streets can be traced back to a long history, vending has increasingly suffered from criticisms related to a concept that has in recent years been fashionably called the "informal economy."[9] The economic order associated with modern capitalism has transformed vending from being seen as a legitimate economic institution that has existed in Chinese society for centuries to what the state currently refers to as the "cancer of cities." Vendors are thus accused of creating disorder and evading taxes. Ironically, in Taiwan, it was only after night markets gradually became more formalized via an influx of stores, fast-food outlets, and department stores that were attempting to capitalize on the crowds attracted to the bargains offered by vendors that night market vending increasingly came under attack for allegedly using unfair business practices. The nature of the relationship between night markets, other sectors of the economy, and the state (via its publicly stated policy concerns) therefore complicates the issue of night market problems. Regardless of the true situation, vending is popularly viewed as serving a social welfare function in providing jobs for the poor, handicapped, and unemployed. As a result, a great disparity exists between stated policies and their enforcement. The ROC government has never been willing to directly confront a myriad of subsequent social and economic problems (i.e., numerous small-firm bankruptcies and their related unemployment) that would result from a concerted effort to control vending. Hence illegal vendor crackdowns are both ambivalent and ineffective, but the state continues to denounce vending through public education campaigns and media reports. Therefore, the relationship between night market vendors and government officials (mostly through police officers) rests upon delicate negotiations, bribes, and simply looking the other way. Today, night markets still play an important role in Taiwan's economy. This has been masterfully negotiated in under-the-table contracts between the state, which realizes its limited alternatives in dealing with vending problems, and vendors, who efficiently utilize what James Scott (1985) has called "weapons of the weak" to resist state attempts at regulation (Yu 1997).[10] The instability of these relationships shows that night markets continue to be sites of competing interests, values, and power relations regarding their legitimacy as pleasure sites, cultural and historical repositories, and consumption centers.

As a result, night markets are positioned in an "in-between" or "neither-this-nor-that" condition—what Victor Turner (1977) termed "liminoid"—in the economic, legal, and cultural systems of Taiwanese society. Their "antistructure" exists through their temporality, consumer behavior patterns, spatial arrangements, interactions among various night market actors, and state policy. Consequently, the contrasting images of legal/illegal, legitimate/illegitimate, modern/traditional, vulgar/tasteful, fashionable/cultural heritage, order/disorder, and so forth tend to coexist in discourses that shape night markets as a popular cultural form. They are alternately described as places full of warmth and genuine personal relationships or as representative of aggressive, chaotic urban competition over cheap goods of questionable taste.

The counterdiscourse describes hardworking Taiwanese selling copies and counterfeits, night market *renao* energy arising from disorder, bargain-hunters' desire for fashionable commodities, modern urbanites enjoying city-centered recreation, and preservation of the "Taiwanese spirit." While doing my fieldwork I was repeatedly surprised at how these competing discourses coexist, sometimes in the opinions of the same person. Whereas in one aspect a night market might be praised as a source of folk culture, in another it would be condemned for promoting bad taste at the expense of traditional values. An individual might impugn popular culture as represented by night markets, but at the same time he or she might find it hard to resist going to famous night markets to enjoy some authentic *xiaochi* treats. Most people overlook the details of how they rationalize these discourses, thus allowing them to be swayed by different reasoning at different times. Unlike department stores, night markets have yet to be accorded a fixed status in Taiwan's society. These discourses have shown that as night markets are increasingly marginalized, their nostalgia and entertainment values are drawing cards that most Taiwanese find hard to resist. It may be their in-between status, characterized by conflicting discourses, that makes them the island's most popular cultural attraction.

NIGHT MARKETS AS TAIWANESE *XIANGTU*

Taiwan's historical context is such that a close bond exists between the issues of Taiwanese indigenous culture and ethnic identity. Most contemporary constructions of "Taiwaneseness" seek divergence from Chinese cultural heritage. The meaning of being Taiwanese, as Bosco (1994) rightly points out, is first in contrast to mainlanders, who came to Taiwan along with the KMT regime in 1949. Being Taiwanese thus becomes defined as Hokkien and Hakka speakers whose ancestors migrated to Taiwan before 1895. Because of Taiwan's current political and economic situation, a second meaning—in which being "Taiwanese" conceptualizes all residents of the island as a group unified in their difference from the PRC—has become important in the construction of a new Taiwanese culture. Based on his nice elaboration, I would further argue that a general state of anxiety exists in contemporary Taiwan concerning potential definitions of an indigenous Taiwanese culture. If Bosco's argument is correct that "the struggle between the orthodoxy of the center and the heterodoxy of the periphery has given way to the unorthodox cosmopolitanism of Taiwanese popular culture," then Taiwanese are certainly treating this popular culture with ambivalence. The country's recent shift toward democratization and globalization has intensified this general sense of anxiety, especially in regard to creating a central consensus from an increasingly pluralistic orientation.

One result has been a utopian construction of Taiwanese indigenousness known as *xiangtu*—a discourse that is frequently illustrated by examples taken from night markets and many other forms of popular culture. The construction is an ahistorical glorification of Taiwanese rural life and folk culture that offers small agricultural communities as its model. Similar to the ethnographic-present mode of presenting anthropological data that was adopted by the early functionalists, this form of discourse freezes time, space, and outside impacts when constructing an image of how Taiwanese would like their culture to be perceived. Hence, urban night markets are said to contain genuine human relationships of the type found only in rural villages and towns. Bargaining is described as an extension of personal relationships in a world marked by alienation, night market *renao* is said to represent a sense of freedom, and *xiaochi* is held up as an example of cultural authenticity.

A list of similar *xiangtu*-related constructions includes the consistent use of rural themes in Taiwanese television soap operas called *xiangtu* drama. These simple stories involving exaggerated figures emphasize traditional values in ahistoric settings. This is in direct contrast to Mandarin dramas that feature more complex stories that take place across a variety of geographic and period settings. In a like manner, Taiwanese antique furniture is called "folk-art furniture" *(minyi jiaju)*—a name promoting its local folk character but short historical depth—instead of "antique" *(gudong)* or "classical" *(gudian) jiaju,* which carries a connotation of mainland origins. A third example is the raincoats made of hemp or woven brush and rough-hewn cattle carriage wheels that have become common Taiwanese motifs in restaurants, teahouses, and other public businesses. In miniature form, they are one of the most common souvenirs given to foreign friends.

According to this *xiangtu* concept, being Taiwanese entails accepting cultural roots associated with rural life and values, manifested in what Taiwanese choose to show to foreign visitors as examples of a Taiwan experience. Along with the world-class Palace Museum (filled with artifacts taken from the mainland by the exiled KMT government) and a handful of historical monuments, night markets are often placed on the itineraries of visiting dignitaries to the island. The monuments and artifacts represent a connection with an older Chinese heritage, but night markets come under the broad definition of Taiwanese *xiangtu.* Just as Shi Wenbin points out in his song, the primary characteristic of

Taiwan's night markets is "all made in Taiwan's night city." The social construction of night market culture focuses on characteristics that can be described as "all made of Taiwanese *xiangtu*"—disregarding the fact that night markets originated as an urban phenomenon and currently serve as a crossroads of global cultural influences.

The emphasis on *xiangtu* has far-reaching impacts. Night markets have become cultural tourism sites emphasizing nostalgia, thus attracting visitors from every sector of the population wishing to partake of the attractive disorder. Many Taiwanese believe that if only the "vendor problem" could be solved, this "cancer of the city" could be turned into cultural landmarks instead. The idea of "tourist night markets" emerged exactly from this context. This new model was jointly developed in 1986 by some businessmen from Taibei's Songshan area, hoping to establish a night market to draw customers to the declining Raohe Street business district. This model was also supported by some scholars invited to propose a night market project that would later gain city government approval. The original attempt, however, was not to transform the night market to attract more foreign tourist consumers, as the title "tourist night market" may imply. Its actual effort was to redefine the boundaries of order/disorder and legal/illegal by establishing a system to regulate internal affairs, thereby reducing sanitation and traffic problems. By reorienting the night market, it was hoped that it would be more in line with a stereotypical *xiangtu* culture, via such folk-art performances as lion dances, giant top-spinning *(tuoluo)* shows, traditional figure-making demonstrations using dough, and handicrafts. Besides finding a solution for the increasingly marginalized urban night markets, this new tourist night market model also strengthens the conception that night markets represent indigenous Taiwanese folk culture. As this is the only model acceptable to both local governments and residents in allowing the continual operation of existing markets, many night markets have attempted to transform themselves into this "modernized" form in recent years. In 1998 the government also proposed a five-year project to gentrify morning and night markets across the island. Its first targets were the large morning and night markets in major cities. The establishment of Taibei's Donghua tourist night market in 1999 was one of the outcomes. Although the entire impact of this project still remains to be accessed, the trend is clearly established.

An enduring influence may be the creation of more tourist night markets as an official form of this unique brand of economic activity. The state's approval of tourist night markets as model examples of the preservation of folk culture marks a trend toward limiting night markets—especially those in big cities—to specific sites as legitimate leisure centers. This trend marks the continuing fragmentation of night markets into sites for folk-art performances, trade shows, and *xiaochi* exhibitions that are more in line with modern standards of order and control. As a result, instead of preserving a carnival atmosphere organized by the people for the people, many night markets may become carnivals controlled by the establishment for the people. If this trend continues, the days of the truly hot and noisy night market may soon be a thing of the past.

8
Disciplined Bodies in Direct Selling
Amway and Alternative Economic Culture in Taiwan
Chien-Juh Gu

EDITORS' INTRODUCTION

Economic changes around the world introduce ever-changing opportunities for profit, for loss, and for social engagement. Commerce has a long history in China, of course, and an intimate relationship with the rise of cities. Taiwan a century ago was an agricultural world, but one with towns and cities full of small shops and wandering peddlers. Today most of the population lives in the island's cities, and the island as a whole has emerged as a powerful marketplace where small shops and wandering peddlers—still on the scene—are joined by department stores, catalog sales, and Internet vendors. In this chapter, Chien-Juh Gu describes the world of "direct selling" by door-to-door vendors partly in the tradition of peddlers of old, but also very much attached to the developing commerce of the present world. She approaches this through a case study of the Amway Corporation in Taiwan.

What makes these modern direct sales agents special is less what they sell or even how they sell it, but rather what selling means to them. In the case of people working for Amway, it is clear that selling means a lot. Recruited from a segment of the Taiwan population with few resources to undertake individual businesses, the sales agents gain from the direct sales corporation a sense of engagement and entrepreneurship that, in its most extreme forms, approaches "religious" dimensions, becoming a core part of the identity of many participants.

Gu describes this to us and seeks to provide an explanation for the remarkable appeal that direct selling has had for urban people in Taiwan. The transformation of society from largely agricultural to largely industrial and from largely rural to largely urban has changed the class structure, Gu explains. In a place without "old money," where all the rich are nouveaux riches, the interest in ending up in a higher rather than a lower social stratum is great. Moving up and getting rich—rapid class mobility—becomes a prime goal for much of the population, and direct selling is seen as a route to this kind of advancement.

It is clear that direct selling is quite different from the door-to-door peddling of earlier eras. The phenomenon is more than economic. It is the playing out of a dream stimulated by the critical importance that money now plays for some people's sense of their place in the world. ∎

Direct selling is a burgeoning labor regime in Taiwan. In the 1990s, more than 2 million Taiwanese people have become distributors, seven hundred thousand of whom are active salespersons in the industry (Xingzhengyuan Gongping Jiaoyi Weiyuanhui 1995).[1] Rather than being an economic activity, direct selling is often described as a religion—or even a cult—in Taiwanese society. In the direct selling community, distributors are trained to behave and talk in a uniform way, and outsiders are often shocked by such an unusual phenomenon. The cultural presentation of direct selling has become a social issue that has yet to be investigated. Many questions remain unanswered: Why do so many Taiwanese people join direct selling? How does direct selling brainwash distributors and unify their vocabularies and behaviors? What sociocultural factors encourage such a unique cultural formation of direct selling in Taiwan? What does direct selling tell us about Taiwanese society today?

In this chapter, I begin by introducing the definition and origin of direct selling and discuss the social context and structural factors that supported the development and growth of this industry in Taiwan. Next, I provide an analysis of a case study—Amway—to demonstrate the alternative economic culture that direct selling has produced in urban Taiwan. Following this analysis, I conclude with the implications of direct selling culture for Taiwanese society.

DEFINITION AND ORIGIN OF DIRECT SELLING ORGANIZATIONS (DSO'S)

Direct selling is the face-to-face (salesperson-to-consumer) sale of products. The salespeople or so-called distributors are independent contractors, not employees. Their earnings come from selling at a profit goods that they buy wholesale from one or more manufacturers or distributors. Sometimes distributors are paid a commission by the wholesaler.

For example, if distributor Mary recruits John, then Mary becomes John's "upline" or "sponsor," while John is Mary's "downline." John recruits Paul and Linda, who become "downlines" for him and also Mary's "leaves." These upline-downline relationships develop a pyramid scheme similar to family trees

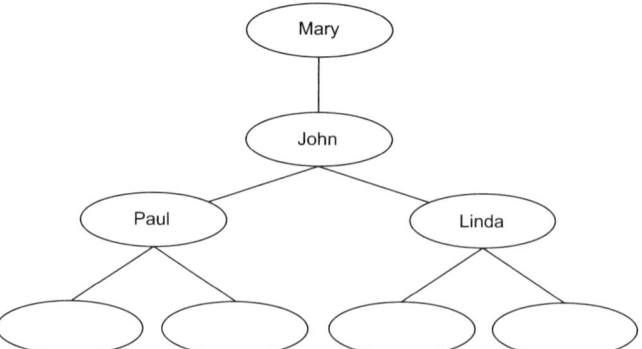

Figure 1. Illustration of the upline-downline network.

(see Figure 1). In this example, John, Paul, and Linda are called Mary's "frontlines" because they belong to Mary's same pyramid scheme. Yet each of them, including Mary, is an independent entrepreneur. Biggart (1989) calls the direct selling industry "network direct selling organizations" (network DSOs), highlighting such pyramidal networks in direct selling.

Distributors have several sources of income in network DSOs. First, they make money on goods personally sold—usually about a 30 percent markup between the wholesale and retail prices. Second, distributors can also earn volume purchase bonuses. In other words, the more one buys wholesale from the company, the less one has to pay. Uplines usually charge their downlines more than they pay for the products, so each upline also profits as a wholesaler. Third, distributors earn royalties from the sales of their frontlines and from the sales of their frontlines' own recruits. This royalty usually ranges from 3 to 5 percent, although different companies might have varying policies.

Colonial peddlers can be regarded as the forerunners of today's distributors, as salesmen sold tools, tea, and liniment door-to-door (Biggart 1989). The contemporary direct selling industry, however, is highly organized and has sophisticated devices of reward systems. The first formal organization of modern direct selling was the Nutrilite Company in the United Sates, whose reward system was designed by Lee Mytinger and William Casselberry in 1934 for marketing vitamins. Later corporations of direct selling, such as Avon, Nu Skin, and Amway, basically adopt similar systems, and the number of DSOs has been increasing since 1950.

A BRIEF HISTORY OF DIRECT SELLING IN TAIWAN

Taiwan Family (Taijia) Company was the first direct selling firm in Taiwan. It was an international corporation established in 1978, capitalized by American,

Japanese, and Taiwanese sources (Liu and Chen 1990). The forerunner of Taiwan Family was the Best Line Company, a corporation that went bankrupt and was accused of illegal business practices in Japan. In the reward system of Best Line, the profits from recruiting downlines exceeded those of selling products to a great extent. Consequently, distributors tended only to recruit new people rather than selling products themselves. Best Line's direct sales became a fraudulent business that had numerous workers but little actual commercial behavior. As a result, Best Line was outlawed in Japan and California; the company then turned to the Taiwanese market with a new firm name—Taiwan Family (Hua 1986).

As with Best Line in Japan, Taiwan Family rewarded its distributors much more for recruiting people than for selling products.[2] Thus many Taiwan Family distributors devoted themselves to recruiting new members instead of selling products. Meanwhile, when joining Taiwan Family, distributors were required to purchase a certain amount of products—mostly detergents. Many distributors paid the membership fee (in other words, bought packages of detergents) for their family members, relatives, or friends out of their own pockets in order to create more downlines. Consequently, most Taiwan Family members ended up accumulating too many products in their home. They were forced to find more downlines by any means possible, not only to earn money but also to seek compensation for the cost of their membership fees. The direct selling in Taiwan Family, therefore, became an expanding web of distributors with little trade.

The consequences of Taiwan Family's reward system soon became a serious problem among members. These distributors requested assistance from the Taiwan Family Company to solve their overstocking problem, but no advice was forthcoming. As a result, they turned to the Consumer's Foundation for help, condemning Taiwan Family for neglecting the problems of its members. The Taiwanese government investigated this case and learned that Taiwan Family not only had an unreasonable reward system, as noted above, but the company had also evaded taxes. The government revealed its investigation to the public and prosecuted Taiwan Family for tax evasion.

This event gave rise to media hype in Taiwan that consequently resulted in an extremely negative public impression of direct selling. In popular thought, direct selling was an illegal business, and distributors were regarded as swindlers. In popular parlance, direct selling enterprises became known as "mouse associations" *(laoshuhui)*—expressing the idea that distributors were like mice, working together for profit but doing nothing decent. After the government's public investigation, the notorious Taiwan Family Company was forced to exit Taiwan. But the notion of direct selling as a mere "mouse association" has existed in Taiwanese society ever since.

Surprisingly, in spite of the notoriety of direct selling in Taiwan in the early 1980s, Amway established a branch in Taiwan and began its marketing in 1982, immediately following the suppression of Taiwan Family. Several direct selling companies, including Avon and Nu Skin, then followed in Amway's footsteps and entered Taiwan's market. Unlike Taiwan Family, these direct marketing firms adopted legal methods of direct selling, and they consequently promoted the development of direct selling in Taiwan (Lin 1994).

In 1991, the Taiwanese government passed a law clearly defining direct selling and establishing specific rules of business management. Since this decree was legalized, the direct selling industry has mushroomed in Taiwan. According to one government survey report, 431 direct selling companies and 2,028,000 distributors were in Taiwan in 1994 (Xingzhengyuan Gongping Jiaoyi Weiyuanhui 1995). It should be noted, however, that most of these distributors were merely consumers (approximately 66 percent)—that is, they only consumed products but did not practice business. Therefore, if we count only the distributors who actually practiced direct selling, 690,000 were active distributors. Direct selling generated a profit of NT $40 billion (U.S. $1.4 billion) in 1994. A later report pointed out that these numbers had increased in 1995 and would continue to increase in the future (Xingzhengyuan Gongping Jiaoyi Weiyuanhui 1995). Lin (1994) also reported that, according to the World Federation of Direct Selling Associations, the business profit of direct selling in Taiwan was the sixth highest in the world, and the number of distributors in Taiwan was the fifth highest in the world in 1992. Undoubtedly, direct selling has prospered in Taiwan's market, and it has also become an alternative labor trend since the 1990s.

As direct selling has become a popular "second job" in contemporary Taiwan, the distribution of this enterprise is disproportionate on this island.[3] Nearly 80 percent of direct selling companies are in the metropolitan areas, especially in northern Taiwan (Xingzhengyuan Gongping Jiaoyi Weiyuanhui 1996). As a result, activities of direct selling such as business meetings, reward ceremonies, and family meetings are much more prevalent in such large cities as Taibei and Taizhong than in rural areas. These activities have become a new social phenomenon in urban Taiwan, and the accompanying cultural presentations are astonishing. Before proceeding to a case study of the Amway Company, I will first illuminate the economic and sociocultural factors within the context of which direct selling emerges in Taiwan.

SOCIAL CONTEXT OF THE DEVELOPMENT OF DIRECT SELLING

Direct selling—an industry that began in Taiwan with a negative and illegal image but turned into a popular business—has absorbed a considerable amount of capital and labor force on the island. In the early 1990s, when the Taiwanese market suffered from economic depression, direct selling was not affected at all. Rather, it began to occupy an important position in Taiwan's economy. Three structural factors supported this development: (1) postindustrial economic structures and labor trends; (2) capitalized social structures; and (3) the social values of economic success.

Postindustrial Economic Structures and Labor Trends

The prevalence of new types of economic activities is closely related to the economic structures of the times. The economic structures that supported the development of direct selling in Taiwan from the 1980s through the 1990s can be attributed to the transformation of two aspects: changes in the larger economic structures and labor trends.

Since 1981, the structural proportions of the agricultural and industrial sectors in Taiwan have been in decline and the service sector has been increasing (see Figure 2). Since 1988, the service sector has occupied more than 50 percent of the whole economic structure and thus dominates Taiwan's economy (Wu

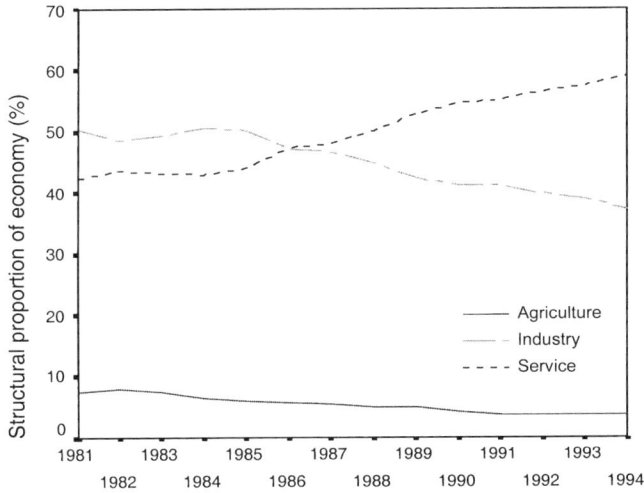

Figure 2. The changing economic structures in Taiwan (1981–1994). *Source:* Xingzheng-yuan Zhujichu (1995).

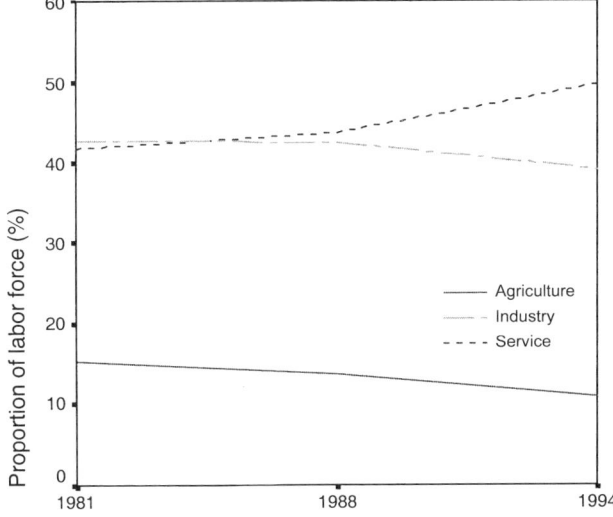

Figure 3. The changing sectional labor force in Taiwan (1981–1994). *Source:* Xingzheng-yuan Zhujichu (1995).

1994). On the other hand, labor structure was confronting a transformation coincident with the change in economic structures. The proportion of the labor force in the service sector was growing, while those in the agricultural and industrial sectors were decreasing (see Figure 3).

According to Wu (1994), this transformation in both the larger economic structure and labor trends is a feature of a "service economy" or a "postindustrial society." In other words, during the period when direct selling was introduced and grew to reign in Taiwan's market, the economic structures once dominated by industry were becoming service dominated. Hence the larger economic environment since the late 1980s provided great advantages for the direct selling industry, as a new form of service economy, to establish and expand its business in Taiwan.

Capitalized Social Structures

In the 1960s, numerous farming tenants became landowners because of the postwar policies of land reform, which consequently allowed real class mobility. Yet the economic structures encountered a transformation in the 1970s, when Taiwan began the process of industrialization and the development of capitalism. The industrial section continued to absorb capital and labor from the agriculture section. As a result, a new working class and a new white-collar class with professional techniques (also called the middle class) emerged in urban areas. Xiao (1988, 1989) uses the term "capitalization" to describe this transformation in social structures as resulting from the change in economic structures. He argues that the change in social structures corresponds to that in the economic development of capitalism; that is, the working class and the white-collar class replace the capitalists and farmers according to the needs of the industrial era. Xiao points out that such "capitalization" has been the main feature of the social structure in Taiwan since the 1970s.

The capitalized social structures have stabilized class structure in Taiwan. For more than two decades, the working class and the middle class have been the main classes in Taiwanese society (Xu 1994). In spite of the continuous differentiation within these two classes, the larger social structure has been very stable. This stability of social structures has made class mobility increasingly difficult in Taiwanese society (Xiao 1988, 1989). From 1950 to 1970, the rapid economic growth in Taiwan created miracles of class mobility. Many small businesses were started because of the prosperous economy during that period. In Taiwanese society, it was believed that the working class, even without capital, could succeed and ascend the social ladder with hard work.

Yet since the 1970s, the social structures in Taiwan have been relatively stabilized, and class mobility is no longer as common as before. Nevertheless, the legacy of "class turnover" from the old times remains in contemporary Taiwanese society. People still believe in the possibility of becoming millionaires and establishing their own businesses, as many capitalists have done in the past. Moreover, the popular folk belief, "Better to be the head of a chicken than the tail of a cow" *(Ningwei jishou, buwei niuhou),* motivates Taiwanese people to work hard and to climb the social class ladder in any way they can.

Within such social contexts, the successful stories of Amway distributors who became millionaires in a short period of time offer people the hope of possible class mobility through the direct marketing industry. The slogan of direct selling, "no investment, no risk" *(ling chengben, wu fengxian),* is also a temptation for those who want to own their businesses but lack the capital to do so. For those people who are tired of their routine jobs, the flexibility of practicing direct selling is also appealing. Therefore, to pursue their dreams of becoming millionaires, numerous Taiwanese people of various classes and occupations have become distributors.

Social Values of Economic Success

Taiwan's rapid economic growth in the 1970s and 1980s has been a historical miracle in Asia. The rich island has become a society within which people hold wealth in great regard, and thus economic success has become one of the major sources of social pressure. A person's success and social status are often judged by his or her financial situation, and this is the criterion upon which social recognition is based. People desire material goods and the capacity of consuming expensive commodities but are not overly concerned about the sources of wealth.

In direct selling, numerous stories regarding how distributors become wealthy in a short time, how they spend tons of money on luxury goods, and how they are respected and envied by others have made this business a dreamland for millions of distributors. In spite of the stigma of being labeled as part of a "mouse association," direct salespeople are willing to confront and conquer potential suspicion and devaluation from outsiders.

DISCIPLINED BODIES IN DIRECT SELLING: ALTERNATIVE ECONOMIC CULTURE IN URBAN TAIWAN

Amway Corporation was founded by Rich DeVos and Jay Van Andel in the United States in 1959. Amway's headquarters are located in Ada, Michigan, and it manufactures more than four hundred products (Anli Taiwan 1993). Amway has also established its branches in more than thirty countries and has had more than 3 million distributors worldwide. During the 1999 fiscal year, Amway generated approximately U.S. $5 billion in sales through this global product distribution network (Amway 2002).

Amway did not begin its Asian operations until 1974, when the Hong Kong Branch was established *(Gongshang zazhi* 1985). In 1982, Amway Corporation Taiwan Branch was launched in Taibei. During the business year of 1993–1994, its operating profit in Taiwan totaled NT $6 billion (U.S. $200 million). More than 180,000 Taiwanese people were registered as Amway distributors in 1996 (Anli Taiwan n.d.).

Stephen Butterfield (1985) and Dominique Xardel (1994) both interpret the term "Amway" as a synonym the "American Way of Life." They indicate that what Amway sells is not just its products but also a value system, a marketing and motivational system, a way of life, and political-religious revivalism. The values that Amway emphasizes—a spirit of free enterprise, cooperation, trust, wealth, and leisure—are all significant characteristics in American life. These values and morality enable Amway to approach the hearts and minds of the American people, an attribute that is often lacking in other corporations. Sociologist Nicole Biggart (1989) also points out that the direct selling industry relies on an "American ethic"—an ideology that creates and legitimates a desire for material wealth. This American ethic is the spirit of capitalism and a belief in the moral virtue of entrepreneurialism.

What happens when such an "American way of life" or "American ethic" is brought to Taiwan? How are the values central to the American society interpreted by Taiwanese people? How does Amway impact on Taiwan's economic culture? I attempt to answer these questions in the following pages.

Fieldwork Methodology

Three informal systems were operated in Amway during my period of fieldwork in 1996: Meihua (Plum Blossom), Feiying (Flying Eagle), and Chengguan (Cap of Maturity). Each system has its own pyramid scheme led by different Crown Ambassadors (the highest title in Amway). I joined the Meihua system, the largest community among these three. Two of the four Taiwanese Crown Ambassadors were from the Meihua system—Ms. Chen Wanfen and Ms. Huang Likai (a downline of Ms. Chen's)—which makes this community the most renowned in Amway. In spite of the fact that these three communities have established their own discourses and culture, their similarities surpass their differences because their behavioral norms are centered on the so-called Amway spirit or Amway values.

Ms. Chen Wanfen, the leader of the Meihua system and the first Amway Crown Ambassador in Taiwan, is a legend in this community. She grew up in a poor family in a rural area of the outlying island of Jinmen, and her father died before she was born. In spite of her outstanding performance in school, Ms. Chen's family could not afford her college education. For this reason, she chose to go to a teachers' school sponsored by the city government after graduating from junior high school and then became an elementary-school teacher. When she was in her thirties, dissatisfied by the fixed and limited salary of being a schoolteacher, Ms. Chen began to work as an Amway distributor in addition to her teaching job. Seeing Amway as an escape from the poverty she suffered throughout her childhood and adolescence, Ms. Chen thus devoted considerable time and effort to direct selling.

Ms. Chen's diligence paid off when she earned the highest title in Amway after nearly twenty years of hard work in the business. She established the Meihua system and began (in a huge pyramid scheme) to teach her downlines in much the same way that an elementary-school teacher does in a Taiwan classroom—that is, emphasizing the importance of life education. Incorporating both Amway's values and her own, Ms. Chen set certain moral and behavioral standards. She also asked distributors to call their uplines "teachers" *(laoshi)* and their downlines "babes" *(baobei)*.[4] These "teacher-student" and "parent-child" relations in the Meihua system not only build the fundamental power structures in this community but also legitimize various forms of regulation and discipline. Ms. Chen also claims that following her teaching is the only way to succeed in Amway, because she is the one who made her dream come true—going from a poor country girl to a multimillionaire.

Ms. Chen Wanfen's story is a legacy in Amway, and she has become a charismatic figure in that community. Distributors want to imitate her personal characteristics—and even to become her. They recite her story over and over to others and follow her teaching everywhere. Whenever Ms. Chen goes overseas, there are always thousands of distributors at the airport to see her off (some distributors even call in sick at work in order to see her in person at the airport). The same phenomenon can be seen when she returns. From my observations, Ms. Chen is not just the leader of this community—she is president of the Amway nation and a goddess of the Amway cult.

During my fieldwork, I saw Ms. Chen only once at a daily meeting. Although I jostled to the front of the crowd that surrounded her, I was able only to shake her hand. While I was feeling frustrated that I did not get the chance to talk to her that night, a distributor said to me in an amazed tone, "Wow, you are the luckiest person tonight! You got to shake Ms. Chen's hand! Congratulations!" This astonishing comment forcefully demonstrated the impact of Ms. Chen's charisma on Amway members. Amway is not just a business, it is a social phenomenon that contains prosperous sociocultural meanings.

THE AMWAY PHENOMENON IN TAIWAN: A PRESENTATION OF COLLECTIVE BODILY ORDER

Amway's direct salespeople are well known in Taiwan for their highly uniform discourses and gestures. Such a unique phenomenon—and its shocking impression to outsiders—can be expressed by a quote from Meiyu,[5] a nondistributor who had attended Amway's meeting and was astonished by what she saw. She said: "Every one of them said the same words, used the same gestures, and even smiled in the same way! It was like they were brainwashed! My goodness!"

Meiyu even described Amway as a "cult"—an organization with religious characteristics. Lihua, another nondistributor, correspondingly described her feeling of the cultlike culture in Amway: "It's really unbelievable! I don't know why they are so crazy about it. The atmosphere in that meeting was like a cult, with a lot of emotions going on. I felt that they were willing to sacrifice everything for this corporation."

Such quasi-religious characteristics and their effect on direct salespeople were well portrayed in an article that won a Documentary Literature Award from *China Times* in 1994: "I realized that whenever mentioning this business [direct selling], Richeng's eyes shine with incredible glory. He looks like a reverent believer who has received the message from God and guidance toward heaven" (Zheng 1994).

"The beautiful dream come true" is the common goal of direct salespeople, and it is also a phrase that is repeatedly emphasized in Amway's TV commercials in Taiwan. This beautiful dream includes wealth, freedom, leisure, success, love, and trust. Amway is depicted as the key, and the only key, to turning this dream into reality. In order to make this wonderful dream come true, therefore, distributors are required to transform themselves into believers of Amway as "the savior," followers of their uplines as "guidance teachers," and advocates of Amway values as their behavioral norms. All of these characteristics feature Amway as a quasi-religious community—or simply as a cult.

Amway's daily meetings serve not only as an exhibition of its cultlike culture but also as the practice of internalizing its behavioral norms and discourses. Once registered with Amway, distributors are expected to attend daily meetings in order to learn and carry out the Amway way of talking, gesturing, perceptions, and behavior—even before beginning to sell products and recruit downlines. Unlike other direct selling companies' OPP[6] meetings that mainly focus on the introduction of direct selling business and reward systems, Amway's daily meetings are organized in a quasi-educational and quasi-religious way. With the exception of one day a week that is dedicated to introducing the business, Amway's meetings have themes such as "The Path to Success," "Skills of Interpersonal Communication," "Self-Growth," "Beauty and Self-Care," "Nutrition and Health," "The Importance of Helping Others," and "The Key to Happiness." Participants are told to learn "the way of life," rather than "the business." By making this claim, Amway legitimates its education of values, attitudes, and behaviors and thereby creates its religious aura. In doing so, Amway not only whitewashes the stigma of direct selling as a "mouse association" that treats social networks as mere commodities—it also disguises its primary goal of profit making. As a result, Amway distributors regard themselves as educators (of Amway's way of life) and preachers (of Amway's values), rather than merely as salespeople.

Certain rituals are routinely held at Amway's daily meetings to assure members' uniform beliefs, discourses, and behavior. The meeting usually starts with short talks by two or three distributors who have earned titles for their sales achievements (see the appendix for a description of Amway's formal reward and title system).

These speakers tell their personal stories about how they succeed in a way not unlike that of a minister speaking about the miracles of Christianity. For instance, they might relate how poor and unhappy they were before becoming

Amway distributors; how Amway changed their lives in the wink of an eye; how Amway gave them the great opportunity to live happily and wealthily; how grateful they are for Amway and their uplines; how Amway provides a hospitable home; and how others who have not yet joined Amway are suffering from misery and poverty.

Becoming wealthy in a short time is the most appealing part of these stories. Speakers repeatedly emphasize that only Amway can make this "miracle" happen, a dream that no ordinary wage worker could ever truly realize. Moreover, these stories attempt to stimulate among the audience another form of desire: that of enjoying other people's envy at their own luxurious lifestyles. Many stories begin with how the speakers were looked down upon before they became rich and end with how other people envy their wealth. In these "before and after" stories, the power of money reinforces the motivation of becoming rich through Amway. The following accounts—stories that I heard from distributors—demonstrate the ways in which Amway members perceive the power of money:

> I have a friend who used to look down upon me when he knew I was a distributor. But ever since I bought a BMW [with earnings from Amway], his attitudes and the way he talks to me have been totally different than before [he became respectful and envious].

> Mr. Yang, a Diamond Direct Distributor in Amway, began his direct selling business in his freshman year. Throughout his college years, his classmates often looked down upon him, teasing him that he was a slave of money. On his graduation day, he donated NT $100,000 [U.S.$ 3,500] to his university. It was only then that he regained his classmates' respect.

Obviously, distributors are aware of the fact that outsiders often stigmatize direct selling, and some of them are even victims of such stigma. Yet after becoming wealthy, especially after being able to exercise the power that money provides, distributors feel entitled to whitewash the stigma and legitimate their business activities.

The same two stories above, along with numerous others, are often recited either in informal conversations in this community or at formal meetings. During my fieldwork in Amway, these stories were repeatedly told by several different distributors. Of course, the details in each story might vary slightly when told by different members, but the main characters and conclusions are all the same. Every time, when any of these stories is recited, a feeling of déjà vu emerges. Consequently, after participating in this community for a while, I could even tell some of the stories to others in a similar way. It is through such storytelling acts that distributors homogenize discourses. This act of storytelling also plays a role similar to that of witnessing in religion. Direct salespeople use these stories to persuade and convince nonmembers that joining Amway can actually make their dreams come true, just like those in the stories. The stories assert, "They did it, so can you!"

The skill of storytelling in this community is not learned just by listening but through diligent work. During the speeches at the daily meetings, Amway members always take notes in order to record important information—words or phrases—that they can apply to their own discourses in the future. Then the members have small group discussions based on their upline-downline connections.[7] In this group discussion, which is called "sharing time" *(fenxiang shijian),* each member repeats what the speakers have just said and praises the valuable wisdom of their words. Most of the time, members have to look at their notes in order to repeat what the speakers say correctly and exactly. Sometimes, when a member mentions a phrase heard at another meeting, others write it down in order to enrich their collections of "Amway wisdom." When this happens, the next person who talks will usually praise and repeat this new wisdom. During this sharing time, members always give their complete attention to the one who is speaking, nod their heads, applaud, and cheer for each other. The more someone can recite the original talks, the more that person earns others' admiration, assurance, and praise. Consequently, participants learn and even memorize a couple of sentences or stories at each meeting, because these words have been repeatedly stated in the same way—and mostly in the same terms—during a three-hour meeting.

Such repetition assures Amway members' uniformity of language, perceptions, and behavior. As their leader Ms. Chen Wanfen claims, "There is only one way to success—that is, the way I succeeded. Follow me, my babes! Copy my ability, my knowledge, and my accomplishment!"

This one-way approach establishes and legitimizes the "requirement" for members to imitate Ms. Chen's ways of thought, speech, and behavior. By replicating her behavior and thoughts, members are assured that they can be "rescued" and will enjoy a "sacred" wealthy life set apart from a secular, ordinary, boring, and restless existence. Hence the importance of imitation is repeatedly emphasized in this community. For example, one day in the daily meeting, a high-level distributor, Guoxiong, reminded everyone that they should show more thoroughness and effort on imitating their leader. He said: "If we want to succeed, we must follow our leader's steps and copy all of her abilities. I feel that we are behind. Last month when I followed Ms. Chen to China, I witnessed how excited and serious those Chinese members were. Many of them videorecorded Ms. Chen's speech and watched the tape over and over at home in order to imitate her every single word and smile. We must reflect upon ourselves and show more efforts to our leader."

Such discourse conveys an image to the members that "once you can act like our leader, you could become her—a wealthy and successful distributor." As a result, the daily meeting becomes a stage where its members perform Amway's way of life based on a standard script day after day. Furthermore, the Amway salespeople's bodies become not only the medium of such acting but also the product of the body plastic that exhibits a collective bodily order. At the individual level, the body is supposed to be both the medium and product of self-expression and self-presentation that depicts unique personal characteristics.

In Amway, this individual bodily performance must be adjusted and smelted to an unvaried collective portrayal. As a result, the Amway people's corporeality becomes a resocialized and reregulated body that carries their organizational features and discourse.

Amway is a direct selling industry that produces disciplined bodies in addition to an alternative economic culture (Gu 1997). Every member is required to act, talk, and even dress in the same fashion, because it is claimed that this is the only way to succeed in Amway. For example, appearance is one of the emphases in Amway's behavioral standards. Members are taught to dress in a "successful way"—that is, men should wear suits and even apply a little bit of foundation to appear neat, while women should wear dresses or suits and definitely wear makeup. Under such a norm, distributors who are college or graduate students and who usually wear T-shirts and jeans during the daytime have to change before attending Amway's nightly meeting. Newcomers who do not dress in the same way, therefore, could be easily recognized—especially a woman without makeup.

As distributor Lifang told me, it is very easy to tell if someone is an Amway member or not just from "the way she or he looks." Members' uniform body language and discourses turn the Amway daily meeting into an exhibition of docile bodies. In Amway, individuals' personal characteristics are replaced with aggregated attributes, and their bodies are well disciplined, socialized, and transformed. As a result, the corporeality in Amway is not an arena of self-expression that demonstrates individual diversities—it is a presentation of the collective bodily order. This feature enables its members to distinguish themselves from outsiders, whose bodies have not been "reproduced" yet by Amway's "corporeal industry."

As an observing researcher participating in Amway's activities, I was forced (either consciously or unconsciously) to adopt Amway's behaviors to a certain extent. For instance, during the early stages of my fieldwork, I felt somewhat awkward that I seemed to stand out easily simply because I wasn't wearing any makeup. Distributors often asked me if I was a newcomer. After a while, I decided to change my style of dress and began to wear some makeup in order to at least appear like an insider and fit in this community by conforming to its customs and behavioral norms. Similar conforming transformations take place much more easily and quickly for new distributors as they commit to this group. Even if new members do not (or do not know how to) dress "correctly," other old birds show concern and give them advice. Consequently, in Amway, any deviant body performance played out by outsiders can be identified, because it breaks the orderliness of this community. For individuals, conforming to this "sameness" also feels more comfortable than being different or odd in a group. In other words, the collective bodily order in Amway is actually produced by both external and internal forces. Thus it is not only organizational norms that create the so-called Amway phenomenon—it is also the members' conformity.

In addition, Amway emphasizes that "direct selling is a way of life, rather than a business" (DeVos and Andel 1992). As Wenhui, a five-year Amway distributor, said: "Direct selling is not a job. Rather, it is life. Each distributor is like a twenty-four-hour department store. Every morning when you wake up, your store is open, and it won't be closed until you go to bed. In other words, Amway is not work but my way of life. We are always doing direct selling in our everyday life without a single break."

As a human "twenty-four-hour department store," every distributor attempts to introduce Amway or sell products to people whenever they can. Direct selling is usually a second job for most distributors, but it is actually practiced without any time constraints in everyday life. At their day jobs, distributors talk about Amway with coworkers whenever they have the opportunity.[8] After work, they usually attend Amway's nightly meetings. On weekends or holidays, Amway people either hold "family meetings" or go shopping together.

In Amway, members who have the same original uplines—or those within the same pyramid scheme—establish a quasi-familial bond. Each "family" holds "family meetings" regularly on weekends. Members take turns to host these meetings in their own houses. The format of these family meetings is similar to that at Amway's daily meetings, but the scale is smaller. Distributors invite their "potential downlines" to these meetings and introduce Amway to them. In other words, members in each quasi-family practice direct selling mostly in a collective way. They often bring friends to these meetings and let other members take on the task of persuasion. By so doing, distributors can avoid possible embarrassment while attempting to sell products to friends or to recruit friends as their downlines (both methods, it should be noted, are attempts to earn money from friends). Although Amway people adopt this collective fashion of doing business, they do not compete for credits or profits. They acknowledge who is whose "potential babe" (potential downline) and help each other to earn the newcomers' trust.

Distributors who belong to the same "family" sometimes go shopping together. Yet their shopping activities actually carry a special "mission"—recruiting strangers as potential downlines. When practicing direct selling, distributors usually start from their own social networks, such as their family members, relatives, friends, and neighbors. In practice, however, solely relying on personal networks will not be enough if a distributor wants to earn titles or millions. Extending downlines beyond personal networks is therefore essential. Recruiting downlines from strangers or remote acquaintances sometimes reduces distributors' anxieties of being perceived by friends as putting profit before friendship. By means of shopping collectively, Amway people attempt to seize the opportunity of recruiting store clerks—and even other customers—as new members. They might talk about Amway with the clerks while shopping or, when in a coffee shop or a restaurant, see people sitting next to them as potential downlines. In other words, Amway distributors practice direct selling whenever they can in everyday life, since they are themselves "twenty-four-hour department stores."

According to such a "working is living" principle, the practice of Amway sellers is limitless in their daily life, in which the distinction between labor/production and leisure/reproduction is negated. Unlike wageworkers whose labor sphere and personal life are separated, Amway members' work and private spheres overlap and are guided by Amway's way of life (an American way of life?). Ergo, they are not just the *agents* of Amway's products but the very *products* of Amway per se. Since "there is only one way to success," as Ms. Chen Wanfen claims, Amway becomes the dominant force that governs how its members' lives should be lived and how members' bodies should act and move. Once a direct salesperson has been resocialized by the Amway's body techniques, his or her individual bodily performance portrays and mirrors the collective regulation within the Amway community.[9] Even when alone, such an aggregate of motions, postures, and gestures can still be observed in one's individual bodily presentation. In the next section, I will demonstrate how such bodily order is formed and maintained in Amway.

REPRODUCING AMWAY BODIES: DISCIPLINE AND SURVEILLANCE OF KNOWLEDGE/POWER

Amway people claim that it is the "knowledge" they possess that distinguishes them from outsiders. As Ms. Chen, leader of the Meihua Amway system, said: "We are here to learn how to live a worthy life. Many people out there are experts in their professional arenas but idiots in running their lives. People's perceptions determine how their lives are, and that is why I'm teaching you my knowledge and perspectives of success. As direct salespeople, we are selling knowledge of life rather than products. Our goal is to help people learn the right ideas about life."

The "knowledge of life" in the Amway community includes the knowledge/philosophy/value of human life, success, marriage, work, nutrition, cooking, and cosmetology, which covers a wide range of everyday life. In the members' views, the act of telling others about Amway and recruiting them is bestowing a favor upon them, because they offer others the opportunity to learn the "right" ideas and knowledge about life. "We are selling knowledge," "We are helping others," state Amway members. From the Amway members' viewpoint, direct selling is not a business or economic activity anymore. Instead, it is a quasi-educational institute, teaching people how to live their lives, and it is a quasi-religious organization, saving people from poverty and endless labor in "traditional" jobs.[10] Based on this recognized ideology, Amway people construct their social reality, perceiving themselves as educators and prophets rather than as salespeople.

Ironically, knowledge of life has its price in Amway. It is not "free of charge." Once I asked a distributor, who was an Amway "nutrition expert," about how to change my diet in order to improve my health. I was expecting some simple advice when raising that question, as a friend or a teacher would offer when one needed help. Yet that distributor's answer was, "You have to attend our nutrition classes." Attending the "basic" nutrition class that contained four sessions costs NT $1000 (U.S. $35), and the "advanced" and "professional" classes, also based on certain product lines, cost even more.

Amway's classes are usually held at the same time and location as daily meetings but in different rooms. Each series contains basic, advanced, and professional classes and charges various fees. Therefore, when preparing themselves for the "knowledge sale," distributors have to pay a lot of money out of their own pockets, even though this contradicts the direct selling slogan: "No business capital is required." In addition to paying and attending various classes, distributors sometimes have to participate in Amway retreats to learn the secrets of the trade. Meetings like the "Gold Producers Retreat" and "Ruby Direct Distributors Retreat" are usually held for certain groups of distributors who then have to pay their own travel and accommodation expenses. Consequently, the reality is that before becoming successful distributors or millionaires, Amway members have to invest a considerable amount of money. For working-class people who lack capital, the "Amway dream" is more of a fantasy than an achievable goal—let alone a means of achieving real class mobility.

Furthermore, since "there is only one way to success," members must believe in this claim and regard Amway's knowledge of life as "the only truth." Regardless of one's class, ethnicity, or gender in the "outside" world, everyone must start over upon entering the Amway community. It is similar to a religion: Once baptized, many start a new life following this religion's values as the only truth in their life.

The "goddess" of Amway, Ms. Chen Wanfen, rules the "cult of the Meihua community." By claiming that her wisdom is "the only path" to success, Ms. Chen's discourse and behavior impose an absolute power over Amway members. In the meantime, the members' desire to become wealthy—as well as their acknowledgement of Ms. Chen's claim—enforces such power hierarchies. As Foucault (1980, 59) states, "Power is strong at the level of desire and also at the level of knowledge." Ms. Chen's fortune and success provoke Amway members' desire and envy. Her utilization of knowledge (of life) as the key to success and the distinction between insiders and outsiders, therefore, works as a spell, governing members' behaviors and perceptions. In other words, Ms. Chen's discourse creates tremendous power in the Amway community, and the members' bodies become the arenas where such power takes effect. Within Amway, the collective constraining force derived from this power/discourse overcomes individuals' subjectivity and thus reproduces numerous docile bodies.

Ms. Chen's discourse, knowledge, and power not only generate voluntary body discipline among Amway members, they also create an automatic mutual surveillance among them. For instance, the "sharing time" in their daily meeting executes the task of such surveillance. By repeating their leader's words and imitating her gestures and behaviors, Amway members earn applause and reassurance. In this community, members mutually supervise each other, verbally and nonverbally, on the "right" way they should act and the "right" thoughts they should think. Not only are all members mirroring the leaders' characteristics, but they are also mirroring other members. Even when the members are alone, they are expected to supervise themselves, because "direct selling is a way of life." When internalizing Amway values and practicing Amway's way of life, distributors' perceptions of the distinctions between work and personal lives and between individual and collective spheres do not exist anymore. Every single distributor turns out to be a corporeal product of the Amway factory, carrying Amway's patent and components. Ms. Chen's teaching serves to provide members with specific meanings of life/work. Through bodily practice, Amway people recognize, experience, and reproduce such meanings. In these ways, the collective bodily order in Amway is formed and maintained.

BODY RESISTANCE IN STRUGGLE: SUCCESS AT COST IN AMWAY

The resocialization and reproduction of Amway bodies is not always a smooth or instant transformation. Instead, it is an ongoing process within which the body is always experiencing two countering forces between the outside-in constraints (from the Amway community) and inside-out enabling (from the previous social self and inner emotion). Before entering the Amway community, each distributor has already been socialized by the broader society and has formed certain perceptions, modes of behavior, and even bodily gestures. Reshaping the self and the body in adulthood thus requires more effort than it does in childhood. The elimination of the division between work and leisure in direct selling entraps distributors in a continuous laboring state and self-surveillance. No matter what emotion they have or what situations they encounter in everyday life, Amway people are expected to act like "standard Amway bodies." This means that Amway distributors not only perform bodily labor but also emotional labor (Hochschild 1983) in that they constantly have to manage and control their own emotions. Mingren, a one-year Amway distributor, once told me his management of personal emotion: "Two months ago, my dad had a heart attack and was hospitalized. I was very sad and worried, but I had to stop crying and come to our daily meeting. In Amway, you have to smile and laugh."

Emotional management is not easy for everyone. As Jialing, a former five-year Amway distributor said: "I felt very tired after a period of hard work. In Amway, you have to maintain a high emotional level every day, no matter what. It was very tiring. I always thought it would be wonderful if I could take off just one day and spend some time with my family. I think Amway is for those people who are strong, because it's very difficult to overcome that kind of fatigue."

Because they think becoming a millionaire will result in unlimited freedom, "laboring for no more labor" (Gu 1997) is the goal of distributors' hard work. But the reward system of direct selling actually prevents distributors from ceasing work, because profits would decrease. As a result, most distributors are trapped in an endless labor process and an incessant disciplining of bodies and emotions in their community (Gu 2000).

Does everyone under the regulation of this community succeed in being blessed by the Amway legacy? The Taiwanese government evaluated distributors of high, medium, and low levels in the direct selling industry.[11] According to this report, only 11.83 percent of distributors are at the higher level, whereas the majority (65.38 percent) are at the lower level (Xingzhengyuan Gongping Jiaoyi Weiyuanhui 1993). Regardless of the fact that only about one-tenth of them are on the top of this pyramid, millions of distributors maintain their faith in direct selling. Also, in spite of the exhaustion resulting from endless work in Amway, numerous members continue to embrace the dream of becoming millionaires.

Amway's strategy of objectifying failure helps to maintain such a dreamy atmosphere, as distributors only see successful cases in this community. In Amway, members' success is said to be an organizational and collective outcome, whereas failure is due to personal factors. Talking about failure is taboo in Amway because "you will become what you talk about and look at." Distributors are encouraged to discuss only successful cases, and any failure is regarded as a "personal problem." They are also told to avoid keeping in touch with those members who quit. Consequently, the downside of direct selling and the frustrations of being distributors are never mentioned in this community. The beautiful dream, therefore, retains its legacy in Amway.

Underneath the disguise of the beautiful dream of direct selling, there are actually numerous distributors who are struggling with feelings of burnout and frustration, and many of them quit after various lengths of hard work. Thus it appears that human corporeality is not merely a docile body passively dominated and manipulated by social forces. Instead, it has its inner drive of emotion that generates a potentiality of resistance. As Foucault argues, "Power, after investing itself in the body, finds itself exposed to a counterattack in that same body" (1980, 56).

Before becoming 100 percent "corporeal products" of Amway, distributors usually wander back and forth between the two opposing forces—Amway's regulatory forces versus their inner emotion and selves. When the outside constraints overcome the inner drive, the uniform Amway body is on the "production line" and distributors become the standardized products of the Amway industry. But when the resistant potentiality exercises its capacity of enabling the self and conquers the external domination, the self regains its empowerment and embodiment. Under such circumstances, distributors are therefore willing and able to escape from the disciplinary forces. Here is what several ex-distributors told me:

> Direct selling is "doing simple stuff repeatedly." Yet you'd feel very tired and bored after a while, because what you do every day is all the same. There's no variation in your life.

I felt exhausted. Every day when I went to the meeting, I had to smile and act energetically. I was really emotionally exhausted. I felt that I just wanted to take a break and be with my family for a day or so.

I ran into a member one day after I quit. He just quit Amway and told me several others did, too. We realized that we experienced the same kind of frustrations and tiredness while in Amway, but we never had the chance to talk about that before. We were not allowed to. In Amway, you only talk about success and joy.

CONCLUSION

Despite the stigma of the Taiwan Family event, direct selling has become a popular second job in Taiwan since the 1990s. The legalization of direct marketing, as well as certain structural factors, helped prepare a beneficial environment for the development and growth of direct selling on the island. As a new labor form of the service economy, direct selling has its advantages in Taiwan's market, in which the economic structure has been dominated by the service sector. As a new path of class mobility, direct selling provides the hope of becoming a millionaire in Taiwanese society, where this mobility has become more and more difficult. The economic opportunities direct selling offers also correspond to the popular social values that place a high regard on financial success. All of these economic, social, and cultural factors have helped to build the direct selling regime in Taiwan. Meanwhile, the popularization of direct selling also reflects these sociocultural characteristics of Taiwanese society.

This case study of Amway provides an analysis of the micropolitics in the direct selling community. In Amway, distributors are taught to behave and talk in a uniform manner that displays a collective bodily order. By claiming that she holds the only path to success, Amway's leader commands members' absolute obedience in that no suspicion or discussion of failures is allowed. Amway becomes a totalitarian community that imposes a powerful disciplinary force on its members' minds and bodies. Under mutual and self-surveillance, distributors are engaging in an endless process of remaking their selves, their bodies, and their emotions. The collective bodily order of Amway is successfully maintained when the disciplinary force overcomes individuals' inabilities. Yet distributors' bodily resistance can also defeat this constraint and revitalize the individuals' subjectivity and embodiment.

When practicing direct selling, distributors claim that they are actually selling knowledge and helping others, with an attempt to whitewash the stigma of the "mouse association." Their economic motivations are disguised by noneconomic purposes, which also serves to legitimatize their cultlike behavior. The quasi-religious and quasi-educational figures of Amway have given direct selling rich social and cultural meanings that go beyond an economic action. The alternative economic culture that direct selling has produced in urban Taiwan has also highlighted certain attributes and trends of Taiwanese culture today.

First, people tend to seek "shortcuts" for achieving economic success. The merit of hard work is not necessarily appreciated in contemporary Taiwan. As a folk proverb goes, "Three features compose a good job: lots of money, little work, and close to home *[qian duo, shi shao, li jia jin]*"—what people desire from work is instant and great financial reward. This phenomenon is similar to Robert Weller's observation (1996) that success seems less likely the result of hard work than of good luck in modern times. Taiwanese people retain the mentality of "better to be the head of a chicken than the tail of a cow" from old times, but nowadays the quick and easy means of "becoming the head of a chicken" is preferred over the ethic of hard work valued in the past.

Second, people tend to "sacralize" their economic motivations. In spite of the desire and social pressure to attain financial success, Taiwanese people are inclined to conceal their intention of making profit, especially in public. In traditional Confucian culture, businessmen are ranked in the lowest category in the order of occupational reputation: "intellectuals, farmers, industrial workers, and businessmen" *(shi, nong, gong, shang)*. Such a cultural heritage shapes Taiwanese people's ambivalent views concerning business or businesslike activities. While society places high pressure on financial achievement, it also devalues profit-oriented behavior. Legitimizing (even "sacralizing") economic actions therefore becomes not only important but necessary for businesspeople to establish their reputations and social status. In the case of Amway, distributors claiming to be "knowledge sellers" and "saviors" represent such an effort, in addition to whitewashing the stigma of direct selling.

Third, there is the common need to seek a group that provides moral guidance and feelings of belonging. Like their Western counterparts who live in the modern era, Taiwanese face increasingly serious moral crisis and alienation. The prosperous economy and advanced technology have brought better material goods, but the meaning of life seems to have been gradually lost. In this vacuum, the traditional moral values Amway advocates, such as trust, love, reciprocity, and respect, as well as the quasi-familial ties in this community, have created a paradise-like atmosphere for distributors. Similar to a religious group, Amway constructs a system of beliefs and behavioral norms that serve to provide moral guidance and meaning for its members. Yet the economic opportunities Amway offers are benefits individuals cannot get from religion. In sum, then, Amway not only meets people's need of searching for meaning and values in modern alienated times, it also meets the need of financial success in a material-oriented secular society.

Western scholars (Biggart 1989; Butterfield 1985; Cross 1999; Xardel 1994) continue to discuss "the American way of life" and "the American spirit." Meanwhile, Amway and other DSOs in Taiwan have incorporated into their "Amway way" many local, social, and cultural characteristics in response to structural changes and contexts. Taiwan's Amway community has taken what was once

Amway's "American way" and used Taiwanese ways of life and culture to influence and transform it in many ways. As David Harvey (1989) correctly points out, capitalism is a revolutionary mode of production. It keeps finding new organizational types, techniques, lifestyles, and new ways of production and exploitation. Like other forms of capitalism, direct selling has created a new mode of production that links both local and global markets and meets both economic and noneconomic needs in modern times. Yet it has also produced a new form of exploitation and false consciousness. While embracing the dream of unlimited wealth and freedom, distributors are actually trapped in an endless process of labor. While believing in love, trust, and equality, distributors are actually manipulated by the invisible power of discipline.

APPENDIX: AMWAY REWARD SYSTEM (SOURCE: CROSS 1999)

Distributor
Earn profits through retail markup on products sold, plus bonuses of 3 to 25 percent based on Point Value (PV), which averages approximately 50 percent of wholesale prices paid on total business volume.

Silver Producer
For one month, generate personal group PV of at least 7,500 points, or sponsoring a 25 percent group (one containing a qualifying Silver Producer or Direct Distributor) and generating at a personal group PV of at least 2,500 points, or sponsor two 25 percent groups in the same month, or foster sponsor a 25 percent group and have PV or 2,500 points.

Gold Producer
Generate three Silver Producer months in a year.

Direct Distributor
For six months of a fiscal year, generate PV of at least 7,500 personal group points, or sponsor a 25 percent group with 2,500 personal group points, or sponsor two 25 percent groups in those months, or foster sponsor a 25 percent group plus achieve PV of at least 2,500 points.

Founders Direct Distributor Pin
Maintain twelve months of Direct Distributor qualification in a fiscal year.

Ruby Direct Distributor
Generate personal group PV of 15,000 or more points in a given month.

Founders Ruby Pin
Maintain Ruby qualification for twelve months within a fiscal year.

Sapphire Pin

Direct Distributors below Emerald who have either three groups qualifying for six months in a fiscal year, or 2,500 Award Volume over the same two qualified groups for each of six months in the fiscal year, or a combination of both.

Emerald Direct Distributor

Direct Distributors who personally, internationally, or foster sponsor three or more qualified groups for at least six months of a fiscal year.

Founders Emerald Pin

Maintain Emerald qualifications for twelve months within a fiscal year.

Diamond Direct Distributor

Direct Distributors who personally, internationally, or foster sponsor six qualified groups for at least six months of the fiscal year.

Additional Pin Levels

Executive Diamond Distributors who personally, internationally, or foster sponsor nine qualified groups for at least six months of the fiscal year; a Double Diamond does so with twelve groups, a Triple Diamond with fifteen groups, a Crown Direct with eighteen groups, and Crown Ambassador with twenty groups.

PART V
Entertainment and the Audience
LIVING FOR THE MOMENT
AND MOMENTS FOR THE LIVING

9
Baseball, History, the Local and the Global in Taiwan
Andrew D. Morris

EDITORS' INTRODUCTION

Baseball, like other sports, is entertainment. Also like other sports, it can be much more than that. Taiwan is a small place, yet its Little League teams became the most famous in the world. How can this possibly have happened? Clearly, baseball is something special in Taiwan. But baseball is an American game. Why would it become special in Taiwan?

In this chapter, Andrew Morris traces the particular case of baseball and shows how it has never been just entertainment for Taiwan. Taiwanese are fully aware of baseball's American and Japanese roots; it was introduced during the Japanese period. These associations make baseball cosmopolitan, international, and globally significant. The success of local teams in foreign fields takes on a cosmic significance as Taiwan shows itself internationally a force to be reckoned with. When its Little League players won international championship after international championship, Taiwan's position as a uniquely important world power simply could not be ignored, at least in this sphere. That was, of course, deeply satisfying.

Furthermore, since participation in amateur baseball is accessible to anyone with a bat and a ball—and since any school can afford the basic equipment for a small baseball team—players of talent can emerge anywhere. The internationally successful teams were drawn from counties and towns all up and down the island, filling baseball with the homey aura of heartland participation and the delicious possibility of rapid fame. A Taiwan baseball team was not just from Taibei or Tainan or Jiayi. It was pan-Taiwanese.

The constant threats of conquest by mainland China over half a century have contributed to a growing sense of Taiwan being separate from China and of Taiwanese being different from Chinese. With the end of martial law, the assertion of independent Taiwanese identity has become far more open, and baseball, like other cultural expressions, reflects this. Baseball may even reflect the difference more than many other areas, because what stands out in Taiwanese baseball is not dependent on a broader Chinese heritage of its participants. It is not, after all, originally a Chinese game. To the extent that athletics involves Taiwan in an international arena, the identity of its teams and its people as Taiwanese in contrast to Chinese is thrown into particularly high relief.

From the beginning, baseball in Taiwan has had wider implications worthy of attention. In Taiwan, baseball was introduced as modernizing under the Japanese administration and evolved into a source of players for Japan's national teams. But as Taiwan's players gained the skills necessary to be taken seriously by Japanese teams, Morris argues, the clear implication was that in other ways, Taiwanese could also be the equal of Japanese, thus subverting the whole notion of Taiwanese subordination in Japan's colonial empire. Generalizing from this example, we may argue that obvious competence in a field as visible as competitive sports is inherently subversive of almost any outside attempt to classify a population as naturally or properly subordinate. Competitive sports, in other words, are inherently democratizing.

It is little wonder, then, that baseball has almost necessarily evolved in our era into a symbol of Taiwan's unique culture and its unique destiny. ∎

On March 25, 2000, Chen Shui-bian (Chen Shuibian) chose a special engagement for his first public appearance as Taiwan's new president-elect. That night, Chen spoke at the Taiwan Major League's opening game, which also served as the opening ceremony of the new Chengqing Lake Stadium in Gaoxiong County. Before the contest between the Taizhong Robots and the Gaoxiong-Pingdong Thunder Gods began, the capacity crowd heard the president-elect describe baseball as a "symbol of the Taiwanese spirit" in announcing that he would designate 2001 "Taiwan Baseball Year" and consider Gaoxiong County Magistrate Yu Zhengxian's proposal to designate baseball as Taiwan's national sport. In his customary self-deprecating fashion, Chen confessed to a childhood fascination with baseball and joked that he decided to be president only after he realized he was not athletic enough to succeed in baseball (*TTO* 2000; *HXXWW* 2000).[1]

President Chen's official attention to the game marks only the latest chapter in the history of Taiwanese baseball, a culture that has become much more than just a sport. It is a colonial legacy that was planted and sunk deep roots during the fifty-year Japanese occupation of the island from 1895 to 1945. The professional version of the game in Taiwan today is experienced as a reminder of the profound influence of American and Japanese culture—and indeed of transnational capitalism in Taiwan at the turn of the century. At the same time that these foreign legacies are crucial to the creation of Taiwanese cultural artifacts like baseball, other "Chinese" factors make the picture even more complicated. More than four decades of living under an authoritarian Chinese Nationalist (Guomindang) regime—combined with the feelings of fear and isolation produced by the blustery nationalism now emanating from the People's Republic of China (PRC)—have also led Taiwanese to fervently and enthusiastically celebrate their uniqueness, linguistic and otherwise, vis-à-vis the "Chinese mainland."

The combination of these interrelated legacies has thus given rise to the remarkable and striking quality of contemporary Taiwanese culture—namely, its strong dual emphases on and blending of the global and the local. Professional baseball in Taiwan is a perfect instance of this self-conscious, ideological combination of the global and the local, the cosmopolitan and the provincial, the international and the Taiwanese. The short history of professional baseball in Taiwan is in many ways nothing more or less than the history of the effort to create a "baseball culture" that could speak to both of these striking and complementary aspects of Taiwanese life.

The conditions outlined above make Taiwanese professional baseball unique in the sporting world. Models of colonial sport, such as that portrayed in the film *Trobriand Cricket,* where natives of the Trobriand Islands of Papua New Guinea transform cricket into a magical, mocking send-up of the colonial game (Leach 1975), are clearly not useful in analyzing contemporary Taiwanese sport. Since World War II, the global relevance of modern sport and the emphasis on international adherence to these models has made it impractical or even impossible to imagine wholesale Taiwanese transformations of baseball.[2] In fact, the application of any standard model of colonialism simply fails to capture the complexity of Taiwan's recent history under the hegemony of Japanese, Chinese Nationalist, and American colonial and military regimes. Instead, this chapter examines the conscious construction of Taiwanese professional baseball as an avenue that leads both to globalization and international acceptance, as well as to a local and unique Taiwanese identity.

BASEBALL IN THE JAPANESE COLONIAL ERA

Baseball in Taiwan, introduced by the Japanese colonial regime, has never thoroughly shed its Japanese heritage. From the name of the game, still called by many in Taiwanese *yagyu* (from the Japanese *yakyū* and not the Mandarin *bangqiu*), to the Taiwanese-Japanese-English playground calls of *"stu-rii-ku"* and *"out-tow,"* baseball's Japanese "origins" are still an important part of Taiwanese heritage. The sport, well developed in Japanese schools by the 1890s (Roden 1980, 520–529), was imported to the colony of Taiwan around 1897, just two years after its incorporation into the Japanese Empire (Cai 1992, 13).[3] Initially played by colonial bureaucrats, bankers, and their sons in Taihoku (Taibei), baseball spread to southern Taiwan by 1910. In 1915, the colonial government formed the Taiwan Baseball Federation, made up of fifteen (all-Japanese) school teams playing the quickly growing sport (Gao 1994, 45; Zhan 1985, 435).

It was not long before Taiwanese youth joined in this new fun. Around 1910, Taiwan Governor-General Sakuma Samata encouraged the development of the sport among Taiwanese youth. As he explained it, this was his humble way of repaying the local Taiwanese deity Mazu, who in 1906 had appeared to his ailing wife in a dream and miraculously cured her (Gao 1994, 41). In 1921, a Hualian native named Lin Guixing formed the Takasago Baseball Team of Ami aborigine boys. Two years later the team changed its name to the High-Ability (Nōkō) Baseball Team when they all enrolled in the Hualian Harbor Agricultural Study Institute. Lin and his Nōkō team achieved great fame when they traveled to Japan in the summer of 1925 and won five of six games against Japanese school teams there.

The most famous of all Taiwanese baseball traditions was that born at the Tainan District Jiayi Agriculture and Forestry Institute (abbreviated Kanō) in the late 1920s. Under the guidance of Manager Kondō Hyōtarō, a former standout player who had toured the United States with his high school team, Kanō dominated Taiwan baseball in the decade before the Pacific War. What made the Kanō team special was its tri-ethnic composition: In 1931, its starting nine comprised two Han Taiwanese, four Taiwan aborigines, and three Japanese players (Su 1996, 10; Zheng 1993, 109–115).[4] Kanō won the Taiwan championship, earning the right to play in the hallowed Kōshien High School Baseball Tournament held at Nishinomiya near Osaka four times between 1931 and 1936. The best of these, the 1931 squad, was the first team ever to qualify for Kōshien with Taiwanese (aboriginal or Han) players on its roster.[5] Kanō placed second in the twenty-three-team tournament that year, their skills and intensity winning the hearts of the Japanese public.[6] Amazingly, this 1931 Kanō team is still a very popular nostalgic symbol even today in Japan (Su 1996, 40). This team of Han, aboriginal, and Japanese players supposedly "proved" to nationally minded Japanese, in an extremely visible fashion, the colonial myth of "assimilation" *(dōka)*—that both Han and aboriginal Taiwanese were willing and able to take part alongside Japanese in the cultural rituals of the Japanese state. Of course, the irony is that the six Taiwanese players on the starting roster probably also saw their victories as a statement of Taiwanese (Han or aborigine) will and skill that could no longer be dismissed by the Japanese colonizing power. But the fact that this Kanō triumph could be understood in such different ways is merely proof of the important and liminal position that baseball held in the Japanese colonial administration of Taiwan.

The great Kanō tradition was not Jiayi's only contribution to the Japanese baseball world; this southern town cemented its reputation as the baseball capital of Taiwan when several of its sons went on to star in baseball in Japan in the 1930s and beyond. The greatest of these was Wu Bo, who starred on Kanō's 1935 and 1936 championship teams, signed with the proud Tokyo Giants baseball team in 1937, and played for the Giants for seven years. In 1943, under the nationalistic pressures of wartime, Wu took the Japanese name Kure Masayuki (keeping the same surname, which is pronounced "Kure" in Japanese). The next year, however, he gave the Japanese baseball community a less polite reminder of his ethnic Chinese identity when he refused to travel to Manchuria with the Giants to arouse Japanese troops stationed there. Wu left the Giants outright, went on to play for another thirteen years with the Hanshin Tigers and Mainichi Orions, and in 1995 became the first Taiwanese player selected to the Japanese Baseball Hall of Fame (Gao 1994, 94–95; Su 1996, 28).[7]

Taiwan did not just produce an elite class of standout baseball players. Baseball became popular at all levels, making it the dominant sport in the colony as it was in the home islands of Japan. Peng Ming-min would later trade his baseball mitt for a pen, enduring much sacrifice as he led the struggle for Taiwanese self-determination and independence during the Chinese Nationalist era. But as a boy in Japanese Gaoxiong during the 1930s, young Peng was the typical Taiwanese schoolboy obsessed with baseball. In a conversation with me in 1999, Peng fondly remembered huddling around the radio with his brother to listen to colonial broadcasts of the Japanese high school championships at Kōshien every spring. As Peng notes in his memoir, *A Taste of Freedom*:

> By this time I was an ardent baseball fan. When Babe Ruth visited Japan I boldly wrote a letter to him and in return received his autograph, which became my treasure. . . . [I] reserved my greatest enthusiasm for baseball. Our school masters took baseball very seriously, treating it almost as if it were a military training program. Although I was a poor batter, I was an excellent fielder, and played on our team when it won a citywide championship. Needless to say, my Babe Ruth autograph gave me great prestige among my classmates. (Peng 1972, 16–17)

The enthusiasm of millions of young people like Peng, who played and paid feverish attention to this Japanese institution, is what made baseball Taiwan's "national game" some seventy years before Chen's presidential remarks in 2000.

This Taiwanese excellence in baseball, the sport of the colonizing power, reflects an important aspect of the experience of almost any colonized people. Edward Said has discussed the "collaborative" aspect of the life of colonized intellectuals, whose long-term strategies for liberation depended on being able to "learn the ways of the [colonizer], translate his works, pick up his habits" (Said 1993, 262). C. L. R. James has extended this model to the sporting world in his discussions of West Indies cricket, where by the early 1900s, the inspired performances of standout black cricketers forced white populations to give West Indians a respect they would not have granted otherwise (James 1986, 118–124).

In Taiwan, baseball likewise was one way in which the colonized population sought to negotiate their relationship with the Japanese colonizing power on terms that the Japanese could not help but accept. There are more explicitly political analogues of this process in colonial Taiwan. One was the Home Rule

Movement, under which Taiwanese students educated in Tokyo—citing the official rhetoric of authoritarian "imperial benevolence"—sought a colonial assembly for Taiwan in the early 1920s (Kerr 1974, 113-129). Taiwan elites' calls in the 1930s for Taiwanese to be allowed to serve in the Japanese military (as more than two hundred thousand Taiwanese later did during World War II) were also explicitly tied to appeals for equal treatment of the Taiwanese as subjects of the emperor (Kondō 1996, 34-36; Lin 1996, 217-227). Baseball was another such liminal realm where Japanese exclusion of Taiwanese baseball teams or players would have given the lie to Japan's entire colonial enterprise.

Baseball allowed the colonized Taiwanese, as Said has written of "native intellectuals" in other settings, to work within the constraints of the system in order to "liberate their energies from the oppressing cultural matrix that produced them" (Said 1993, 269). Indeed, this physical realm of baseball was one fraught with many tensions and contradictions; participation in Japan's "national game" allowed Taiwanese people to prove and live their acculturation into the colonial order at the very moment that Taiwanese baseball successes worked to subvert it.[8] Taiwanese subjects, both Chinese and aborigine, could use baseball skills and customs taught by the Japanese to appeal for equal treatment within the national framework that baseball represented in so many ways. Yet the Taiwanese baseball community, through its many triumphs, was able to use this arena to offer the final proof, in a "national" language that the Japanese had to understand, that the colonial enterprise that aimed to shackle the Taiwanese population in permanent subservience was bound to fail.

BASEBALL IN GUOMINDANG TAIWAN, 1945–1980S

When the Guomindang state took the reins of Taiwan's government in late 1945, it set out to effect two related transformations of the Taiwan polity. To truly achieve a Chinese "Retrocession" (Guangfu) of Taiwan, the Nationalists would have to strip Taiwanese culture of its Japanese legacies, while at the same time restoring to it an essential and timeless "Chineseness" for which the Taiwanese people presumably had been longing for a half century. Policies of "de-Taiwanization" were enforced, officially degrading any distinctively Taiwanese cultures or customs. These policies were designed not only to cut the colonial links to Japan, but also to nip in the bud any heretical links between a culturally distinctive and politically separate Taiwan (Chang 1993, 142-145). These policies were even applied to the baseball realm as well; the Japanese stigma that the game carried in the late 1940s was so potent that it was rare to find a Guomindang-fearing school administrator willing to accept the presence of a baseball team on his campus (Su 1996, 27).

At the same time, however, state agents involved in Retrocession efforts also realized what a valuable exception baseball could be to this rule of erasing any and all colonial remnants. The Guomindang state had promoted physical culture in planning the construction of a strong and healthy Chinese populace and state on the mainland for two decades. Official endorsement of baseball soon became one method of officially "sinicizing" a cultural realm that still represented a Pandora's box of colonial thinking and customs. Baseball was included at the First Taiwan Provincial Games, held in October 1946 at National Taiwan University, with twenty counties, cities, colleges, and government organizations sending baseball teams to this meet overseen by Chiang Kai-shek (Jiang Jieshi) and Song Meiling, in Taiwan for the first anniversary of Retrocession (Taiwan sheng 1946, 7, 15–52, 82–84; Su 1996, 27).[9]

A baseball tournament was held in Taiwan in August 1947, even as government "anticommunist" forces continued their massacres, begun that March, of thousands of Taiwanese elites seen as a threat to Chiang's regime. It is telling that the baseball world was not able to escape this horror. Lin Guixing, coach of the great Hualian Nōkō teams of the 1920s, was killed on August 1, 1947, during the violent and sustained aftermath of the 228 Incident (Gao 1994, 47–50). Fudan University and Shanghai Pandas teams also came to play against teams from Taibei, Taizhong, Taiwan Power, Taiwan Sugar, and Taiwan Charcoal, as if all was well that bloody summer (31). In 1949, a Taiwan Province Baseball Committee was formed, chaired by future ROC vice president Xie Dongmin, organizing annual provincial baseball tournaments at all levels of play (Zhan 1985, 436).

What is interesting about these Guomindang efforts to promote baseball in Taiwan in the immediate postwar period is that Taiwan was clearly the only region of the Republic of China with any baseball tradition whatsoever. When the Taiwan Province Baseball Team won the championship at China's Seventh National Games in Shanghai in 1948, there were only three other teams entered: the national Police and Air Force teams, both of which were stacked with Taiwanese players, and the Filipino Overseas Chinese team (*Di qi jie* 1948, 30). In other words, the Guomindang could hardly promote baseball as a "Chinese" custom. Thus their work to hijack the game's unique popularity in Taiwan for their own uses still had to be in explicitly Taiwanese terms. The game of basketball soon became fashionable in Taiwan, promoted by the sizable *waisheng* mainlander population concentrated in the north. But baseball remained an arena in which Taiwanese people could successfully—and without any fear of reprisal—challenge the Guomindang's policies of "de-Taiwanization" and their claims to represent a true Chinese culture that Taiwanese needed for their own good.

Baseball, then, is also central to the story of Taiwan's rapid and traumatic transition from wartime to decolonization to a new oppression delivered in the rhetoric of Retrocession to Chinese rule. Said's model predicts decolonized intellectuals' work for the "rediscovery and repatriation of what had been suppressed in the natives' past by the processes of imperialism" (Said 1993, 210). But in Taiwan after February 28, 1947, this process was unthinkable. At this moment, original support for Chinese rule of Taiwan had been dashed violently and unmercifully by the actions of tens of thousands of carpetbagging Guomindang troops, bureaucrats, and hangers-on. The relieved and enthusiastic searching for a "Chinese" Taiwan among Taiwanese thus quickly gave way to a yearning for cultural artifacts from the good old colonial days. Baseball was one of these artifacts, and this complicated picture of a Taiwan stuck between a Japanese rock and a Guomindang hard place explains much of baseball's continued popularity after the Japanese were long gone from Taiwan.

Yet the vagaries of decolonization and Retrocession do not provide the full extent of this history. The Taiwanese people now had to contend with the reality of an invigorated American Cold War imperialism that sought to dictate affairs in Taiwan and throughout Asia as a whole. Taiwan's baseball history offers a look at this process as well. In 1951, the first ever All-Taiwan baseball team was organized for a series of games versus Filipino teams in Manila. The Manila sporting public fell in love with the All-Taiwanese, especially the astounding home run hitting of Penghu native Hong Taishan. But the young team from Taiwan made an even deeper impression when they "volunteered" to give blood to American soldiers recuperating in Manila hospitals from casualties sustained in the Korean War (Gao 1994, 13–16). This episode, though anecdotal, thus provided a most profound metaphor to describe life in small Asian nations during the depths of the Cold War. In the end, the greatest triumphs that could be won were in activities (like baseball) defined and approved by the United States, in locales dependent on and exposed to American beneficence and greed, and in ways that figuratively sucked life from these locales as they were integrated into America's new postwar empire.

This incredible tightrope walk between Japanese colonialist legacies and Guomindang–U.S. hegemony in Taiwan continued into and was in many ways exemplified by the international success of Taiwanese Little League baseball (Shaonian bangqiu, or Shaobang) teams beginning in the late 1960s. In a tremendous run perhaps unmatched in the history of international sport, Taiwanese teams won ten Little League World Series titles between 1969 and 1981[10] and sixteen in the twenty-seven-year period from 1969 to 1995. This success brought desperately needed attention to Taiwan in a time when its most important ally, the United States, was gradually shunning the island in favor of ties to the People's Republic of China. But it also allowed the playing out of a very complicated jumble of national and racial tensions that make a study of Taiwanese baseball crucial to a deeper understanding of Taiwanese society during this era.

This Little League success began in August 1968 with two great victories by the Maple Leaf (Hongye) Elementary School team over a visiting team from Wakayama, Japan. This Hongye Village team—made up of Bunun aborigine youth representing their tiny Taidong County school of just a hundred students—earned the right to play Wakayama after winning the islandwide Students' Cup tournament held in Taibei. They then became superstars after their victories over Wakayama at the Taibei Municipal Stadium. The twenty thousand fans who managed to get tickets for each of these historic games were joined by an islandwide television audience treated to more than thirteen hours of Taiwan

Television broadcasts on the first game alone (Wang 1994, 66–74). The overall significance in Taiwan of the Maple Leaf boys' success is hard to measure. Virtually all of Taiwanese society was energized in a way that has few parallels in American history—the Olympic triumphs of Jesse Owens or the 1980 hockey team being perhaps the closest examples. To this day, the Maple Leaf's 1968 victories against Wakayama are cited as a defining moment in the history of Taiwanese nationalism. In fact, a print advertisement for a set of two books chronicling twentieth-century Chinese history, published in Taiwan in 2000, featured five photographs of the crucial moments of this century: the 1911 revolution, the 1945 surrender of Japan after World War II, the Great Leap Forward famine of the early 1960s, Taiwan's withdrawal from the United Nations in 1971, and the Maple Leaf baseball triumphs of 1968 (Changrong 2000, 85)!

Unfortunately, the jubilation at these victories was soon dampened by an unfortunate revelation. On their roster of eleven players, the Maple Leaf team included nine ineligible boys who were playing under false names (Wang 1994, 5–6).[11] Nonetheless, these great victories by aboriginal village youths from Taidong County constituted a tremendous moment in modern Taiwanese sports and cultural history and announced to the world that Taiwan was ready to join—in this realm of competition at least—the powers of world sport.

The next year, 1969, was Taiwan's first entry into the Little League World Series, operated by the U.S. Little League establishment and held in Williamsport, Pennsylvania. The youth of Taiwan spared no time in making this tournament a yearly blowout of any and all challengers. The Taizhong Golden Dragons, Taiwan's 1969 champions, "surprised everyone from Japan to the U.S.," as the *Sporting News* put it, sweeping opponents from Ontario, Ohio, and California to take the world title. An impressed—if politically incorrect—*Sporting News* described the skill and infectious enthusiasm of "the Orientals":

> Thousands of gong-clanging, cheering fans in the stands at Williamsport adopted the Chinese as their favorite team.
>
> [Chen Zhiyuan] captured the fans' imagination when, after every out, he'd turn around and shout to his fielders, raising the ball above his head. In return they yell in Chinese the American equivalent of, "Go men!" (Keyes 1969)

Guo Yuanzhi—one of the stars of this team who went on to become a legend in Japan, pitching for the Chunichi Dragons for sixteen years—later remembered his teammates' racial jitters at being the only "yellow" players in Williamsport. They overcame these fears by using the taller physiques of their Western opponents against them, throwing them numerous curve balls that they felt the longer-armed North Americans would have more trouble hitting (Guo 1998, 45). Their confidence was also boosted by the presence at their games of thousands of delirious Taiwanese and Chinese flag-waving fans—residents of the United States who would make these yearly baseball pilgrimages to Williamsport for decades to come.

Fans at home in Taiwan were even more jubilant, glued to their radios into the wee hours of that humid summer night. One radio DJ remembered thirty years later how "the Taipei night nearly boiled over. When the game finished at 3 A.M., the streets of the city erupted with the constant banging of firecrackers, as ordinary citizens opened their windows and yelled out to the night sky, 'Long live the Republic of China!'" (Li 1999, 101). At a time when Taiwan's standing in the international community was becoming less and less stable, this, like the Maple Leaf triumphs the year before, was a satisfying victory indeed.

Yet this championship, unfortunately, was also plagued by irregularities. It was common knowledge in Taiwan that the 1969 world champions—technically a school team from Taizhong in central Taiwan—had actually been recruited as a national all-star team *(guojia daibiaodui),* a fact that clearly violated the Williamsport charter. Only two of the team's fourteen players actually came from Taizhong! Nine of the starting players were from Jiayi and Tainan in the south of the island. Star Yu Hongkai, from Taidong, had played illegally as a ringer for the 1968 Maple Leaf team and was recruited from across the island for the 1969 Golden Dragons. Guo Yuanzhi, the future Japanese pro star, was also recruited from far Taidong for the World Series (Su 1996, 43; Wang 1994, 48).

This trend would not end soon. The 1970 "Jiayi Seven Tigers," the only Taiwan team not to win at Williamsport over the next decade, included only seven Jiayi boys, supplemented by five Tainan and two Gaoxiong players. As late as 1979, the Puzi Elementary School Tornadoes world championship team included two ringers from elsewhere in Jiayi County (Su 1996, 55, 71). These teams—and rightfully so—generated great suspicion on the part of an American public unable to fathom the source of this invincible Taiwan baseball dynasty. In fact, by the end of this run, the phrase "Taiwanese Little League baseball," like "Texas high school football" or "East German women's swimming," became a standard metaphor for those who would use youth sports to achieve victory with no regard for the rules of "fair competition."

Yet this view of their Little League program mattered little to the Taiwanese public of the time. In 1971, when the Tainan Giants won the Williamsport championship, some 10 million people in Taiwan—an incredible two-thirds of the island's population—watched the game on television from 2:00 to 5:00 A.M. (Appleton 1972, 37). Baseball stardom became an almost universal aspiration among the boys and young men of Taiwan. Li Kunzhe, who starred professionally for the China Trust Whales in the late 1990s, remembers: "I grew up watching baseball.... I remember the days when everyone would wake up in the middle of the night to watch our national teams perform in the international competitions. They were national heroes. We all wanted to represent our country and be a hero" (Li 2000, 8).

These triumphs were especially thrilling for Taiwanese people given the island's unique geopolitical squeeze described above. The sight of these Taiwanese boys annually making mincemeat of the strong and confident American teams was pure bliss to anyone hoping to strike back and prove the strength and general worth of Taiwan to their American "allies" so busy selling out Taiwan in favor of relations with the PRC during the 1970s. Indeed, the humbled Americans were reduced to booing these Taiwanese youngsters (when the Tainan Giants won again in 1973, as it happens, on their third consecutive no-hitter) and eventually even banning all foreign teams for a year in 1975 in order to guarantee an American "winner" (*NYT* August 26, 1973, V-5; *NYT* November 12, 1974, I, 51).

Most importantly, success in this Taiwanese (and not mainland Chinese) sport of baseball invigorated dissidents and critics of the Chiang Kai-shek regime thirsting for tangible measures of uniquely Taiwanese accomplishment. Williamsport soon became a "new battlefield" for Taiwanese dissidents and independence activists (*Taiwan duli* 2000, 58). In 1969, frenzied Taiwanese fans shouted upon the Golden Dragons' victory, "The players are all Taiwanese! Taiwan has stood up!" (Guo 1998, 48). Taiwanese supporters soon raised the stakes in this implicit protest against the Guomindang government. In 1971, as the Tainan Giants swept to a world championship, Taiwanese Independence activists at Williamsport hired an airplane to fly over the stadium towing a bilingual banner reading, "Long Live Taiwan Independence *[Taiwan duli wansui]*, Go Go Taiwan" (*Taiwan duli* 2000, 58).[12] The Taiwan teams' games attracted fans from all points of the political spectrum, so each Taiwan Independence flag or banner was matched by pro-Nationalist mainlander fans waving national flags and cheering for the "Chinese" team. The pro-state fans had an advantage, however, in the dozens of New York Chinatown thugs hired by the Guomindang to identify and rough up Taiwan Independence activists at the games. That same year of 1971, the championship game was interrupted when a dozen of these toughs ran across the field to rip down a banner reading in English and Chinese, "Team of Taiwan, Go Taiwan *[jiayou Taiwandui]*" (*Taiwan duli* 2000, 58; Taipingshan 1971, 54–55).

In 1972, when the Taibei Braves challenged for the world title, the Guomindang was better prepared, renting every single commercial aircraft for miles around to keep the Taiwan Independence crowd from repeating their coup (*Taiwan duli* 2000, 58). Some seventy to eighty military cadets training in the United States were also recruited to Williamsport, where they shouted while beating Taiwanese male and female supporters with wooden clubs, "Kill the traitors *[Shasi hanjian]!*" (Yi wei 1972, 45–46). One wonders what American fans at Williamsport thought of all this violence, but these concerns did not stop either side from carrying out their battles. In 1973 at the Senior Little League Championships in Gary, Indiana, four activists wore T-shirts reading *Tai, Du, Wan,* and *Sui* (Long Live Taiwan Independence), only to have Guomindang officials in attendance order that they be arrested by Gary police as terrorists (*Taiwan duli* 2000, 59). At Gary in 1975, Taiwanese activists floated a balloon with this same independence message, and thanks to the generous and curious ABC cameramen on the scene, this sky-high subversion flashed across millions of

Taiwanese television screens for the first time in history.[13] Thus, through the manipulation of satellite technology and the tweaking of the connection between sports and nationalism that the Guomindang itself had tried to disseminate in Taiwan, Little League baseball became one of the most effective and joyous ways of challenging Chinese Nationalist hegemony in Taiwan.

Finally, the world of baseball was an important site for the expression of strength and pride among Taiwan's aboriginal tribes. Many of Taiwan's early championship teams were from the aboriginal areas of eastern Taiwan. These youngsters and their adult followers could only have taken an ironic pleasure in winning such great honors for—and being feted by—the oppressive Guomindang state that only continued to ignore and impoverish these representatives of a pre-Chinese Taiwan past. In fact, their baseball and sporting success in general became one of the most important ways in which Taiwan's aboriginal citizens represented and understood their identity and position in Taiwan society (Guo 1998, 26; *TTO* May 28, 2000).

Yet clearly, this gratifying annual attention paid to the original inhabitants of Taiwan and their baseball prowess was not enough to truly sustain the aboriginal populations. It is telling that Taiwan's two greatest exports to Japanese baseball—Guo Yuanzhi (Kaku Genji) and Guo Taiyuan (Kaku Taigen)—were both Little League icons of aboriginal descent. Both Guos left Taiwan as very young men, settled and married in Japan, and only returned to the Taiwan baseball world in the late 1990s after their careers in Japan came to a close.[14]

The many jumbled and precarious directions along which Taiwanese baseball developed in the first four decades of Guomindang rule did not resemble in the least the neat white straightness of the baseball diamonds that were home to this movement. In the martial law days of mainlander domination of the Guomindang Party and state, baseball was one realm in which Taiwanese people could register their own contributions to Taiwan culture and society. This mixture of mild pro-Japanese nostalgia,[15] resistance against Guomindang hegemony in Taiwan and American hegemony in East Asia, and even aboriginal resistance to the double oppression of the mainlander and Taiwanese Han presence could all be voiced in the language of baseball. But what made this dissent safe was the Guomindang's own understanding of the role of sports in modern society. Their standard two-part philosophy, developed when the party ruled China in the late 1920s and 1930s, was that popular participation in sports served to integrate a diverse population into a single nation-state and that outstanding sporting performances on international stages were valuable opportunities to win national face, sympathy, and even allies in the ever-changing world of the twentieth century.[16] Thus, in many ways baseball represented a table of negotiation in which Taiwanese baseball communities exchanged measures of integration for measures of independent expression, measures of "Chinese" identity for measures of pro-Japanese nostalgia, and measures of the autocratic martial law Guomindang state for measures of an independent Taiwanese culture and society.

CHINESE PROFESSIONAL BASEBALL LEAGUE: BEGINNINGS, 1990–1994

Planning for a Taiwanese professional baseball league began in late 1987, the year that martial law was lifted in Taiwan (Zeng 1997, 22). The events of this year marked the end of four decades of naked authoritarian rule by the Guomindang and signaled the beginning of a new era in Taiwan, where there was now space to redefine identities and historical memories once drawn along the lines of Japanese, Chinese, and American hegemony. By this time, two different movements had emerged in this new Taiwan. The first was to define a unique identity for the Chinese-but-not-really-Chinese island nation. This "uniqueness" in turn would aid in the second—the scramble to ensure Taiwan's inclusion in a new globalizing world order. Both of these impulses, along with the entrepreneurial drive perfected in 1980s Taiwan, came together perfectly with the 1988 public announcement that the Chinese Professional Baseball League (CPBL, or Zhonghua Zhiye Bangqiu Lianmeng) would begin play in 1990.[17]

The new CPBL consisted of four corporate-owned teams: the Weichuan Dragons, Brother Elephants, President Lions, and Mercuries Tigers.[18] These teams' uniforms clearly demonstrated the CPBL's efforts to present a product that was a pleasurable mix of the global and the Chinese: The teams' names and parent companies were represented on the jerseys and caps in various mixtures of English and Chinese lettering. The four corporate-owned teams did not represent cities, as teams do in most professional leagues; instead, the teams toured up and down the island's west coast together, playing weekly round-robin series in Taibei, Taizhong, and Gaoxiong. Each of these cities (plus Tainan, Xinzhu, and Pingdong, where a few games were scheduled every year) had their own fan clubs organized to support each of the CPBL's four teams. The majority of these fan club members were male high school or university students, but these fan clubs were also filled with significant numbers of female students, businessmen, and laborers (Shih 1998, 37–39, 80). The enthusiastic rooting of these fan clubs *(houyuanhui,* from the Japanese *kōenkai)* could at times very easily turn violent. The sight of angry fans—Lions fans in the President Corporation's hometown of Tainan were particularly famed for this—hurling bottles, cans, eggs, and garbage at opposing players or even surrounding the opposing team's bus in a mob was not uncommon in the league's early years, giving the lie to the notion of a united Taiwan cheering on a united CPBL.

Another important element of the new Chinese Professional Baseball League was the presence of foreign players (usually called *yangjiang,* or "foreign talents") culled from the rosters of American Double-A minor-league teams.[19] Twenty-three players, American and Latin American in origin, went to Taiwan in the winter of 1989–1990 for tryouts. Sixteen were selected to join the CPBL (with a league limit of four *yangjiang* per team). The presence of these players was meant to add an international flavor to the league and also to provide an external stimulus for the improvement of the quality of CPBL play. In a 1993 conversation, Jungo Bears pitcher Tony Metoyer described to me how these foreign players also served as "silent coaches" who could share their knowledge of American strategies and training methods with the Taiwanese players. Their many contributions allowed the Taiwanese game to become closer in strategy to the more open or risky style of baseball played in the Americas and less like the conservative game that suited Taiwan so well in its years of Little League dominance.

Steps were also taken to sinicize the identities of these foreign players as well. Each of the players was given a "Chinese name," usually sounding something (if only vaguely) like the player's original name, and one which usually bestowed fine and admirable qualities on the foreigner. Elvin Rivera, a Dominican pitcher selected by the Tigers, became "Li Wei"—"Li" as the common Chinese surname and "Wei" meaning "great" or "mighty." Freddy Tiburcio, the Elephants' star Dominican outfielder, was called "Dibo," or "imperial waves and billows." Luis Iglesias, the Tigers' home run champion from Panama, was called "Yingxia," or "chivalrous eagle." These players were photographed for magazine covers dressed in "traditional" Chinese scholars' caps and robes, as Taiwan's baseball public was taught that even in the realm of baseball, a game having explicitly foreign origins, the Chinese ability to assimilate outsiders was as powerful as ever.

Yet this "assimilation" could occur on the most materialistic terms, as many of the foreign players' "Chinese" names were just advertisements for products sold by their team's parent corporation. The Mercuries Tigers inflicted names of noodle dishes (Qiaofu, Quanjiafu) from their chain restaurants onto pitchers Cesar Mejia and Rafael Valdez. The President Lions, whose parent company specialized in convenience stores and prepackaged foods, did the same with the names Shengmaige (San Miguel beer), A-Q (instant noodles), and Baiwei (Budweiser) for pitchers Aguedo Vasquez, Jose Cano, and Ravelo Manzanillo. Later, the China Times Eagles resourcefully used names from their minor corporate sponsors, dubbing pitcher Steve Stoole "Meile" (Miller Beer), calling the Afro-Dominican outfielder Jose Gonzalez "Meilehei" (Miller Dark!), and former New York Mets infielder Brian Giles "Aikuai" (Alfa Romeo). Practices like this served to maintain some distance between the Taiwanese and these foreigners, assimilated or not.

Real outsiders from the larger world of baseball came to Taiwan to endorse the CPBL enterprise as well, as the league in its early years won several valuable publicity coups. The Chunichi Dragons[20] and San Diego Padres sent minor-league teams to Taiwan for exhibition series against CPBL teams after the 1991 and 1992 seasons. Then in 1993, the Los Angeles Dodgers major-league squad visited, only to be beaten in two of three games by Taiwan's CPBL teams! The presence in Taiwan's ballparks of these representatives of the great American and Japanese baseball traditions only boosted the status of the CPBL in the eyes of Taiwanese and foreign baseball communities.

Besides this conscious effort to connect Taiwanese baseball and culture to the greater international baseball and cultural worlds, efforts were also made to emphasize the CPBL's local composition in marketing the league. The most di-

President Lions Guo Yuanzhi and Zeng Zhizhen at spring training, 1997. (Photo by Zhuang Ping)

rect connection was the presence of former Little League heroes who had won such great honors for Taiwan in the 1970s. During their prime years in the 1980s, before the Chinese Professional Baseball League was founded, these heroes could play only in Japanese or Taiwanese semipro leagues. The CPBL was extremely fortunate to have begun play while this celebrated group still was in command of most of their skills; after a few years of play, it was obvious that the careers of some of these ex-child stars were heading south. But their presence in the CPBL's first years of play was crucial in making the league a viable enterprise.

Other accoutrements of "traditional Chinese culture" helped cement the league's special Chinese characteristics as well. Fan favorites like Dragon pitcher Huang Pingyang and Lions captain Zeng Zhizhen (known as "The Ninja Catcher") were often featured in magazines that told of their pursuits of self-consciously Chinese or Taiwanese customs, like drinking fine tea, taking in traditional Taiwanese puppet theater, or collecting teapots or Buddhist paintings. Popular television variety shows even featured noted numerologists and geomancers using these "traditional" Chinese sciences to predict the results of upcoming baseball seasons.

Thus the roots of the CPBL's early success lay in this important effort to combine the local and global. International symbols of sporting culture were carefully balanced with aspects of the local, expressed through the involvement of particular individuals identified with past Taiwanese sporting successes or through linguistic or cultural particulars that remained a part of CPBL baseball. This strategy, the key to the CPBL's successes in the early 1990s, is strikingly different from the model by which Tokyo's Yomiuri Giants became such a powerful symbol of Japanese pride and strength during the late 1960s and 1970s. Anthropologist William Kelly has outlined the history of the Giants' nine-year run of consecutive championships won from 1965 to 1973, a reign that "precisely mapped postwar Japan's double-digit boom years that catapulted the country to the first rank of industrial powers" (Kelly 1998, 105). The Giants organization insisted on maintaining a "pure" Japanese team, refusing even to allow the great Japanese-Hawaiian star and three-time batting champion Wally Yonamine to remain a Giant. The Giant cult was constructed atop beliefs of "uniquely Japanese" elements of a "fighting spirit" *(konjō)* and strategies of "managed baseball" that mimicked new forms of corporate organization and became an important brick in the wall of an essentialist, culturally and racially defined postwar Japan (105–107).

Yet there is literally no analogue between the cult of the Yomiuri Giants and the rise of professional baseball in Taiwan. For an island that has always been as politically and ethnically complicated as Taiwan, this kind of national or racial chauvinism was impossible. There was tension, however, between notions of a uniquely "Taiwanese" identity emerging in 1990s Taiwan and some of the essential "Chinese" gimmicks used to show how baseball was being assimilated into Taiwanese/Chinese culture. In the CPBL, explicit "Taiwan consciousness" took second stage to the exaggerated "Chineseness" of the league's image, and this crack in the CPBL's fun mixture of international and local cultures would be exploited by later competitors.

MINOR-LEAGUE FOREIGNERS AND TENSIONS IN "CHINESE" BASEBALL

The CPBL reached its peak popularity, measured by crowd attendance, in its third through fifth seasons, 1992–1994 (see Table 1). In 1993, the league was joined by two new teams—the Jungo Bears and the China Times Eagles—each loaded with seven young, popular members of Taiwan's 1992 silver medal Olympic baseball team. That same season, the all-sports station TVIS paid NT $90 million (U.S. $3.6 million) to broadcast CPBL games over the next three seasons—hardly American network money, but a great improvement over the NT $3,000 (U.S. $120) per-game fee paid by Taiwan's major broadcast stations up to that point (Chen 1996, 80). CPBL games were being televised in thirty-eight different countries covered by Rupert Murdoch's STAR-TV enterprise (Wilson 1993, 3). At the same time, the league also actively expanded its schedule into the Xinzhu, Tainan, and Pingdong markets, bringing quality baseball to the hometowns of more baseball-starved Taiwanese.

But somehow, despite all these signs of vigorous growth, the league's popularity began to wane seriously by 1995, as the game began to lose the local Taiwan flavor it had worked so hard to cultivate. The CPBL mishandled the important balance between the local and the international that was so crucial in sustaining public interest in the league, as owners developed a dependence on international networks that made the league simply less appealing.

Table 1 CPBL and TML average attendance, 1990–2002

YEAR	CPBL ATTENDANCE	TML ATTENDANCE
1990	5,000	—
1991	5,836	—
1992	6,878	—
1993	5,928	—
1994	5,954	—
1995	5,488	—
1996	4,548	—
1997	2,041	2,041
1998	2,191	3,442
1999	1,786	3,296
2000	1,676	3,922
2001	1,876	N/A
2002	2,957	N/A

Source: "Zhonghua" 2002; *Naluwan* 2000.

Perhaps the most visible form of this dependence was the CPBL's reliance on the foreign ballplayers invited to Taiwan to supplement the native rosters. Although most of these foreign players were AA-level minor leaguers who would never reach the American major leagues, several of them were able to excel in Taiwan. It became apparent in the league's first year that a team's success could depend heavily on the performance of their foreign "supplements." Teams began putting more emphasis on the foreign element of their roster, seeing it as the quickest path to improvement; it was certainly easier to wave money at a foreigner with proven skills than to dedicate several years to developing a Taiwanese player from scratch. The situation was exacerbated more when, in 1994, the board of CPBL owners raised the foreign player maximum to seven per team. (By contrast, Japanese and Korean pro teams today are allowed to carry only four and two foreigners on their rosters, respectively.) In 1995 this ceiling was raised to ten foreigners per team, and in March 1997, the league owners voted to eliminate all limits whatsoever on roster composition.

Public interest in the league fell consistently as the CPBL became less and less "Chinese" or Taiwanese and more and more reliant on American and Dominican players. By 1995, fully 44 percent of the CPBL's players came from outside Taiwan. Many of these *yangjiang* made the situation even worse. Some admitted far too candidly to being baseball mercenaries in Taiwan solely for the relatively high salaries they could demand there. Others alienated local residents and fans with their promiscuous and sometimes even brutish behavior; in fact, an entire book was published on the topic, entitled *Foreign Pro Baseball Players' Sex Scandals* (Gu 1997).

In 1998, commenting on the dominance of foreign pitchers in the CPBL, a *Liberty Times* columnist summoned up ugly images from modern Chinese his-

Table 2 Number of foreigners and total players on all CPBL teams, 1990–2002

YEAR	FOREIGN PLAYERS	TOTAL PLAYERS	AS % OF TOTAL
1990	19	99	19.2
1991	24	100	24.0
1992	33	111	29.7
1993	48	153	31.4
1994	58	169	34.3
1995	78	177	44.1
1996	61	172	35.5
1997	93	221	42.1
1998	116	226	51.3
1999	N/A	N/A	N/A
2000	11	115	9.6
2001	13	110	11.8
2002	17	114	14.9

tory in calling the league's pitching mound a "foreign concession" *(waiguo zujie)*.[21] Indeed, the predominance of foreign pitchers that season reached ridiculous heights. Of the hundred CPBL pitchers who took the mound that year, only twenty-two were Taiwanese. The 1998 CPBL champion Weichuan Dragons carried twelve foreign pitchers on their roster (combined record 56 wins, 48 losses, and one tie) but only two Taiwanese pitchers (combined record 0-0-0).[22] Not only were a great percentage of the players foreign, but many teams preferred to hire foreign managers, thought to have a more worldly grasp of strategy than native Taiwanese managers. The success of Elephants Manager Yamane Toshida, who led his team to three straight championships from 1992 to 1994, made quite an impression on league owners searching for that extra edge. By 1995, five of six CPBL teams were managed by Japanese helmsmen.

The baseball community's mixed feelings about these foreigners who took over their league were manifested in many ways. Chen Dashun, a Dragon star first baseman turned columnist, reflected on the difficulty of creating a "local *[bentu]* baseball culture" in a league dominated by foreign players, and described Taiwan baseball culture as ultimately and frustratingly "not Chinese and not Western" *(bu zhong bu xi)* (Chen 2000, 19).

Popular baseball cartoons drawn by artist Ao Youxiang demonstrate aspects of this ambivalence in a much less sensitive way. Some cartoons show foreign players (particularly players of African descent) as simply big and dumb, unable to comprehend any but the most corporeal of sensations. In one, a black batsman (with absurdly exaggerated "Negroid" facial features) is hit in the groin by a pitch. As the batter rushes the mound, players of both teams follow, fearful of the damage to be done to the Taiwanese pitcher by this enraged black behemoth. But all are stunned when he arrives at the mound, evidently unfazed by pain that would fell any normal man, and thanks the pitcher for breaking up his kidney

"How brave of you, to dare to hit me!" (Cartoon by Ao Youxiang, from *Pro Baseball Rhapsody*, 1994: 28.)

stones (Ao 1994, 28). Another cartoon shows a black baserunner, styling himself as "the American stolen base king," vainly assured in his attempt to steal second base. But he is fended off by a wily Taiwanese shortstop, who sends the silly American scampering back to first base by waving a plate of "stinky tofu" his way (42). These stereotypes of the clever and rational Chinese versus the physically gifted but dimwitted black man were tired, ignorant, and tellingly provincial, but these cartoons did show the degree to which many felt betrayed by what was supposed to be Taiwan's own baseball league.

In an editorial written in March 1997, a Taiwan sportswriter addressed in a different manner the problem of the dominance of foreign players in Taiwan baseball. He credited the *yangjiang* with aiding the development of pro baseball in Taiwan. But he reminded fans that the use of these foreigners truly came down to one question: Would these "AAA-level [minor-league] foreigners *[laowai]*" ever be able to help Taiwan win an Olympic medal in baseball (*MSB* March 9, 1997, 5)? In terms of national loyalty or the crucial international baseball stage, these foreign players could never truly contribute anything to Taiwan's future.

Fans' own wishes for a more Taiwan-centric CPBL could be seen in voting for the annual All-Star Game. In a 1997 season marked by foreign dominance more than any other,[23] fans did not select a single foreigner to the All-Star teams, picking marginal (at best) players like Whales outfielder He Xianfan (batting average .218) and pitcher Huang Qingjing (1 win and 9 losses, 5.65 ERA) to the teams over the dozens of foreign players who were more deserving by any statistical standard. From artists to columnists to fans themselves, the CPBL community began making explicit statements about the kind of local flavor they wished the league had retained since its more successful early years. The presence of these foreign players and managers achieved one of the original goals of this *yangjiang* strategy in that the quality of CPBL play improved greatly over the league's first few years. Yet it is also telling that as the CPBL improved in technical terms, it simultaneously became a subject of such little interest to Taiwanese baseball fans.

Even the baseball clubs themselves seemed to mock the foreign players who had overtaken the CPBL game. In 1998, after the practice had been prohibited for years, some teams resumed the awarding of outright, even crudely commercial Chinese names to foreign players. Al Osuna, who pitched for the Astros, Dodgers, and Padres in the American major leagues, was signed by the Mercuries Tigers that year and given the Chinese name Napoli—the same name as the local pizza restaurant that gave away a hundred free pizzas every night Osuna started a game (*ZYSB* May 28, 1998, C-10). The Sinon Bulls (formerly Jungo Bears), owned by the huge Sinon Agrochemical Corporation, in 1997 cleverly named several of its foreign players after the conglomerate's best-selling pesticides (*ZYSB* March 11, 1998, C-6)!

There were other ways in which an overdependence on international parties and networks hurt the CPBL in the eyes of its fans. The Sinon Bulls management has long-standing ties with Los Angeles Dodgers owner Peter O'Malley.

Since 1997, the Bulls have held their spring training camps at the famed Dodgers Baseball Academy at Campo Las Palmas in the Dominican Republic. In February 1997, the Bulls announced that they and the Dodgers planned to cooperate in building a Professional Baseball Academy in Xiamen, China, based on the model of the Dodgers Dominican facility (*TWRB* February 17, 1997, 9).[24] This Dodgers influence, however, was viewed by many Taiwanese fans as more threatening than the all-American franchise would have liked. In May 1997, when the Bulls decided to fire Korean manager Kim Yong Woon and his coaches, hiring outfielder Wang Junlang as player-manager, rumors flew through the CPBL that a group of Dodgers coaches soon would come to take over the team. In fact, Teddy Martinez, a coach in the L.A. system, did arrive soon after to serve as Manager Wang's "special assistant." Martinez stayed well within his defined "assistant" role, but this instance showed just how fragile the public imagined Taiwanese control of the team to be. If the imagined Dodgers takeover did not take place, it is still useful to see just how much power the Dodgers organization—one of the most fitting symbols of American paternalism and cultural hegemony—was imagined to have in this Taiwanese league on the other side of the Pacific Ocean. Indeed, this ominous view of the Dodgers proved to hold much truth when, in January 1999, the team signed twenty-one-year-old Taiwanese superstar Chen Chin-feng (Chen Jinfeng) to a seven-year contract in clear violation of all Chinese Taipei (ROC) Amateur Baseball Association regulations (*TWRB* January 6 and 7, 1999, B-7).

Having been established at an important turning point in modern Taiwanese history, when Taiwan's society, culture, and Taiwanese identity itself were being redrawn, the CPBL originally was able to capitalize on and define the trends of the times. It held great appeal for many in Taiwan, who sought both to explore and to learn more about the world that was now so much more accessible to them—and also to finally establish what it really meant to be "Taiwanese." The league's attempt to establish connections with international baseball and cultural networks while at the same time retaining a self-consciously local identity was a perfect strategy for the time. But after just five seasons, the league's popularity went into decline when this fine balance was lost by careless and short-sighted team owners entranced by the quick-fix talents of American and Dominican players. This overdependence on the foreign only served to make the CPBL seem a slave to the hegemonic forces of American sport that the league was supposed to mediate and resist in the first place and extinguished much of the enthusiasm so evident in the early 1990s for this enterprise.

THE TAIWAN MAJOR LEAGUE

In December 1995, a new chapter in the story of Taiwan baseball began. A group of investors, led by Qiu Fusheng and Chen Shengtian of the Era Communications and Sampo Electronics dynasties, announced the formation of a new Naluwan Corporation that would operate a Taiwan Major League (TML, or Taiwan Da Lianmeng) to begin play in 1997. Qiu, a major figure in the Taiwan baseball world ever since his sports network TVIS began broadcasting CPBL games in 1994, gambled that one baseball league was not enough for the island.

The new TML was designed to trump the CPBL—not with better quality baseball, but with a media-savvy and authentically "Taiwanese" approach that made the old league's "Chinese" identity look like cheap outdated gimmickry. This explicitly politicized strategy would fit perfectly within the dialectic between globalization and local Taiwanese identity that drives so much of contemporary Taiwan society and culture. Pride in the unique aspects of Taiwanese culture and in the unique contributions that Taiwan can make to today's world justifies a place for Taiwan in the international community. Likewise, the pursuit of international (often specifically American or Japanese) trends and symbols can also be understood as solidifying a status for a Taiwan independent of the PRC and its threats of reunification. Mastering this dialectic between the uniquely Taiwanese and the international or universal is necessary for the success of any cultural, social, commercial, or political enterprise in contemporary Taiwan. And the Taiwan Major League was an endeavor that fit all of these categories.

Contacts with foreign baseball networks, as with the CPBL, were an important priority for the Taiwan Major League. In April and May 1996, top TML officials traveled to Japan and the United States, making important top-level connections with representatives of league offices and top teams like the Orix Blue Wave, Seibu Lions, and the Atlanta Braves (Gao 1997, 2).[25]

The Taiwan Major League worked to avoid being overwhelmed by the American influence that came to plague the CPBL so. To be sure, TML teams employed many American and Latin American players in their quest for championships, and the league made the most of its connections to American baseball, even playing "Take Me Out to the Ballgame" during the middle of the seventh inning of each TML game. Yet the league made no secret of its preference for what it calls a "Japanese way" *(heshi fengge)* or "Oriental wind" *(dongyang feng)* in recruiting Japanese coaches and players (*TWRB* August 14, 1998, 20, and December 30, 1998, B-7). In recruiting foreign players, TML team officials admit their fondness of Japanese players, praising their skill and personal discipline that make them "more manageable" than Latin American ballplayers (*HXXWW* June 13, 2000). These gestures to a shared Taiwanese-Japanese past and future serve both as a marker of the TML's cosmopolitan distinctiveness and as a claim to a proud supranational Asianism for the twenty-first century (Ching 2000, 236).

Unlike the CPBL, the Taiwan Major League did not allow these productive connections with the international to overshadow the league's explicitly "Taiwanese" character.[26] Where the CPBL clung to dry stereotypes of "traditional China," the TML's identity is squarely based in Taiwan's unique culture and history. The name of the Naluwan Corporation that runs the TML and the names of the four teams—Agan (Jin'gang, Robots), Fala (Leigong, Thunder Gods), Gida (Taiyang, Suns), and Luka (Yongshi, Braves)—were taken from the languages of Taiwan's aboriginal tribes that, as described above, made such great contributions to the history of Taiwan baseball. Team uniforms were designed to reflect "the special characteristics of the aboriginal peoples," but also only after "consideration of the colors and design of professional baseball uniforms of other nations" (*Naluwan Weekly* 1997b, 3). In case these measures did not make the Taiwan-centric flavor of the league distinctive enough, the TML chose as its 1999 league slogan: "Focus on Taiwan, the local comes first" *(Taiwan youxian, bentu di yi)* (*TWRB* December 4, 1998, B-6).

Another important choice made by the Taiwan Major League was to follow what it calls a "territorial philosophy" *(shudi zhuyi),* in which each team has a city or region that it calls home, unlike the CPBL, whose teams never enjoyed a true "home-team advantage."[27] The TML teams play half of their games in their home city or region—the Suns in Taibei, the Robots in Taizhong, the Braves in Jiayi-Tainan, and the Thunder Gods in Gaoxiong-Pingdong. The "territorial" doctrine of *shudi zhuyi* dictates that teams take these "home" connections seriously. Before the 1997 season, teams took part in New Year's ceremonies in their home cities and took oaths before city officials to serve as loyal and morally upright representatives of these cities. The Robots' team oath, taken on January 17, 1997, before the Taizhong Municipal Assembly, went as follows:

1. We will love and cherish Taizhong, and will work together with our Taizhong neighbors to promote the baseball movement.
2. We will sink roots in Taizhong, and will join together with our Taizhong neighbors in working for the public good.
3. We will have the fervent spirit of a rainbow, and are determined to win the highest glories in this first baseball season for our Taizhong neighbors.
4. Our hearts are full of sincerity, and we will work together with our Taizhong neighbors to create a healthy baseball movement.
5. We will play conscientiously and diligently, vowing to work with our Taizhong neighbors to make this the new home of "power baseball" [*qiangli bangqiu*]. (*Naluwan Weekly* 1997a, 6)

These hometown loyalties took on more significance with the tragic earthquake that struck central Taiwan in September 1999. The Robots quickly dubbed themselves "The Disaster Area Team," and set up their own Robots Van that delivered disinfectants, vitamins, and medicines to the residents of the epicenter at Zhongliao Village, Nantou County (*SJRB* October 8, 1999, B-6).

The Jiayi-Tainan Braves took their municipal vows seriously as well, canceling one of their 1997 preseason games against the Thunder Gods so that players could attend *miaohui* temple festivals in Beigang, Xingang, Puzi, and Dongshi during the Lantern Festival in late February (*TWRB* February 12, 1997, 9). That fall, during Jiayi County Magistrate Li Yajing's bid for reelection, Braves Manager Zhao Shiqiang (interestingly, a second-generation mainlander) registered as an official member of Li's campaign team. He and his coaching staff put in tireless hours drinking with, feting, and entertaining Jiayi County's many power brokers, as well as participating in local religious festivals (*ZYSB* November 8, 1997, C-8). The Braves capturing the TML championship in early November certainly did nothing to hurt Li, who weeks later recaptured the magistrateship by a comfortable margin.

The most spectacular demonstrations of the Taiwan Major League's distinctively "Taiwanese" character come in two of the league's trademarks. The first was its "tradition" of holding its season openers on February 28 (228) at the Jiayi Municipal Stadium. Little explanation need be given of the colossal significance of this date in Taiwan's history. Yet the TML stripped the powerful date of the anti-Nationalist/mainlander acrimony that marked private, subversive observances of the 1947 massacre for almost five decades. Instead, it transformed 228 into a celebration of everything that is truly "Taiwanese." President Lee Teng-hui (Li Denghui) threw out the first pitch at the 1997 Opening Game, after ignoring the CPBL's repeated invitations for him to appear at their opening game, as he had in 1996 (*HXXWW* January 21, 1998). Leaders of Taiwan's nine official aboriginal tribes also were honored in the game's opening ceremonies. The decision to honor Jiayi with this tradition (and with the TML's marquee team, the Braves), was a very conscious one as well, as the TML paid its respects to this "baseball capital" of Taiwan.

The symbolism of the Taiwan Major League's new "228 Opening Game" tradition is powerful and complex. The TML's 1997 opener showed off the league's international connections, with official representatives of the American, Japanese, and Korean major baseball leagues and even stars like Jackie Chan in attendance. But the chief emphasis of the "228 Opening Game" is clearly on the local—the "Taiwanese." Where the CPBL—perhaps constrained by the politics of the late 1980s and early 1990s—presented itself as a "Chinese" baseball league, the TML did everything it could to be a truly "Taiwanese" league. Local politics, local religion, tribute to the aboriginal tribes of Taiwan, and even modern Taiwanese history's most sacred date, February 28, were all included in the elaborate rituals of the new Taiwan Major League.

Participation in the international sport of baseball and impressive connections to powerful baseball networks all over the world created a cosmopolitan image for the TML. Yet the early success of the TML came from its bold celebration of the local, the authentic, the Taiwanese. Even though the new league offered an inferior quality of baseball than the old CPBL, the Taiwan Major League consistently outdrew its rival at the gates. One random (but telling) example was a night in September 1998, when 14,385 Jiayi fans attended a TML Braves-Robots game, compared to crowds of just 629 and 1,113 that showed up for CPBL games in Taibei and Gaoxiong (*LHB* September 23, 1998, 29).

Finally, the Taiwan Major League's official theme song, "Naluwan—True Heroes" (Naluwan—Cheng-keng e Eng-hiong) was perhaps the finest example of the fascinating mixture of historical and cultural legacies that makes Taiwan society so unique and dynamic and so difficult to fit within most standard models of historical, economic, cultural, social, or political development. The TML anthem, supposedly based on rhythms and patterns of several types of aboriginal tribal songs,²⁸ consists of lyrics (see below) in Mandarin, Taiwanese, English, Japanese, and Aboriginal languages:

> *Naluwan—True Heroes*
> Take charge—the fervent spirit of the rainbow,
> Our hearts are filled—with great fire shining bright,
> Struggle on—with hopes that never die,
> Start anew—a space for us alone.
> Fight! Fight! Fight, fight! Speed just like the wind,
> K! K! K! Power stronger than all,
> *Homu-ran batta*—truly strong and brave,
> Aaa . . . Na-Lu-Wan, the true heroes!²⁹

Each singing, each playing of this league anthem became a neat and tidy recreation of the last several centuries of Taiwan history and culture. To be sure, little room for critical analysis of or retrospection on this history was allowed in this rousing, commercial theme song. But the tune was one more way in which the TML sought to portray itself as the true heirs and "the true heroes" of the proud, complicated history of Taiwan.

"YOU'VE GOT THE F---ING TROUBLE": THE DECLINE OF TAIWANESE PRO BASEBALL, 1997–2001

In the winter of 1997, the future of Taiwan's pro baseball enterprise looked bright. The CPBL was beginning the first year of a rich new television contract with the China Trust conglomerate worth NT $1.5 billion (U.S. $60 million) over three years—seventeen times more than the league's previous deal with TVIS. The new Taiwan Major League, while stirring up controversy by stealing some of the CPBL's best players, promised to provide healthy competition for the old league.

The CPBL enterprise was also newly energized by a revival in Jiayi, described earlier as the traditional home of Taiwanese baseball. Jiayi's new fourteen-thousand-seat municipal baseball stadium was completed in 1997, with twenty-four CPBL games scheduled there for that summer. The new China Trust Whales, the CPBL's seventh team, chose Jiayi as their home base. This city also happened to be the hometown of Whales manager Li Laifa, another 1970s Little League star who played pro ball in Japan and managed Taiwan's 1992 Olympic team.

Unfortunately, 1997 would bring only disgrace, both domestic and international, to the CPBL. In late January 1997, law enforcement uncovered a gambling scandal that revolved around the fixing of CPBL games by ballplayers in return for huge payoffs—often double a player's monthly salary. The nation was shocked by the front-page news that some of the game's greatest and most popular stars had accepted payoffs of NT $300,000–500,000 (U.S. $11,000–18,000) per game that they threw for the local gangs handling the "gambling" on each team. The China Times Eagles threw games most spectacularly; it was revealed that the entire team was bought off regularly for a single team fee of NT $7.5 million (U.S. $270,000) per game (*TWRB* February 2, 1997, 1).[30]

This scandal, later found to be linked to gambling interests in Hong Kong and Macao as well as southern Taiwan, nearly led to the unraveling of the league as the baseball public learned the sordid details of this enterprise. And, unfortunately for the home of Taiwanese baseball, the scandal was centered in the city of Jiayi. Three Eagles players from Jiayi[31]—all members of the 1992 Olympic team—were at the core of that team's game-fixing plans with the powerful Xiaos of Jiayi, a crime gang whose three brother/leaders also embellished their illicit might by occupying top posts in local government.[32] Jiayi native Jiang Taiquan, 1992 Olympic team captain and a Lions star outfielder who was to join the Whales for their inaugural season, was also indicted for fixing games for the hometown Xiao Gang.[33] This was a tricky business: Jiang and Lions star pitcher Guo Jinxing lost some NT $200 million (U.S. $7.3 million) of the Xiaos' money in one game (Lions vs. Bulls, August 28, 1996) by "accidentally" winning after assuring gamblers that the Lions would lose (*TWRB* February 14, 1997, 3, 9; *LHB* February 14, 1997, 3). The powerful Xiaos were not men to suffer gambling losses like this gladly. Another Lions outfielder and Jiayi native may have learned this lesson the hard way; Wu Linlian went missing without a trace after he became a target of investigation in the scandal in February 1997 (*TWRB* February 12, 1997, 9).

No team or player was safe from these gangs and their members' frustrations when their favorite teams won. Loyal Elephant gamblers furious at their team's winning ways kidnapped five Elephant players, pistol-whipping one and shoving a gun down the throat of another. Seven Tigers players (including two Americans and two Puerto Ricans) were abducted at the Gaoxiong Stardust Hotel by gun-packing thugs who used similarly violent ways of requesting the players to throw games (*TWRB* August 7, 1997, 5). And one day while picking his daughter up at school, Dragon manager Xu Shengming was stabbed in the lower back by a representative of yet another gambling outfit.[34]

Understandably, fewer and fewer fans decided to pay much attention to a league whose games they feared were still being decided by sleazy mob kings. Attendance fell by 55 percent for 1997, a change also due to the easier availability of American and Japanese baseball games via Taiwan's booming cable TV market. Over the next two years, the CPBL tried to find new ways of appealing to Taiwan's increasingly inattentive public. Yet nothing—new slogans for the league, such as "Continuing our traditions and looking to the future" and "Exciting and good baseball, extremely lively" (*TWRB* February 6, 1999, B-8), promotional events with movie star Kevin Costner and Vice President Lian Zhan (*HXXWW* January 20, 1998; *ZYSB* February 6, 1998, C-6), or even plans for the Sinon Bulls and Weichuan Dragons to play China's national team in Xiamen (*TWRB* July 31, 1998, 20; *ZYSB* August 1, 1998, C-8)—was enough to convince

Taiwan's baseball public of the league's continuing relevance. By the 1999 season, fan attendance for most games was below a thousand. One day in October 1999, the two scheduled CPBL games, both crucial to the late-season pennant race, drew just 176 and 116 fans respectively (*SJRB* October 8, 1999, B-6). During the winter after the 1999 season, the league lost two more teams, as the Mercuries Tigers and three-time defending champions Weichuan Dragons both cited financial pressures in folding their baseball operations.[35]

This sad series of events came at the exact moment when American and Japanese major-league teams were beginning to aggressively scout young Taiwanese baseball talent. In 1999–2000, seven young players who would have starred in Taiwan signed lucrative contracts with American and Japanese teams. The Los Angeles Dodgers, well connected in Taiwan, struck first by signing young outfielder Chin-Feng Chen. Chen was named League MVP (Most Valuable Player) in his first U.S. minor-league season (California League, Class A) in 1999, and at age twenty-four he made his celebrated major-league debut in September 2002.[36] The Colorado Rockies were next, bagging eighteen-year-old Tsao Chin-hui (Cao Jinhui), toast of the 1999 World Junior Championships, with a U.S. $2.2 million contract in 2000. Tsao, who had been scouted by major-league teams since junior high school, has since been called "the Hope Diamond of the Rockies' minor league system" (Renck 2001). The New York Yankees, Seibu Lions, and Chunichi Dragons also invested heavily in young Taiwanese players whose talent the CPBL and TML—already crippled by the events described—now had to live without.

A final humiliation came in March 2001, on the opening night of the TML's fifth season of play. The Taiwan Major League, although not tainted directly by the CPBL's gambling problems, had also seen the popularity of its inferior quality of baseball wane since 1997. By 2001, the two rival leagues, both plagued by several consecutive money-losing seasons, were seriously considering a merger and a further downsizing of the baseball enterprise. The TML shortened team schedules from eighty-four to just sixty games each and desperately tried to attract fans with a new marketing gimmick—naming four pop stars as official "spokespeople" for each of the league's teams. Rapper Zhang Zhenyu, spokesman of the Gaoxiong-Pingdong Thunder Gods, was scheduled to kick off the festivities at Chengqing Lake Stadium, along with ROC Legislative Yuan Speaker Wang Jinping (also TML chairman) and Ronald McDonald. The game itself was to be a milestone in TML history, marking the debut of Taibei Suns Manager Li Juming, the former Little League and Brother Elephant star idolized as Taiwan's "Mr. Baseball." The season got off to an unbecoming start, however, when Zhang enthusiastically performed his song "Trouble," repeatedly screaming in English before the sellout crowd and a national TV audience, "You've got the f---ing trouble! You've got the f---ing trouble!" (*CP* April 1, 2001). Zhang's league handlers, not to mention Ronald McDonald, were surely humiliated by this display of bad judgment, but his words were also a very accurate diagnosis of the state of Taiwanese pro baseball at the beginning of the twenty-first century.

CONCLUSION

On December 31, 2000, Taiwan's President Chen Shui-bian made his first New Year's address to the nation, remarks meant to sum up his first seven months in office and also to "Bridge the New Century." Chen had much to discuss, from the political revolution completed by his own victory and his once-illegal party's climb to power, to the world economic recession and entry into the World Trade Organization, to Taiwan's tense relations with China and the increasing possibility of an armed conflict across the straits. The president summed up his remarks with comments on the unique "Taiwan spirit" forged during the twentieth century and closed his address with an interesting symbol of the Taiwan experience:

> I recently had the opportunity to read some of Taiwan's historical records and was deeply inspired by one picture in particular: a portrait of the Maple Leaf Little League baseball team. In this black-and-white photograph, there was a barefoot aboriginal boy at bat. His face showed full concentration, as he focused all of his energy on his responsibility. Meanwhile, his teammates stood by on the sidelines anxiously watching and giving encouragement. Such a beautiful moment perfectly captures twentieth-century Taiwan and is a memory that I will never forget.
>
> My dear fellow countrymen, history has passed the bat to us, and it is now our turn to stand at the plate. The twenty-first century will undoubtedly throw us several good pitches, as well as one or two dusters [*huaiqiu*]. Regardless of what is thrown to us, however, we must stand firm and concentrate all of our strength and willpower for our best swing. (Chen 2000; Chen 2001, 3)

Again, it is no accident that Chen chose this Maple Leaf image to encapsulate Taiwan's history and identity (although he may be understating the case by calling a possible Chinese invasion of Taiwan a mere "duster"). I have tried to theorize here that a history of Taiwanese baseball is an appropriate and crucial window for understanding the complicated histories and cultures of modern Taiwan. Starting with the game's Japanese origins, followed by the high-profile successes of Taiwanese Little League baseball from the 1960s to the 1980s, baseball was an important avenue by which Taiwanese people have navigated the historical relationships with the Japanese, the Chinese Nationalists, and their American allies. Now, at the turn of the century, as the search for a uniquely Taiwanese identity is given official sanction, baseball is a crucial element of this identity.[37]

Despite the depths to which the professional game's popularity has sunk, recent events still demonstrate the centrality of baseball in Taiwan. Taiwan successfully hosted the 2001 International Baseball Association amateur championships, a development that speaks to the weight that Taiwan carries in the world baseball community despite efforts by the PRC to shut down this type of international Taiwan presence. Many rejoiced when, in early 2003, it was announced that the rival CPBL and TML would end their six-year rivalry and merge into a single six-team league. Taiwan's baseball heritage has the attention of the art world. Taiwan's 1999 Golden Horse Award for Best Documentary went to director Xiao Juzhen's "Maple Leaf Legend" (Hongye Chuanqi), a film about the men who made baseball history for Maple Leaf Elementary School, Hongye Village, Taidong County, and all of Taiwan so many decades ago.

More than one century ago, Mark Twain wrote that baseball was the perfect expression of the American society of his day, declaring that the game had become "the outward and visible expression of the drive and push and rush and struggle of the raging, tearing, booming nineteenth century!" (Guttmann 1994, 79). Robert Whiting and William Kelly have both seen Japanese baseball as the perfect symbol of different elements of that nation's modern history and culture.[38]

The same can be said for Taiwan. Baseball's position at the center of a new Taiwanese nationalism and project of self-definition is illustrated perfectly by the NT $500 bill issued in December 2000. As the sage visage of the iron-fisted Generalissimo Chiang Kai-shek is removed from Taiwan's currency for the new millennium, what better indigenous symbol to replace him than an image of the young Little Leaguers who won his regime so much fame in the 1970s? Now, instead of facing the gaze of the Chinese military leader forced on Taiwanese youth for four decades as "Savior of the People," Taiwan consumers handing over NT $500 are inspired by the smiles on the faces of the Puyuma aborigine boys from Taidong County whose Pacific Cup victory celebration is portrayed on the bill (*LHB* December 16, 2000, 6). At the turn of the twenty-first century, these are the healthy and "authentic" faces that Taiwanese people today take to represent their island nation and—as they have for nearly a century—express through their national sport of baseball.

10
Yang-Sucking She-Demons
Penetration, Fear of Castration, and Other Freudian Angst in Modern Chinese Cinema
Marc L. Moskowitz

EDITORS' INTRODUCTION

Movies, like baseball, are entertainment. Also like baseball, they are more than entertainment—they are reflections and sources of popular understandings about the world and our place in it.

Most movies shown in Taiwan are not made in Taiwan. Some are Chinese versions of movies made for many other audiences—often in Japan, Europe, or especially America. Of the films made for Chinese audiences, a very large proportion are made in Hong Kong for an audience of Chinese around the world, including especially Taiwan. To an audience representing the global "Greater China," Hong Kong films provide a culturally synthesizing medium that creatively blends the anxieties and satisfactions of modern life with the symbolic heritage of Chinese traditions. (To a non-Chinese audience, they are often flat and foolish, as the audience lacks the necessary cultural heritage and appreciates little of the ingenuity with which it is manipulated.)

In this chapter, Marc Moskowitz analyzes the extravagantly successful film *A Chinese Ghost Story* and shows us how it is understood by a Taiwan audience. The film is a blend of grotesque demons, tragic ghosts, reincarnation, martial arts, and deeds of courage and adventure, all set in the distant past. It is based on a well-known story, so suspense is not part of the appeal. Instead the Chinese audience enjoys a combination of eternally interesting motifs (such as the triumph of good over evil) and the artistry with which the tale is retold.

For a story to "sell" to a modern audience, it cannot be a stilted museum piece. Commercial success comes from making the story fresh, even while it remains familiar. Furthermore, a film is not a book, and what reads well doesn't always look appealing, just as what can best be represented with the sound and motion of a movie screen is not always effective in print. Analysts of the film industry have often commented on how Hollywood or its foreign equivalents change tales. Apologists for these changes argue that they are improvements—or at least necessary compromises—as the tale moves from one period or one medium to another.

To make the successful film version of *A Chinese Ghost Story*, several changes were made. Comparing the movie version with the Qing era short story on which it is based provides Moskowitz a view of the changes (and continuities) in three very specific areas of life: gender roles, heterosexuality, and the unconscious fear of men that women are potentially dangerous to them (technically called "castration anxiety").

What are we to make of these changes, introduced by the Hong Kong filmmaker and so winning with Taiwan audiences? Moskowitz shows that many of the changes, like many changes in the society they reflect, are less drastic than they seem. As he recounts and analyzes each change and balances the evidence, he shows that many old assumptions about gender and family still remain, sometimes comically inverted, sometimes locked away under symbolic restatements, and sometimes betrayed by a single offhand remark.

To the Chinese viewer, the analysis is not a conscious operation, but the message must be clear enough: The world is complicated but there are verities—and here they are. The film reinforces a prevailing and in the end rather traditional view of life, even while celebrating the complexities of its manifestations. The symbolic complexities that Moskowitz analyzes for us arguably represent also the complexities of life in modern Taiwan, and that is what makes the film so intriguing to its Taiwanese audience. ∎

When the Hong Kong movie *Ghost Story*[1] was first shown in Taiwan's cinemas in 1987, it captured public imagination in a way that might be compared to *Star Wars* in the United States. It not only gained enormous popularity of its own but became a model for many later films of its kind. Even today this film can frequently be seen on television, and it is rare to meet a Taiwanese person between the ages of fifteen and forty who has not seen it. Thus, unlike the other chapters of this volume, the subject of this essay was not produced in Taiwan, but it can rightfully be said, by virtue of its popularity, to reflect Taiwanese concerns. To some degree it has also become part of a great many Taiwanese lives. In the following pages I will present this film and compare and contrast it with the traditional ghost story that inspired it.

The movie *Ghost Story* was adapted from the eighteenth-century short story "Nie Xiaoqian," named after the female protagonist of the tale. The story is in a Qing dynasty collection of ghost stories written by Pu Songling (1640–1715) entitled *The Strange Tales of Liaozhai (Liaozhai zhiyi)*. The movie *Ghost Story* is part of a genre of films called *wuxia* that are set in traditional China and feature enlightened martial artists with supernatural powers. To compare it to a film that is more familiar to an American audience, it is something akin to the fantastic nature of Ang Lee's movie *Crouching Tiger, Hidden Dragon,* in which swordsmen jump stories high and do other miraculous feats (Lee 2000). *Ghost Story,* with its ghosts and demons, is far more surreal but relies on the same set of cultural understandings about martial artists' supernatural powers and morality. Unlike other films about ghosts that could be categorized as horror movies, this genre places more emphasis on martial arts, comedy, and a love story.

Hong Kong and Taiwan have quite distinctive histories and cultures, yet both have been occupied by foreign forces and have traditionally been on the periphery of China.[2] In addition to this there is a certain degree of crossover with actors and actresses. The main actress[3] in *Ghost Story,* for example, is from Taiwan. Therefore, the Hong Kong movie industry becomes a central cultural zone between mainland China, Hong Kong, and Taiwan. This reaffirms a common background of "Chinese culture" in an era in which Taiwanese identity is frequently at the forefront of sociopolitical movements. This is not to discount the dramatic cultural differences of modern-day Taiwan, Hong Kong, and mainland China. Yet it is important to remember that just as the United States and England are vastly different nations that share many common values because of a partially shared history, Taiwan, Hong Kong, and mainland China have transformed into distinctive entities that still share many cultural values and concerns that must be remembered to fully understand what they have become.

In looking at how *Ghost Story* has selectively been changed to make it more amenable to a modern audience, we see a shift from the traditional ideal of polygynous households to one of monogamous love matches. This in turn provides a different set of expectations for ideal manhood, a woman's place in the patriline, and modern conceptions of proper relationships between lovers. In short, "modernizing" the plot transforms the story to show dramatic disparities between traditional and modern concerns and norms—or does it?

In fact, the only thing that is more striking than the changes that I have just outlined are the underlying cultural continuities. The themes that I will address in the following pages are: gender roles, enforced normative heterosexuality, and castration anxiety—the last of which is evinced by traditional fears of male loss of power and of women as sexually, socially, and spiritually dangerous to men. Thus, in comparing the film to the original story, we see which gendered conceptual frameworks have been preserved from the past, which have shifted in meaning, and which have taken on entirely new forms.

YIN AND YANG, DAOIST SEX TRACTS, AND FOX SPIRITS

To understand the stories that I am about to present, some background information is necessary. The first piece of this puzzle is yin and yang. Yin represents women, darkness, passivity, and often sickness and death. Yang, in turn, stands for men, light, activity, and life force. It was—and is—thought that one needs both yin and yang in the universe. Although yang undoubtedly has more positive connotations, to have only yang would be as unbalanced as having only daytime. Maintaining a proper balance, therefore, stresses the need to have both yin and yang, and to some extent becomes a metaphor for conjugal union in that either man or woman alone is incomplete.

It is believed, however, that a little more yang essence in one's life is never a bad thing. Thus, illness in both traditional and modern China and Taiwan is often described by traditional Chinese doctors and religious practitioners as having an excess of yin. Similarly, it is thought that ghosts are more yin, whereas the living are more yang.

Daoist bedchamber manuals also play an important role in providing the necessary background information for the movie. These were Daoist tracts that told men of the medical benefits of having sex with as many young women as possible and warned of the harmful effects of using improper techniques. The man was warned that ejaculation would deplete his life energy *(yang qi)*. Instead, when climaxing, he was instructed to send this vital energy up his spine to be stored in the brain (van Gulik 1961, 78). This would then turn his hair black, allow lost teeth to grow back, and possibly even help him to attain immortality (136). More relevant to this study, however, is the fear that women might gain the knowledge of such secret arts and that they would use the techniques to profit at men's expense instead, thereby preserving their beauty and becoming more youthful but leaving the men wasted and sickly (75, 158–159).

In modern Taiwan people do not seem to believe in these arts anymore. For that matter, most people I have spoken with in Taiwan have not even heard of them. Yet fear of the depletion of life energy through sexual intercourse continues to be strong in both modern Taiwan (Moskowitz 2001) and in mainland China (Evans 1997, 42–44).

Traditional stories about fox spirits draw on these same conceptions of yang energy and the danger of losing one's life force through sexual activity. Fox spirits *(hulijing)* were thought to be beings that could transform themselves into human form. Although they could be either men or women, they were most often portrayed as sexually rapacious female tricksters who seduced men to steal their yang essence. In some tales, fox spirits could gain immortality if they accumulated enough male life force in this fashion (Wu 1986, 123). In other stories they seemed to do it just to have a good time. In some of the stories the fox spirits could have intercourse with men without harming them. In most stories, however, the men would become weak, sickly, and either be rescued or die.

In modern Taiwan such spirits are no longer thought to exist, yet the term "fox spirit" is still commonly used in a derogatory fashion to refer to a loose woman. Traditional stories about fox spirits also carried thinly veiled messages about the living. For example, if we compare the following eighteenth-century stories we see strikingly similar views of sexual exploitation. In the first story, a man knowingly has relations with a fox spirit. When he attempts to leave her, she becomes angry. This is his response:

Don't act like that. Men carry full authority in matters pertaining to men and women. . . . What's more, you have come to sap my vital energies. I do not owe you an emotional debt, for we are never united by feelings. You've been with so many men that it would be hard to talk of chastity: I was not the cause of your fall. The gentleman derides the practice of abusing a woman and in the end abandoning her, but that holds true for humans, not for creatures of your type. (Chan 1998, 71)

The second story is almost identical to the first, only in this case it is the fox spirit that leaves her human lover.

When reprimanded for her lack of feelings, the fox retorted in anger, "There are no marital obligations between us; I came for the specific purpose of getting spiritual nourishment. The cream and essence of your being has been exhausted. With nothing more to gain, why should I not go? This is like liaisons built on power and influence that are broken when there is no more power or influence. Liaisons built on wealth, too, are severed when there is no more wealth. Humans curry favor with those whose wealth and power have aroused their attention, not out of any genuine feelings. Previously didn't you ingratiate yourself with so-and-so, whom you now no longer care about? And I am being reproached!" (Chan 1998, 204)

Initially one might consider these two accounts to be quite different: In the first story the man is in control and in the next it is a woman. Their reasoning is also slightly different in the two tales, reflecting their gendered realities. Yet both stories serve as parables concerning a wider morality that revolves around female/male exchanges of sustenance for pleasure, whether that exchange is in the form of marriage or prostitution. It is presented as being excusable for fox spirits to pursue physical pleasure, just as it is expected that men will do so because that is thought to be their nature (Chan 1998, 122). The first story suggests that a woman who fails to remain chaste has only herself to blame if things go wrong. The second tale evinces a fear of the manipulative prostitute[4] and, by extension, comments on female "exploitation" of men. The allegory sets up a logical set of consequences: Men "naturally" pursue pleasure, women "naturally" exploit this desire for their livelihood. Thus we see different schemas for morality that are sharply divided along gender lines.

THE TRANSFORMATION OF A TALE

Earlier I noted that *Ghost Story* was adapted from a short story in the Qing dynasty collection, *The Strange Tales of Liaozhai,* perhaps the most famous set of ghost stories in Chinese fiction. It contains stories about a wide range of ghosts and supernatural happenings, and a number of the tales are about fox spirits. As a whole, Pu Songling's stories portray fox spirits in a more positive light than other stories of their kind (Wu 1986, 136, 139). Yet some other stories about fox spirits also portray them in often surprisingly sympathetic and vulnerable terms (Huntington 1996, 41, 56). The spirits' noble deeds are often used to highlight the ignoble actions of the living and are held up as exemplars for proper behavior (Huntington 1996, 150; Wu 1986, 140–141, 145).

The heroine of the story, Xiaoqian (Nie Xiaoqian), is not explicitly referred to as a fox spirit, but she has many of the same traits: She is intelligent, stunningly beautiful, deceiving, mischievous, and a seductress of unsuspecting living males. As with Xiaoqian, fox sprits are associated with the depletion of men's yang essence through sexual intercourse. Unlike fox spirits, however, Xiaoqian does not directly benefit from this exchange.

Fox spirits often serve as thinly veiled metaphors for prostitution (Chan 1998, 52, 232; Huntington 1996, 145–147). Men are portrayed as insatiably lustful, and the female spirits use their sexuality to meet other needs (Huntington 1996, 179). In the movie, the ghosts' home is essentially a house of prostitution in which an evil tree witch acts as the madam and yang essence is the currency. Xiaoqian's job is to seduce men. Once the men are aroused, the tree witch can suck out their life essence. The hero of the story, Caichen (Ning Caichen), shares lodging at an old abandoned temple with Swordsman Yan (Yan Dajiao), who has supernatural powers that keep the ghosts at bay. Because Caichen is an upright and moral person, he resists Xiaoqian's temptation where others failed and died.

These basic elements of the plot can also be seen in the movie *Ghost Story*, but there are also many significant departures. In the short story, Caichen is already married and the plot is equally divided between his encounter with Xiaoqian at the abandoned temple and the ways in which she is integrated into his family once he frees her from her evil master and she returns home with him. The short story emphasizes familial concerns when Caichen introduces Xiaoqian to his mother, who is at first concerned that a ghost marriage would not produce heirs. Xiaoqian explains that Caichen has a good fate, which will bring him three children and success in the imperial examinations, bringing honor both to his family in the world of the living and to Xiaoqian in the realm of the dead. Xiaoqian understands his mother's concerns, however, and suggests that she enter the family as Caichen's sister.[5] Because Caichen's wife is deathly ill and unable to perform her household duties, Caichen's mother is slowly won over by Xiaoqian's ability to perform these tasks. When Caichen's wife dies, his mother agrees to allow a marriage ceremony between her son and Xiaoqian.[6] Later Caichen takes an additional (living) wife who bears him a child, and Xiaoqian bears him two additional living children (Pu 1766, 47–57).[7]

This story is moving, as Anthony Yu points out, not only because it has a happy ending, but also because of Xiaoqian's "progressive reintegration into the human community" (Yu 1987, 428). More specifically, the story purposefully integrates her into her lover's patriline (429). In other words, she is not passive by any means but she is presented as having overcome her sordid past and proven herself worthy precisely because she accepts the "superiority" of her husband, the importance of filial piety, and because she prioritizes adjusting to the needs of her husband's patriline. Caichen's dominance is unquestioned and he shows no weakness of character or fear throughout the story. Xiaoqian's desire to be a member of a polygynous union is taken as a matter of course, and her stated reason for being there has less to do with the modern concept of love than the recognition that he is a righteous man worthy to be her husband because of his potential success in the imperial government.

In contrast, Caichen of the movie is a common person with no foreseeable rise in status. In fact, the movie ends as he and Swordsman Yan ride off to follow a rainbow, indicating that, if anything, he has become more distant from mainstream society instead of showing promise of upward mobility within it. Significantly, the familial aspect of the story is completely absent from the movie. If Caichen is married it is never even hinted at, and his youth, status, and actions would suggest otherwise. Neither his parents nor the problem of progeny is ever mentioned.

In both the short story and the movie, Xiaoqian falls in love with Caichen because he proves himself to be righteous by resisting her sexual advances. Yet the two versions of Caichen resist for different reasons. Caichen of the story is a flawless person. He is not tempted by Xiaoqian's sexual advances, nor is he afraid of ghosts. This would seem to point to the most fundamental difference between the short story and the movie and can largely be explained by the intended audience. In Imperial China, the only people who could have read Pu's stories would have been the literate elite. As Joseph Esherick and Mary Rankin have pointed out, unlike modern American sensibilities about class, in traditional China "it was taken for granted that a society should have an elite. The only questions involved what type of elite it should be" (Esherick and Rankin 1990, 1). Pu Songling's characters, therefore, were part of a larger discourse on the proper behavior of a gentleman and a scholar. In many stories about fox spirits, the characters demonstrate the human foibles of the elite; but in the case of Caichen, we are presented with an idealized exemplar of proper behavior. In contrast, in dealing with the movie version we have a wider intended audience, most of whom are not from the elite classes. Presumably to create characters with whom such an audience could identify, Caichen of the movie is transformed into a poor tax collector who is generally scorned and abused by the public. This version of Caichen is fearful, harassed, and clearly desires Xiaoqian—but he acts honorably because he is a good person.

Unlike the original plot, in the movie Xiaoqian falls in love with Caichen rather than just finding him to be worthy. She does so in part because of his righteousness and in part because he has shown chivalric valor by protecting her from Swordsman Yan, who seeks to destroy her because she is a ghost. Perhaps most importantly, however, she falls in love with him because she finds his imperfections to be endearing—specifically, his fearfulness, his gullibility, and his innocence. In the second sequel,[8] *Ghost Story 3*, we have essentially the same set of themes, but this time the hero is a poor apprentice monk who spends most of the movie being hungry and fearful. What we see, then, is a direct shift in popular cultural models of manhood that both allows for a romanticization of the common man and presents the ideal man as allowing for "feminine" weakness rather than being an invulnerable, "perfect" male.

In the short story, Xiaoqian is fairly passive until she arrives at Caichen's home, whereupon she sets out to prove her worthiness to become part of the patriline by performing domestic duties. In the movie, however, when she is not playing the role of seductress, she is portrayed as a woman warrior who effortlessly kills wolves and poisonous snakes, pushes Caichen around, and does battle with other ghosts. Both the short story and the movie highlight her beauty and her ability to seduce men. The other side of her character, however, could not be more different in the two portrayals.

In the movie, Xiaoqian and Caichen make love. Because she does not beckon the tree witch as she had done with other men, Caichen is not harmed. Thus it is in her power to spare him or to surrender him to his enemies. Unlike the short story in which Caichen presents a uniformly invulnerable persona, Caichen of the movie is lovable precisely because of his weakness. Unlike the short story, in which she has a platonic relationship with Caichen until they are married, in the movie they consummate their love with no formal ties. They have a reciprocal relationship—he protects her from the living, and she hides and protects him from the dead. This mutual need and assistance further emphasize their romantic bond.

Contrasting the movie and the original plot, therefore, one can see a reflection of changing conceptions of manhood, love, sexuality, and gendered power disparities within relationships. There is also a marked shift from a view of women as domestic servants in polygynous households to women of balancing—though not equal—power vis-à-vis the men with whom they have romantic monogamous relationships.

MALE DESIRE AND FEMALE PERFORMANCE

Ghost Story and its second sequel *Ghost Story 3* are very playful with their presentation of male desire and female performance. A man in such stories is often portrayed as being unable to control his sexual impulses, which inevitably leads to his own destruction and often the ruination of his entire family (Epstein 1996, 123). Therefore, an essential component of the performative comedy in both the short story and the movies is a comedic role reversal in which women pursue men and men fight to preserve their purity.

In the short story this can be seen when Xiaoqian, failing to seduce Caichen, offers him money.[9] In a comic twist, Caichen angrily refuses the money, saying, "This kind of unearned money would dirty my pocket!" *(Zhe zhong buyi zhi cai, zang wo de koudai!)* (Pu 1766, 49).

A representative scene in *Ghost Story 3* that also uses role reversal for comic effect can be seen when the heroine tries to seduce the hero of the movie, a young apprentice monk who is traveling with his Buddhist master:

The heroine, who is a ghost, knocks at the temple door, "Save me! There are Ghosts [out here]."

The apprentice monk reasons that if she needs to be saved from ghosts, she must not be a ghost, so he lets her in. She then runs around the room screaming, "Ghosts! Ghosts!" before falling to the ground. Lying on the floor she seductively whispers, "There's a ghost. I'm so scared. Quick, help me up."

He seems hesitant to get too near her, for he is a monk and she is a woman. "Your clothing is very thin, where are the ghosts?"

"Let me hide beside you," she says as she trips him and rolls on top of him. "Look, something's moving over there. Protect me." She rolls under him and wraps her leg around him.

He stammers, "Your leg."

She grabs his hand and places it on her breast. "Feel my heart. See how quickly it is beating? Caress me."

He pulls back in fear. "I almost broke my vows! I'm not allowed to touch women. I know, why don't we take out the Buddhist scriptures and read them together! That way the ghosts won't come!"

She smiles, clearly amused by his innocence. He rolls away from her on the ground and she rolls behind him. "I don't want to recite the scriptures, let's do something else."

She lies on top of him and they roll across the floor together.

He exclaims in surprise, "Hey, how did we get stuck together again?"

"You know, you are my first man. Shall I help you undress?"

"Undress? Did I hear you right? If my master hears us like this he will never believe I was saving your life! Let's pray!"

Part of the entertainment of the role reversal in these movies is the woman's insistence on her purity when it is obvious that this is not the case, combined with the man's concern with preserving *his* purity in the face of her unexpected sexual assertiveness. As in the short story, in the movies the heroine uses her feminine guile in an attempt to seduce the innocent hero. An equally comedic twist in these movies is women's deceit and the ease with which men are deceived. This form of comedy plays with traditional gender stereotypes, and the Taiwanese audience, at least those I have spoken with, laughingly recognize the exaggeration of the games that are played in real life.

Though women become the sexual aggressors in these movies, it does not represent reversed gender roles as it might first appear, for part of the humor is based on the premise that women do not normally pursue men and that men do not naturally resist their sexual impulses. The hero's ability to stumble away from temptation sets him apart from the other men in the movie and is the endearing and comedic factor that wins over the heroine's love.

I have suggested that in both *Ghost Story* and *Ghost Story 3*, the female ghosts are portrayed as women warriors who can effortlessly injure or kill mortal men. This female power is contextual, however. In the movie the heroine is inevitably rescued by the hero, in spite of his human frailty. Also, the enlightened man, Swordsman Yan, can easily defeat the female ghosts; his only real adversary is the tree witch, who is strong precisely because she has absorbed so many men's yang essence. In other words, the movie opens with images of women warriors who are fearless and strong and can easily defeat men in battle. But it concludes, as do many films of this genre, with images of women's femininity, vulnerability, and their grateful dependence on men.

In the end of *Ghost Story 3*, for example, the swordsman and the hero part ways. Once the swordsman is out of sight, he laughingly pulls out the heroine's urn that holds the ashes to which her spirit is bound. But upon opening the urn, he finds that it is empty because the hero has transferred her ashes to a pouch that he hangs from his neck. It is a happy ending, for the romantic partners have not been separated either by malicious spirits or the mischievous living. But it is also an unintentionally unsettling message. In an important sense, the heroine's status has not changed; she has been passed from owner to owner, and her fate lies not so much with her own agency as with her lover's ability to outwit other men in a battle for possession of her physical body. Again, patriarchal control is restored.

PENETRATION, CONSUMING ORIFICES, AND CASTRATION ANXIETY

One of the more striking images of *Ghost Story* is the villain, a one-thousand-year-old female tree witch who wears female clothing and makeup but who is played by a stocky male actor with an extremely masculine facial structure. The tree witch's voice switches back and forth from an exaggeratedly baritone male voice to a dubbed, shrill female voice. This is presumably because she has absorbed so much yang essence from men—a deviation from more prevalent traditional conceptions of yang suckers, who were thought to become younger and more beautiful with each victim they seduced. In addition to her ghastly appearance and her rather formidable tongue, which I will discuss at further length in a moment, she is intended to frighten and amuse precisely because of her transgendered identity. The movie quickly becomes a war, then—not only between the living and the dead but between "natural" heterosexual identities and this sexually ambiguous persona. Thus, her inevitable downfall is not simply a victory of good over evil—it is a restoration of normative heterosexuality in which those who deviate from the sexual norm are expelled.

In the traditional tales of fox spirits, as in the Daoist bedchamber manuals, stories of female succubi warn that uncontrolled desire is inherently perilous. The danger that such female spirits present occurs on an individual level but also represents a larger disintegration of the sociopolitical order (Epstein 2001, 121). In Pu Songling's story, Xiaoqian seduces her victims and pricks their feet so that her master can drink their yang essence (Pu 1766, 50). In the movie, the tree witch also sends her more feminine ghostly vassals to seduce men. Once the men are aroused, Xiaoqian beckons the tree witch by ringing her ankle bracelet. The tree witch then penetrates the male victims' mouths (which are inevitably open because the men are screaming in horror) with her seemingly infinitely extendable tongue and sucks out their yang essence until they are nothing but shriveled corpses—literally skin and bone.

The tree witch's tongue becomes a major feature in the movie as it penetrates, stretches hundreds of feet into the air, crosses floors, and breaks rafters and whatever else crosses its path. The tongue itself is slimy, veiny, and looks like an erect penis. In one scene, when Swordsman Yan stabs the tongue with his sword—thereby penetrating the penetrating object—he is covered with the white sticky effluvium that spurts out. In several other scenes, the tree witch attacks the heroes with her tongue and they desperately grasp its tip, which wiggles inches from their faces, to prevent it from entering their mouths and sucking the life out of them.

It is important to note that the danger here is not presented as harm from the gradual depletion of yang essence due to sexuality itself, as was presented in the Daoist bedchamber manuals. Nor is it presented as the danger of ejaculation as it once had been. Instead, arousal itself is presented as opening a gateway that allows the tree witch to enter. In other words, this carries less a sense of gradual depletion of life energy than of yang-essence rape.

Penetration becomes a recurrent theme in the movies. There is, of course, the tree witch's formidable tongue. Also, I have already mentioned Swordsman Yan stabbing the tree witch's tongue with his sword and the visual similarity to ejaculation that results. Second only to the tree witch's penetration in graphicness is the heroine's use of her own tongue. In *Ghost Story 3*, the heroine tricks the hero into letting her put her tongue in his mouth, ostensibly to suck out the venom of a snake. (She convinces him he will be poisoned because he sucked the venom out of the snakebite on her leg.) The camera shot shows her tongue inside of his mouth and follows it as it wiggles its way deep down his throat. When her tongue reaches the inside of his stomach, he pushes her away in fear, and she laughs at her own deception and at the hero's gullibility. Again, the man is portrayed as innocent and as trying to maintain his purity as the more worldly woman takes advantage of him and penetrates him.

Fear of engulfment is another prominent theme in the movies. In one scene in the movie, the tree witch's hundred-foot-long tongue splits open to reveal jagged teeth as tendrils shoot out to try to pull Caichen into it. The tree witch's face is deep in the back of the crocodile-like mouth, waiting to devour her prey. Suddenly, the phallus is transformed into a jagged engulfing orifice that threatens to consume with its bloody teeth.

Bhaskar Sarkar has eloquently argued that the anxiety demonstrated in Hong Kong cinema evinces larger fears in Taiwan, Hong Kong, and the PRC concerning modernization and a "crisis in national identity" as they are faced with Western economic hegemony (Sarkar 2001, 169–170). I argue, however, that while his analysis may point to some of the reasons that this genre of cinema is so popular in modern Asia, a more important factor is that these tales

The tree witch attacks with her tongue. *(A Chinese Ghost Story 1)*

The attempted seduction of the young monk. *(A Chinese Ghost Story 3)*

Swordsman Yan covered in goo after stabbing the tree witch's tongue. *(A Chinese Ghost Story 1)*

draw on ongoing fears concerning the loss of male privilege in a patriarchal system. The image of these supernatural women therefore exemplifies a long-standing fear that men will lose their privilege to castrating women as the men enter the bedroom and expose themselves—both literally and figuratively.

The prevalence of severed arms and heads combined with copious menstrual and nuptial blood points to the prevalence of castration anxiety in fox spirit tales (Epstein 2001, 138–141).[10] In the movies, both the images of engulfing orifices and the penetrating phallus point to castration anxiety. Inescapable orifices that pull men into awaiting sharp, jagged teeth offer perhaps a more overt expression of this, but if we take castration anxiety to represent a fear of losing male power and agency, we can see the same elements in fear of penetration or loss of yang essence. The fact that the tree witch is both male and female enhances this imagery, for the she-demon penetrates with a phallus that does not ejaculate but sucks the men dry of their "male essence," leaving them powerless. In the context in which sexuality is presented as inevitably leading to painful and complete loss of male energy and death, it is no surprise that the most powerful or potent male characters (Swordsman Yan and the older monk) are free from sexual desire.

The traditional fear of losing yang essence is also inherently linked with castration anxiety, for in using one's male member, the man is in danger of losing his vital energy and risks becoming sick and weakly—or even dying. There is a long-standing fear of women as supernaturally dangerous.[11] The image of female ghosts sucking the life energy out of men is a continuance of this age-old fear of women as sexual agents and as potential bringers of chaos.

CONCLUSION

Because of space limitations, I have not directly addressed other movies of this genre here, but although the details vary from film to film, elements of all the underlying themes that I have outlined here can be seen in many other films of this kind.[12] To the unfamiliar eye, the movie might seem like a bad acid trip: Evil sprites wiggle their tongues at the camera, swordsmen leap stories high into the air, and body parts have the surreal potential to move, extend, or expand in unexpected ways. Yet as one watches more of these films, certain patterns begin to emerge as mortals and immortals, living and dead, do battle, make alliances, and fall in love.

In spite of the bizarre nature of this genre of cinema, anyone familiar with American Westerns would find these movies strangely familiar. The heroes are strangers who come to town, do battle with their enemies, and ride off toward the horizon after they win the climactic fight scenes. Xiaoqian is presented as the hooker with the heart of gold—a character also familiar in Westerns. She begins by seducing men for a living and is won over by the goodness of the heroes. As the film progresses, she risks her own life to protect the hero against the establishment that she had previously served. The fact that she is a ghost and that the currency is yang essence is admittedly an added twist, but in general the same guidelines for honor, evil, and morality about greed and corruption apply.

To review, on first inspection *Ghost Story* seems to have taken on very different meanings to please a modern audience that has different concerns—perhaps even different realities—from the readership of the original story. This is in some senses true, for we saw the assumption in the Qing era story that both women and men would be content in polygynous households, that respect and reverence for elders took precedence over one's individual desires, and that a proper woman obeyed her husband—whom she married because of his worth and status rather than because of love in the modern sense of the term. We saw that as a reflection of differing audiences, the movie version of this tale chooses "the common man" rather than elite scholars as its heroes. We also saw that conceptions of ideal manhood are widening to allow the expression of human emotions such as fear and caring.

Underlying the apparent proof that times have changed, however, traditional assumptions manifest themselves concerning the "naturalness" of women's subordination, in spite of the more overt portrayal of strong women warriors. We are also witness to traditional fears of women's sexuality and male anxieties concerning loss of potency, whether that loss was demonstrated as a fear of consuming orifices, penetration, or loss of yang essence. If we take these same elements to be the basis of castration anxiety, these seemingly bizarre plots depict strangely familiar anxieties.

In the end, things have been "set right"—transgendered demons have been disposed of and their harmful castrating, penetrating, and draining potential has been controlled. Women's deceit and promiscuity have been uncovered, forgiven, and replaced by monogamous love. Male heroes, previously protected by women warriors, triumph by rescuing the women who have turned out to be vulnerable and grateful to be saved by their men after all. Paradoxically, then, in the midst of portrayals of such surprisingly strong, assertive, and capable women, coexisting themes of normative heterosexuality and patriarchal order have been restored. Hence this seemingly unworldly plot, far from being a series of unrelated images as it might first seem, reveals itself to be a parable for spoken and unspoken understandings about the relationship between yin and yang, ghosts and the living, women and men.

Notes

CHAPTER 1. TAIWAN'S HISTORY

1. Despite the important protestations of Lydia Liu (1999, 131–134), "barbarian" still seems the best English term available for translating the character *"yi,"* which, before it was used to describe westerners, referred to less-civilized peoples from homelands located to the east of China proper.

2. For explanations of some of these terms, see Cao 1980, 43; Carrington 1977, 79; Fang 1994, 13; Goddard 1966, 129; Hsu 1980a, 9; Nakamura 1954, 114; Phillips 1999, 277; Stainton 1999b, 37.

3. Even by the mid-eighteenth century, the popular novel *Yesou puyan* (A country codger's words of exposure) still portrayed Taiwan as an island fundamentally different from China and orthodox Confucian values, an "allegoric wilderness" populated with lethal female sex-demons (Epstein 2001, 219–221).

4. These various names were meant to transliterate the native Austronesian name "Tayouan," which in the native Sirayan language means "coastal area" and actually designated only the area now called Tainan on the southern coastal plain (and which was purchased from the Siraya by the Dutch for fifteen pieces of cloth in 1625) (Hsu 1980a, 12).

5. In Hokkien, *"U bou khaqhou cit-e thi: -gong-cuo."* Thanks to David Schak and Ricky Pai for supplying this information.

6. In addition, seventeen were classified as native Austronesian anti-Qing movements, and several other revolts were organized through pioneer and native cooperation (Chen 1987, 11–12; Shepherd 1993, 130–132).

7. Annual population growth was 2.2 percent over the period 1683–1811 (Ka 1995, 39), a rate resulting in a doubling every thirty-three years!

8. The Japanese lost several hundred troops to these rebel attacks—but also several thousand troops to malaria (Fraser 1988, 94).

9. Nitobe would become the first chair of Colonial Studies at Tokyo University, and he was immortalized on the 5,000 yen bill.

10. These Indian-fighting techniques were also complemented by the Japanese regime's own contribution to "savage" management: the first air raids in Asian history, carried out on unruly mountain villages in 1913–1914 (Kerr 1974, 104).

11. The Japanese government even enlisted the services of a British official adviser to help implement the "successful" techniques of British colonial rule in Egypt (Townsend 2000, 102).

12. Other Taiwanese elites, refusing to become totally "Japanized," accepted the antiqueue movement but resented the attack on the traditional Chinese scholars' robe, forming Societies to Cut the Queue but Keep the Clothes (Duanfa Bugaizhuang Hui) (Wang 1960, 20).

13. By the late 1920s, many Taiwanese student organizations in China had also come to call explicitly for independence as the solution to the exploitation of their island (Lan 2000, 16–23).

14. The population, still 95 percent rural, was 4.6 million, including 228,000 Japanese, most of whom were professionals, merchants, industrialists, and bureaucrats (Fraser 1988, 100).

15. Scholar Ō Ikutoku, cited in Tsurumi 1977, 177.

16. The Japanese government has never compensated those Taiwanese wounded or the families of those killed in World War II on the grotesquely legalistic grounds that after 1945 they were not Japanese nationals.

17. In fact, during the first several months of the war, more than a thousand cases were reported of Taiwanese cursing Japanese officials and police (Lai et al. 1991, 26).

18. Technically, the British did not agree to this condition, only that Taiwan "shall be renounced by Japan" (Chiu 1973, 205–207). What is more, this Cairo Declaration, which British Prime Minister Winston Churchill noted "merely contained a statement of common purpose," and the 1945 Potsdam Declaration that confirmed Cairo, are not documents that under international legal norms could create Chinese title to Taiwan (Chen and Reisman 1972, 635–637).

19. The question is complicated enough that an entire academic subgenre has grown around this topic. For example, see Peng and Huang 1976 and Chen and Reisman 1972.

20. Andō soon would be convicted and sentenced to death as a war criminal, but he evidently felt obligated to honor the precise details of the surrender signed by his emperor.

21. Also annoying was the fact that the residents of Taiwan cared more about the Japanese treatment of *them* than they did about Japanese war crimes and brutalities carried out in far-off Chinese places like Nanjing or Manchuria.

22. The PRC made several strikes back against the ROC regime on Taiwan. One memorable example was the drugging of Taiwanese Olympic decathlete C. K. Yang (Yang Chuanguang), the world record holder and overwhelming favorite to win gold at the 1964 Tokyo Olympics, by two traitorous teammates who spiked his event-day orange juice and then defected to the PRC (*CP* 1997).

23. This did not stop ROC postal authorities from issuing an "International Year for Human Rights" set of stamps for 1968.

24. One reason that this peaceful pro-Taiwan sentiment was acceptable to Chiang was that the alternative was the rise of a pro-independence terrorist movement. In 1970, Chiang had been shot at by radical pro-independence assassins in New York. In 1976, extremists sabotaged a power station in southern Taiwan and sent a letter bomb to Provincial Governor Xie Dongmin that blew off his left hand (Martin 1985, 24–29). In all, these pro-independence terrorists carried out twenty-one attacks on ROC officials or offices throughout the world between 1978 and 1981 (Tyson 1987, 165).

25. As of August 2001, there were ninety-five political parties in Taiwan, representing every possible social, economic, and political platform (*CP* 08/01/2001).

26. See Stainton 1999a, 419–435 on the "Aboriginal self-government" movement in the 1990s.

27. At the end of 1999, foreign exchange reserves were U.S. $106.2 billion, the third highest in the world (*Republic of China Yearbook* 2001).

28. One unique aspect of this development, seen by many as a possible model for development in mainland China, is the overwhelming role of the state in Taiwan's economy.

In the late 1990s, the ROC government and the then-ruling Guomindang owned or controlled about 50 percent of all corporate assets on the island, which accounted for 30 percent of Taiwan's gross national product (Johnson 2000, 155).

29. Since Nixon's visit to China, the United States has recognized this claim for thirty years, in order to keep healthy economic relations with the PRC. Many argue that the United States has definite interests in keeping Taiwan and the PRC separate and in avoiding competition with this potential super-rich pan-Chinese power. The United States reserves the right to sell arms to Taiwan under the Taiwan Relations Act of 1979, and thus it wins great profits for America's arms dealers. In 1996, when the PRC engaged in provocative war games and live-fire missile tests in order to disrupt Taiwan's first-ever direct presidential election, the United States sent two aircraft carriers into the region (although not into the straits themselves) to guard Taiwan.

But on the whole, the United States has been very complicit in the PRC's claims on the island. Perhaps the firmest show of support for the PRC came during President Bill Clinton's administration. When Taiwan President Lee Teng-hui stopped in Honolulu on his way to Central America in 1994, the U.S. State Department denied him a visa even for one night after consulting with PRC officials on the issue (Mann 1999, 315). In China in 1998, Clinton made a "deep, deep kowtow" to his hosts, volunteering in a speech in Shanghai that the United States would support no future for Taiwan other than absorption into the PRC (*BG* 1998, A-11). Then, in 1999, the United States for the first time opposed Taiwan's bid to rejoin the United Nations (He 2001, 8).

30. The PRC Ministry of Foreign Affairs, claiming to represent the people of Taiwan, then proceeded to "thank" the international community for its concern and donations, an abhorrent move that Taiwan foreign minister Jason Hu likened to China "looting a burning house" (Reuters 1999).

31. In accordance with this "public opinion," plans relating to such an invasion of Taiwan make up 52 percent of the current PRC military budget (He 2001, 9).

32. The French foreign ministry did agree to allow First Lady Wu Shuzhen to receive the award on Chen's behalf, under the following illiberal conditions: that she not pass through Paris, that she leave France immediately after accepting the award, and that she not speak to reporters while in France (TTO 2001).

CHAPTER 2. FOWL PLAY

Author's note: I would like to thank David K. Jordan, Marc Moskowitz, Andrew Morris, and the two anonymous reviewers for the University of Hawai`i Press for all their helpful comments and suggestions.

1. For more on these issues, see Ch'ü T'ung-tsu 1961; Esherick and Rankin 1990; Goodman 1995; Kuhn 1991; and Rowe 1989.

2. See, for example, Allee 1994; Lamley 1981; Ownby 1996; and ter Haar 1998.

3. See the following groundbreaking works: Chiu Hei-yuan 1988; Harrell and Huang 1994; and Rubinstein 1994.

4. See, for example, Bernhardt and Huang 1994; Huang 1996; Karasawa 1993; Macauley 1994, 1998; Reed 2000; Zhou 1995.

5. I have already published extensively on these rituals (see Katz 2000, 2001, n.d.) and plan to write a book-length manuscript on this subject in the future.

6. The use of the term "elder brother" suggests that Ch'en and Wang may have been sworn brothers.

7. For more on this cult, see Harrell 1974; Lin 1995; Tai 1997; and Thompson 1975.

8. For a discussion of scapegoats in the context of Chinese religion, see Katz 1995a, 1995b.

9. Implying that the deceased will not enjoy the benefits of mortuary rites intended to transform a ghost into an ancestor.

10. See also Kataoka 1921, 7.

11. I am deeply grateful to David K. Jordan for his guidance in formulating the above analysis.

12. For similar data from other parts of China, see Duara 1988, 138; Wu 1988.

13. For more on the overlap between judicial rituals and the legal system, see Katz n.d.

14. For more information, see Katz 2000, 2001.

15. See also ter Haar 1992, 173–195, 263–281.

16. See, for example, Hayden 1978; Johnson 1989a.

17. For more on this, see David Jordan's essay (chapter 3) in this volume.

18. For more on the quantification of morality in Chinese culture, see Brokaw 1991; see also Eberhard 1967; Goodrich 1981.

CHAPTER 3. POP IN HELL

1. They are sometimes also referred to as "the underground courts of Fengdu" (Fengdu or Fengdu *difu*). Fengdu is a county seat in Sichuan Province, outside of which there was once a dry well thought to be the entrance to the lower realms.

2. The most famous one circulating today is *Laozi's Essay on Response and Retribution (Taishang ganying pian)*, containing long lists of ways to be annoying—theft, gossip, betrayal, and so on—and assurances that people committing these acts will be held to account eventually. In Taiwan, the text is routinely reprinted by individuals as an act of merit and distributed freely from temples. The most readily available English rendering is by Suzuki and Carus (1906) and includes a collection of moral tales sometimes circulated with it.

3. Perhaps the most conspicuous and constant association between hell and Buddhism is the presence in the popular pantheon of a bodhisattva, the "Earth Vault King Bodhisattva" (Dizangwang Pusa), who has sworn not to move on to Buddhahood while there are yet souls suffering in hell. His compassion in excusing people from their punishments when they truly repent figures in some stories. He is called Ksitigarbha in Sanskrit, and a Chinese scripture about him has been rendered into English under the title *Sutra of the Past Vows of Earth Store Bodhisattva* (Hsüan Hua 1974).

4. "Mulian" is the Chinese transcription of Maudgalyayana, one of the disciples of the historical Buddha. Hinduism has a rite for the release of souls from hell, perhaps the origin of this association. In China, Mulian's filial piety easily becomes a symbol of the cosmic superiority of indigenous popular morality over imported religious rule making. See Johnson (1989b) for a book-length analysis of the Mulian tale.

5. See Jordan and Overmyer 1986 for a discussion of trance-writing societies. Although such organizations engage in a range of religious exercises and sometimes subscribe to idiosyncratic doctrines, they have been a prime source of "virtuous books" *(shanshu)* and "valued scrolls" *(baojuan)* for several centuries. One type of such writing is a general account of the courts of hell or of a visit to hell by a deceased human or supernatural, with descriptions of what is found there. Because mediums may write of hell at any time, the genre easily adjusts itself to new moral challenges arising in a changing society such as that of Taiwan.

6. *"Dian"* literally refers to a very large hall or palace and is occasionally used in names of temples because of its grandiose connotations. The implication in the case of the courts of hell is of a large official hall or place of imperial business. The conventional English translation—"court"—builds upon the legal implications but fails to capture the notion of gravity and immense size that is implied by the Chinese.

7. One of the characters sometimes used for "almanac" *(li)* is also a verb (to pass through).

8. A full description of the ten courts of hell can be found in Doré (1920, 250–302). A translation of the "Precious Manuscript" can be found in Giles (1916, 467–485), who retitles it "The Divine Panorama." Another translation, with the Chinese original on facing pages, has been included in Wieger (1913, 344–403). A description and analysis of different

editions makes up chapter 2 of Eberhard (1967), and a remarkably detailed description of the courts of hell as represented in proverbs is provided by Plopper (1935, 319–357). In preparing this essay I have used a copy (RSBJ) reprinted in Hong Kong in 2000 (with introductions dating from 1906 to 1954) and a 1992 Taiwan reprint of an early twentieth-century "colloquial" version (Xiao 1992).

9. For a Taiwanese table of the ten main halls, each divided into sixteen subhalls, see Huang Wenbo 1992 (154–155).

10. The series went by the name of *Special Cartoon Issues on Karma (Yingguo manhua zhuankan)* and was a project of the Shengxin Tang religious society in Dali City, Taizhong County. To the best of my knowledge at least ten books were issued, all competitive in quality with commercial cartoon books targeting children.

11. I am grateful to Marc Moskowitz for bringing these films to my attention as a potentially significant source of pop culture ideas about hell. In his essay (chapter 10 in this volume), Moskowitz correctly argues that, although a large proportion of films shown in Taiwan are made in Hong Kong, our concern is with the reaction of the Taiwanese who watch them, and it is quite clear that the Hong Kong and Taiwan film markets are for all practical purposes parts of a single Greater China market.

12. The three films in the series, which began in 1987 (Cheng 1987, 1990, 1991), were joined in 1997 by a cartoon version (Tsui 1997), winner of the 1997 Golden Horse Award for Best Animated Film. Somewhat confusingly, the films with human actors are named *A Chinese Ghost Story*, *A Chinese Ghost Story 2*, etc., in English; the cartoon is also called *A Chinese Ghost Story*.

13. Cartoonist Hu Rong, from Jiangsu Province, won the 1966 East Asia Comics Special Award for a comic book adaptation of the same story in 1996, and Taiwan Cartoonist Tsai Chih Chung (Cai Zhizhong) of Zhanghua County included it as one of two tales making up one of his many volumes. Both comic books have been released in English (Hu 1996; Tsai 1997).

14. Yanluo Wang or Yan Wang is the name of a particular king in hell, but *yanwang* is sometimes also used as a generic term to refer to all of them, suggesting that to most speakers, *yan* simply refers to hell. The name is a Chinese transliteration of the Sanskrit Yama, an ancient Indian god who presided over the afterworld. The characters used for this name are merely taken for their sound value to approximate the Sanskrit. However, *"yan"* literally refers to a gate and *"luo"* is literally a net of the kind that might be used to catch birds. Someone seeking meaning beyond merely sound transcription—and there are many such people among religious Chinese—might therefore explicate the name as meaning "entry net king" and associate it with entrapment in hell.

15. The pantheon is large, and local temples—while always defining a central patron—inevitably include a range of other gods as well. The use of a temple for memorial, mediumistic, or other specialized purposes evolves in response to local need more than from the identity of its main object of worship.

16. A collection of paintings made by Professor Paul Vidor (Wei Boru) was contributed to the National Museum of History in Taibei and was the object of an exhibit in 1984. The bilingual exhibition catalog (Ho 1984) provides reproductions of the paintings with full translation of all their annotations and an analysis of the contents. Neil Donneley (1990) describes and analyzes three contrasting graphic representations from Taiwan, a set of scrolls painted by "Ho Hsin yen," an early nineteenth-century folk artist from Xinzhu, a set by an unknown artist formerly belonging to an anonymous Daoist priest in Xinzhu and probably dating to the late seventeenth or early eighteenth century, and a set of woodblock prints that originally were pages from an edition of the "Jade Almanac" reprinted in the mid-nineteenth century from an original produced (it claims) at the turn of the eighteenth to nineteenth centuries. In an appendix, he briefly describes murals of the courts of hell from a twentieth-century restoration of the temple of Baosheng Dadi in Xiamen in Fujian Province.

17. At one time, slipping into a trance was regarded as especially dangerous to the

youths who played these roles, and their attendants were skilled in exorcism to revive them if they began to lose control of their performance. In recent decades, slipping into a trance in these cases has come to be expected, and Eight Generals groups are now interpreted by some observers as a specialization within the general cover category of spirit mediums. This error, if it is an error, is not limited to foreigners. See Liu Huanyue (1994, 100).

18. English speakers are quick to point out that Milton and Dante portrayed hell quite explicitly. English speakers do not, however, produce frequent films and comic books based on Milton and Dante.

19. An appendix includes my translation of the original Yuan dynasty collection. The translation is also available, with the Chinese text, on my web site: http://anthro.ucsd.edu/~dkjordan.

20. Arguably, some people believe that their deceased parent was so unblemished in life as not to be at risk of any punishment in the hereafter. I know of one family in which the adult sons claimed that their deceased father had been appointed a god after death. Nevertheless, even they had funerary ritual performed to help facilitate his passage through hell and to mitigate his punishments. Either they did not in fact consider him to have been blameless throughout life or they did not consider the courts of hell to be dependably just. Either way, they apparently thought it prudent to provide for the likelihood of infernal torment.

21. It may be argued that the deceased do have the power to harm the living if the living do not provide at least minimal memorializing, but such tales typically also stress the dependency of the ghost upon the living and thus tend to reinforce the notion of the ghost as pathetic.

CHAPTER 4. FROM HIDDEN KINGDOM TO RAINBOW COMMUNITY

1. In fact, the lesbian group Between Us (Women Zhi Jian) began publishing the magazine *Girlfriend* in 1994.

2. The Defense of Marriage Act was a bill designed to establish the legal definition of marriage as "a union between one man and one woman." It is binding on all agencies and programs of the federal government and prevents them from recognizing gay marriages in any states that may hypothetically legalize them in the future. The bill passed the House of Representatives 342 to 67 on July 12. It passed the U.S. Senate 85 to 14 on the same day. President Clinton signed it into law on September 21.

3. The construction of lesbian identity in Taiwan merits further research but lies outside the scope of this study. In Taiwanese lesbian circles, women make a clear distinction between "t" and *"po"* lesbians, categories that function almost as separate genders (for research on lesbian identity, see Gian 1998 and Zheng 1997). "T" is an abbreviated version of the English word "tomboy" and refers to masculine lesbians. They refuse to conform to gender expectations for women in Taiwanese society. They usually crop their hair short, dress in blue jeans or shirt and tie, and smoke profusely. They often discuss their mannish appearance as a way of affirming their sexual identities. *"Po,"* which means "woman," refers to feminine lesbians. They dress and behave according to the widely accepted gender expectations for women and thus are not visibly distinguishable from heterosexual women.

4. This man, who is an active member of the Mormon Church and educated in Utah, enjoys comparing Taiwan to (Mormon) America. At the time of this conversation in 1998, he was engaged to an American Mormon woman. By 2001, he had ended that relationship and started affirming a gay identity with no intention of marriage.

5. In July 1969, New York police raided a gay club in Greenwich Village, and the gays responded with riots that lasted for several hours. That event is remembered as a turning point in the American gay rights movement.

6. Although such laws have been rescinded in England, many U.S. states still prohibit

homosexual behavior through laws forbidding oral and anal sex. Gays are also not permitted to serve in the military; even under Clinton's "Don't ask, don't tell" policy, gays in uniform continued to be persecuted and dismissed from service if discovered (Shilts 1994).

7. Ironically, some gay men themselves have argued for such a policy, hoping to use sexual identity as a way to avoid universal conscription to military service. In the past, some men have avoided conscription by using homosexual behavior as evidence of mental deficiency. That argument has not worked in recent years.

8. Since most of the men involved were not participating in illegal activities, this is clearly a case of illegal harassment on the part of the police against people they perceive as deviant. Identity checks at night are still frequent in Taiwan, and not just in places frequented by gays.

9. Thanks to the Gay/Lesbian Hotline for providing firsthand accounts of the incident, as collected by Ke Fei.

10. Since public obscenity laws forbid both homosexual and heterosexual sexual acts in public and are also enforced against heterosexual violators, this law is not an example of discrimination against gays in the same way as antisodomy laws that explicitly forbid homosexual behavior. It must be recognized, however, that public obscenity laws are frequently used by the police to harass gays in Taiwan as well as elsewhere, including the United States and Canada. In September 2000, for example, Toronto police raided a lesbian party at a bathhouse and sparked a similar protest from the local gay and lesbian community. Ontario law still requires that gay saunas collect the names of their clients.

11. There is intense political rivalry between President Chen Shui-bian (DPP) and Mayor Ma Yingjiu (KMT). Ma's victory over incumbent Chen in the Taipei mayoral election ironically gave Chen the opportunity to run for president. Chen is a Native Taiwanese, Ma is a mainlander, and they have very different visions for the future of Taiwan. Since they may meet in another election in the future, both strive to portray themselves as progressive in terms of human rights.

CHAPTER 5. TAIWAN'S MASS-MEDIATED CRISIS DISCOURSE

1. *2100: All People Open Talk,* Taiwan's first TV call-in program, was largely influenced by *Larry King Live,* from its superficial adaptation of the set's curvilinear desk separating host and guest speakers to the host's imitation of King's sartorial style of colorful shirts and patterned suspenders, as well as King's trademark elbow-leaning, hunched posture.

2. It should be noted that at the time of writing, some TV stations were considering bringing and adapting reality shows to Taiwan.

3. For instance, call-in show guest panelists judged the New Party (Xindang) to be obsolete, or "dissolving into bubbles" *(paomohua),* following its poor showing in the 2000 presidential election.

4. This assessment is based on Taiwan's A. C. Nielsen ratings from January to August 2000, to which call-in shows and TV stations in general have access on a daily basis.

5. The use of "show" here represents a double entendre that references both the call-in show itself as well as the transliterated Mandarin term *"xiu,"* which in the colloquial phrase *"zuoxiu"* means "to put on an act."

6. "Saliva wars" represent the local equivalent of the American notion of mudslinging or verbal attacking.

7. Aside from the two leading political TV call-in programs, *2100* and *8 o'clock,* other call-in programs have a more difficult time in achieving high ratings and attaining financial success.

8. In the United States, daytime talk shows began in the 1940s, while political talk shows emerged in the late 1960s. For further reading on U.S. talk shows, refer to Abt and Mustazza 1997, Alterman 1999, Gamson 1998, Hirsch 1991, Lowrey 1999, Munson 1993, and Shattuc 1997.

9. Predominantly scheduled in mid-morning and late afternoon, daytime talk shows

were originally created as a programming transition from early morning talk shows to the evening news.

10. A *New York Times* article on the political talk show phenomenon noted, "They may not reach huge, prime-time audiences, but they reach many of the people who run the country" (Gamarekian 1987).

11. During martial law, opposition groups were locally dubbed as the *dangwai,* which literally means "outside the [Guomindang] party."

12. Cable television in Taiwan was originally transmitted through Common Antennas Television (CATV) systems set up by cable television pirates and the political opposition (Rawnsley and Rawnsley 2001).

13. In 1994, TVBS only had one news channel or division. It has since created several channels separately devoted to news, sports, and general entertainment.

14. As of August 2000, the date when research for this study concluded, Taiwan's five all-news stations included TVBS, ETTV (Dongsen), FTV (Minshi), Global TV (Huanqiu), and CTN (Dadi).

15. Although Taiwan's airwaves also feature call-in programs on topics such as relationships, finance and investment, and social issues (especially those addressing women, children, and education), the programs that discuss political topics are by far the most widely viewed.

16. Several viewers and guests, however, told me that Li Tao appears biased in his moderating, but they differed in their interpretations of exactly which political parties/candidates or guests enjoy his favor.

17. Another call-in show moderator who shares Yu Fu's attitude is Li Ao, a historian and former New Party presidential candidate. Li Ao flaunted his mockery of the moderate call-in host philosophy with his ultraconservative and provocative speaking style in a call-in show that aired during the 2000 presidential campaign. Since Li Ao does not attempt to conceal his openly biased views, viewers know that "what they see is what they get."

18. Italics indicate speaker's switch from Mandarin to English.

19. Italics indicate speaker's switch from Mandarin to English.

20. TVBS' *2100: All People Open Talk* aired live broadcasts from Jiji, while both *2100* and *Always Speak Your Mind* provided special broadcasts from the United States in the months prior to the 2000 presidential elections.

21. The DPP was officially founded in 1986 by *dangwai* activists. For more reading, see Rigger 1999 and Arrigo 1994.

22. The Guomindang's reunification platform requires that a unified "China" be under a democratic leadership. In contrast, the NP does not make such a stipulation.

23. For instance, former Taiwan provincial governor James Soong (Song Chuyü) and former ROC president Lee Teng-hui have campaigned on building a "new Taiwanese" (*xin* Taiwanren) identity that attempts to transcend Taiwanese-mainlander distinctions.

24. The New Party claims a pro-China reunification agenda from which it cites the Guomindang as having strayed. In contrast, the PFP has endeavored to chart a middle course that attempts to distance itself from the political corruption—locally known as black-gold *(heijin)* politics—that surrounds the Guomindang and from the conservative pro-unification stance of the NP. In comparison, the TSU continues to promote former ROC president and Guomindang chairman Lee Teng-hui's "Taiwanization" or "nativization" *(bentuhua)* agenda that increases *benshengren* membership and promotion to high-ranking party positions. As a *benshengren* himself, former president Li epitomized the "nativization" of Guomindang Taiwan during his twelve-year (1988–2000) presidency.

25. In his inaugural address on May 20, 2000, President Chen introduced his "one if and five no's" cross-straits policy. This list cited that if the PRC "has no intention to use military force against Taiwan," then Taiwan would maintain the status quo, including not declaring Taiwan independence, not changing the national title from the "Republic of China," not altering the ROC constitution, not holding a referendum on Taiwan independence, and not abolishing the Guidelines for National Unification (*Taipei Journal* 2001).

26. Programs on all these topics aired between 1997 and 2001.

27. Respondents to this question could feasibly answer "none of the above." From my observations of call-in show coverage of this topic, however, participants do not entertain this option.

28. Most call-in programs prefer a set number of guests on each episode. Again, *2100*'s approach to inviting guests differs from other call-in programs. Most call-in shows invite anyone who can appear on that evening's program who is familiar with the topic. As the top-ranked call-in program, *2100* is in a coveted position and can be more selective in its choice of guests. The other shows do not have this clout and therefore are often left with "second tier" guests that *2100* does not seek.

29. Phone-in polling was frequently included during the 2000 presidential election cycle, but call-in shows only sporadically added this feature in the months immediately after the election in March 2000.

30. During the months leading up to a highly contested national election, weekly political TV call-in programs air on weekends as well.

31. Derived from personal interviews with various call-in production units and data from A. C. Nielsen during the period of January to August 2000.

32. Most guests are given two to three minutes to introduce their perspective on the topic at the beginning of the program and then fifteen to thirty seconds to summarize their arguments at the end.

33. The *2100* program restricts callers to twenty seconds each, while other call-in shows do not enforce a consistent time limit. Before *2100* implemented a twenty-second speaking rule, viewers complained that the program was biased toward certain political views. Reasons why other call-in programs do not establish a set caller speaking time include allowing callers to fully express their opinions and to provide opportunities for follow-up questions between callers and panelists or moderator.

34. The number of calls per show on *2100* ranges from several hundred to several thousand, depending upon the topic and whether it is an electoral season.

35. Li Tao uses this unique intonation pattern when moderating the program, but, as I observed, not when he is "off camera" and interacting with the production staff and guests, such as before the program and during commercial breaks.

36. This episode aired May 31, 2000, on *2100: All People Open Talk*. For more reading on the issue of Taiwan's national identity dilemma and ethnopolitical tensions, see Wachman (1994).

37. Verbal cues in brackets represent shifts in Li Tao's prosodic delivery.

38. The Legislative Yuan (Lifayuan) is Taiwan's national legislature.

39. The notion "constructed dialogue" asserts that so-called quoted speech or reported speech rarely represents the direct reporting of another person's words and thus represents constructed or reconstructed speech. For further reading on this subject, see Tannen (1989).

40. This episode aired on June 12, 2000, three weeks after President Chen's inauguration.

41. The DPP male panelist is a legislator in the Legislative Yuan.

42. The New Party male panelist is a legislator in the Legislative Yuan.

43. The use of "we" refers to the male guests on the panel, which included four male legislators. Earlier in the episode, the sole female guest panelist—a spokesperson for a women's organization—had accused the male panelists of exhibiting gender bias toward Lu.

44. Guests are introduced by their title and name; for example, "Legislator Li Yingyuan of the DPP" (Li Yingyuan Minjindang *liwei*).

45. Yü Fu represents the exception, as he consistently finds ways to provoke his guest panel into heated debate.

46. The episode entitled "Taiwanese, Mainlander: Is There Still a Distinction?" (Bensheng, waisheng hai yao fen ma?) aired May 2, 2000, on *2100*.

47. "*Hua*" is comparable to the term "Cathay," which serves as a poetic, archaic refer-

ence to China assumed to be unified through a shared cultural, historical, and linguistic background. The term is also more conceptual, evoking an indistinct image of splendor that is applied to the Chinese nation rather than the Chinese polity. For this reason, Chinese people who do not want to associate themselves with the Chinese state may identify themselves as Huaren rather than Zhongguoren (Wachman 1994, 39).

48. Speakers in mainland China refer to Mandarin as the "common language" *(putonghua),* while speakers in Singapore generally use Huayu, which also carries ideological meanings in those geopolitical settings.

49. As another way to express their Taiwanese-consciousness sentiments, independence activists refer to the Taiwanese language as the "Formosan" language. In reappropriating this Portuguese term for the island of Taiwan, speakers avoid the use of "Taiwanese," which as a Chinese-derived descriptor indexes the island as a province that is marginal to China—and subordinate within a Chinese perspective. The term "Formosan language" can also encompass Taiwan's aboriginal languages (of which there are eleven), recognizing them as non–Han Chinese languages and their speakers as the original inhabitants of "Formosa."

50. Ethnically, Zhang Huimei is from the Puyuma (Beinan) tribe, one of eleven aboriginal groups in Taiwan. As with many of Taiwan's contemporary artists, Amei maintains an apolitical stance in that she openly advocates neither Taiwan independence nor reunification with mainland China. This is aimed in part to create marketing appeal beyond Taiwan, such as attracting fans in the PRC, Hong Kong, and Singapore. As a transnational pop star, Amei has performed throughout Asia, including a successful PRC concert tour in 2000 (*Newsweek* 2001, 14–18).

51. The "misunderstanding" that Xie and the other panelists cite refers to the PRC's misinterpretation of the ROC anthem as symbolizing Taiwan independence, a reading that fails to recognize that the anthem's lyrics specifically denote allegiance to the Guomindang.

52. Taken from an episode entitled "Is the PRC Banning Amei?" (Zhonggong fengsha Amei?) that aired on May 24, 2000, on *2100: All People Open Talk* and occurred four days after President Chen Shui-bian's inauguration as the eleventh ROC president.

53. DPP supporters frequently criticize the ROC national anthem's lyrics for pledging allegiance to the Guomindang and not the nation, be it the ROC or Taiwan.

54. Callers are introduced as, for example, "Ms. Lin from Taipei County" (Taibei Xian de Lin Xiaojie).

55. The vocal presence of call-in teams was particularly evident during the 2000 presidential elections. Many guests, production staff, and viewers accused the Guomindang of setting up call-in teams in their party headquarters, although party members denied doing so. Personal interviews with Guomindang officials, however, revealed that such practices were used. Other political parties and candidates were rumored to establish "voluntary" call-in teams that were not organized by the party per se but were nonetheless tacitly (or not so tacitly) encouraged.

56. Political TV call-in programs repeat their programs later in the night and sometimes the next day. For instance, *2100* rebroadcasts its program from midnight to 1 A.M. and again from 3:30 to 4:30 P.M. the following afternoon.

57. Several call-in shows, most notably *2100*, have attempted to combat call-in teams by automatically deleting calls with succeeding phone numbers, a strategy that has had limited success.

58. This fear refers to the notion of a "sense of fear among mainlanders" *(waishengren kongjugan)* linked to the Guomindang's descent from power.

59. The exception in this case would be the presence of call-in teams. Their participation, however, is limited to the two-to-three-month campaign season prior to national elections.

CHAPTER 6. THE OTHER WOMAN IN YOUR HOME

1. In my research, I use "migrant domestic workers" to refer to foreign workers who are categorized as domestic helpers and domestic caretakers in the 1992 act. The common usage in Taiwan to refer to this group of women, however, is *waiji nüyong*, which literally means "maids of foreign nationality." This term is widely used by the general public and scholars in discussion. Another prevailing colloquial usage is Feiyong (Filipina maid), because the majority of workers were from the Philippines. I do not wish to use the term "maid" to refer to domestic workers because "maid," in the Taiwanese context, is a word loaded with implications of class inferiority. When I interviewed one Taiwanese domestic worker and asked whether she would protest in the street against her declining working opportunities, she replied: "If factory workers protest, at least they have the factory's name in front of them. We are *nüyong*. We do not want people to know that we are helping out as maids *[chulai bangyong]*." The racial overtones of "Filipina maids" as "maids" is further explored in this chapter. I do not intend to reinforce existing prejudices by addressing domestic workers as "maids"; however, to retain its original meaning in everday language, I have deliberately placed the term "foreign maids" within quotation marks throughout this chapter.

2. Similar arguments are also heard in the migration debates in Britain. Migration Watch, a right-wing research group organized by Sir Andrew Green, retired British ambassador, and David Coleman, professor of demography at Oxford University, argued that mass immigration would drive up the population with disastrous consequences for the environment, social cohesion, and public health (Bright et. al. 2002).

3. Zhan became vice president of the Council of Labor Affairs in 1994.

4. The legislator's previous job was news reporter. The male veteran assumed that her previous job as a news reporter would give her more time to take care of "her family" than her current job as a legislator, which was regarded as a man's job by this veteran.

5. Taiwan is not the only country that utilizes state sexism on female migrant workers. The prohibition of migrant workers' pregnancy is also found in Singapore (S. J. Cheng, 1996, 147) and Malaysia. State sexism relating to female migrant workers is not the privilege of Asian countries alone. Inhumane vaginal and health examinations were enforced in British immigration laws on Asian migrant women in the 1970s in the name of state benevolence (Parmar 1982, 245–246).

6. This includes a chest X-ray examination, tests for pregnancy, HIV antibodies, syphilis, hepatitis B, malaria, intestinal parasites, amphetamines, and morphine. If they fail any of these examinations (except for the parasites; a month of medical treatment is permitted for this), they will be expelled from Taiwan. No other foreigners in Taiwan are subjected to such intensive and detailed health checks. Moreover, these health checks are humiliating because of the hidden assumptions behind them.

7. In recent years, there are increasing regulations concerning AIDS examinations imposed on foreigners in general, especially for those who want to marry Taiwanese women. Since a significant number of these foreigners are white, this probably suggests a stigmatization process occurring for westerners as well. Nevertheless, so far at least, westerners need not experience the same complicated health checks as *waiji laogong* in order to work in Taiwan. The degree of their health check depends on the foreigner's class status in Taiwan.

8. Recently there has been a tendency to extend the working period, primarily in the interests of the employer. In 1992, migrant workers were allowed to work for only one year, and they could extend the contract for a second year. In 1997, the maximum stay was extended to three years.

9. Exceptions are given when the patient dies or the employer emigrates. In these cases, the caretaker can be given other work as a domestic helper in the same household or transferred to a new employer. If the employer wants to terminate the contract for reasons other than the fault of the worker, the worker can also be transferred to a new employer. Still, this measure concerns the employer more than the worker. It benefits friends and rel-

atives of the employers who wish to continue employing workers whom they know. Regarding workers, on the other hand, it is very difficult for them to provide evidence to prove abuse, so it is not easy for them to change employers.

10. Workers can get the money back only when they finish their working periods in Taiwan. Although this is not enforced in every working contract, the law provides strong support for employers who intend to do so.

11. There is no quota limitation for domestic caretakers, but a quota limit of fifteen thousand domestic helpers has been set, to work for families with children under the age of twelve and the elderly over the age of seventy.

12. For detailed analysis of the contents and effects of the Foreign Maid Policy, please refer to C. J. Lin (2000).

13. Cases are exemplified in *United Daily News* 1995a, 3; *United Daily News* 1995b, 3; and *United Daily News* 1995c, 3.

14. According to the news report on October 11, 1995, Angelina had seen a doctor for insomnia, lack of appetite, and sickness. Dr. Lau found that she had slightly high blood pressure, which according to him was not serious. Nevertheless, since she worried so much about her illness, Dr. Lau gave her tablets to calm her down. According to this description, it appears to me that Angelina was more likely under stress than mentally ill. In May 1997, Angelina was sentenced to twelve years in prison. Her "mental illness" was not considered sustainable by the judge (Wang Yinfan 1997, 5).

15. At home, they are told to obey employers' requests, entertain visitors, and so on. In public, they are preached at to wear neat clothes, not to throw rubbish anywhere, to keep out of mischief, not to make noises in public places, to obey traffic regulations, and so forth (Southeast Asia Human Capital Management Company 1997, 7–8).

16. Many Filipina workers paid half of the broker's fee by borrowing money from relatives or brokers and paid the rest with their first year's incomes in Taiwan. The heavy debts of working abroad have rendered Filipina workers especially vulnerable. When confronting abuses, they usually choose to endure their hardships rather than revoke their contracts, for the very simple reason that it is extremely difficult to pay off the debts without working in Taiwan for at least a year. There is, however, a constant push for the government to adopt "direct hiring" to avoid workers' exploitation by the brokers.

17. This view corresponds to the public discourse of warning the parents of the negative influences of Filipina maids' accents on children's English pronunciation.

18. Filipina workers' names are pseudonyms.

19. Since industrialization, the autonomy of both daughters-in-law and domestics has increased. The power relations between mothers-in-law and daughters-in-law have been reversed (Gallin 1984; Lin 2003). Moreover, it is less likely for employers to impose these humiliating practices on autonomous Taiwanese workers because of the risk of losing them (Lin 2000).

CHAPTER 7. HOT AND NOISY

1. The stanza "All made in nine-city" is sung in English. Shi appears to use "nine" as an English homonym for "night," probably in an attempt to make it easier to pronounce in Taiwanese.

2. "Strive to Win" became well known in 1989 when the legendary Taiwanese singer Ye Qitian publicized this song. It strongly reflected the socioeconomic conditions at the time when martial law had just been abolished, all kinds of social movements were rampant, and Taiwan's economy was at a pinnacle. "Strive to Win" symbolized not only the mentality of adapting to this historical conjunction but also the former generations of hardworking Taiwanese who created an economic niche in the world economy through family-based small-scale enterprises. The song was quickly employed by the KMT Party in its election campaign as a symbol of self-inspiration and party union. It also became a favorite song among Taiwanese businessmen in the early 1990s, especially for those who ex-

panded their businesses to mainland China. Ironically, "Strive to Win" has also become self-ridicule, depicting the hardworking Taiwanese as overly opportunistic and individualistic, sacrificing civilized approaches to a modern capitalist economy.

3. The Cantonese dialect does not have a special term for "night market." Hong Kong residents use *"dapaidang"* to refer to clusters of cooked-food vendors operating at night. The English term "night market" was probably utilized by the Hong Kong Tourist Bureau to promote two major night markets—Temple Street and Tungchoi Street—to foreign tourists.

4. Vendors are actually fined by traffic rules.

5. This particular segment of restaurants and stores is expanding in certain night markets as more and more chain stores open there.

6. Tempura is made from fish paste that is deep-fried to golden brown. Japanese generally cook tempura with vegetables and seaweed in a big pot of soup. One tempura vendor in Jilong's Temple-Front Night Market earned its special reputation by serving freshly fried tempura with a typical Taiwanese red sauce.

7. Stories of small snack-food stall owners accruing big fortunes have always been favorites with Taiwan's media. Taiwanese do believe that these stories are to some extent "real," although they also understand that this situation occurs only among some vendors. On the other hand, these stories also attract attention from the city tax bureau and interrogations by city councillors on vendor tax issues.

8. Taiwan's industries have suffered from a labor shortage since at least the early 1970s (Gates 1979). The problem has intensified in the past decade due to the reluctance of younger workers to take on manual labor jobs. Workers from Thailand, Indonesia, and the Philippines are now being imported to perform jobs refused by Taiwanese. At the same time, Taiwan's economy has begun to deteriorate for a number of reasons, including the loss of confidence associated with a major change in political power. As a result, in 2002 the unemployment rate jumped to over 4 percent the first time in over thirty years.

9. "Underground economy" *(dixia jingji)* was once a more commonly used term than "informal economy" *(feizhengshi jingji)* in Taiwan. The latter term, however, has gained some publicity in the media since it was introduced by local Taiwanese sociologists in the mid-1980s.

10. Vendors use many tactics. Attracting pedestrian sympathy to create difficulties for police to proceed with fining is probably the most common one. Subtle forms of showing solidarity among vendors against the police as a way of resisting regulation comprise another.

CHAPTER 8. DISCIPLINED BODIES IN DIRECT SELLING

1. Most people become distributors for the purpose of obtaining member discounts (usually 20–25 percent) while purchasing direct selling products. They are mainly consumers and do not actually practice direct selling as salespersons. They also seldom join the daily meetings to learn how to act like distributors. The target population of this study is those distributors who actually practice direct selling and attend daily meetings regularly.

2. These upline-downline relations are critical in direct selling because they establish a web of business networks from which distributors profit in addition to product sales. Ideally, the relationships between uplines and downlines in direct selling are partnerships, with an attempt to provide a contrast to the hierarchies in other industries. Yet in reality, the upline-downline relationships often take on the form of teacher-student or even parent-child relationships, because uplines are those who bring downlines into the business. Downlines are expected to feel grateful toward their uplines.

3. Practicing direct selling as a second job is the main form of this industry. Distributors are encouraged to give up their first job only when the profit of direct selling exceeds their regular salary.

4. This term represents quasi-family ties between upline and downline. During my fieldwork, people often asked me, "Whose babe are you?" This means, "Who is your upline?" Although it seems intimate, the term "babe" in Mandarin is rarely used, especially among nonfamily members. This usage somewhat contradicts the conservative feature of Chinese vocabulary and culture in relational expression. It is also part of the reason why outsiders often regard Amway members to be affectatious.

5. Pseudonyms have been used here and throughout to ensure informants' anonymity.

6. In the direct selling industry, "OPP" is the abbreviation of "opportunity." Direct selling companies hold regular meetings to explain their company histories, reward systems, and products and to introduce the opportunity represented by the direct selling business.

7. Members who have the same original uplines establish a quasi-familial bond. They are highly involved with each other in this small group and participate in formal and informal meetings together.

8. Amway members—especially if they are students or have not yet earned any title—do not usually initiate conversations about direct selling in the work setting. Many hesitate to reveal their distributor status at work, fearing that coworkers may think of them as "money slaves," ruining their reputation and relations with their colleagues. Therefore, distributors usually practice direct selling implicitly at work. For instance, they might "casually" use Amway cosmetics or multivitamins in front of coworkers and begin to talk about Amway only when colleagues show interest or curiosity about the products.

9. This concept from Foucault (Martin et al. 1988) refers to the means with which the self, medical techniques, or social forces are used to transform the body.

10. Amway people call all occupations except direct selling "traditional jobs" because these jobs cannot offer people what direct selling can: wealth and freedom at the same time.

11. This report provided an overall review of the distribution of direct salespeople, whereas the statistics of any single company were not available. The Amway Company refused to release any statistical data regarding its distributors' information, so I was not able to show the pyramidal distribution of Amway members in this chapter.

CHAPTER 9. BASEBALL, HISTORY, THE LOCAL AND THE GLOBAL IN TAIWAN

Author's note: Previous versions of this essay were presented at the North America Taiwan Studies Conference, University of Texas at Austin, May 29–31, 1998, the Western Conference of the Association for Asian Studies Annual Meeting, Long Beach, October 6–7, 2000, and the Fifth Annual RGTHC Conference on the History and Culture of Taiwan, Los Angeles, October 12–15, 2000. I hereby thank the participants of these conferences, as well as Chunwei Yu and Jeffrey Wilson, for their helpful comments.

1. Emphasizing his official commitment to baseball, Chen invited members of the Jiayi-Tainan Braves of the Taiwan Major League to perform a skit about Taiwan's 1969 Little League world championship team at his inaugural celebration (*HXXWW* May 21. 2000).

2. Exceptions to this universal adherence could only really come in ideological attacks on modern sport or on modern capitalist society altogether. In 1952, American feathers were ruffled when the Soviet magazine *Smena* published a piece on American baseball, calling it "beastly battle, a bloody fight with mayhem and murder," a harsh capitalist venture that discarded players "with ruined health and also often crippled . . . [to] increase the army of the American unemployed." The game, according to *Smena,* was merely a typically awful American perversion of the Russian game *lapta,* which had been "played in Russian villages when the United States was not even marked on the maps" (*NYT* September 16, 1952, 1, and September 17, 1952, 30).

3. Baseball was not played in Taiwan under Qing rule, although Chinese studying in the United States were playing baseball as early as 1873.

4. One roster (Zheng 1993, 115) lists aborigine shortstop Chen Gengyuan under his Japanese name, Agarimatsu Kōichi.

5. The Kōshien tournament, founded in 1915, began inviting Taiwan representatives in 1923. From 1923 to 1930, all the Taiwan teams that qualified for Kōshien were Japanese teams from Taihoku (Taibei) (Gao 1994, 54–55).

6. Kanō won their first three games by the combined score of 32-9 before finally losing in the championship game (Zheng 1993, 124).

7. Wu led the Japanese League in batting in 1942 and 1943, was named League MVP in 1943, pitched a no-hitter in 1946, and retired with a .272 batting average over twenty seasons (Zheng 1993, 121). There were Taiwan aborigine standouts in the Japanese leagues as well. Luo Daohou of the famed Hualian Ami tribal baseball teams played for the Tokyo Senators from 1936 to 1938, and Ye Tiansong, another Ami, starred for the Nankai Hawks from 1940 to 1949 (Gao 1994, 99–101).

8. This was not a uniquely Taiwanese strategy by any means; elsewhere in the Japanese Empire, the Korean nationalist martyr Yŏ Un-hyŏng sponsored athletics in the 1930s as a similarly indirect mode of resistance to the forces of the colonial power (Deane 1999, 48).

9. Provincial Chief Administrator Chen Yi served as meet chairman.

10. Foreign teams were not even allowed to compete at Williamsport in 1975, so the Taiwanese boys won ten titles in twelve years of competition.

11. Months after these victories, the Maple Leaf Elementary School principal, coach, and head administrator were all sentenced to a year's imprisonment by the Taidong County Local Court for these gross violations (Wang 1994, 79).

12. And to boot, the Chinese on the banner was written in mainland-style simplified characters that were illegal to use in Taiwan!

13. This shot drew harsh protests from the ROC government, which asked ABC to avoid pointing their cameras at Chinese-language messages that could possibly be subversive.

14. Many baseball players of aboriginal backgrounds thrived in Taiwanese professional baseball in the 1990s. But old stereotypes die hard, and no matter how much glory these players have won for Taiwan, they are still treated differently from Han Taiwanese. A recent example is the Taibei Suns Fan Club's coordinated chants of "Savage [*hoan-á*] get out!" directed at Jiayi-Tainan Braves pitcher Chen Yixin during the 1997 Taiwan Major League Championship Series (*ZYSB* November 3, 1997, C-8).

15. For example, the Chuiyang Elementary School team, always a force in their home city of Jiayi, wore caps emblazoned with an interlocked "CY" that was a dead ringer for the Tokyo Yomiuri Giants' trademark "YG" design (Su 1996, 64).

16. In fact, the Nationalist government could even use baseball as a mode of anticommunist propaganda. In 1987, an official article told of how several mainland fishermen taking refuge from a typhoon in the port of Taoyuan were absolutely stymied by the experience of watching "Free China [i.e., ROC] sluggers pound Japan 9-3 in a live telecast of the 14th Asian Amateur Baseball Championships from Tokyo.... The most difficult thing was convincing the mainland fishermen that the game they were watching their ROC compatriots play in Japan was actually taking place at that very time and being beamed by satellite to Taiwan" (*Free China Journal* 1987, 3).

17. Tellingly, the ROC Professional Baseball Preparatory Committee stated that one reason for launching the CPBL was to "[stem] the import of Taiwan's best players by Japanese teams" (*Free China Journal* 1988, 2).

18. These four corporations had sponsored semipro teams in Taiwan before 1990.

19. Of the nineteen foreigners who played during the CPBL's first season, only two had major-league experience: Tiger infielder Jose Moreno (1980 NY Mets, 1981 San Diego Padres, 1982 California Angels) and Elephant pitcher Jose Roman (1984–1986 Cleveland Indians).

20. The Chunichi minor leaguers were joined by the big-league Dragons' two Taiwanese stars, Guo Yuanzhi and Chen Dafeng.

21. After thirty-eight CPBL games that year, foreign pitchers had won thirty-five decisions and thrown 81 percent of the innings (*ZYSB* March 25, 1998, C-8).

22. Of the second-place Sinon Bulls' eleven pitchers, nine were foreign. The foreign pitchers' combined record was 57-45-2 that year; the two Taiwanese pitchers were 1-0-0.

23. An indication of foreign dominance of the CPBL in 1997 can be seen in the season statistical leaders. In the major categories given, there were the following number of foreign players in the top ten: batting average: eight; home runs: eight; runs batted in: seven; victories: seven; and earned run average: six.

24. A week later, O'Malley attended the CPBL's Opening Night in Tainan and addressed the crowd, calling the game "the 1997 Opening Game for professional baseball the world over" (*TWRB* February 24, 1997, 9).

25. A deal made with the International Division of America's Major League Baseball (MLB) has sent distinguished coaches like Bill Plummer, Greg Riddoch, Fernando Arroyo, and Jim Lefevbre to serve as official MLB advisors to the league's teams. The Taiwan Major League sent all eight of its umpires to the MLB–approved Brinkman-Froemming Umpire School in Florida for a thirty-one-day training session (*TWRB* February 5, 1997, 9).

26. In 1997, 42.7 percent of the TML's players came from abroad. But the TML wisely lowered this limit to seven *yangjiang* per team for 1998, which reduced the ratio of foreign players on TML rosters to less than 30 percent (*ZYSB* October 13, 1997, C-8).

27. This concept is very possibly based on the Japanese professional soccer J-League's official "Mission" of community sport.

28. The official recording of the anthem, performed by seven aboriginal singers, was made into a baseball music video and also sold in stores on an official Taiwan Major League CD *(Naluwan Weekly* 1997c, 5*)*.

29. The first four lines of the anthem are in Mandarin, the fifth in Taiwanese, the sixth in English and Taiwanese, the seventh in Japanese and Taiwanese, the eighth in "Aborigine" and Taiwanese (Huang 1997, 5).

30. Dubbed the "Black Eagles" (Heiying), the team was suspended from the league in late 1997 and formally disbanded in 1998 (*ZYSB* November 17, 1997, C-8; *ZGSB* September 16, 1998, 31).

31. They were Zhuo Kunyuan, Cai Minghong, and Zhang Zhengxian. Cai and Zhang were also members of the Puzi Tornados team that won the 1979 Little League World Series.

32. They served as Jiayi City assembly speaker, Jiayi City agricultural cooperative manager, and Jiayi County assembly speaker (*LHB* February 14, 1997, 3).

33. After being banned from Taiwan professional baseball, Jiang got a second chance five years later in mainland China as coach of the Tianjin Lions of the new China Baseball League and manager of the PRC national team. The Tianjin team, which evidently has a poor vetting process, also hired fallen Taiwan stars Guo Jiancheng and Zheng Baisheng—also banned in 1997 for throwing CPBL games—as coaches (*TTO* May 9, 2002).

34. Although no one admitted it at the time, these underworld connections and violence associated with the CPBL were a main factor in the defection of so many of the league's stars to the new Taiwan Major League before the 1997 season. One player who attempted to make the jump but was also found to have thrown games in the CPBL was Lion pitcher Guo Jinxing, the finest pitcher in Taiwan during the mid-1990s. He was banned from playing in either league—but soon made headlines another way, when he was arrested in 1999 for using a knife to hold up a woman at an ATM (*ZYSB* June 29, 1999, 6).

35. If nothing else, the downsizing to four CPBL teams has solved the problem of foreign players' dominance of the league. Whereas there were too few good Taiwanese players to fill seven CPBL team rosters, which prompted the need for so many *yangjiang,* there are enough to fill four. As of the 2000 season, CPBL teams carried only two foreign players at a time.

36. At Chen's debut at Dodger Stadium, a celebratory message from Taiwan President Chen Shui-bian was shown on the big-screen scoreboard before the game. Nike also

planned for a December 2002 release of Chen's own signature baseball cleats, "Air Zoom Respect SP" (*TTO* September 13, 2002).

37. A recent example is President Chen Shui-bian's public statement that Taiwanese culture should not be a marginalized segment of Chinese culture, calling it instead a substantial and unique civilization of its own (*TTO* August 5, 2000).

38. Where Whiting has privileged essential "Japanese" or "samurai" qualities such as "unity and team spirit," Kelly concentrates on the postwar invention of racially pure or authoritarian categories that were part and parcel of the 1960s–1970s Japanese rise to economic dominance (Whiting 1989; Kelly 1998, 102–108).

CHAPTER 10. YANG-SUCKING SHE-DEMONS

Author's note: This is a revised version of a presentation I gave at the 2001 Association of Asian Studies Conference under the same title. I am grateful for the insightful responses of the audience members at that time.

1. The full title of the movie is *A Chinese Ghost Story (Qian nü youhun)*, but for brevity's sake I will refer to it simply as *Ghost Story*.

2. Indeed, to say "Hong Kong cinema" is something of a misnomer in that it is heavily influenced by Taiwanese capital investment and creates films with an eye to pleasing Taiwanese and mainland audiences (Lo 2001, 261). Since the early 1980s, Hong Kong films have become a dominant force in Taiwan's cinemas, and Taiwanese investment and influence on the film industry has increased accordingly. Hong Kong cinema can thus be seen to be transnational cinema and reflects Taiwanese concerns as much as those of people living in Hong Kong.

3. Joey Wong (Wang Zuxian).

4. For more on the historical images of Chinese prostitutes as manipulative and scheming, see Hershatter (1994, 1997).

5. Historically in mainland China and until the last few decades in Taiwan, it was common for families to adopt young girls and raise them with the intent of marrying them to their sons (A. Wolf 1976, 1980, 1995; M. Wolf 1968, 1972). Thus, even this unexpected twist was a culturally valid option at that time.

6. People who die before they are wed are structurally anomalous. To remedy this situation, "ghost marriages" take place in which a living person will marry a ghost and take on the responsibility for providing religious offerings to that ghost. For more on ghost marriages, see Jordan 1972.

7. It is surprisingly common for ghosts to bear living children in such tales (Yu 1987, 423).

8. *A Chinese Ghost Story 3 (Dao dao dao: Qian nü youhun 3)*. The first sequel, *A Chinese Ghost Story 2 (Renjian dao: Qian nü youhun 2)*, has many of the same actors and actresses. In *Ghost Story 2*, however, the heroine is not presented as a ghost, so I will not address the film here.

9. Later she confesses that other men who took the money had their hearts or livers torn out (Pu 1766, 50).

10. The link between castration anxiety and fox spirit's depletion of male essence is reinforced by the culture-bound syndrome of *koro*, in which men become convinced that their penises are shrinking away. Victims of *koro*, it has been reported, often state that the cause of their maladies is fox spirits who are believed to "collect" men's penises to transform to human form (Prince 1992, 123, 128–129; Tseng et al. 1988, 1,539), to cause penile shrinkage by "pulling at the other end" (Cheng 1997, 62), or more generally by collecting male energy (yang essence) to gain immortality (Prince 1992, 128; Cheng 1996, 76).

11. See Ahern 1975, 193, 202 and 1988, 165; Andors 1983, 50; Gates 1996, 185–187; Harrell 1986, 113–114; Hsu 1948, 209; Moskowitz 2001; Seaman 1981, 395 and 1981, 388–389; A. Wolf 1974, 151; and M. Wolf 1974, 160.

12. To cite a few examples of this, in the movie *The Demon's Baby* (Liang 1998), we see the fear of consuming orifices as women bearing fetus demons have their stomachs open up like slimy clams. The fetus demon then shoots out tendrils and drags its struggling victims to it to eat the flesh off their skulls with its sharp, bloody fangs. (This is a very unusual depiction of fetus demons. For more on fetus demons and fetus ghosts, see Moskowitz 2001.)

For transgendered characters, in *Field of Flowers Wedding Event* (Gao 1993), the hero's mother is played by a male actor. In *The Mad Monk* (Du 1993), a masculine-looking actor plays a female deity and both wears women's clothing and has a dubbed female voice. There is also a scene in which the hero is coronated in the heavens for his meritorious deeds. He is dressed up as a woman, and the whole scene is a parody of a beauty pageant in which they give him a staff and crown and he cries with joy as he gives his acceptance speech. In *A Chinese Odyssey Part 1* (Liu 1995a), there is a scruffy-looking male bandit who has a dubbed female voice; we discover in the sequel, *A Chinese Odyssey Part 2* (Liu 1995b) that he is in actuality a woman who, because of a magic spell, changed bodies with a man. In *The Bride with White Hair* (Yu 1993), the villain is a Siamese twin—half man and half woman—who is constantly at odds with her/his twin. At the end of the movie, they are killed when the link between them is severed.

Role-reversal seduction and/or rape, such as the heroine's seduction of the hero in *Ghost Story 1* and *3*, can be seen in a number of movies. In *Royal Tramp* (Wang 1992), the princess has the queen's servants cut off the hero's clothes with their swords, wrap him up in a carpet, and bring him to her bedroom. In the film *Mr. Vampire* (Liu 2002), a female religious master ties a male religious master to her bedposts while she soaks her clothing in water, hoping that the sight of her wet clothing clinging to her body will arouse him—though he clearly wants to escape. In a later scene, he has sex with her as a condition for her to agree to help him battle an evil spirit. In the following scene they have clearly made love, and she laughs and smokes, using stereotypical male body language while he looks ashamed and hides under the covers. In *Field of Flowers Wedding Event* (Gao 1993), a woman lassos and rapes a man. In *A Chinese Odyssey* (Liu 1995a), an older sister threatens to rape and kill the man with whom her younger sister is in love, and she often beats the father of her child. He in turn tearfully talks of enduring the abuse because he loves her so dearly.

The theme of women seemingly being in charge but then subverting to male authority in the end of the movie can also be seen in *A Chinese Odyssey* (Liu 1995a), when an immortal woman brands the hero's foot to mark him as her property and spends a good deal of the movie physically abusing him. In other scenes of this movie, when the men offer to defend the women, the women contemptuously push them aside to do battle with their supernatural foes. Yet by the end of the sequel (Liu 1995b), the main male characters reveal themselves to be the reincarnated monkey king and his assistant the pig-man. Once their transformation is complete, the men become infinitely stronger than the women and must defend them against their supernatural foes. Though less obvious, *Crouching Tiger, Hidden Dragon* (Lee 2000) follows a similar plot line: The younger heroine and the older female villain, Jade Fox, can both effortlessly kill the average man. Their power seems limitless until they must face the hero, who is clearly a superior swordsman and rescues the young heroine from both the villain and herself. Jade Fox, it should be noted, is a man-hating feminist who is more masculine in appearance than the other female characters. She is also the only female character who has no romantic interest in men. Thus in killing her, the hero not only vanquishes evil but restores normative heterosexuality, as I have discussed for *Chinese Ghost Story*.

Glossary of Terms and Abbreviations

228 Incident. February 28, 1947. On the evening of February 27, a forty-year-old widow was severely beaten by ROC agents for selling black market cigarettes. The next morning this sparked widespread protests against the already unpopular KMT government. The result was four days of riots in urban areas throughout Taiwan, followed by a brutal crackdown by police and military forces. It is estimated that, over the next several months, the Nationalist government killed as many as twenty thousand Taiwanese people as part of this crackdown. Many others were arrested in their homes, imprisoned for long sentences, or even "disappeared." The date on which the uprising began—February 28, shortened to 228—has become a potent symbol of the tyranny of the Nationalist regime during its early years of power in Taiwan and has become a focal point for pro-Taiwanese (or anti–KMT) movements to this day.

Benshengren. Inhabitants of Taiwan, of Chinese descent, who were born in Taiwan before the arrival of the Nationalists in 1945–1949. The term also includes their children and descendents. The term is often simply glossed as "Taiwanese" in English and contrasts with *waishengren*. In other contexts, the term "Taiwanese" is limited to speakers of Southern Fujianese (Hokkien), the Chinese "dialect" shared with the mainland coastal area in southern Fujian Province, and thus it excludes speakers of Hakka, who were also among the early Chinese settlers of Taiwan. In yet other contexts, including this book, the term "Taiwanese" is extended to all the people of Taiwan.

Chen Shui-bian (Chen Shuibian). The first president in Taiwan from a non–KMT political party, the Democratic Progressive Party (DPP), elected in 2000. Like his predecessor, Lee Teng-hui, Chen is a native Taiwanese. He rose to fame as a lawyer for Taiwanese anti–KMT activists in the 1980s.

Chiang Ching-kuo (Jiang Jingguo). Son of Chiang Kai-shek, named premier in 1972 and elected ROC president by the National Assembly in 1978. Because Chiang Ching-kuo spent over half of his life in Taiwan, he was far more engaged with the conditions of everyday life in Taiwan than his father. He was responsible for opening the gates for both democratization and a more tolerant governmental stance toward the Taiwanese population. Chiang Ching-kuo worked for the election of Lee Teng-hui, a native Taiwanese, as his vice president, lifted martial law, and generally set the way for Taiwan's liberalization. When he died in 1988, Lee Teng-hui became president.

Chiang Kai-shek (Jiang Jieshi). Leader of the Nationalist government (KMT), Chiang Kai-shek was officially the ROC president from 1950 until his death in 1975. Chiang Kai-shek's administration implemented a series of economic policies that have been credited as the basis for Taiwan's current economic success. Politically, however, "the Generalissimo" is remembered for running the nation with an iron fist and is held responsible by many Taiwanese for the 228 crackdown, the implementation of martial law, and the resulting White Terror.

DPP (Democratic Progressive Party). An opposition (anti–KMT) party for the first thirteen years of its existence, as of 2003 the DPP holds the presidential office and is the strongest party in the national legislature. In 2000, when the DPP's Chen Shui-bian won the presidential election, the world witnessed the first peaceful transition of power by popular electoral process in Chinese or Taiwanese history. Traditionally, the DPP has actively represented the native Taiwanese population rather than concerning itself with the mainlanders *(waishengren)*, the refugees who fled to Taiwan between 1945 and 1949. Before winning the election, the DPP was also a strong vocal advocate for Taiwan's formal independence from the mainland. Since 2000, however, President Chen and the DPP as a whole have had to backtrack on this issue, because the mainland PRC government has threatened that it would respond to any declaration of independence with a military invasion. The United States has also cautioned the DPP leadership against openly advocating independence. In spite of this, the DPP owes its popularity largely to its association with the movement toward full independent statehood for Taiwan.

KMT (Kuomintang, traditional spelling of Guomindang). The Chinese Nationalist Party (KMT) dominated the ROC government, which was awarded Japanese-ruled Taiwan by the Allies at the end of WWII. Taiwan came under KMT rule in October 1945. The Nationalist government, under the leadership of the KMT, fled mainland China when it was defeated by the armies of the Chinese Communist Party, which established the People's Republic of China in 1949 but had not yet gained control of Taiwan. Thus Taiwan Province (and two small islands off the coast of Fujian) became the sole remaining domain of the KMT. Were it not for military and economic aid from the United States after the beginning of the Korean War, there is little doubt that the Communists also would have overtaken Taiwan. The KMT had a fifty-five-year monopoly on political power in Taiwan until the 2000 presidential election won by the DPP.

Languages. There are several languages spoken in Taiwan. The official language is the Mandarin "dialect" of Chinese, and this is the language spoken in schools and in most corporate settings. Mandarin, however, is a second language for the majority of people in Taiwan. Most people speak Hokkien—often called Taiwanese—at home. Ethnic minorities, such as the Hakka and members of some of the aboriginal tribes, speak their own languages among themselves.

Lee Teng-hui. The first native Taiwanese president of the ROC on Taiwan. Lee Teng-hui continued in the tradition of his predecessor Chiang Ching-kuo in liberalizing Taiwan. It was after eight years of Lee's rule as president that, in 1996, the first popular presidential election was held in the history of China or Taiwan. He won this election, but there was some doubt, both at home and abroad, as to whether or not Taiwan could truly be called a democracy in light of the fact that the KMT continued its rule. When the DPP won the presidential election in 2000, however, Lee stepped down in a peaceful transition of power.

Martial Law. In the aftermath of the 228 Incident, the Nationalists imposed martial law, which included the suppression of free speech and freedom of the press and the implementation of curfews, among other restrictions. As part of a general liberalization of the nation, President Chiang Ching-kuo lifted martial law in 1987.

PRC (People's Republic of China). The Communist-led government in mainland China. Like the ROC, the PRC has never conceded that their military victory in 1949 drew clear boundaries between China and Taiwan. The PRC has done everything in its power, short of an all-out invasion, to reclaim Taiwan. This has included bullying or bribing countries throughout the world to refuse to recognize Taiwan as an independent nation. In 1996 they went so far as to conduct a series of "missile tests," shooting missiles near and sometimes over Taiwan in an effort to intimidate Taiwanese voters and influence the result of Taiwan's first presidential election.

ROC (Republic of China). Established in 1912 by Sun Yat-sen, this was the first government in China after the end of the 2,100-year imperial system. After the KMT's defeat by the Communists, Chiang Kai-shek and his followers moved the seat of the ROC government to Taiwan in 1949. Although this was seen as a temporary solution at the time, it soon became clear that the KMT would never retake the mainland, and their "provisional" ROC government came to be seen as the de facto government only of Taiwan. But the formal claim to be the government of all of China—combined with the formal claim of the PRC government on the mainland that *it* is the only legitimate government of Taiwan—produces the diplomatic stalemate so central to Taiwan politics and international relations.

Waishengren. People who came from mainland China to Taiwan with the Nationalists in 1945–1949. Now that there have been almost six decades of contact between *benshengren* and *waishengren* in Taiwan, these strict divisions are breaking down somewhat. One example of this is the difficulty—and the futility—of labeling those who have one *benshengren* and one *waishengren* parent. Most commonly, this is traced through one's father. The term "mainlander" is usually used in English to refer to *waishengren.*

White Terror. The "white terror" was a campaign of general intimidation and brutality against Taiwanese elites and dissidents. The campaign began as a response to the 228 Incident in 1947. By the mid-1950s, the government had executed an estimated one to two thousand people and was holding approximately fourteen thousand political prisoners in jail. This movement took its name from the fact that white has traditionally been the color of death in Chinese culture.

Glossary of Characters

Note: Japanese names and terms are followed by (J).

Agarimatsu Kōichi (J)　上松耕一
Ài pīn cái huì yíng　愛拼才會贏
Àikuài　愛快
Andō Likichi (J)　安藤利吉
Áo Yòuxiáng　敖幼祥
Ā-Q　阿Q
Bādiǎn Dà Xiǎo Shēng　八點大小聲
Bāguā Shān　八卦山
Bái Bīngbīng　白冰冰
Bái Xiānyǒng　白先勇
báiliǎn　白臉
báimiàn　白麵
báisè kǒngbù　白色恐怖
Bǎiwēi　百威
bājiājiàng　八家將
bàngqiú　棒球
Bāo Gōng　包公
Bāo Qīngtiān　包青天
bǎobèi　寶貝
bǎojuàn　寶眷
Bǎoshēng Dàdì　保生大帝
bāozi　包子
Běijīng　北京
Běijīngyǔ　北京語
Běnshěng, wàishěng hái yào fēn ma?
　　本省，外省還要分嗎？
běnshěngrén　本省人
běntǔ　本土

běntǔ yìshì　本土意識
běntǔhuà　本土化
Brother Elephants (Xiōngdì Xiàng)
　　兄弟象
bù yuànyì　不願意
bù zhōng bù xi　不中不西
bunmei kaika (J)　文明開化
bùxiào yǒu sān, wúhòu wéi dà
　　不孝有三，無後為大
cài　菜
Cài Mínghóng　蔡明宏
Cài Zhìzhōng　蔡志忠
Cǎichén (Níng Cǎichén)　采臣 (寧采臣)
càishìchǎng　菜市場
Cáo Jǐnhuī　曹錦輝
Chén Dàfēng　陳大豐
Chén Dàshùn　陳大順
Chén Dì　陳第
Chén Dìngnán　陳定南
Chén Gēngyuán　陳耕元
Chén Jǐnfēng　陳金鋒
Chén Ruòxiān　陳若仙
Chén Shèngtián　陳盛沺
Chén Shuǐbiǎn (Chen Shui-bian)　陳水扁
Chén Wǎnfēn　陳婉芬
Chén Yí　陳儀
Chén Yìxìn　陳義信
Chén Yǒuyì　陳有義

Chén Zhìyuán　陳智源
Chéngguān　成冠
Chénghuáng　城隍
chéngshì　成市
Chiang Ching-kuo (Jiǎng Jīngguó)
　　蔣經國
Chiang Kai-shek (Jiǎng Jièshí)　蔣介石
chihō jitsu (J)　地方自治
China Times Eagles (Shíbào Yīng)
　　時報鷹
China Trust Whales (Héxìn Jīng)　和信鯨
chūlái bāngyòng　出來幫佣
Chǔlǐ wěiyuánhuì　處理委員會
Dà héjiě: wǒmen shì shénme rén?
　　大和解：我們是甚麼人？
dà páidàng　大排檔
Dàdì　大地
Dàjiā lái shěnpàn　大家來審判
Dàlǐ　大里
dǎngwài　黨外
Dàwān　大灣
Dàyuán　大員，大圓
diàn　殿
diǎnxīn　點心
Dìbō　帝波
dìsìtái　第四台
dìxià jīngjì　地下經濟
dìyù　地獄
Dìzàng Ān　地藏庵
Dìzàngwáng púsà　地藏王菩薩
dōka (J)　同化
Dōngfān jì　東番記
Dōnghuá　東華
Dōngjīng mènghuá lù　東京夢華錄
Dōngsēn　東森
dōngyáng fēng　東洋風
Dōngyuè dàdì　東嶽大帝
Duànfǎ Bùgǎizhuàng Huì　斷髮不改壯會
duìtiān lìshì　對天立誓
dǔzhòu　賭咒
Employment Service Act (Jiùyè Fúwù Fǎ)
　　就業服務法
Èrshísì Xiào　二十四孝
fàn　飯
Fàn Yún　范雲
fànggào　放告
Fēiyīng　飛鷹
Fēiyōng　菲傭
fēizhèngshì jīngjì　非正式經濟
Fēngdū　酆都
Fēngdū *dìfǔ*　酆都地府
Fēngsú Gǎiliáng Huì　風俗改良會
fēnlèi xièdòu　分類械鬥
fēnxiǎng shíjiān　分享時間

Fó'ér huà　佛爾話
Fújiàn　福建
fùshí　副食
gào yīnzhuàng　告陰狀
Gāoshānguó　高山國
Gaoxiong-Pingdong Thunder Gods
　　(Gāo-Píng Léigōng)　高屏雷公
gōng　工
Gōng Wǔ　恭武
Gotō Shimpei (J)　後藤新平
Guān Dì　關帝
Guāngfù　光復
Guānyīn　觀音
gǔdiǎn　古典
gǔdǒng　古董
Guō Jiànchéng　郭建成
Guō Jìnxīng　郭進興
Guō Tàiyuán (Kaku Taigen)　郭泰源
Guō Yuánzhì (Kaku Genji)　郭源治
guójiā dàibiǎoduì　國家代表隊
Guómíndǎng (KMT)　國民黨
guóyǔ　國語
Gǔsǒu　瞽搜
Hàojiǎo　號角
Hé Chūnruǐ (Josephine Ho)　何春蕤
Hé Xiànfán　何獻凡
hēijīn　黑金
hēiliǎn　黑臉
Hēiyīng　黑鷹
héshì fēnggé　和式風格
Ho, Josephine (Hé Chūnruǐ)　何春蕤
hoan-á (Taiwanese) *(fān zǎi)*　番仔
Hóng Tàishān　洪太山
Hóngyè　紅葉
Hóngyè Chuánqí　紅葉傳奇
hòuyuánhuì (kōenkai)　後援會
Hú Róng　胡蓉
huá　華
huàiqiú　壞球
Huáng Píngyáng　黃平洋
Huáng Qīngjìng　黃清境
Huánqiú　環球
Huárén　華人
Huáyǔ　華語
húlíjīng　狐狸精
isshi dōjin (J)　一視同仁
Itō Hirobumi (J)　伊藤博文
Jiǎng Jièshí (Chiang Kai-shek)　蔣介石
Jiǎng Jīngguó (Chiang Ching-kuo)
　　蔣經國
Jiāng Tàiquán　江泰權
Jiāngsū　江蘇
jiàohún　叫魂
jiǎozi　餃子

Jiayi-Tainan Braves (Jiā-Nán Yǒngshì)
　　嘉南勇士
jiāyóu Táiwānduì　加油台灣隊
jiéshì　結市
Jíjí　集集
Jìn　晉
Jīn Chéngwǔ (Kaneshiro Takeshi)
　　金城武
Jīn Píng Méi　金瓶梅
Jīn Xiùlì　靳秀麗
Jīngāng　金剛
jìnjì　禁忌
Jīnmén　金門
Jungo Bears (Jùnguó Xióng)　俊國熊
kāijiǎng　開講
kaiseimei (J)　改姓名
Kanō (J)　嘉農
Kē Fēi　喀飛
Kē Nǎiyíng　柯乃熒
Keihatsukai (J)　啟發會
Kim Yong Woon (Korean)　金容雲
KMT (Guómíndǎng)　國民黨
kōenkai (J)　後援會
kokugo hukaisha o issōsu (J)
　　國語不解者を一掃す
kōminka undō (J)　皇民化運動
Kondō Hyōtarō (J)　近藤兵太郎
konjō (J)　根性
Kōshien (J)　甲子園
kǒushuǐ zhàn　口水戰
kòuyìng　叩應
kòuyìng bùduì　叩應部隊
kòuyìng jiémù　叩應節目
kòuyìng rècháo　叩應熱潮
Kure Masayuki (J)　吳昌征
Lài Zhèngzhé　賴正哲
lǎobǎn　老闆
lǎoshī　老師
lǎoshǔ huì　老鼠會
lǎowài　老外
Lǎozǐ　老子
Lee Teng-hui (Lǐ Dēnghuī)　李登輝
Léigōng　雷公
lěngqīng　冷清
lì　曆,歷,历
Lì　歷
Lǐ Áo　李敖
Lǐ Dēnghuī (Lee Teng-hui)　李登輝
Lǐ Hóngzhāng　李鴻章
Lǐ Jūmíng　李居明
Lǐ Kūnzhé　李坤哲
Lǐ Láifā　李來發
Lǐ Tāo　李濤
Lǐ Wěi　李偉

Lǐ Yǎjǐng　李雅景
Lǐ Yìngyuán　李應元
Lǐ Yìngyuán Mínjìndǎng lìwěi
　　李應元民進黨立委
Lián Zhàn　連戰
Liào Tiāndīng　廖添丁
Liáozhāi zhìyì　聊齋誌異
Lìfǎyuàn　立法院
Lǐjì　禮記
Lín Guìxīng　林桂興
Lín Yìxióng　林義雄
líng chéngběn, wú fēngxiǎn
　　零成本，無風險
lìshì　立誓
Liú Yuánqīng　劉元卿
lòuxí　陋習
Lǚ Xiùlián　呂秀蓮
luàn　亂
lùdiàn　露店
luó　羅
Luó Dàohòu　羅道厚
lǜsè xì dǎo　綠色矽島
Mǎ Yīngjiǔ　馬英九
Máo Zédōng　毛澤東
Māzǔ　媽祖
Méihuā　梅花
Měilè　美樂
Měilèhēi　美樂黑
Mèng pó　孟婆
Mèng Zōng　孟宗
Mèngliánglù　夢梁錄
Mèngzǐ　孟子
Mercuries Tigers (Sānshāng Hǔ)　三商虎
miàohuì　廟會
mínbiàn　民變
Míng　明
mǐngǎn　敏感
míngjiān　冥間
Mínjìndǎng　民進黨
Mínshì　民視
mínyì jiājù　民藝家具
Mínzhǔ jìnbù dǎng　民主進步黨
míxìn　迷信
mǒhēi　抹黑
Mùlián　目蓮
naichi enchō (J)　內地延長
Nàlǔwān　那魯灣
Nàlǔwān—Chèng-kêng ê Eng-hiông
　　那魯灣—正港的英雄
nanshin (J)　南進
Nápōlǐ　拿坡里
Nǐ/ěr (yě) lái le　你/爾[也]來了
níng wéi jīshǒu, bù wéi niúhòu
　　寧為雞首，不為牛後

níngjìng gémìng　寧靜革命
Nitobe Inazō (J)　新渡戶稻造
Nōkō (J)　能高
nóng　農
nǚyōng　女傭
Ō Ikutoku (J)　王育德
Ozaki Hotsuki (J)　尾崎秀樹
Pān Jīnlián zhī Qiánshì Jīnshēng
　　潘金蓮之前世今生
pànguān　判官
pǎo jiānghú　跑江湖
pàomòhuà　泡沫化
pèi　配
Péng Míngmǐn　彭明敏
pó　婆
President Lions (Tǒngyī Shī)　統一獅
Pú Sōnglíng　蒲松齡
pǔtōnghuà　普通話
Puzi Tornados (Pǔzi Xuànfēng)　朴子旋風
qián duō, shì shǎo, lí jiā jìn
　　錢多、事少、離家近
qiánglì bàngqiú　強力棒球
Qiànnǚ Yōuhún　倩女幽魂
Qiǎofú　巧福
Qīngdǎo　青島
Qīnmíndǎng　親民黨
Qiū Fùshēng　邱復生
Quánjiāfú　全家福
Quánmín kāijiǎng　全民開講
qūwáng tái　驅忘台
ràng wǒ duǒ zài nǐ shēn biān
　　讓我躲在你身邊
Regulations Governing Employment and
　　Control of Foreigners (Wàiguórén
　　pìn gù xǔkě jí guǎnlǐ bànfǎ)
　　外國人聘僱許可及管理辦法
rènaò　熱鬧
rénqíngwèi　人情味
rōshū (J)　陋習
Sakariba (J)　盛り場
Sakuma Samata (J)　佐久間左馬太
sànshì　散市
Shāndōng　山東
shāng　商
Shànghǎirén　上海人
shāngrén guójiā　商人國家
shāngzhǎn　商展
shànshū　善書
Shàobàng　少棒
Shàonián bàngqiú　少年棒球
shāsǐ hànjiān　殺死漢奸
shēngfān　生番
shěngjí qíngjié　省籍情結
Shèngmàigé　聖麥格

Shèngxīn Táng　聖心堂
shì　士
shì　市
Shī Láng　施琅
shì nóng gōng shāng　士農工商
Shī Wénbīn　施文彬
Shíbā Dìyù Miào　十八地獄廟
Shinminkai (J)　新民會
shǔdì zhǔyì　屬地主義
shúfān　熟番
shūfáng　書房
Shùn　舜
Sìchuān　四川
Sinon Bulls (Xīngnóng Niú)　興農牛
sīxíng　私刑
Sòng　宋
Sòng Chǔyú (James Soong)　宋楚瑜
Sòng Měilíng　宋美齡
Soong, James (Sòng Chǔyú)　宋楚瑜
Táiběi　台北
Taibei Braves (Táiběi Yǒngshì)　台北勇士
Taibei Suns (Táiběi Tàiyáng)　台北太陽
Táiběixiàn de Lín Xiǎojiě
　　台北縣的林小姐
Táidú　台獨
Táidú wànsuì　台獨萬歲
Táijiā　台家
Tainan Giants (Táinán Jùrén)　台南巨人
Tàishàng Gǎnyìng Piān　太上感應篇
Táiwān　台灣
Taiwan Bunka Kyōkai (J)　台灣文化休會
Táiwān Dà Liánméng　台灣大聯盟
Táiwān dúlì wànsuì　台灣獨立萬歲
Taiwan Gikai Kisei Dōmei (J)
　　台灣議會規制同盟
Táiwān Gònghéguó　台灣共和國
Táiwān Mínzhǔguó　台灣民主國
Taiwan Seinen (J)　台灣青年
Táiwān Tuánjié Liánméng　台灣團結聯盟
Táiwān Xìngbié Rénquán Xiéhuì
　　台灣性別人權協會
Táiwān yōuxiān, běntǔ dì yī
　　台灣優先、本土第一
Táiwānrén　台灣人
Tàiyáng　太陽
Táiyǔ　台語
Táiyuán　台員
Táizhōng　台中
Taizhong Golden Dragons (Táizhōng
　　Jīnlóng)　台中金龍
Taizhong Robots (Táizhōng Jīngāng)
　　台中金剛
Takasago (J)　高砂
tānfàn　攤販

244　*Glossary of Characters*

Táng Jǐngsōng　唐景崧
Tiānjīn　天津
Tiānránzú Huì　天然足會
Tóngfēng Huì　同風會
Tóngguāng Jiàohuì　同光教會
tóngzhì　同志
tóngzhì kōngjiān zhènxiàn　同志空間陣線
tuóluó　陀螺
Tǔyǔ Jìnzhǐ Huì　土語禁止會
U bou khaqhou cif-e thi: -gong-cuo
　　有"女"較好一個天公祖
wàiguó zūjiè　外國租界
wàijí láogōng　外籍勞工
wàijí nǚyōng　外籍女傭
wàiláo wèntí　外勞問題
wàishěng　外省
wàishěngrén　外省人
wàishěngrén dì'èr dài　外省人第二代
wàishěngrén kǒngjùgǎn　外省人恐懼感
wáng　王
Wáng Bùrén　王不仁
Wáng Jīnpíng　王金平
Wáng Jùnláng　王俊郎
Wáng Lìkǎi　王儷凱
Wáng Píng　王蘋
Wáng Zǔxián　王祖賢
wángye　王爺
Wànhuá　萬華
Wèi Bórú　魏伯儒
wèi jì shōurù bǎntú　未既收入版圖
Weichuan Dragons (Wèiquán Lóng)
　　味全龍
wèntí　問題
Wǒmen Zhījiān　我們之間
Wú Bō　吳波
Wú Línliàn　吳林煉
Wú Měng　吳猛
Wú Shèng　吳晟
Wú Shūzhēn　吳淑珍
wǔwèi chá　五味茶
wǔxiá　武俠
wǔxíng　五行
Xī Shènglín　奚聖林
Xiáhǎi Chénghuáng Miào　霞海城隍廟
Xiàmén　廈門
xiànchǎng　現場
Xiàng　象
Xiāng duì lùn　相對論
xiāngtǔ　鄉土
xiāngtǔ xiǎochī　鄉土小吃
Xiāngyāo láiguàng yèshì　相邀來逛夜市
xiànshēn　現身
xiào　孝
Xiāo　蕭

Xiǎo dōng dǎo　小東島
Xiāo Júzhēn　蕭菊貞
xiǎo lǎopo　小老婆
Xiǎo Liúqiú　小流求
Xiǎoběi　小北
xiǎofàn　小販
Xiǎoqiàn (Niè Xiǎoqiàn)　小倩 (聶小倩)
xiǎozhòng　小眾
Xiè Dōngmǐn　謝東閔
Xīméndīng　西門町
Xīn Nányáng　新南洋
xin Táiwānrén　新台灣人
Xīndǎng　新黨
Xīnzhú　新竹
Xiōngdì Xiàng　兄弟象
xiù　秀
Xú Shēngmíng　徐生明
Xǔ Yòushēng　許佑生
yakyū (J)　野球
Yamane Toshida (J)　山根俊英
yán　閻
Yàn Dàjiǎo (Yàn Bǔtóu)　燕大佼 (燕捕頭)
Yán Qīngbiāo　顏清標
Yán Wáng　閻王
yáng　陽
Yáng Chuánguǎng　楊傳廣
yáng qì　陽氣
yángjiāng　洋將
Yánluó　閻羅
Yánluó wáng　閻羅王
Yáo　堯
Yè Qǐtián　葉啟田
Yè Tiānsòng　葉天送
Yěsǒu Pùyán　野叟曝言
yí　夷
yīn　陰
Yīnguǒ Mǎnhuà Zhuānkān　因果漫畫專刊
Yīngxiá　鷹俠
yīnjiān　陰間
Yízhōu　夷洲，夷州
Yomiuri Giants (J)　讀賣巨人
Yonamine, Wally (J)　與那嶺要
yǒngshì　勇士
Yǒu huà lǎoshi jiǎng　有話老實講
Yú　虞
Yú Hóngkāi　余宏開
Yú Zhèngxiàn　余政憲
Yuán　元
Yuánhuán　圓環
yuánzhùmín　原住民
Yuè Fēi　岳飛
Yufū　魚夫
yùlì　玉曆
Yùlì Bǎochāo　玉曆寶鈔

zájì 雜技
Zēng Zhìzhēn 曾智偵
zhǎn jītóu 斬雞頭
zhàndòu wényì 戰鬥文藝
Zhāng Xiǎohóng 張小紅
Zhāng Zhèngxiàn 張正憲
Zhāng Zhènyù 張震獄
Zhānghuà 彰化
Zhào Shìqiáng 趙士強
Zhè zhǒng bùyì zhī cái, zāng wǒ de kǒudài!
　　這種不義之財，髒我的口袋
Zhènlán gōng 鎮瀾宮
Zhèng Bǎishèng 鄭百勝
Zhèng Chénggōng 鄭成功
Zhèng Jīng 鄭經
zhèntóu 陣頭

Zhōnggòng fēngshā Āmèi? 中共封殺阿妹？
Zhōngguórén 中國人
Zhōnghuá Zhíyè Bàngqiú Liánméng
　　中華職業棒球聯盟
zhōnglì 中立
Zhōu Ēnlái 周恩來
Zhōu Jìnshēng (Jonathan Chou) 周晉昇
zhòuzǔ 咒咀
Zhū Wěichéng 朱偉誠
Zhū Yīguì 朱一貴
zhǔfùhéyī 主副合一
Zhuō Kūnyuán 桌琨原
zhǔshí 主食
zìzhǔ 自主
zòngzi 粽子
zuòxiù 做秀

References

Abt, Vicki, and Leonard Mustazza. 1997. *Coming after Oprah: Cultural Fallout in the Age of the TV Talk Show.* Bowling Green, OH: Bowling Green State University Popular Press.
AFP (Agence France Presse). Various dates.
Ahern (Martin), Emily. 1975. "The power and pollution of Chinese women." In *Women in Chinese Society*, ed. Margery Wolf and Roxanne Witke, 193-214. Stanford: Stanford University Press.
———. 1988. "Gender and ideological differences in representations of life and death." In *Death Ritual in Late Imperial and Modern China*, ed. James Watson and Evelyn S. Rawski, 164-179. Berkeley: University of California Press.
Allee, Mark A. 1994. *Law and Local Society in Late Imperial China: Northern Taiwan in the Nineteenth Century.* Stanford: Stanford University Press.
Alterman, Eric. 1999. *Sound and Fury: The Making of the Punditocracy.* Ithaca, NY: Cornell University Press.
Amarles, Bienvenida M. 1990. "Female migrant labor: Domestic helpers in Singapore." *Philippine Journal of Public Administration* 34(4): 365-387.
Amway Corporation. 2002. "Our story." http://www.amway.com/ourstory/0-intro.asp, accessed November 27, 2002.
An Keqiang 安克強. 1997. *Hong taiyang xia de hei linghun: Zhongguo dalu tongzhi xianchang baodao* 紅太陽下的黑靈魂：中國大陸同志現場報導 (Black spirits under the red sun: A report on mainland Chinese comrades). Taibei: Reai Chubanshi 臺北：熱愛出版社.
Anderson, Benedict. 1991. *Imagined Communities: Reflections on the Origin and Spread of Nationalism.* London: Verson.
Andors, Phyllis. 1983. *The Unfinished Liberation of Chinese Women, 1949-1980.* Bloomington: Indiana University Press.
Anli Taiwan Fengongsi 安麗台灣分公司 (Amway Corporation, Taiwan Branch). 1993. *Renshi Anli* 認識安麗 (Knowing Amway). Taibei: Anli Taiwan Fengongsi.
———. n.d. "Anli Taiwan xiaodang'an" 安麗台灣小檔案 (Amway Taiwan file). http://www.amway.com.tw/1knewamw/taiwan.html, accessed November 27, 2002.
Ao Youxiang 敖幼祥. 1994. *Zhibang kuangxiangqu* 職棒狂想曲 (Pro baseball rhapsody). Taibei: Zhonghua Zhibang Shiye Gufen Youxian Gongsi 中華職棒事業股份有限公司.

AP (Associated Press). Various dates.
Appadurai, Arjun. 1996. *Modernity at Large: Cultural Dimensions of Globalization.* Minneapolis: University of Minnesota Press.
Appleton, Sheldon L. 1972. "Taiwan: The year it finally happened." *Asian Survey* 12(1): 32–37.
Arrigo, Linda Gail. 1994. "From democratic movement to bourgeois democracy: The internal politics of the Taiwan Democratic Progressive Party in 1991." In *The Other Taiwan: 1945 to the Present*, ed. Murray A. Rubinstein, 145–180. Armonk, NY: M. E. Sharpe.
Babcock, Barbara A. 1978. "Introduction." In *The Reversible World: Symbolic Inversion in Art and Society*, ed. Barbara A. Babcock, 13–36. Ithaca, NY: Cornell University Press.
Bai, Xianyong. 1995. *Crystal Boys*. Trans. Howard Goldblatt. San Francisco: Gay Sunshine Press.
Bakan, Abigail B., and Daiva K. Stasiulis. 1995. "Making the match: Domestic placement agencies and the racialization of women's household work." *Signs* 20(2): 303–332.
Bernhardt, Kathryn, and Philip C. C. Huang, eds. 1994. *Civil Law in Qing and Republican China.* Stanford: Stanford University Press.
BG (Boston Globe). Various dates.
Bi Hengda 畢恆達. 2001. "Caihong de guodu" 彩虹的國度 (Rainbow country). In *Kongjian jiu shi quanli* 空間就是權力 (Space is power), ed. Bi Hengda, 113–126. Taibei: Xingling Gongfang 臺北：心靈工坊.
Biggart, Nicole Woolsey. 1989. *Charismatic Capitalism: Direct Selling Organizations in America.* Chicago: University of Chicago Press.
Bishop, Ryan, and Lilian Robinson. 1998. *Night Market: Sexual Cultures and the Thai Economic Miracle.* London: Routledge Press.
Blum, Susan D. 2001. *Portraits of "Primitives": Ordering Human Kinds in the Chinese Nation.* Lanham, MD: Rowman and Littlefield.
Bosco, Joseph. 1994. "The emergence of a Taiwanese popular culture." In *The Other Taiwan: 1945 to the Present*, ed. Murray A. Rubinstein, 392–403. Armonk, NY: M. E. Sharpe.
Bright, Martin, Burhan Wazir, and Emma Flatt. 2002. "Onward march of lobby against immigration." *The Observer*, December 1, accessed December 10, 2002, http://www.observer.co.uk/race/story/0,11255,851676,00.html.
Brokaw, Cynthia. 1991. *The Ledgers of Merit and Demerit.* Princeton: Princeton University Press.
Butterfield, Stephen. 1985. *Amway: The Cult of Free Enterprise.* Boston: South End Press.
Cai Hongjin 蔡宏進. 1991. "Taiwan waiji laogong keneng zaocheng de buliang shehui yingxiang" "台灣外籍勞工可能造成的不良社會影響" (The possible negative social impacts that foreign workers might bring about). *Zhongguo shibao* 中國時報 *(China times)*, July 29: 3.
Cai Zongxin 蔡宗信. 1992. "Riju shidai Taiwan bangqiu yundong fazhan guocheng zhi yanjiu—yi 1895 (Mingzhi 28) nian zhi 1926 (Dazheng 15) nian wei zhongxin" 日據時代台灣棒球運動發展過程之研究—以1895（明治28）年至1926（大正15）年為中心 (Research into the development of Taiwanese baseball during the Japanese occupation). M.A. Thesis, National Taiwan Normal University, Physical Education Department.
Company, Robert Ford. 1996. *Strange Writing: Anomaly Accounts in Early Medieval China.* Albany: State University of New York Press.
Cao Yonghe 曹永和. 1980. "Ming-Zheng shiqi yiqian de Taiwan" 明鄭時期以前的臺灣 (Taiwan before the Ming dynasty and Zheng Chenggong eras). In *Taiwanshi luncong, di yi ji* 臺灣史論叢第一輯 (Collected essays on Taiwan history, vol. 1), ed. Huang Fusan 黃富三 and Cao Yonghe 曹永和, 39–97. Taibei: Zhongwen Tushu 眾文圖書.
Carrington, George Williams. 1977. *Foreigners in Formosa, 1841–1874.* San Francisco: Chinese Materials Center, Inc.

Chan, Tak-hung Leo. 1998. *The Discourse on Foxes and Ghosts: Ji Yun, an Eighteenth-Century Literati Storytelling.* Honolulu: University of Hawai'i Press.

Chang, Gordon G. 1988. "To the nuclear brink: Eisenhower, Dulles and the Quemoy-Matsu crisis." *International Security* 12(4): 96-123.

———. 2001. *The Coming Collapse of China.* New York: Random House.

Chang Mau-Kuei. 1993. "Middle class and social and political movements in Taiwan: Questions and some preliminary observations." In *Discovery of the Middle Classes in East Asia*, ed. Hsin-Huang Michael Hsiao, 121-176. Taipei: Academia Sinica Institute of Ethnology.

Changrong Kongzhong Shangdian 長榮空中商店 (EVA Sky Shop). 2000. Taoyuan: Changrong Guoji Gufen Youxian Gongsi 長榮國際股份有限公司.

Chao, Y. A. 1999. "Performing like a p'o and acting as a big sister: Reculturating into the indigenous lesbian circle in Taiwan." In *Sex, Sexuality, and the Anthropologist*, ed. F. Markowitz and M. Ashkenazi, 128-144. Urbana: University of Illinois Press.

Chen Cheng-siang. 1956. *The City of Taipei.* Taipei: Fu-Min Geographical Institute of Economic Development.

Chen Dashun 陳大順. 2000. "Zhaochu wenti, jiejue wenti" 找出問題，解決問題 (Locate the problem, solve the problem). *Zhiye bangqiu* 職業棒球 (Professional baseball) 219: 19-21.

Chen, Edward I-te. 1977. "Japan's decision to annex Taiwan: A study of Itô-Mutsu diplomacy, 1894-95." *Journal of Asian Studies* 37(1): 61-72.

———. 1984. "The attempt to integrate the empire: Legal perspectives." In *The Japanese Colonial Empire, 1895-1945*, ed. Ramon H. Myers and Mark R. Peattie, 240-274. Princeton: Princeton University Press.

Chen, Jackie. 1996. "Major league controversies: Professional baseball enters a new era." Trans. Phil Newell. *Sinorama* 21(3): 76-87.

Chen Kongli 陳孔立. 1990. *Qingdai Taiwan yimin shehui yanjiu* 清代台灣移民社會研究 (Research into the immigrant society of Qing Taiwan). Xiamen: Xiamen Daxue Chubanshe 廈門大學出版社.

Chen, Lung-chu, and W. M. Reisman. 1972. "Who owns Taiwan: A search for international title." *Yale Law Journal* 81(4): 599-671.

Chen, Sheue Yun. 1998. "State, media and democracy in Taiwan." *Media, Culture, and Society* 20: 11-29.

Chen Shui-bian 陳水扁. 2000. "Zongtong fabiao kua shiji tanhua" 總統發表跨世紀談話 (The president's century-bridging address). Taibei: Office of the President of the Republic of China. December 31. http://www.president.gov.tw/1_news/index.html, accessed June 30, 2001.

———. 2001. "Bridging the new century: President Chen's New Year's Eve address, Dec. 31, 2000." *Taipei Update* 2(2): 1-3.

Chen Yundong 陳運棟. 1987. "Yimin hu? Bu yi zhi min hu?" 義民乎？不義之民乎？(People with a sense of justice? Unjust people?). *Santai zazhi* 三台雜誌 *(Three highest magazine)* 14: 10-20.

Cheng, Sheung-Tak. 1996. "A critical review of Chinese *koro*." *Culture, Medicine and Psychiatry* 20: 67-82.

Cheng Shu-ju Ada. 1996. "Migrant women domestic workers in Hong Kong, Singapore and Taiwan: A comparative analysis." *Asian and Pacific Migration Journal* 5(1): 139-152.

Cheng Xiaodong 程小東, director. 1987. *Qian nü youhun* 倩女幽魂 (A Chinese ghost story). Xianggang: Jin Gongju Dianying Zhizuo Youxian Gongsi 香港：金公主電影製作有限公司.

———. 1990. *Renjian dao: Qian nü youhun 2* 人間道：倩女幽魂2 (A Chinese ghost story 2). Xianggang: Jin Gongju Dianying Zhizuo Youxian Gongsi 香港：金公主電影製作有限公司.

———. 1991. *Dao dao dao: Qian nü youhun 3* 道道道：倩女幽魂3 (A Chinese ghost story 3). Xianggang: Jin Gongju Dianying Zhizuo Youxian Gongsi 香港：金公主電影製作有限公司.

Cheng Zhiyue 成之約. 1997. "Waiji banyong zhengce jiqi yingxiang de tantao" 外籍幫傭政策及其影響的探討 (Exploring the foreign maid polity and its effects). Paper Presented at the Conference on Foreign Maid Policy and State Development, April. Taibei.

Chi Yifeng and Liu Qingjian. 1987. *Zhongguo jingji zui zuei* 中國經濟之最 (The most known of Chinese economy). Beijing: Zhongguo Lüyou (北京：中國旅遊).

Chin, Ko-lin, 1996. *Chinatown Gangs: Extortion, Enterprise, and Ethnicity*. New York: Oxford University Press.

China Times. 1995. "The first case of a Filipina maid killing her employer breaks out in our nation." 1995. "Guonei baofa shouzong Feiyong shasi guzhu an" 國內爆發首宗菲傭殺死雇主案. *Zhongguo shibao* 中國時報 *(China times)*, November 10: 1.

Ching, Leo. 2000. "Globalizing the regional, regionalizing the global: Mass culture and Asianism in the age of late capital." *Public Culture* 12(1): 233–257.

———. 2001. *Becoming "Japanese": Colonial Taiwan and the Politics of Identity Formation*. Berkeley: University of California Press.

Chiu, Fred Y. L. 2000. "Suborientalism and the subimperialist predicament: Aboriginal discourse and the poverty of state-nation imagery." *Positions: East Asian Cultures Critiques* 8(1) (spring): 101–149.

Chiu Hei-yuan 瞿海源. 1988. "Taiwan diqu minzhong de zongjiao xinyang yu zongjiao taidu" 臺灣地區民眾的宗教信仰與宗教態度 (Popular religious beliefs and attitudes in the Taiwan region). In *Bianqian zhong de Taiwan shehui* 變遷中的臺灣社會 *(Taiwan society in transition)*, ed. Yang Kuo-shu 楊國樞 and Chiu Hei-yuan, 239–276. Nankang: Institute of Ethnology, Academia Sinica.

Chiu, Hungdah, ed. 1973. *China and the Question of Taiwan: Documents and Analysis*. New York: Praeger.

Ch'iu, K'un-liang. 1989. "Mu-lien 'operas' in Taiwanese funeral rituals." In *Ritual Opera, Operatic Ritual*, ed. David Johnson, 105–125. Berkeley: IEAS Publications.

Chiu Peilin and Sylvia M. Chan-Olmsted. 1999. "The impact of cable television on political campaigns in Taiwan." *Gazette* 61(6): 491–509.

Chou Wah Shan 周華山. 1994. *Tongzhi lun* 同志論 (On comrades). Xianggang: Tonzhi Yanjiu Shi 香港：同志研究社.

———. 1997 *Houzhimin tongzhi* 後殖民同志 (Postcolonial comrades). Xianggang: Tonzhi Yanjiu Shi 香港：香港同志研究社.

Chou Wan-yao 周婉窈. 1995. "Taiwanren di yi ci de 'guoyu' jingyan: xilun Rizhi moqi de Riyu yundong jiqi wenti" 台灣人第一次的「國語」經驗：析論日治末期的日語運動及其問題 (The Taiwanese people's first experience with a "national language": An analysis of the Japanese language movement during late Japanese rule). *Xin shixue* 新史學 *(New historiography)* 6(2): 113–159.

Ch'ü, T'ung-tsu. 1961. *Law and Society in Traditional China*. Paris: Moulon.

Chu Wei-cheng 朱偉誠. 1998. "Taiwan tongzhi yundong de houzhimin sikao: Lun 'xianshen' wenti." 台灣同志運動的後殖民思考：論「現身」問題 (Coming out or not: Postcolonial autonomy and gay activism in Taiwan). *Taiwan shehui yanjiu jikan* 台灣社會研究季刊 *(Taiwan: A radical quarterly in the social sciences)* 30: 35–62.

———. 2000. "Jianli tongzhi guo? Chaoxiang yige xing yiyi zhengti de wutuobang xiangxiang" 建立同志「國」？朝向一個性異議政體的烏托邦想像 (Taking queer nation/alism seriously: The vista of a utopian polity of sexual dissidents). *Taiwan shehui yanjiu jikan* 台灣社會研究季刊 *(Taiwan: A radical quarterly in the social sciences)* 40: 103–152.

CLA (Council of Labor Affairs) (勞委會 Laoweihui). 1991. *Dui waiji nüyong kanfa ji guonei nüyong guyong xiankuang yu gongxu yiyuan tongji baogao* 對外籍女傭看法及國內女傭僱用現況與供需意願統計報告 (The statistics of current supply and demand of recruiting foreign domestic servants in the Taiwan area). Taipei: Laoweihui.

———. 1996. *The Management Problems of Foreign Laborers and Its Related Legal Issues.* Taipei: Laoweihui.
———. 1997a. *The Management Reports of Foreign Labor in Taiwan Area, August 1996.* Taipei: Laoweihui.
———. 1997b. *A Guidance for Employers Who Recruit Foreign Workers.* Taipei: Laoweihui.
———. 1997c. *Monthly Bulletin of Labor Statistics, Taiwan Area*, March. Taipei: Laoweihui.
———. 1997d. *Statistics Index.* June. Taipei: Laoweihui.
———. 1998a. *A Handbook for Foreign Workers Working and Living in the Republic of China*, May. Taipei: Laoweihui.
———. 1998b. *Handbook for Foreign Workers in the Republic of China.* Taipei: Laoweihui.
———. 2001. Council of Labor Affairs' website, accessed on June 18. http://www.cla.gov.tw/acdept/month/tab1102.xls.
CND (China News Digest). Various dates. Gaithersburg, MD: China News Digest International, Inc. http://www.cnd.org.
Constable, Nicole. 1997. *Maid to Order in Hong Kong: Stories of Filipina Workers.* London: Cornell University Press.
CP (China Post). Various dates.
Cross, Wilbur. 1999. *Amway: The True Story of the Company that Transformed the Lives of Millions.* New York: Berkley Books.
Davidson, James W. 1903. *The Island of Formosa: Historical View from 1430 to 1900.* New York: Macmillan.
de Groot, Jan J. M. 1892–1910. *The Religious System of China.* 6 vols. Leiden: E. J. Brill.
Deane, Hugh. 1999. *The Korean War, 1945–1953.* San Francisco: China Books and Periodicals.
DeGlopper, Donald R. 1980. "Lu-kang: A city and its trading system." In *China's Island Frontier: Studies in the Historical Geography of Taiwan*, ed. Ronald G. Knapp, 143–165. Honolulu: University of Hawai'i Press.
D'Emilio, John. 1993. "Capitalism and gay identity." In *The Lesbian and Gay Studies Reader*, ed. H. Abelove, M. Barale, and D. Alperin, 467–476. London: Routledge.
DeVos, Richard M., and Jan Van Andel. 1992. *Huahanji* 華翰集 (Wisdom from the Amway founders). Trans. Anli Taiwan Fengongsi 安麗台灣分公司 (Amway Corporation, Taiwan Branch). Taibei: Anli Taiwan Fengongsi.
Di qi jie quanguo yundonghui huikan 第七屆全國運動會會刊 (Publication of the seventh National Games). 1948. Shanghai: Shenbaoguan 申報館.
Dickson, Bruce J. 1993. "The lessons of defeat: The reorganization of the Kuomintang on Taiwan, 1950–1952." *China Quarterly* 133: 56–84.
Dikötter, Frank. 1992. *The Discourse of Race in Modern China.* London: Hurst.
———. 1997. *The Construction of Racial Identities in China and Japan.* London: Hurst.
Donnelly, Neal. 1990. *A Journey through Chinese Hell: Hell Scrolls of Taiwan.* Taipei: Artist.
Doré, Henry. 1920. *Researches into Chinese Superstitions.* Trans. M. Kennelly. Shanghai: T'usewe Printing Press.
DPA (Deutsche-Presse Agentur). 2000. "Präsident von Taiwan unterstützt rechte der homosexuellen." *Meldung* (September 4).
Du Qifeng 杜琪峰, director. 1993. *Jigong* 濟公 (The mad monk). Xianggang: Daduhui Dianying Zhizuo Youxian Gongsi 香港：大都會電影製作有限公司.
Duara, Prasenjit. 1988. *Culture, Power, and the State: Rural North China, 1900–1942.* Stanford: Stanford University Press.
Dudbridge, Glen. 1995. *Religious Experience and Lay Society in T'ang China: A Reading of Tai Fu's Kuang-i chi.* Cambridge: Cambridge University Press.
Eberhard, Wolfram. 1967. *Guilt and Sin in Traditional China.* Berkeley: University of California Press.
Economic Daily News. 1989. "Zhengshi waiji laogong suo zisheng de wenti" 正視外籍勞工所滋生的問題. (Face the social problems that foreign laborers would cause). *Jiinji ribao* 經濟日報 *(Economic daily news).* Editorial, December 20: 2.

The Economist. 2000. "Behind the smiles." 8193: 48–49.
Edelman, Murray. 1988. *Constructing the Political Spectacle.* Chicago: University of Chicago Press.
Epstein, Maram. 2001. *Competing Discourses: Orthodoxy, Authenticity, and Engendered Meanings in Late Imperial Chinese Fiction.* Cambridge, MA: Harvard University Press.
Esherick, Joseph W., and Mary Backus Rankin. [1990] 1994. *Chinese Local Elites and Patterns of Dominance.* Berkeley: University of California Press.
Evans, Harriet. 1997. *Women and Sexuality in China.* Cambridge: Polity Press.
Executive Yuan. 1991. *Special Issues on Foreign Labor.* 42. Taipei: Executive Yuan.
Fairclough, Norman. 1992. *Discourse and Social Change.* Cambridge: Polity Press.
Fang Hao 方豪. 1994. *Taiwan zaoqi shigang* 台灣早期史綱 (A historical outline of early Taiwan). Taibei: Taiwan Xuesheng Shuju 台灣學生書局.
Faure, David. 1990. "What made Foshan a town? The evolution of rural-urban identities in Ming-Qing China." *Late Imperial China* 11(2): 1–32.
Foucault, Michel. 1980. *Power/Knowledge: Selected Interviews and Other Writings, 1972–1977.* Brighton: Harvester Press.
Fraser, Andrew. 1988. "First fruits of empire: Japan's colonial administration in Taiwan, 1895–1934." *Papers on Far Eastern History* 38: 93–101.
Free China Journal. 1987. "Live catches." September 7: 3.
———. 1988. "ROC pro ball in 1990." September 8: 2.
Fulda, Andreas Martin. 2002. "Reevaluating the Taiwanese democracy movement: A comparative analysis of opposition organizations under Japanese and KMT rule." *Critical Asian Studies* 34(3): 357–394.
Gallin, Rita S. 1984. "Women, family and the political economy of Taiwan." *Journal of Peasant Studies* 12(1): 76–92.
Gamarekian, Barbara. 1987. "Come the weekend, it's Talk-Show City." *New York Times*, March 1: 52.
Gamson, Joshua. 1998. *Freaks Talk Back.* Chicago: University of Chicago Press.
Gao Lisan 高立三. 1997. "Yong mengxiang ji xinxin, dazao di er ge wangguo" 用夢想及信心，打造第二個王國 (Using dreams and faith to build a second kingdom). *Naluwan zhoubao* 那魯灣週報 (Naluwan weekly) 5: 2.
Gao Zhengyuan 高正源. 1994. *Dong sheng de xuri: Zhonghua bangqiu fazhan shi* 東昇的旭日：中華棒球發展史 (Rising sun in the East: The history of the development of Chinese baseball). Taibei: Minshengbao She 民生報社.
Gao Zhishen 高志森, director. 1993. *Huatian xishi* 花田囍事 (Field of flowers wedding events). Xianggang: Fang Dianying Chengping Youxian Gongsi 香港：方電影山品有限公司.
Gardella, Robert. 1999. "From treaty ports to provincial status, 1860–1894." In *Taiwan: A New History*, ed. Murray A. Rubinstein, 163–200. Armonk, NY: M. E. Sharpe.
Garver, John W. 1997. *The Sino-American Alliance: Nationalist China and American Cold War Strategy in Asia.* Armonk, NY: M. E. Sharpe.
Gates, Hill. 1979. "Dependency and the part-time proletariat in Taiwan." *Modern China* 5(3): 381–408.
———. 1996. *China's Motor: A Thousand Years of Petty Capitalism.* Ithaca, NY: Cornell University Press.
Geertz, Clifford. 1973. "Deep play: Notes on the Balinese cockfight." In *The Interpretation of Cultures*, Clifford Geertz, 412–453. New York: Basic Books.
Gian Jia-shin 簡家欣. 1998. "Jiuling niandai Taiwan nütongzhi de rentong jiangou yu yundong jijie: Zai kanwu wanglu shang xingcheng de nütongzhi xin shequn." 九零年代台灣女同志的認同建構與運動集結：在刊物網路上形成的女同志新社群 (Taiwanese lesbians' identification under the queer politics since 1990). *Taiwan shehui yanjiu jikan* 台灣社會研究季刊 (Taiwan: A radical quarterly in the social sciences) (30): 63–115.

Giles, Herbert A., trans. and ed. 1916. *Strange Stories from a Chinese Studio*. Shanghai: Kelly and Walsh.

Girard, Rene. 1979. *Violence and the Sacred*. Trans. Patrick Gregory. Baltimore: Johns Hopkins University Press.

Glenn, Evelyn Nakano. 1992. "From servitude to service work: Historical continuities in the racial division of paid reproductive labor." *Signs* 18(1): 1–43.

Goddard, William G. 1966. *Formosa: A Study in Chinese History*. East Lansing: Michigan State University Press.

Gong Zhaojian 龔招健. 1997. "Danxin Feiyong de weisheng xiguan" "當心菲傭的衛生習慣" (Mind Filipina maids' hygiene habits). *Zhongguo shibao* 中國時報 *(China times)*, July 22: 13.

Gongshang zazhi 工商雜誌 *(Industry and business magazine)*. 1985. "Anli de jueqi yu pengbo" 安麗的崛起與蓬勃 (The emergence and development of Amway). 33(9): 59–61.

Goodman, Bryna. 1995. *Native Place, City, and Nation: Regional Networks and Identities in Shanghai, 1853–1937*. Berkeley: University of California Press.

Goodrich, Anne Swan. 1981. *Chinese Hells: The Peking Temple of Eighteen Hells and Chinese Conceptions of Hell*. St. Augustin: Monumenta Serica.

Gordon, Leonard H. D. 1976. "The cession of Taiwan: A second look." *Pacific Historical Review* 45(4): 539–567.

Gu Chien-Juh. 1997. "The cultural formation of direct sales in Taiwan." Paper presented at the North American Taiwan Studies Association Annual Conference. University of California at Berkeley.

——— . 2000. "Volatile-structurative corporeality: Disciplined bodies in direct selling." Paper presented at the North America Taiwan Studies Association Annual Conference. Harvard University.

Gu Hong 孤紅. 1997. *Zhibang yangjiang xing chouwen: Jiefa nüqiumi yu yangjiang de taose jiaoyi* 職棒洋將性醜聞：揭發女球迷與洋將的桃色交易 (Foreign pro baseball players' sex scandals: Exposing the illicit relations between female baseball fans and foreign players). Taibei: Rizhen Chubanshe 日臻出版社.

Guo Yuanzhi 郭源治. 1998. *Reqiu* 熱球 (Hot ball). Taibei: Xin Zhongyuan Chubanshe 新中原出版社.

Guttmann, Allen. 1994. *Games and Empires: Modern Sports and Cultural Imperialism*. New York: Columbia University Press.

Halliday, Jon. 1975. *A Political History of Japanese Capitalism*. New York: Pantheon Books.

Harrell, C. Stevan. 1974. "When a ghost becomes a god." In *Religion and Ritual in Chinese Society*, ed. Arthur P. Wolf, 193–206. Stanford: Stanford University Press.

——— . 1986. "Men, women, and ghosts in Taiwanese folk religion." In *Gender and Religion*, ed. Caroline Walker Bynum, Stevan Harrell, and Paula Richman, 97–116. Boston: Beacon Press.

Harrell, C. Stevan, ed. 1995. *Cultural Encounters on China's Ethnic Frontiers*. Seattle: University of Washington Press.

Harrell, C. Stevan, and Chün-chieh Huang, eds. 1994. *Cultural Change in Postwar Taiwan*. Boulder: Westview Press.

Harvey, David. 1989. *The Condition of Postmodernity: An Enquiry into the Origins of Cultural Change*. New York: Blackwell.

Hauptman, Laurence M., and Ronald G. Knapp. 1977. "Dutch-aboriginal interaction in New Netherlands and Formosa: An historical geography of empire." *Proceedings of the American Philosophical Society* 121(2): 166–182.

Hayden, George A. 1978. *Crime and Punishment in Medieval Chinese Drama: Three Judge Bao Plays*. Cambridge, MA: Harvard University Press.

He Baogang. 2001. "The question of sovereignty in the Taiwan Strait: Re-examining Peking's policy of opposition to Taiwan's bid for UN membership." *China Perspectives* 34: 7–18.

Henninger, Joseph. 1987a. "Sacrifice." Trans. Matthew J. O'Connell. In *The Encyclopedia of Religion*, vol. 12: 544–557. New York: Macmillan.

——. 1987b. "Scapegoat." Trans. Matthew J. O'Connell. In *The Encyclopedia of Religion*, vol. 13: 92–95. New York: Macmillan.

Hershatter, Gail. 1994. "Modernizing sex, sexing modernity: Prostitution in early twentieth-century Shanghai." In *Engendering China: Women, Culture, and the State*, ed. Christina K. Gilmartin, Gail Hershatter, and Tyrene White, 147–174. Cambridge, MA: Harvard University Press.

——. 1997. *Dangerous Pleasures: Prostitution and Modernity in Twentieth-Century Shanghai*. Berkeley: University of California Press.

Heyzer, Noeleen, Greertje Lycklama a Nijeholt, and Nedra Weerakoon. 1994. *The Trade in Domestic Workers: Causes, Mechanisms and Consequences of International Migration*. London: Zed Books.

Hirsch, Alan. 1991. *Talking Heads: Political Talk Shows and Their Star Pundits*. New York: St. Martin's Press.

Ho Hao-tien 何浩天, ed. 1984. *Ten Kings of Hades: An Exhibition Held at the National Museum of History, August 8–17, 1984*. Taipei: National Museum of History.

Ho, Samuel P. S. 1979. "Decentralized industrialization and rural development: Evidence from Taiwan." *Economic Development and Cultural Change* 28(1): 77–96.

Hochschild, Arlie R. 1983. *The Managed Heart: Commercialization of Human Feeling*. Berkeley: University of California Press.

Hsiao, Frank S. T., and Lawrence R. Sullivan. 1979. "The Chinese Communist Party and the status of Taiwan, 1928–1943." *Pacific Affairs* 52: 446–467.

——. 1983. "A political history of the Taiwanese Communist Party, 1928–1931." *Journal of Asian Studies* 4(2): 269–289.

Hsiau, A-chin. 2000. *Contemporary Taiwanese Cultural Nationalism*. New York: Routledge.

Hsing, You-tien. 1998. *Making Capitalism in China: The Taiwan Connection*. New York: Oxford University Press.

Hsu, Francis. 1948. *Under the Ancestor's Shadow*. New York: Columbia University Press.

——. 1983. "Chinese kinship and Chinese behavior." In *Rugged Individualism Considered*, ed. F. L. K. Hsu, 332–356. Knoxville: University of Tennessee Press.

Hsu Min-tao. 1998. "'Fitting in' to the 'no return trip': Women's perceptions of marriage and family in Taiwan." *Proceedings of the National Science Commission, ROC (C)* 8(4): 527–538.

Hsu, Wen-Hsiung. 1980a. "From aboriginal island to Chinese frontier: The development of Taiwan before 1683." In *China's Island Frontier: Studies in the Historical Geography of Taiwan*, ed. Ronald G. Knapp, 3–29. Honolulu: University of Hawai'i Press.

——. 1980b. "Frontier social organization and social disorder in Ch'ing Taiwan." In *China's Island Frontier: Studies in the Historical Geography of Taiwan*, ed. Ronald G. Knapp, 87–105. Honolulu: University of Hawai'i Press.

Hsüan Hua. 1974. *Sutra of the Past Vows of Earth Store Bodhisattva*. Trans. Heng Ching. San Francisco: Sino-American Buddhist Association.

Hu Rong 胡蓉. 1996. *Romance of the Ghost Maiden Nie Xiaoqian*. Story adapted by Wang Yongsheng 王庸聲. Trans. Wu Jingyu 吳敬瑜. *Qiannü youhun* 倩女幽魂. Singapore: Asiapac.

Hu Yu-hwey 胡幼慧. 1997. "Cong funü jioye de kunjing yu xuqio tan waiyong zhengce de yihan" 從婦女就業的困境與需求談外傭政策的意涵 (To discuss the implications of foreign maid policy in light of the predicament and the needs of working women). Paper presented at the Conference on Foreign Maid Policy and State Development, April. Taipei.

Hua Baoluo 華保羅. 1986. "Taijia sinüe ying longzhao: Taijia laoshuhui de zheng mianmu weihe bei jiechuan" 台家肆虐影籠罩：台家老鼠會的真面目為何被揭穿 (The true face of the Taiwan Family Mouse Association). *Caixun zazhi* 財訊雜誌 *(Finance journal)* 56: 258.

Huang Guihua 黃貴華 and Yang Pei-ling 楊佩玲. 1993. "Wailao kaifan, jianglai yao ruhe baituo, defa jingyan lingren you" 外勞開放，將來要如何擺脫，德法經驗令人憂 (After lifting the ban, how do we get rid of them in the future? German and French experiences worry people). *Lianhe bao* 聯合報 *(United daily news)*, July 18: 6.

Huang Jianming 黃建銘. 1997. "'Naluwan: Zhenggang de yingxiong' (Naluwan Zhibang lianmeng zhuti gequ)" 那魯灣—正港的英雄 (那魯灣職棒聯盟主體歌曲) ("Naluwan: True heroes" [Taiwan major-league theme song]). *Naluwan zhoubao* 那魯灣週報 *(Naluwan weekly)* 5: 5.

Huang, Philip C. C. 1996. *Civil Justice in China*. Stanford: Stanford University Press.

Huang Wenbo 黃文博. 1989. *Taiwan xinyang chuanqi* 臺灣信仰傳奇 (Popular beliefs in Taiwan). Taipei: Taiyuan 臺原.

———. 1992. *Taiwan minghun chuanqi* 臺灣冥魂傳奇 (Traditions about ghosts in Taiwan). Taipei: Taiyuan 臺原.

Huang Xiuzheng 黃秀政. 1986. "Maguan yihe de ge Tai jiaoshe (shang)" 馬關議和的割臺交涉 (上) (The Treaty of Shimonoseki and negotiations over the cession of Taiwan, Part 1). *Jindai Zhongguo* 近代中國 *(Modern China)* 55: 239–263.

Huang Yijing 黃以敬. 1996. "Jiayio Feiyong haizi biandiao" 家有菲傭，孩子變調 (Filipina maids at home, children change their accents). *Zhongyang ribao* 中央日報 *(Central daily news)*, July 1: 11.

Huang Zhanyue 黃展岳. 1986. "Shenpanfa yu 'xiezhi' juesong" 神判法與獬豸決訟 (Divine justice and the use of *xiezhi* to decide legal disputes). In *Gudai lizhi fengsu mantan* 古代禮制風俗漫談 (Discussions on ancient manners and customs), 2: 13–18. Beijing: Zhonghua Shuju.

Huntington, Rania A. 1996. "Foxes and Ming-Qing fiction." Dissertation: East Asian Languages and Civilizations, Harvard University.

HXXWW (Huaxun xinwenwang 華訊新聞網 *[Taiwan today news network])*. Various dates. State College, PA: Quintet, Inc. http://www.ttnn.com/.

Itō Kiyoshi 伊藤潔. 1993. Taiwan: yonhyakunen no rekishi to tenbō 台灣：四百年の歷史と展望 (Taiwan: Four hundred years of history and views). Tokyo: Chūō Koronsha 中央公論社.

Jacoby, Neil H. 1966. *U.S. Aid to Taiwan: A Study of Foreign Aid, Self-Help, and Development*. New York: Frederick A. Praeger.

James, C. L. R., and Anna Grimshaw, eds. 1986. *Cricket*. New York: Allison and Busby.

Ji Wuzi 薊午子. 1990. *Mantan shengui shijie* 漫談神鬼世界 (Chats on the world of gods and ghosts). Harbin: Beifang Wenyi 北方文艺.

Jiang Guosheng 蔣國聖. 1985a. *Diyu zhi mianmu* 地獄之面目 (The face of hell). 2 vols. Taipei: Miaowen 妙文.

———. 1985b. *Mingwang zhi shenpan* 冥王之審判 (Judgments of the kings of hell). 2 vols. Taipei: Miaowen 妙文.

Johnson, Chalmers. 2000. *Blowback: The Costs and Consequences of American Empire*. New York: Henry Holt and Company.

Johnson, David. 1989a. "Actions speak louder than words: The cultural significance of Chinese ritual opera." In *Ritual Opera, Operatic Ritual: "Mu-lien Rescues His Mother" in Chinese Popular Culture*, ed. David Johnson, 1: 1–45. Berkeley: University of California.

Johnson, David, ed. 1989b. *Ritual Opera, Operatic Ritual: "Mu-lien Rescues His Mother" in Chinese Popular Culture*. Papers from the International Workshop on the Mu-lien Operas, Berkeley, 1987. Publications of the Chinese Popular Culture Project, vol. 1. Berkeley: University of California. (Distributed by IEAS Publications.)

Joint Communiqué of the United States of America and the People's Republic of China. 1972. Los Angeles: Taiwan Documents Project. http://www.taiwandocuments.org/communique01.htm, accessed August 27, 2001.

Jordan, David K. [1972] 1985. *Gods, Ghosts, and Ancestors: Folk Religion in a Taiwanese Village*. Berkeley: University of California Press.

———. 1981. "'Causes and effects' tales in sectarian revelation." In *Proceedings of the International Conference on Sinology*, 73–99. Academia Sinica, August 15–20, 1980, Section of Folklore and Culture.

———. 1983. "The repression of hostility and the representation of hell in south Taiwan religious processions." In *Concepts of Hell in Asia*, vol. 1, ed. Ruth-Inge Heinze, 17–31, 82–83. Berkeley: Folklore Institute.

———. 1986. "Folk filial piety in Taiwan: 'The twenty-four filial exemplars.'" In *The Psycho-Cultural Dynamics of the Confucian Family: Past And Present*, ed. Walter H. Slote, 47–112. Seoul: International Cultural Society of Korea.

———. 1998. "Filial piety in Taiwanese popular thought." In *Confucianism and the Family*, ed. Walter H. Slote and George A. DeVos, 267–283. Albany: State University of New York Press.

Jordan, David K., and Daniel L. Overmyer. 1986. *The Flying Phoenix: Aspects of Sectarianism in Taiwan*. Princeton: Princeton University Press; Taipei: Caves Books.

Ka Chih-ming 1993. *Taiwan dushi xiaoxing zhizaoye de chuangye jingying yu shengchan zuzhi: yi Wufenpu chengyi zhizaoye wei anli de fenxi* 台灣都市小型製造業的創業、經營與生產組織：以五分埔成衣製造業為案例的分析 (Market, social networks, and the production organization of small-scale industry in Taiwan: The garment industries in Wufenpu). Taibei: Zhongyang Yanjiuyuan Minzuxue Yanjiusuo 台北：中央研究院民族學研究所 (Institute of Ethnology, Academia Sinica).

———. 1995. *Japanese Colonialism in Taiwan: Land Tenure, Development, and Dependency, 1895–1945*. Boulder: Westview Press.

Karasawa, Yasuhiko. 1993. "Composing the narrative: A preliminary study of plaints in Qing legal cases." Paper presented at the Conference on Code and Practice in Qing and Republican Law, Los Angeles.

Kataoka Iwao 片岡巖. [1921] 1981. *Taiwan fengsu zhi* 臺灣風俗誌 (Gazetteer of Taiwan customs). Trans. Ch'en Chin-t'ien 陳金田 and Feng Tso-min 馮作民. Taipei: Ta-li Publishing Company.

Katz, Paul R. 1995a. *Demon Hordes and Burning Boats: The Cult of Marshal Wen in Late Imperial Chekiang*. Albany: State University of New York Press.

———. 1995b. "The pacification of plagues: A Chinese rite of affliction." *Journal of Ritual Studies* 9(1): 55–100.

———. 2000. "Hanren shehui de shenpan yishi chutan: Cong zhan jitou shuoqi" 漢人社會的神判儀式初探：從斬雞頭說起 (A preliminary study of judicial rituals in Han Chinese society based on chicken-beheadings). *Bulletin of the Institute of Ethnology, Academia Sinica* 88: 173–202.

———. 2001. "Divine justice: Chicken-beheading rituals in Japanese occupation Taiwan and their historical antecedents." *Proceedings of the International Conference on Society, Ethnicity, and Cultural Performance*, ed. Wang Ch'iu-kuei, Chuang Ying-chang, and Chen Chung-min, 111–160. Taipei: Center for Chinese Studies.

———. n.d. "Divine justice in late Imperial China: A preliminary study of indictments, oaths, and ordeals." In *Taoism and Local Religion in Modern China*, ed. John Lagerwey. Paris: Publications de l'École Française d'Extrême Orient. In press.

Kellerman, Aharon. 1991. "The decycling of time and the reorganization of urban space." *Cultural Dynamics* 4(1): 38–54.

Kelly, William W. 1998. "Blood and guts in Japanese professional baseball." In *The Culture of Japan as Seen through Its Leisure*, ed. Sepp Linhart and Sabine Frühstück, 95–111. Albany: State University of New York Press.

Kerr, George H. 1965. *Formosa Betrayed*. Boston: Houghton Mifflin.

———. 1974. *Formosa: Licensed Revolution and the Home Rule Movement, 1895–1945*. Honolulu: University of Hawai'i Press.

Keyes, Ray. 1969. "Taiwan team springs upset ... Tops Santa Clara in L. L. final." *Sporting News*, September 6.

Knapp, Ronald G., and Laurence M. Hauptman. 1980. "'Civilization over savagery': The Japanese, the Formosan frontier, and United States Indian policy, 1895-1915." *Pacific Historical Review* 49(4): 647-652.

Kondō Masami 近藤正己. 1996. *Soryokusen to Taiwan: Nihon shokuminchi hokai no kenkyu* 總力戰と台灣：日本殖民地崩壞の研究 (Total war and Taiwan: Research into the collapse of Japanese colonialism). Tokyo: Tosui Shobo 刀水書房.

Kuhn, Philip A. 1991. *Soulstealers: The Chinese Sorcery Scare of 1768.* Cambridge, MA: Harvard University Press.

Kuo Ting-yee. 1973. "The internal development and modernization of Taiwan, 1863-1891." In *Taiwan in Modern Times*, ed. Paul K. T. Sih, 171-240. Jamaica, NY: St. John's University Press.

Lai, Tse-han, Ramon H. Myers, and Wei Wou. 1991. *A Tragic Beginning: The Taiwan Uprising of February 28, 1947.* Stanford: Stanford University Press.

Lai Zhengzhe. 2000. "Zai gongsi shang ban: Xin gongyuan zuowei nan tongzhi yanchu dijing zhi yanjiu" 在公司上班—新公園作為男同志演出地景之研究 (Working at the office: Research on the New Park as a setting for male gay performance.) In *Xing/bie Zhengzhi yu Zhuti Xinggou* 性/別政治與主體形構 (Sexual politics and subject formation), ed. Josephine Ho, 131-186. Taibei: Shuangtian Chubanshi 臺北：麥田出版社.

Lamley, Harry J. 1964. "The Taiwan literati and early Japanese rule, 1895-1915: A study of their reactions to the Japanese occupation and subsequent responses to colonial rule and modernization." Ph.D. dissertation, University of Washington.

———. 1977. "The formation of cities: Initiative and motivation in building three walled cities in Taiwan." In *The City in Late Imperial China*, ed. G. William Skinner, 155-209. Stanford: Stanford University Press.

———. 1981. "Subethnic rivalry in the Ch'ing period." In *The Anthropology of Taiwanese Society*, ed. Emily Martin Ahern and Hill Gates, 282-318. Stanford: Stanford University Press.

———. 1999. "Taiwan under Japanese rule, 1895-1945: The vicissitudes of colonialism." In *Taiwan: A New History*, ed. Murray A. Rubinstein, 201-260. Armonk, NY: M. E. Sharpe.

Lan Bozhou 藍博洲. 2000. "Zai Xiamen de Taiwan xuesheng yundong" 在廈門的台灣學生運動 (The Taiwanese student movement in Xiamen). In T*aiwan ernü zuguo qing: Ji Xiamen de Taiwan shengji renshi* 台灣兒女祖國情：記廈門的台灣省籍人士 (Taiwanese sons and daughters' love for the motherland: A record of Taiwan provincials in Xiamen), ed. Zeng Xiong 曾雄, 1-27. Beijing: Taihai Chubanshe 台海出版社.

Leach, Jerry W., director. 1975. *Trobriand Cricket: An Ingenious Response to colonialism.* Office of Information, Government of Papua New Guinea.

Lee, Ang, director. 2000. *Crouching Tiger, Hidden Dragon.* Los Angeles: Sony Pictures.

Lee, J. S., and Wang, S. W. 1996. "Recruiting and managing of foreign workers in Taiwan." *Asian and Pacific Migration Journal* 5(2-3): 281-302.

———. 1995. "Notions of space, time, and harmony in Chinese popular culture." In *Time and Space in Chinese Culture*, ed. Huang Chün-chieh and Erik Zürcher, 383-398. Leiden: E. J. Brill.

Lee Yikun 李易昆. 1995. *Tamen weishenue bu xingdong? Waiji laogong xingdong celue chabei zhi yanjiu* 他們為什麼不行動？外籍勞工行動策略差別之研究 (Why do they not act? A study on different acting strategies of migrant workers). MA thesis, Fu-jen Catholic University.

LeGendre, Charles. 1874. *Is Aboriginal Formosa a Part of the Chinese Empire? An Unbiased Statement of the Question, with Eight Maps of Formosa.* Hong Kong: Lane, Crawford and Co.

Lewis, Mark Edward. 1990. *Sanctioned Violence in Early China.* Albany: State University of New York Press.

LHB. *Lianhe bao* 聯合報 *(United daily news)*. Various dates.

Li Daoming 李道明. 1995. "Riben tongzhi shiqi dianying yu zhengzhi de guanxi" 日本統治時期電影與政治的關係 (The relationship between movies and politics during Japanese rule). *Lishi yuekan* 歷史月刊 *(Historical monthly)* 94: 123–129.

Li Huilin et al. 黎慧琳等. 1996. "Xinzhu yiyuan zhuicha yisi shirouxing lünong ganjun zhisi bingli faxian: Liunü Feilao yi chaofu quchongyao" 新竹醫院追查疑似噬肉性綠膿桿菌致死病例發現：六女菲勞疑超服驅蟲藥 (Xinzhu hospital further pursues the cases that were suspicious of scrub typhus infection and result in death: Six Filipina laborers were suspicious of taking an overdose on anti-parasitic drugs). *Lianhe bao* 聯合報 *(United daily news)*, August 21: 5.

Li, Laura. 1999. "Empowering the people: 50 years of struggle." Trans. Brent Heinrich. *Sinorama* 24(10): 100–107.

———. 2001. "Shanghai or bust! Taiwanese high-tech descends on eastern China." Trans. Phil Newell. *Sinorama* 26(6): 6–16.

Li, Paul. 2000. "Baseball tries to make a comeback." *Taipei Journal* 17(45): 8.

Li Qiao. 2001. *Wintry Night*. Trans. Taotao Liu and John Balcom. New York: Columbia University Press.

Li Yih-yuan 李亦園. 1983. "Zhan jitou" 斬雞頭 (Chicken-beheading rituals). In *Shitu, shenhua, yu qita* 師徒，神話及其他 (Master-pupil, myth, and other things). Taipei: Cheng-chung.

Li Yuanzhen 李元貞. 1991. "Funü zhengce yu waiji nüyong" 婦女政策與外籍女傭 (Women's policies and foreign maids). *Zili wanbao* 自立晚報 *(Independence evening post)*, June 6: 3.

Liang Hongfa 梁宏發, director. 1998. *Menggui shi rentai* 猛鬼食人胎 (The demon's baby). Xianggang: Zuijia Paidang Dianying Zhizuo Gongsi 香港：最佳拍檔電影製作公司.

Liang Yufang 梁玉芳. 1996. "Feiyong chaoji guanjia, keneng dailai zhauji mafan." 菲傭超級管家，可能帶來超級麻煩. (Superb Filipino managers may bring special troubles). *Lianhe bao* 聯合報 *(United daily news)*, April 4: 3.

Liberty Times 自由時報 *(Ziyou shibao)*. Various dates.

Lien, Chan. 1973. "Taiwan in China's external relations, 1683–1874." In *Taiwan in Modern Times*, ed. Paul K. T. Sih, 87–170. St. John's University Press.

Lin Chin-ju 林津如. 1999. *Filipina Domestic Workers in Taiwan: Structural Constraints and Personal Resistance*. Taipei: Taiwanese Grassroots Women Workers' Center.

———. 2000. "Waiyong zhengce yu nüren zhizhan: Nüxing zhuyi celue zai sikao"「外傭政策」與女人之戰：女性主義策略再思考 (The state policy that divides women: Rethinking feminist critiques of the "Foreign Maid Policy" in Taiwan). *Taiwan shehui yanjiu jikan* 台灣社會研究季刊 *(Taiwan: A radical quarterly in social studies)* 39: 93–151.

———. 2003. "Transforming patriarchal kinship relations: Four generations of 'modern women' in Taiwan, 1900–1999." Ph.D. dissertation, University of Essex, Colchester, UK.

Lin Fu-shih 林富士. 1995. *Guhun yu guixiong de shijie: Bei Taiwan de ligui xinyang* 孤魂與鬼雄的世界：北台灣的厲鬼信仰 (The world of lonely souls and heroic ghosts: Cults to vengeful spirits in northern Taiwan). Banchiao: Taipei County Government.

Lin Heng-tao. 1975. "Origins of Taiwanese place names." *Echo* 5: 5–8, 52.

Lin Jiwen 林繼文. 1996. *Riben ju Tai moqi (1930–1945) zhanzheng dongyuan tixi zhi yanjiu* 日本據台末期(1930–1945)戰爭動員之研究 (Research into the wartime mobilization structure of the late Japanese colonial period (1930–1945). Banqiao: Daoxiang Chubanshe 稻鄉出版社.

Lin Xunmin 林訓民. 1994. *Chuanxiao quan fangwei zhinan* 傳銷全方位指南 (Handbook of direct selling). Taibei: Taiwan Yingwen Zazhishe 台灣英文雜誌社.

Lishi Jiaoxue Yuekan She 歷史教學月刊社 (Historical Education Monthly Publishing House), ed. 1954. *Zhong-Ri jiawu zhanzheng lunji* 中日甲午戰爭論集 (Collected essays on the 1894 Sino-Japanese War). Beijing: Wushi Niandai Chubanshe 五十年代出版社.

Liu Guangwei 劉觀偉, director. 1992. *Xin jiangsi xiansheng*. 新殭屍先生 (Mr. Vampire). Xianggang: Wanli Dianying Youxian Gongsi 香港：萬里電影有限公司.

Liu Huanyue 劉還月. 1994. *Taiwan minjian xinyang xiao baike: Lingmei juan* 臺灣民間信仰小百科：靈媒卷 (Concise encyclopedia of Taiwan popular belief: Spirit mediums). Taipei: Taiyuan 臺原.

Liu, Lydia H. 1999. "Legislating the universal: The circulation of international law in the nineteenth century." In *Tokens of Exchange: The Problem of Translation in Global Circulations*, ed. Lydia H. Liu, 127–164. Durham: Duke University Press.

Liu Yongping. 1998. *Origins of Chinese Law*. Hong Kong: Oxford University Press.

Liu Yuanqin 劉元卿 and Chen Ruoxian 陳若仙. 1990. *Renshi chuanxiao zhidu* 認識傳銷制度 (Understanding direct selling). Taibei: Daolue 韜略.

Liu Zhenwei 劉鎮偉, director. 1995a. *Qitian dasheng dongyouji 1* 齊天大聖東遊記 (A Chinese odyssey part one: Pandora's box). Xianggang: Caixing Dianying Gongsi 香港：彩星電影公司.

———. 劉鎮偉, director. 1995b. *Qitian dasheng dongyouji 2* 齊天大聖西遊記 (A Chinese odyssey part two: Cinderella). Xianggang: Caixing Dianying Gongsi 香港：彩星電影公司.

Livingstone, Sonia, and Peter Lunt. 1994. *Talk on Television: Audience Participation and Public Debate*. London: Routledge.

Lo, Kwai-cheung. 2001. "Transnationalization of the local in Hong Kong cinema of the 1990s." In *At Full Speed: Hong Kong Cinema in a Borderless World*, ed. Esther C. M. Yau, 261–276. Minneapolis: University of Minnesota Press.

Lowrey, KathLin S. 1999. *Baring Our Souls: TV Talk Shows and the Religion of Recovery*. New York: Aldine de Gruyter.

Lü Lizheng 呂理政. 1992. *Chuantong xinyang yu xiandai shehui* 傳統信仰與現代社會 (Traditional beliefs and modern society). Panchiao: Tao-hsiang.

Lu Xiuyi 盧修一. 1992. *Riju shidai Taiwan gongchandang shi (1928–1932)* 日據時代台灣共產黨史 (1928–1932) (History of the Taiwanese Communist Party during the era of Japanese occupation (1928–1932). Taibei: Qianwei chubanshe 前衛出版社.

Luo Zhuoyao 羅卓瑤, director. 1989. *Pan Jinlian zhi Qianshi Jinsheng* 潘金蓮之前世今生 (The reincarnation of Golden Lotus). Hong Kong.

Ma Shutian 馬書田. 1998. *Zhongguo mingjie zhushen* 中國冥界諸神 (China's underworld deities). Beijing: Tuanjie Chubanshe.

Macauley, Melissa. 1994. "Civil and uncivil disputes in southeast coastal China." In *Civil Law in Qing and Republican China*, ed. Kathryn Bernhardt and Philip C. C. Huang, 85–121. Stanford: Stanford University Press.

———. 1998. *Social Power and Legal Culture: Litigation Masters in Late Imperial China*. Stanford: Stanford University Press.

Macgowan, The Rev. J. 1910. *Chinese Folklore Tales*. London: Macmillan.

———. 1912. *Men and Manners of Modern China*. London: T. Fisher Unwin.

Mair, Denis C., and Victor H. Mair, trans. and ed. 1989. *Strange Tales from Make-Do Studio*. Beijing: Phoenix Books.

Mann, James. 1999. *About Face: A History of America's Curious Relationship with China, from Nixon to Clinton*. New York: Alfred A. Knopf.

Martin, Joseph. 1985. *Terrorism and the Taiwan Independence Movement: A Preliminary Study*. Taipei: Institute on Contemporary China.

Martin, Luther H., Huck Gutman, and Patrick H. Hutton, eds. 1988. *Technologies of the Self: A Seminar with Michel Foucault*. Amherst: The University of Massachusetts Press.

Marx, Karl. [1847] 1995. *The Poverty of Philosophy*. New York: Prometheus Books.

Masuda Fukutaro 増田福太郎. [1942] 1996. *Minzoku shinkyō o chūshin toshite: Tōa hōsei jōsetsu* 民族信仰中心：東亞法制徐序説 (An introductory study of East Asian law centering on folk religion). Taipei: Southern Materials Center reprint.

Mendel, Douglas. 1970. *The Politics of Taiwanese Nationalism*. Berkeley: University of California Press.

Meng Yuanlao. [1922] 1980. "Dongjing menghualu" 東京夢華錄 (The eastern capital: A dream of splendors past). In *The Collected Works of Dongching Menghualu Wai Sizhong* 東京夢華錄外四種, 1–88. Taibei: Dali 台北：大立.

Minnick, Wendell L. 1995. "Target: Zhou Enlai: Was America's CIA working with Taiwan agents to kill Chinese premier?" *Far Eastern Economic Review* 158(28): 54–55.

Mishima, Yukio. [1951] 1968. *Forbidden Colors.* Trans. Alfred H. Marks. New York: Perigree Books.

Morris, Andrew. 2002. "The Taiwan Republic of 1895 and the failure of the Qing modernizing project." In *Memories of the Future: National Identity Issues and the Search for a New Taiwan*, ed. Stephane Corcuff, 3–24. Armonk, NY: M. E. Sharpe.

Moskowitz, Marc L. 2001. *The Haunting Fetus: Abortion, Sexuality, and the Spirit World in Taiwan.* Honolulu: University of Hawai'i Press.

MSB. Minshengbao 民生報 *(People's livelihood times).* Various dates.

Munson, Wayne. 1993. *All Talk: The Talkshow in Media Culture.* Philadelphia: Temple University Press.

Murray, Stephen. 1992. "The 'underdevelopment' of gay homosexuality in Mexico, Guatemala, Peru and Thailand." In *Modern Homosexualities*, ed. K. Plummer, 29–38. London: Routledge.

Nakamura Takashi 中村孝志. 1954. "Taiwan-shi gaiyō (kindai)" 台灣史概要 (近代) (The modern history of Formosa). *Minzokugaku kenkyū* 民族學研究 *(Anthropological research)* 18(1–2): 113–122.

Naluwan Weekly. 1997a. "Jin'gang chuan qing, xiangqin xian'ai" 金剛傳情，相親獻愛 (Robots profess their devotion, local folk present their love). *Naluwan zhoubao* 那魯灣週報, February 1, 7: 6.

———. 1997b. "Qiuyuan quan chong mote'er: Zhanpao shanliang xianshen" 球員權充模特兒，戰袍閃亮現身 (Ballplayers moonlighting as models: Battle gear unveiled in its glory). *Naluwan zhoubao* 那魯灣週報, February 1, 7: 3.

———. 1997c. "'Zhenggang de yingxiong' qianggong xuanchuan tantou" 「正港的英雄」搶攻宣傳灘頭 ("True heroes" attacking the publicity beachheads). *Naluwan zhoubao* 那魯灣週報, January 4, 5: 5.

NCH (North-China Herald and Supreme Court and Consular Gazette). Various dates. Shanghai.

Newsweek (Asia Edition). 2001. "Back in the spotlight." January 8: 14–18.

Niida Noboru 仁井田陞. 1964. *Chūgoku hōseishi kenkyū: Hō to kanshū, hō to dōtoku* 中國法制史研究：法と慣習，法と道德 (A study of Chinese legal history: Law and custom, law and morality). Tokyo: Tokyo Daigaku.

Norris, Robert S., William M. Arkin, and William Burr. 1999. "Where they were." *Bulletin of the Atomic Scientists* 55(6): 26–35.

NYT (New York Times). Various dates.

Overmyer, Daniel. 1989–1990. "Attitudes toward popular religion in the ritual texts of the Chinese state: The collected statutes of the great Ming." *Cahiers d'Extrême-Asie* 5: 191–221.

Ownby, David. 1996. *Brotherhoods and Secret Societies in Early and Mid-Qing China.* Stanford: Stanford University Press.

Palmer, Phyllis M. 1989. *Domesticity and Dirt: Housewives and Domestic Servants in the United States, 1920–1945.* Philadelphia: Temple University Press.

Parmar, Pratibha. 1982. "Gender, race and class: Asian women in resistance." In *The Empire Strikes Back: Race and Racism in 70s Britain,* Center for Contemporary Cultural Studies, University of Birmingham. London: Hutchinson.

Peattie, Mark R. 1984. "Japanese attitudes toward colonialism, 1895–1945." In *The Japanese Colonial Empire, 1895–1945,* ed. Ramon H. Myers and Mark R. Peattie, 80–127. Princeton: Princeton University Press.

Peng, Mingmin. 1972. *A Taste of Freedom: Memoirs of a Formosan Independence Leader.* New York: Holt, Rinehart and Winston.

Peng Mingmin 彭明敏 and Huang Zhaotang 黃昭堂. [1976] 1995. *Taiwan zai guojifa shang de diwei* 臺灣在國際法上的地位 (The status of Taiwan in international law). Trans. Cai Qiuxiong 蔡秋雄. Taibei: Yushan She 玉山社.

Phillips, Steven. 1999. "Between assimilation and independence: Taiwanese political aspirations under Nationalist Chinese rule, 1945–1948." In *Taiwan: A New History*, ed. Murray A. Rubinstein, 275–319. Armonk, NY: M. E. Sharpe.

Plopper, Clifford H. [1935] 1969. *Chinese Religion Seen through the Proverb.* New York: Paragon Book Reprint Corp.

Prince, Raymond. 1992. "Koro and the fox spirit on Hainan Island (China)." *Transcultural Psychiatric Research Review* 29: 119–132.

Pu Songling. [1766] [1981] 1992. *Nie Xiaoqian* 聶小倩. *Jingxuan baihua liaozhai zhiyi* 精選白話聊齋誌異 (Selected works in contemporary Chinese from the strange tales of Liaozhai), ed. Qi Lizi 齊力子, 47–58. Taiwan Shangwu Yinshuguan Banfen Youxian Gongsi 台灣商務印書館股份有限公司.

Quan Jiali 全嘉莉. 1992. "Waiji nüyong jiang dengtang rushi, shehui wenti yi fanhuan weiran" 外籍女傭將登堂入室、社會問題宜防患未然 (Foreign maids will come, social problems should be prevented from becoming disasters). *Taiwan shibao* 台灣時報 *(Taiwan times)*, July 27: 3.

Rampal, Kuldip R. 1994. "Post-martial law media boom in Taiwan." *Gazette* 53: 73–91.

Rawnsley, Gary, and Ming-Yeh T. Rawnsley. 2001. *Critical Security, Democratization and Television in Taiwan.* Aldershot, UK: Ashgate.

Reed, Bradly W. 2000. *Talons and Teeth: County Clerks and Runners in the Qing Dynasty.* Stanford: Stanford University Press.

Ren Li 任力. 1996. *Kangxi tongyi Taiwan shimo* 康熙統一台灣始末 (The history of the Kangxi emperor's unification of Taiwan [into the Qing Empire]). Beijing: Jiefangjun Chubanshe 解放軍出版社.

Renck, Troy E. 2001. "Hampton returns." ColoradoRockies.com, May 4. http://rockies.mlb.com/NASApp/mlb/col/news/col_news_story.jsp?article_id=col_20010504_pre_newsandteam_id=col, accessed August 21, 2001.

Republic of China Yearbook. 2000. Taipei: Government Information Office. http://www.gio.gov.tw/info/book2000/0content.htm, accessed August 31, 2001.

Republic of China Yearbook: Taiwan. 2001. Taipei: Government Information Office. http://www.gio.gov.tw/taiwan-website/5-gp/yearbook/, accessed June 14, 2001.

Reuters. Various dates.

Rigger, Shelley. 1999. *Politics in Taiwan: Voting for Democracy.* New York: Routledge.

Roden, Donald. 1980. "Baseball and the quest for national dignity in Meiji Japan." *American Historical Review* 85(3): 511–534.

Rollins, Joel D. 1996. "The continuing crisis: An analysis of educational crisis rhetoric from 1951–1985." Dissertation, University of Texas at Austin.

Romero, Mary. 1992. *Maid in the U.S.A.* New York: Routledge.

Rowe, William T. 1989. *Hankow: Conflict and Community in a Chinese City, 1796–1895.* Stanford: Stanford University Press.

RSBJ. 2000. *Rensheng baojian yuli baochao* 人生寶鑑，玉歷寶鈔 (Precious mirror of human life: "The Jade Almanac Precious Manuscript"). Hong Kong: Privately reprinted.

Rubin, Gayle. 1975. "The traffic in women: Notes on the political economy of sex." In *Toward an Anthropology of Women*, ed. R. R. Reiter, 157–210. New York: Monthly Review Press.

Rubinstein, Murray A. 1999a. "Taiwan's socioeconomic modernization, 1971–1996." In *Taiwan: A New History*, ed. Murray A. Rubinstein, 366–402. Armonk, NY: M. E. Sharpe.

Rubinstein, Murray A., ed. 1994. *The Other Taiwan: 1945 to the Present.* Armonk, NY: M. E. Sharpe.

———. 1999b. *Taiwan: A New History.* Armonk, NY: M. E. Sharpe.

Said, Edward W. 1993. *Culture and Imperialism.* New York: Alfred A. Knopf.

Sarkar, Bhaskar. 2001. "Hong Kong hysteria: Martial arts tales from a mutating world." In *At Full Speed: Hong Kong Cinema in a Borderless World*, ed. Esther C. M. Yau, 159–176. Minneapolis: University of Minnesota Press.

Schivelbusch, Wolfgang. 1988. *Disenchanted Night: The Industrialization of Light in the Nineteenth Century*. Trans. Angela Davis. London: University of California Press.

Scott, James. 1985. *Weapons of the Weak: Everyday Forms of Peasant Resistance*. New Haven: Yale University Press.

Seaman, Gary. 1981. "The sexual politics of karmic retribution." In *The Anthropology of Taiwanese Society*, ed. Emily Martin Ahern and Hill Gates, 381–396. Stanford: Stanford University Press.

———. 1989. "Mu-lien dramas in Puli, Taiwan." In *Ritual Opera, Operatic Ritual*, ed. David Johnson, 155–190. Berkeley: IEAS Publications.

Shattuc, Jane. 1997. *The Talking Cure*. New York: Routledge.

Shen, Mary Chin-Hui. 1999. "Participatory current-affairs talkshows: Public communication revitalized on television." Dissertation, University of Amsterdam.

Shepherd, John R. 1993. *Statecraft and Political Economy on the Taiwan Frontier, 1600–1800*. Stanford: Stanford University Press.

———. 1999. "The island frontier of the Ch'ing, 1684–1780." In *Taiwan: A New History*, ed. Murray A. Rubinstein, 107–132. Armonk, NY: M. E. Sharpe.

Shi Yongqian 施永乾. 1990. "Wailao fanzuilu pingjun meiyue jin baiqi" 外勞犯罪率平均每月近百起 (Foreign laborers commit almost 100 crimes per month). *Qingnian ribao* 青年日報 *(Youth daily news)*, September 29: 3.

Shih, Chih-pin. 1998. "A study of the relationship between media coverage, audience behavior, and sporting events: An analysis of Taiwan professional baseball booster club members." Ph.D. dissertation, University of Northern Colorado.

Shilts, Randy. 1994. *Conduct Unbecoming: Gays and Lesbians in the U.S. Military*. New York: Ballantine Books.

SJRB. Shijie ribao 世界日報 *(World daily)*. Various dates.

Simon, Scott 史國良. 1998. "Zouchu ziji de lu: Taiwan dushi de nütongzhi kongjian yu chuangye" 走出自己的路，台灣都市的女同志空間與創業 (Forging their own paths: Entrepreneurship and lesbian space in urban Taiwan). *Xingbie yu kongjian yanjiushi tongxun* 性別與空間研究室通訊 *(Report of the research group on gender and space)* 5: 73–82.

———. 2001. "Xing yishi, wenhua, yu zhengzhi jingji: Minnan 'tongzhimen' de yanjiu" 性意識，文化，與政治經濟學：閩南「同志們」的經驗 (Sexuality, culture and political economics: Experiences of Minnan 'comrades'). In *Tongzhi Yanjiu* 同志研究 (Queer research), ed. Josephine Ho 何春蕤, 51–88. Taibei: Chuliu Chubanshi 臺北：巨流出版社.

Skoggard, Ian. 1996. *The Indigenous Dynamic in Taiwan's Postwar Development: The Religious and Historical Roots of Entrepreneurship*. Armonk, NY: M. E. Sharpe.

Smart, Josephine. 1988. "How to survive in illegal street hawking in Hong Kong." In *Traders Versus the State: Anthropological Approaches to Unofficial Economies*, ed. Gracia Clark, 99–118. Boulder: Westview Press.

Southeast Asia Human Capital Management Company. 1997. *The Discipline Book of Filipino Maids and Caretakers*. Taipei: SAHCMC.

Stainton, Michael. 1999a. "Aboriginal self-government: Taiwan's uncompleted agenda." In *Taiwan: A New History*, ed. Murray A. Rubinstein, 419–435. Armonk, NY: M. E. Sharpe.

———. 1999b. "The politics of Taiwan's aboriginal origins." In *Taiwan: A New History*, ed. Murray A. Rubinstein, 27–44. Armonk, NY: M. E. Sharpe.

Studwell, Joe. 2002. *The China Dream: The Quest for the Last Great Untapped Market on Earth*. New York: Atlantic Monthly Press.

Su Jinzhang 蘇錦章. 1996. *Jiayi bangqiu shihua* 嘉義棒球史話 (Items from the history of Jiayi baseball). Taibei: Lianjing Chuban Shiye Gongsi 聯經出版事業公司.

Suzuki, Teitaro, and Paul Carus. 1906. *T'ai-shang Kan-ying P'ien: Treatise of the Exalted One on Response and Retribution.* La Salle, IL: Open Court.

Szonyi, Michael. 2002. *Practicing Kinship: Lineage and Descent in Late Imperial China.* Stanford: Stanford University Press.

Tai Po-fan. 戴伯芬. 1994. "Shei zuo tan fan? Taiwan tanfan de lishi xinggou" 誰作攤販？台灣攤販的歷史形構 (Who are vendors? The historical formation of vendors in Taiwan). *Taiwan shehui yanjiu jikan* 台灣社會研究季刊 *(Taiwan: A radical quarterly in social studies)* 17: 121–148.

Tai Wen-feng 戴文鋒. 1997. "Taiwan minjian xinyang Youying Gong kaoshi" 台灣民間信仰有應公考實 (An investigation of cults to the lords of response in Taiwanese popular religion). *Taiwan fengwu* 台灣風物, 46(4): 53–109.

Taipei Government Information Office. 2001. "Taiwan's leader to receive 2001 prize for freedom." http://www.gio.gov.tw/taiwan-website/freedom/, accessed October 17, 2001.

Taipei Journal. 2001. "Taiwan's Chen Shui-bian: A president's progress." July 20.

Taipingshan 太平山. 1971. "Wei-lian-si-bao guan qiu ji" 威廉斯堡觀球記 (A record of watching the game at Williamsport). *Duli Taiwan* 獨立台灣 *(Viva Formosa)* 38: 54–55.

Taiwan Documents Project. 1945. "Surrender order of the Imperial General Headquarters of Japan, 2 September 1945." http://www.taiwandocuments.org/ghq.htm, accessed July 18, 2001.

Taiwan duli jianguo lianmeng de gushi 台灣獨立建國聯盟的故事 (WUFI: A history of World United Formosans for Independence). 2000. Taibei: Qianwei 前衛.

Taiwan Sheng Di Yi Jie Quansheng Yundong Dahui Xuanchuan Zu 臺灣省第一屆全省運動大會宣傳組 (First Taiwan Provincial Games information section), eds. 1946. *Taiwan sheng di yi jie quansheng yundong dahui* 臺灣省第一屆全省運動大會 (The First Taiwan Provincial Games). Taiwan Sheng Di Yi Jie Quansheng Yundong Dahui Xuanchuan Zu 臺灣省第一屆全省運動大會宣傳組.

Tang Funian 唐復年. 1996. "Wailao fanzuilu jienwan shansheng" 外勞犯罪率漸往上升 (The percentage of foreign laborers committing crime rises gradually). *Lianhe bao* 聯合報 *(United daily news)*, Taipei County Edition. June 20: 6.

Tannen, Deborah. 1989. *Talking Voices: Repetition, Dialogue, and Imagery in Conversational Discourse.* Cambridge: Cambridge University Press.

Taylor, Jay. 2000. *The Generalissimo's Son: Chiang Ching-kuo and the Revolutions in China and Taiwan.* Cambridge: Harvard University Press.

Teiser, Stephen F. 1988. "'Having once died and come back to life': Representations of hell in medieval China." *Harvard Journal of Asiatic Studies* 48(1): 433–464.

———. 1993. "The growth of purgatory." In *Religion and Society in T'ang and Sung China*, ed. Patricia B. Ebrey and Peter N. Gregory, 115–145. Honolulu: University of Hawai'i Press.

———. 1994. *The Scripture on the Ten Kings and the Making of Purgatory in Medieval Chinese Buddhism.* Honolulu: Kuroda Institute.

Teng, Emma. 1999. "Taiwan as a living museum: Tropes of anachronism in late-Imperial Chinese travel writing." *Harvard Journal of Asiatic Studies* 59(2): 445–484.

ter Haar, Barend. 1992. *The White Lotus Teachings in Chinese Religious History.* Leiden: E. J. Brill.

———. 1995. "Local society and the organization of cults in early modern China: A preliminary study." *Studies in Central and East Asian Religions* 8: 1–43.

———. 1998. *Ritual and Mythology of the Chinese Triads: Creating an Identity.* Leiden: E. J. Brill.

Thompson, E. P. 1965. *The Making of the English Working Class.* New York: Vintage Press.

Thompson, Laurence G. 1975. "Yu Ying Kung: The cult of bereaved spirits in Taiwan." In *Studia Asiatica: Essays in Felicitation of the Seventy-Fifth Anniversary of Professor Ch'en Shou-yi*, ed. Laurence G. Thompson, 266–277. San Francisco: Chinese Materials Center.

Townsend, Susan C. 2000. *Yanaihara Tadao and Japanese Colonial Policy: Redeeming Empire.* Richmond, UK: Curzon Press.

Tsai Chih Chung 蔡志忠. 1997. *Hungu xianguai* 魂孤仙怪 (Ghosts, fox fairies, and the supernatural). Trans. Wu Jingyu. Singapore: Asiapac.

Tsang, Steve. 1994. "Target Zhou Enlai: The 'Kashmir Princess' Incident of 1955." *China Quarterly* 139: 766–782.

Tseng, Wen-Shing, Kan-Ming Mo, Jing Hsu, Li-Shuen Li, Li-Wah Ou, Guo-Qian Chen, and Da-Wei Jiang. 1988. "A sociocultural study of koro epidemics in Guangdon, China." *American Journal of Psychiatry* 145(12): 1,538–1,543.

Tsu, Timothy. 1998. "Between superstition and morality: Japanese views of Taiwanese religion in the colonial period, 1895–1945." *Zinbun* 33: 31–56.

Tsui Hark. 1997. *A Chinese Ghost Story: Tsui Hark's Animation.* Polygram KK Win's Entertainment Ltd. Cathay Asia.

Tsurumi, E. Patricia. 1977. *Japanese Colonial Education in Taiwan, 1895–1945.* Cambridge: Harvard University Press.

TTO (Taipei Times Online). Various dates. Taipei: Liberty Times Group. http://www.taipeitimes.com/news.

Tuan, Yi-Fu. 1982. *Segmented Worlds and Self: Group Life and Individual Consciousness.* Minneapolis: University of Minnesota Press.

Turner, Bryan. 1996. *The Body and Society.* London: Sage Publications.

Turner, Victor. 1977. "Variations on a theme of liminality." In *Secular Ritual*, ed. Sally F. Moore and Barbara G. Myerhoff, 36–52. Amsterdam: Van Gorcum.

TWRB. Taiwan ribao 臺灣日報 *(Taiwan daily).* Various dates.

Tyne, James A. 1994. "The social construction of gendered migration from the Philippines." *Asian and Pacific Migration Journal* 4(2–3): 589–617.

Tyson, James. 1987. "Christians and the Taiwanese independence movement: A commentary." *Asian Affairs: An American Review* 14(3): 163–170.

United Daily News. 1995a. "Feiyong anqi, bingren zhaogu bingren, niangcheng beiju" 菲傭安琪、病人照顧病人、釀成悲劇 (Filipina maid Angelina, patient took care of patient, caused tragedy). *Lianhe bao* 聯合報 *(United daily news),* November 10: 3.

———. 1995b. "Wailao anxin, zhengfu yaopin zhanglaoshi." 外勞安心，政府要聘「張老師」 (Foreign laborers don't worry, government will employ counselors). *Lianhe bao* 聯合報 *(United daily news),* November 11: 3.

———. 1995c. "Zhiwuren wangxiaomin jiazhong, yeyou guyong wailao kunrao" 植物人王曉民家中，也有雇用外勞困擾 (In Wang Xiaomin's family, there is also trouble employing the foreign laborer). *Lianhe bao* 聯合報 *(United daily news),* November 12: 3.

van Gulik, R. H. [1961] 1974. *Sexual Life in Ancient China.* Leiden, Netherlands: E. J. Brill.

van Veen, Ernst. 1996. "How the Dutch Ran a seventeenth-century colony: The occupation and loss of Formosa, 1624–1662." *Itinerario* 20: 59–77.

Vecchione, Judith, director. 1998. *Tug of War: The Story of Taiwan.* Boston: WGBH.

Wachman, Alan. 1994. "Competing identities in Taiwan." In *The Other Taiwan: 1945 to the Present*, ed. Murray Rubinstein, 17–80. Armonk, NY: M. E. Sharpe.

Wang Ching-Feng and Chian Mei-Fen. 1997. "The Japanese government's legal liability to Comfort Women: A note for Taiwanese Comfort Women's request of restitution to Japan." Taipei: Taipei Women Rescue Foundation. http://taiwan.yam.org.tw/womenweb/conf_women/conf_japan2e.htm, accessed July 18, 2001.

Wang Huimin 王惠民. 1994. *Hongye de gushi* 紅葉的故事 (The story of Maple Leaf). Taibei: Minshengbao She 民生報社.

Wang, I-Shou. 1980. "Cultural contact and the migration of Taiwan's aborigines: A historical perspective." In *China's Island Frontier: Studies in the Historical Geography of Taiwan*, ed. Ronald G. Knapp, 31–54. Honolulu: University of Hawai'i Press.

Wang Jing 王晶, director. 1992. *Xin ludingji* 新鹿鼎記 (Royal tramp). Xianggang: Yongsheng Dianying Gongsi 香港：永盛電影公司.

Wang Li-rong 王麗容. 1997. "Waiyong zhengce yu funü laodong zhengce zhi guanxi" 外傭政策與婦女勞動政策之關係 (The relations between the Foreign Maid Policy and

Women's Labor Policy). Paper presented at the Conference on Foreign Maid Policy and State Development, April. Taipei.

Wang Peiyuan 王培元. 1996. "Zhuyi wu feilao, yiganran banzhen shanghan, yixue zhuanjia zhuancheng nanxia huizhen 竹醫五菲勞，疑感染斑疹傷寒，醫學專家專程南下會診 (Five Filipino laborers in Xin-zhu Hospital are suspicious of infection with scrub typhus, medical specialists take a special trip down south to check it out). *Zili zaobao* 自立早報 *(Independent morning post)*, August 24: 5.

Wang, Peter Chen-main. 1999. "A bastion created, a regime reformed, an economy reengineered, 1949–1970." In *Taiwan: A New History*, ed. Murray A. Rubinstein, 320–338. Armonk, NY: M. E. Sharpe.

Wang Weifan 王偉芳. 1995. "Wailao jianjian 59 ren amibaliji, qizhong ren shi Feiji nüyong, waishu yu guzhu danxin quebao jiating chengyuan jiankan" 外勞健檢59人阿米巴痢疾，其中五人是菲籍女傭，衛署籲雇主當心確保家庭成員健康 (The health check of foreign laborers found 59 cases of amoebic dysentery, five of them were Filipina maids, Department of Health called upon employers' attention to ensure the health of the family members). *Zhonghua ribao* 中華日報 *(Chinese daily news)*, December 23: 13.

Wang Yigang 王一剛. 1960. "Riju chuqi de xisu gailiang yundong" 日據初期的習俗改良運動 (The customs-improvement movement of the early Japanese occupation). *Taibei wenwu* 台北文物 *(Cultural relics of Taibei)* 9(2–3): 13–22.

Wang Yinfan 王吟芳. 1997. "Wailao sha guzhu, panxing shier nian" 菲勞殺雇主，判刑十二年 (The foreign laborer who killed employer is sentenced to 12 years). *Zili zaobao* 自立早報 *(Independence morning post)*, May 23: 5.

Ward, J. S. M., and W. G. Stirling. 1925. *The Hung Society or the Society of Heaven and Earth*. Vol 1. London: Baskerville Press.

Webster's Collegiate Dictionary (10th ed.). 1995. Springfield, MA: Merriam-Webster Inc.

Weller, Robert P. 1996. "Matricidal magistrates and gambling gods: Weak states and strong spirits in China." In *Unruly Gods: Divinity and Society in China*, ed. Meir Shahar and Robert P. Weller, 250–268. Honolulu: University of Hawai'i Press.

———. 1999. *Alternate Civilities: Democracy and Culture in China and Taiwan*. Boulder: Westview Press.

Weng Chia-yin 翁佳音. 1995. *Zaoqi Taiwan shi* 早期台灣史 (Early Taiwan history). National Taiwan University course, fall semester.

Whiting, Robert. 1989. *You Gotta Have Wa*. New York: Vintage Books.

Wieger, Léon. [1913] 1981. *Moral Tenets and Customs in China*. Trans. L. Davrout. Ho-kien-fu: Catholic Mission Press. Reprinted New York: Garland Publishing.

Williams, C. A. S. 1941. *Outlines of Chinese Symbolism and Art Motives*. Shanghai: Kelley and Walsh.

Williams, Jack F. 1980. "Sugar: The sweetener in Taiwan's development." In *China's Island Frontier: Studies in the Historical Geography of Taiwan*, ed. Ronald G. Knapp, 219–251. Honolulu: The University of Hawai'i Press.

Williams, Jack F., and Ch'ang-yi Chang. 1994. "Paying the price of economic development in Taiwan: Environmental degradation." In *The Other Taiwan: 1945 to the Present*, ed. Murray A. Rubinstein, 237–256. Armonk, NY: M. E. Sharpe.

Wills, John E., Jr. 1999. "The seventeenth-century transformation: Taiwan under the Dutch and the Cheng regime." In *Taiwan: A New History*, ed. Murray A. Rubinstein, 84–106. Armonk, NY: M. E. Sharpe.

Wilson, Jeffrey P. 1993. "Taiwan enters the big leagues: A look at disputes involving foreign professional baseball players." *For the Record* 4(5): 3–4.

Wolf, Arthur P. 1974. "Gods, ghosts, and ancestors." In *Religion and Ritual in Chinese Society*, ed. Arthur Wolf, 131–182. Stanford: Stanford University Press.

———. 1976. *Childhood Association, Sexual Attraction, and Fertility in Taiwan*. Albuquerque: University of New Mexico Press.

———. 1995. *Sexual Attraction and Childhood Association: A Chinese Brief for Edward Westermarck*. Stanford: Stanford University Press.
Wolf, Arthur P., and Chieh-shan Huang. 1980. *Marriage and Adoption in China, 1845-1945*. Stanford: Stanford University Press.
Wolf, Margery. 1968. *The House of Lim*. New York: Meridith Corporation.
———. 1972. *Women and the Family in Rural Taiwan*. Stanford: Stanford University Press.
———. 1974. "Chinese women: Old skills in a new context." In *Women, Culture and Society*, ed. Michelle Zimbalist Rosaldo and Louise Lamphere, 157–172. Stanford: Stanford University Press.
Woo, Jennie Hay. 1991. "Education and economic growth in Taiwan: A case of successful planning." *World Development* 19(8): 1,029–1,044.
Wu, Cheng-han. 1988. "The temple fairs in late Imperial China." Ph.D. dissertation, Princeton University.
Wu, Fatima. 1986. "Foxes in Chinese supernatural tales (Part 1)." *Tamkang Review* 17(2): 121–154.
Wu Huilin 吳惠林. 1994. "Taiwan chanye jiegou zhuanbian yu chanye kongdonghua" 台灣產業結構轉變與產業空洞化 (The structural changes of industry in Taiwan). In *Taiwan jingji de qiji, weiji yu zhuanji* 台灣經濟的奇蹟，危機與轉機 (The miracle, crisis and transformation of economics in Taiwan), 183–206. Taibei: Zhengzhong 正中.
Wu Micha 吳密察. 1996. *Zhimindi yu zhanzheng* 殖民地與戰爭 (The colonial and wartime eras). National Taiwan University course, spring semester.
Wu Wenxing 吳文星. 1986. "Riju shiqi Taiwan de fangzu duanfa yundong" 日據時期臺灣的放足斷髮運動 (The antifoot-binding and hair-cutting movements in Japanese-occupied Taiwan). *Zhongyang yanjiuyuan Minzuxue yanjiusuo zhuankan yizhong zhi 16* 中央研究院民族學研究所專刊乙種之16 (Academia Sinica Anthropological Institute special publication no. 16), 69–108.
———. 1987. "Riju shiqi Taiwan zongdufu tuiguang Riyu yundong chutan" 日據時期臺灣總督府推廣日語運動初探 (An investigation into the Taiwan colonial administration's Japanese language promotion campaigns during the Japanese occupation). *Taiwan fengwu* 臺灣風物 (Taiwan folkways) 37(1, 4): 1–31, 53–86.
———. 1995. *Riju shidai Taiwan* 日據時代台灣 (Taiwan in the Japanese era). National Taiwan Normal University course, fall semester.
Wu Ying-t'ao 吳瀛濤. 1987. *Taiwan minsu* 臺灣民俗 (Taiwanese folkways). Taipei: Chungwen.
Wu Yuanhua 吳媛華. 1992. "Feifa wailao, tainan feinü zuiduo" 非法外勞，泰男菲女最多 (Most illegal foreign laborers are Thai males and Filipina). *Lianhe bao* 聯合報 (United daily news), April 29: 6.
Wu Zimu. [1921] 1980. "Menglianglu" 夢梁錄 (Record of the splendors of Hangzhou City). In *The Collection of Dongjing menghualu wai shizhong* 東京夢華錄外四種, 129–328. Taibei: Dali 台北：大立.
Xardel, Dominique. 1994. *The Direct Selling Revolution: Understanding the Growth of the Amway Corporation*. Cambridge: Blackwell.
Xia Zhiqian 夏之乾. 1990. *Shenpan* 神判 *(Divine justice)*. Shanghai: Sanlian shudian.
Xiao Xinhuang 蕭新煌 (Hsiao, Michael Hsin-huang). 1988. *Shehuixue de ziwei* 社會學的滋味 (The taste of sociology). Taibei: Dongdai 東大.
———. 1989. "Jiegou zhuanxing yu shehuili de chongzu" 結構轉型與社會力的重組 (Structural transformation and the restructuring of social forces). In *Shehuili: Taiwan xiang qian kan* 社會力：台灣向前看 (Social forces: Taiwan looking forward), 37–48. Taibei: Zili Wanbao 自立晚報.
Xiao Xueliang 蕭學良. 1992. *Baihua yuli* 白話玉曆 (Colloquial "Jade Almanac"). Taipei: privately published reprint. (Original date probably second quarter of twentieth century.)
Xingzhengyuan Gongping Jiaoyi Weiyuanhui 行政院公平交易委員會 (Fair Trade Commission, Executive Yuan, ROC). 1993. *Zhonghua minguo bashiyi nian Taiwan diqu*

duo cengci chuanxiao shiye ji canjiaren jingying gaikuang diaocha baogao 中華民國八十一年台灣地區多層次傳銷事業暨參加人經營概況調查報告 (The 1992 survey report of direct selling in Taiwan). Taibei: Xingzhengyuan Gongping Jiaoyi Weiyuanhui 行政院公平交易委員會.

——. 1995. *Zhonghua minguo bashisan nian Taiwan diqu duo cengci chuanxiao shiye ji canjiaren jingying gaikuang diaocha baogao* 中華民國八十三年台灣地區多層次傳銷事業暨參加人經營概況調查報告 (The 1994 survey report of direct selling in Taiwan). Taibei: Xingzhengyuan Gongping Jiaoyi Weiyuanhui（行政院公平交易委員會）.

——. 1996. *Zhonghua minguo bashisi nian Taiwan diqu duo cengci chuanxiao shiye ji canjiaren jingying gaikuang diaocha baogao* 中華民國八十四年台灣地區多層次傳銷事業暨參加人經營概況調查報告 (The 1995 survey report of direct selling in Taiwan). Taibei: Xingzhengyuan Gongping Jiaoyi Weiyuanhui (行政院公平交易委員會).

Xingzhengyuan Zhujichu 行政院主計處 (Directorate General of Budget Accounting and Statistics, Executive Yuan, ROC). 1995. *Zhonghua minguo tongji nianjian* 中華民國統計年鑑 (Annual statistical report of the Republic of China). Taibei: Xingzhengyuan Zhujichu 行政院主計處.

Xiu Ruiying (修瑞瑩). 1997. "Feiyong lihuan mafongbing, guzhu keneng be chuanran, tongyi wuyang xia, shenghuo jin yinian, kejie feimo kongqi ji pifu jiechu ganran, qianfuqi chang, binghuan shanyue yi chujing" 菲傭罹患痲瘋病，雇主可能被感染，同一屋簷下，生活近一年，可籍飛沫空氣及皮膚接觸感染、潛伏期長，病患上月已出境 (Filipina maid diagnosed with leprosy, the employer might be infected for they had lived together under the same roof for almost one year. Leprosy can be transmitted through air and skin contact. The incubation period is long. The patient had left Taiwan last month.) *Lianhe wanbao* 聯合晚報 *(United evening news)*, March 7: 5.

Xu Guotu 徐國涂. 1997. "Wailao fanzuilu you piangao xianxiang" 外勞犯罪率有偏高現象 (The crime rate of foreign labor appears to be high). *Lianhe bao* 聯合報 *(United daily news)*, Jan. 17: 6.

Xu Jiayou 許嘉猷. 1994. "Jieji jiegou de fenlei, dingwei yu guji: Taiwan he Meiguo de shizheng yanjiu" 階級結構的分類，定位與估計：台灣和美國的實證研究 (The categories, definitions, and estimation of class structures: An empirical comparison of Taiwan and the U.S.). In *Jieji jiegou he jieji yishi bijiao yanjiu lunwenji* 階級結構和階級意識比較研究論文集 (Collection of comparative studies of class structures and consciousness), ed. Zhongyang Yanjiuyuan 中央研究院 (Academia Sinica), 21–72. Taibei: Zhongyang Yanjiuyuan 中央研究院.

Xu Rongshu zhanbao 許榮淑戰報 (Xu Rongshu's war bulletin). 1991. 3.

Yan Xiang-luan 嚴祥鸞. 1997. "Waiyong zhengce zai guojia fazhang de yiyi: Cong nüxing zhuyi tanqi" 外傭政策在國家發展的意義—從女性主義談起 (The meaning of the Foreign Maid Policy in state development: A feminist perspective). Paper presented at the Conference on Foreign Maid Policy and State Development, April. Taipei.

Yan, Yunxiang. 1997. "The triumph of conjugality: Structural transformation of family relations in a Chinese village." *Ethnology* 36: 191–212.

Yang, Martin M. C. 1970. *Socio-Economic Results of Land Reform in Taiwan*. Honolulu: East-West Center Press.

Yao Han-ch'iu 姚漢秋. 1981. "Cong Minnan fengsu tan Taiwan de yifeng yisu" 從閩南風俗談台灣的移風移俗 (A discussion of the spread of customs to Taiwan based on a study of southern Min customs). *Taiwan wenxian* 台灣文獻 32(2): 99–122.

Yeh, Michelle, and N. G. D. Malmqvist. 2001. *Frontier Taiwan: An Anthology of Modern Chinese Poetry*. New York: Columbia University Press.

Yi wei Taiwanren 一位台灣人. 1972. "Binzhou qiusai changbian wuda xiaoji" 賓州球賽場邊武打小記 (A short record of the fighting outside the ballpark in Pennsylvania). *Duli Taiwan* 獨立台灣 *(Viva Formosa)* 50: 45–46.

You Jianming 游鑑明. 1988. *Riju shiqi Taiwan de nüzi jiaoyu* 日據時期臺灣的女子教育 (Female education in Taiwan during the Japanese occupation). Taibei: Guoli Taiwan Shifan Daxue Lishi Yanjiusuo 國立台灣師範大學歷史研究所.

Yu, Anthony C. 1987. "Rest, rest, perturbed spirit: Ghosts in traditional Chinese prose fiction." *Harvard Journal of Asiatic Studies* 47(2): 397–434.

Yu Renqin 于仁泰, director. 1993. *Bai fa mo nü zhuan* 白髮魔女傳 (The bride with white hair). Xianggang: Dongfang Dianying Faxing Gongsi 香港：東方電影發行公司.

Yu, Shuenn-Der. 1995. "Meaning, disorder, and the political economy of night markets in Taiwan." Ph.D. dissertation, University of California at Davis.

———. 1997. "Duili yu tuoxie: Shilun yeshi yu guojia de guan xi." 對立與妥協：試論夜市與國家的關係 (Opposition and compromise: An analysis of the relationship between night market traders and Taiwan's state). *Zhongyang Yanjiuyuan Minzuxue Yanjiusuo Jikan* 中央研究院民族學研究集刊 (*Bulletin of the Institute of Ethnology, Academia Sinica*) 82: 115–174.

Yung, Wing. [1909] 1978. *My Life in China and America.* New York: Arno Press.

Zeng Wencheng 曾文誠. 1997. "Zhibang caochuang: Bilu lanlü" 職棒草創蓽路藍縷 (The early years of professional baseball: The hard life of pioneers). *Zhiye bangqiu* 職業棒球 (*Professional baseball*) 167–168: 21–24.

Zerubavel, Eviatar. 1981. *Hidden Rhythms: Schedules and Calendars in Social Life.* Chicago: University of Chicago Press.

ZGSB. *Zhongguo shibao* 中國時報 (*China times*). Various dates.

Zhan Deji 詹德基. 1985. "Woguo bangqiu yundong de fawei yu zhanwang" 我國棒球運動的發微與展望 (The development of and perspectives on our nation's baseball movement). *Jiaoyu ziliao jikan* 教育資料季刊 (*Educational information quarterly*) 10: 433–483.

Zhan Huosheng 詹火生. 1991. "Wailao yu waiyong" 外勞與外傭 (Foreign laborers and foreign maids). *Zhongshi wanbao* 中時晚報 (*China evening times*), February 29: 3.

Zhang Guanzi 張冠梓. 2000. *Lun fa de chengzhang: Lai zi Zhongguo nanfang shandi falu minzuzhi de quanshi* 論法的成長—來自中國南方山地法律民族誌的詮釋 (The development of law: Interpretations of ethnographies on law from the mountains of south China). Beijing: Shehui Kexue Wenxian Chubanshe.

Zhang Liwen 張黎文. 1996. "Feinügong chuxian bumin zhengzhuang, youyou wuqi" 菲女工出現不明症狀、又有五起 (There are five more cases of Filipina workers suffering from unknown illness). *Zhongguo shibao* 中國時報 (*China times*), December 5: 9.

Zheng Lizhong 鄭禮忠. 1994. "Zhumeng de ren" 逐夢的人 (The people chasing dreams). *Zhongguo shibao* 中國時報 (*China times*), November 26: 29.

Zheng Meili 鄭美里. 1997. *Nüerquan: Taiwan nütongzhi de xingbie, jiating yu quannei shenghuo* 女兒圈：台灣女同志的性別、家庭與圈內生活 (Girls' circle: Gender, family and community life of Taiwanese lesbians). Taibei: Nushu Wenhua 臺北：女書文化.

Zheng Sanlang 鄭三郎, ed. 1993. *Jianong koushu lishi* 嘉農口述歷史 (Oral histories of the Jiayi Agriculture and Forestry Institute). Jiayi: Guoli Jiayi Nongye Zhuanke Xuexiao Xiaoyouhui 國立嘉義農業專科學校校友會.

Zheng Xifu 鄭喜夫, ed. 1981. *Minguo Qiu Canghai xiansheng Fengjia nianpu* 民國丘倉海先生逢甲年譜 (A chronological biography of Mr. Qiu Canghai [Fengjia] of the republic). Taibei: Taiwan Shangwu Yinshuguan 台灣商務印書館.

Zhong Jie 鍾傑. 1991. "Gei liwei zhouquan de gongkai xin" 給立委周荃的公開信 (A public letter to legislator Zhouquan). *Taiwan shiba* 台灣時報 (*Taiwan times*), March 14: 8.

"Zhonghua Zhibang lianmeng jianjie" 中華職棒聯盟簡介 (Brief introduction to the CPBL). 2002. Taibei: Zhonghua Zhiye Bangqiu Lianmeng. http://www.cpbl.com.tw/html/cpbl.asp, accessed November 17, 2002.

Zhou Guangyuan. 1995. "Beneath the law: Chinese local legal culture during the Qing." Ph.D. dissertation, University of California at Los Angeles.

Zhou Mi. 周密. [1922] 1983. *Wulin jiushi* 武林舊事 (Former events in Wulin [Hangzhou]). Taibei: Shangwu (台北：商務).

ZYSB. *Ziyou shibao* 自由時報 (*Liberty times*). Various dates.

Contributors

Alice Chu received her Ph.D. from the Anthropology Department at the University of Texas at Austin. Her dissertation, entitled "Political TV Call-in Shows in Taiwan: Animating Crisis Discourses through Reported Speech," examines the linguistic strategies that call-in show participants use to produce, contest, and reconfigure Taiwan's sociopolitical crisis discourses. She has also published an article, "Pop Politics and TV Call-in Shows in Taiwan: (Re)framing Sociopolitical Discourse and Identities through Verbal Utterances," on this topic in *East Asia Forum* (vol. 8/9, fall 1999).

Chien-Juh Gu is a Ph.D. candidate in the Department of Sociology at Michigan State University. She received her M.A. in sociology from National Taiwan University, investigating direct selling culture. Her present research interests include gender and mental health, medical sociology, and the sociology of the body. She has published an article on gendered body images among Taiwanese immigrants in 2001, and another one is forthcoming on gender issues in Taiwan. Currently Gu is working on her dissertation, which examines how transnational context interplays with gender in shaping Taiwanese Americans' emotional life.

David K. Jordan is professor of anthropology at the University of California, San Diego, where he has taught since receiving his Ph.D. in anthropology from the University of Chicago in 1969. He is the author of *Gods, Ghosts, and Ancestors: Folk Religion in a Taiwan Village* (1976, 1985) and coauthor with Daniel L. Overmyer of *The Flying Phoenix: Aspects of Sectarianism in Taiwan* (1986). In recent years he has also headed one of UCSD's six undergraduate colleges.

Paul R. Katz is an associate research fellow at the Institute of Modern History, Academia Sinica, Taiwan. His main publications include: *Demon Hordes and Burning Boats: The Cult of Marshal Wen in Late Imperial Chekiang* (Albany: SUNY Press, 1995), *The Cult of the Royal Lords in Taiwan* (in Chinese) (Taipei: Shang-ting Publishing Company, 1997), and *Images of the Immortal: The Cult of Lü Dongbin at the Palace of Eternal Joy* (Honolulu: University of Hawai`i Press, 1999). At present, he is completing research on an anti-Japanese religious rebellion that erupted in southern Taiwan during the summer of 1915.

Chin-ju Lin is a post-doctoral research fellow in the Institute of Sociology, Academia Sincia. She received her Ph.D. in sociology from the University of Essex. Her Ph.D. thesis, "Transforming Patriarchal Kinship Relations: Four Generations of 'Modern Women' in Taiwan, 1900–1999," explores the interconnections between employment and reproductive work and examines the relationships between patriarchal kinship and exploitation of women in the family. Her publications include *Filipina Domestic Workers in Taiwan: Structural Constraints and Personal Resistance* (Taipei: Taiwanese Grassroots Women Workers Center, 1999) and "The State Policy that Divides Women: Rethinking Feminist Critiques of the 'Foreign Maid Policy' in Taiwan" in *Taiwan: A Radical Quarterly in Social Studies* 39 (2000).

Andrew D. Morris is assistant professor of history at the California Polytechnic State University, San Luis Obispo, specializing in modern Chinese and Taiwanese history. He received his Ph.D. in modern Chinese history at the University of California at San Diego in 1998. His book *Marrow of the Nation: A History of Sport and Physical Culture in Republican China* will be published by the University of California Press in 2004. He also has published several articles in journals and edited collections on sports and physical culture in Republican-era and contemporary China and on the Taiwan Republic of 1895.

Marc L. Moskowitz is an assistant professor in the Department of Sociology and Anthropology at Lake Forest College. He received his Ph.D. in cultural anthropology at the University of California at San Diego in 1999. He has also published *The Haunting Fetus: Abortion, Sexuality, and the Spirit World in Taiwan* (University of Hawai'i Press, 2001).

Scott Simon is assistant professor in the Department of Sociology, University of Ottawa. His research is focused primarily on minority entrepreneurs and development in Taiwan, including the gay and lesbian business community. He is the author of *Sweet and Sour: Life Worlds of Taipei Women Entrepreneurs* (Rowman and Littlefield, 2003).

Shuenn-Der Yu is an assistant research fellow in the Institute of Ethnology, Academia Sinica. He received his Ph.D. from the University of California at Davis in 1995. His dissertation was entitled "Meaning, Disorder, and the Political Economy of Night Markets in Taiwan." He has published several articles in Chinese on both economic and medical anthropology.

Index

References to illustrations are in **boldface**.

Aborigines: in contemporary era, 28, 220n.26, 228nn.49, 50, 238; under Dutch rule, 8, 219n.4; under Japanese rule, 14, 16-17, 132, 219n.10; as original population, 3, 6, 7; under Qing rule, 11, 219n.6; in Taiwan baseball, 178, 182, 186, 196-197, 198-199, 203, 233nn.7, 14
Academia Sinica, 71, 85
A. C. Nielsen, 92, 225n.4
AG Gym Incident, 79, 81-82, 84
AIDS, 78, 229n.7
Amei. *See* Zhang Huimei
Ami tribe, 178, 233n.7
Amway Corporation, 150, 151, 152, 154, 157-172, 232n.11; and collective bodily order, 159, 162-165, 166-167, 168; history, 157-158; as quasi-educational institute, 160, 165; quasi-familial bonds, 159, 164, 169, 232nn.4, 7; as quasi-religious organization, 158, 159-162, 165, 169; reward system, 160, 166, 171-172; value system, 158, 159, 160, 163-167, 170-171
Andō Likichi, 19, 220n.20
anti-footbinding movement, 15
anti-KMT opposition movement *(dangwai)*, 21-23, 95, 226nn.11, 12, 21, 237, 238; dissidents, 25, 26, 185-186; pro-independence terrorism, 220n.24
anti-Qing revolts, 10-12, 219n.6
Ao Youxiang, 192-194
assimilation, official doctrine under Japanese. *See* Japan, *dōka* assimilation policy

Austronesians. *See* Aborigines
Avon, 152, 154

Bai Bingbing, 99
Bai Xianyong, 68-69, 76, 82
bars, gay, 74, 76, 77, 79
baseball, 175-203; and Cold War, 182-184; and global/local dialectic, 177, 196; International Baseball Association Championships (2001), 202; in Japanese colonial era, 175, 176, 177-180, 202; Little League baseball in Nationalist era, 175, 180-186; as mode of assimilation and resistance to Japanese, 178-180; as national game, 176, 179, 203; and national image, 175, 182-186; in 1992 Olympics, 190, 199, 200; in Qing, 232n.3; Taiwan Baseball Federation (1915), 178; Taiwan Baseball Year (2001), 176; Taiwan Province Baseball Committee, 181; and Taiwanese identity, 176, 182-186. *See also* Chinese Professional Baseball League; Taiwan Major League
baseball teams, Chinese Professional Baseball League: Brother Elephants, 187, 188, 192, 200; China Times Eagles, 188, 190, 200, 234n.30; China Trust Whales, 184, 194, 199, 200; Jungo Bears, 188, 190, 194; Mercuries Tigers, 187, 188, 194, 200, 201; President Lions, 187, 188, 200, 234n.34; Sinon Bulls, 194-195, 200, 234n.22; Weichuan Dragons, 187, 192, 200, 201
baseball teams, Major League Baseball (US): Atlanta Braves, 196; California Angels,

233n.19; Cleveland Indians, 233n.19; Colorado Rockies, 201; Houston Astros, 194; Los Angeles Dodgers, 188, 194–195, 201; New York Mets, 233n.19; New York Yankees, 201; San Diego Padres, 188, 194, 233n.19
baseball teams, Nippon Professional Baseball (Japan): Chunichi Dragons, 183, 188, 201, 233n.20; Hanshin Tigers, 179; Mainichi Orions, 179; Nankai Hawks, 233n.7; Orix Blue Wave, 196; Seibu Lions, 196, 201; Tokyo (Yomiuri) Giants, 178, 189–190, 233n.15; Tokyo Senators, 233n.7
baseball teams, PRC: PRC National Team, 200, 234n.33; Tianjin Lions, 234n.33
baseball teams, ROC: Shanghai Pandas, 181; Taiwan Charcoal, 181; Taiwan Power, 181; Taiwan Sugar, 181
baseball teams, Taiwan Little League: Jiayi Seven Tigers, 184; Maple Leaf (Hongye) Elementary School team, 182–183, 202, 203, 233n.11; Puzi Elementary School Tornadoes, 184, 234n.31; Taibei Braves, 185; Tainan Giants, 184, 185; Taizhong Golden Dragons, 183
baseball teams, Taiwan Major League: Gaoxiong-Pingdong Fala (Thunder Gods), 176, 196, 197, 201; Jiayi-Tainan Luka (Braves), 196, 197, 198, 232n.1, 233n.14; Taibei Gida (Suns), 196, 197, 233n.14; Taizhong Agan (Robots), 176, 196, 197, 198
baseball teams, youth (Japanese era): Kanō (Jiayi Agriculture and Forestry Institute), 178; Nōkō (High-Ability) Team, 178, 181; Takasago Baseball Team (Ami tribe), 178
benshengren. *See* Taiwanese
Best Line Company, 153
Between Us, 83, 87, 224n.1
blackfacing, 105
blood covenant, 36, 47
Buddhism, 43, 52–58, 63, 73, 134, 211–212, 222n.3, 222n.4
Bunun tribe, 182

Cai Hongjin, 115
Cai Minghong, 234n.31
Cairo Declaration, 18, 220n.18
call-in shows, 89–108; *Always Speak Your Mind* (*You hua laoshi jiang*), 92, 96, 97, 100, 226n.20; audience, 92–95, 98, 107; callers, 100, 105–107, 108; crisis frame, 89, 91, 97, 99–101, 105, 107, 108; *8 o'clock Loud and Soft Voices* (*Badian da xiao sheng*), 91, 96, 100, 101, 225n.7; *Everyone Let's Deliberate* (*Dajia lai shenpan*), 100; *Face-to-Face Debate* (*Xiang dui lun*), 91, 92, 100; format, 94, 96, 97–98, 100–103, 104–105, 227nn.28, 33; as *kouying*, 91, 94; mania, 91; phone-in polling, 100, 227n.29; ratings, 92–93, 225nn.4, 7; *2100 All People Open Talk* (*2100 Quanmin kaijiang*),

91–92, 95, 96, 97, 100, 101, 103, 104, 225nn.1, 7, 226n.20, 227nn.29, 33, 34, 228nn.56, 57
camphor, 12, 14
Cano, Jose, 188
capitalism, 74–75, 77, 86, 133, 137, 145, 158
Casselberry, William, 152
castration anxiety, 205, 206, 216, 217, 235n.10
CCP. *See* Chinese Communist Party
Changde Street Incident, 79, 80–81, 82, 83, 84
chastity/purity, 208, 211, 212, 214
Chen Chin-feng (Chen Jinfeng), 195, 201, 234n.36
Chen Dafeng, 233n.20
Chen Dashun, 192
Chen Di, 7
Chen Dingnan, 85
Chen Gengyuan, 233n.4
Chen Shengtian, 195
Chen Shui-bian (Chen Shuibian), 28, 30–31, 79, 80, 99, 144, 225n.11, 227n.40, 235n.37, 237, 238; as *bailian*, 102; and baseball, 176, 202, 234n.36; and gay issues, 71, 84, 85, 88; 2000 presidential inauguration, 104, 226n.25, 228n.52, 232n.1
Chen Wanfen, 158–159, 162, 165, 166, 167
Chen Yi, 233n.9
Chen Yixin, 233n.14
Chen Zhiyuan, 183
Chiang Ching-kuo (Jiang Jingguo), 26–27, 220n.24, 237–238, 239
Chiang Kai-shek (Jiang Jieshi), 18, 20, 23–24, 76, 181, 203, 237, 238, 239
chicken-beheading ritual, 35–49, 50; in mainland China, 44–47
Chinese Communist Party, 5, 20, 23, 70, 98, 238
Chinese medicine, 207
Chinese Nationalist Party. *See* KMT
Chinese Professional Baseball League (CPBL, 1990–), 187–195, 196, 197, 198, 199–201, 203, 233nn.17, 19; as "Chinese," 188, 189, 190, 196, 198; foreign players and managers, 187, 191–195, 200, 234n.21, 22, 23, 35; gambling scandal, 199–200, 201, 234nn.30, 31, 33, 34; as global, 187–188, 189, 190, 195; as local, 187–189, 190, 192, 195. *See also* baseball teams, Chinese Professional Baseball League
Chinese Taipei, 6, 29, 195
Christian organizations and beliefs, 73, 84, 85, 87
Churchill, Winston, 220n.18
class (socioeconomic), 86, 113, 116–117, 120, 151, 156, 210, 229n.1
class mobility, 145, 146, 151, 156–157, 160–161, 210
Clinton, William, 71, 99, 221n.29, 224n.2
cockfights, 48–49
Cold War, 23, 182
collective bodily order, 159, 162–165, 166–167, 168
"comfort women," 18

coming out, 80, 85–86, 87. *See also* gay
commodification of sexuality, 77–78
concubinage, 67
Confucian thought and writings, 36, 51, 52, 59–63, 67, 72
conjugality, 72
corruption, 20, 21, 42
Costner, Kevin, 200
Council of Labor Affairs (ROC), 114, 115, 117, 118, 229n.3
CPBL. *See* Chinese Professional Baseball League
cricket, 177, 179
crisis discourse, 89, 91, 97, 99–101, 105, 107, 108
cross-Straits relations, 24, 26, 29–31, 90, 91, 98, 99, 102, 104, 202
cursing, 39; contingent curses, 44

dangwai. *See* anti-KMT opposition
Dante, 224n.18
Daoist bedchamber manuals, 207, 213, 214
decolonization, 180–182
"deep play," 49
Defense of Marriage Act (USA), 71, 224n.2
democracy, 27–28, 31, 92, 94, 99, 148, 238
Democratic Progressive Party (DPP), 27, 28, 69, 70, 79, 95, 98, 99, 103, 104, 106, 226n.21, 228n.53, 237–238
de-Sinicization, 17
de-Taiwanization, 20, 180, 181
DeVos, Rich, 157
direct selling, 150–172; as alternative economic culture, 151, 154, 158, 163, 169, 231n.3, 232n.10; defined, 151–152; history, 152–154; organizations (DSO), 152, 170; role and behavior of distributors, 151–152, 153–154, 164, 166, 167–168, 231n.1, 232n.8; sociocultural factors, 151, 154–157, 170; upline-downline networks, 151–152, 153, 158, 159, 164, 231n.2, 232n.4
discourses, racial/social, 112, 113, 114, 116, 117, 161
dispute resolution/mediation, 35–49
divine justice/punishment, 39, 40, 44, 63
documentary films. *See* movies and documentaries
domestic workers: Filipina, 111–128; Taiwanese, 122, 229n.1
DPP. *See* Democratic Progressive Party
DSO. *See* direct selling, organizations
Dutch, 6, 8, 9

education: under Japanese, 14–15, 20; ROC era, 25, 180
elections. *See* presidential elections
emotional labor, 167
environmental gradation (ROC era), 29
Era Communications, 195
"ethnic other," 113, 114, 118, 126
ethnocentricism, 112–113, 128

ethnopolitical relations, 19–23, 24, 25, 26, 28, 91–92, 97, 98, 101, 106–107, 147, 181, 185–186, 198, 237–238, 239. *See also* Taiwanese, *benshengren;* "mainlanders"
Exodus Prayer and Ministry Center, 84

face, 22, 72, 186
family values, 68
fan clubs, 187
Fan Yun, 85
filial piety, 67–68; in fiction, 60–62, 209–210, 222n.4; and gay sons, 72, 73–74; and hell, 51–52, 59–63
Filipina maids. *See* domestic workers, Filipina; "foreign maids"
films. *See* movies and documentaries
folk culture, 26, 133
food, 135, 140–144; oyster omelets, 130, 143; *xiaochi*, 130, 134, 135, 137, 139, 140–144, 147; Western, 141
foreign domestic workers, 112, 118. *See also* "foreign maids"
"foreign laborers," 118, 119–121
"foreign maids," 112–128; as backward, 112, 121, 127; causing social problems and disorder, 112, 115, 116, 118; and crime, 115, 120; defined, 229n.1; and dirt, 112, 124, 127; and disease, 112, 115, 120–121, 127; exploitation and abuse of, 112, 116, 117, 123–125; feminist opinions on, 116–118; legal status and subjugation, 118–119, 126, 229nn.5, 8, 9, 230n.10; and mental illness, 120, 230n.14; public opinion, 113, 115–118, 120–121; relations with employers, 116, 119, 121–125
Foreign Maid Policy, 114–121, 230n.12
Formosa, 16, 228n.49. *See* Taiwan
fox spirits, 207–209, 210, 213, 235n.10
France, 116, 221n.32; interest in Taiwan, late nineteenth century, 6, 12, 13
Free China, 23–24, 25
Front for Gay/Lesbian Space, 80
Fujian Province (China), 3, 8, 9–11, 44–45
Fudan University, 181
funerals, 58, 63, 73

G&L Magazine, 69, 71, *82, 83*
gambling. *See* Chinese Professional Baseball League, gambling scandal
Gaoxiong Eight, 26
gay: culture in West, 85, 87; Gay and Lesbian Hotline, 86, 225n.9; gay marriage rights, 70, 71, 82, 84–85; gay meeting places and public space, 68–69, 73, 75–76, 79, 85; Gay Pride Movement, 70–71, 82, 83, 85; pressure toward heterosexual conformity, 68, 69, 85; state pressure vs., 79, 80–83, 84, 225n.8. *See also* bars, gay; saunas, gay; United States, homosexuality and gay movement in

Index   273

gay and lesbian commercial establishments, 69, 74, 76–79, 82–83, 86–87
gay community, 68, 70, 71, 74–75, 78–79, 82–85, 86–87; defined, 72
gay identity, 68, 74–75, 78, 82; defined, 72, 79
gender: bias, 102, 227n.43; division of labor, 116; role reversal, 211–212, 216, 236n.12; roles, 205, 206, 211–216, 217. *See also* male fears of women; marriage; sex
Gender/Sexuality Rights Association (Taiwan), 82, 84, 85
Germany, 115; interest in Taiwan, late nineteenth century, 6, 11
ghosts, 56, 204–206, 208–213, 217, 221n.9, 224n.21, 235nn.6, 7, 8, 236n.12
Giles, Brian, 188
Gin Gin Bookstore, 69, 83
globalization, 74–75, 87, 128, 148, 177, 196
GMD. *See* KMT
Gonzalez, Jose, 188
Gotō Shimpei, 14
Great Britain, 36, 47, 220n.11, 229nn.2, 5; interest in Taiwan, late nineteenth century, 6, 11
green silicon island, 6, 29
Guangdong Province (China), 9, 10–11
guest workers. *See* "foreign laborers"; "foreign maids"; migrant workers
Guo Jiancheng, 234n.33
Guo Jinxing, 234n.34
Guo Taiyuan (Kaku Taigen), 186
Guo Yuanzhi (Kaku Genji), 183, 184, 186, **189**, 233n.20
Guomindang. *See* KMT

Hakkas, 10, 28, 103, 147, 237, 238
Haojiao Publishing Company, 79
Harriman, Grey, 84
He Xianfan, 194
hell, 50–63, 222nn.3, 4, 5; and art, 56–58, **57, 60**; and Buddhism, 50, 52–58, 63; and filial piety, 51–52, 59–63. *See also* underworld bureaucracy
heterosexuality: as normative, 72, 205, 206, 213, 217, 236n.12
Ho, Josephine, 84
Hodge, John, 19
Hokkien. *See* Taiwanese, as language
Hoklo, 10, 29. *See* Taiwanese, *benshengren*
Home Rule Movement, 16, 179–180
homophobia, 73
homosexual relationships, 68
homosexuality, 54, 67–88. *See also* gay; lesbian culture
Hong Kong, 90, 116, 132, 157, 200, 206, 214, 228n.50, 231n.3; movie industry, 204, 205, 206, 223n.11, 235n.2
Hong Taishan, 182
Hu, Jason, 221n.30

Huang Pingyang, 189
Huang Qingjing, 194
Huang, Tracy, 80
human rights, 26, 30, 71, 81, 82, 84, 85, 86, 87, 114, 116, 225n.11
Human Rights Bill, 71, 86
Hunter, Nan, 84

Iglesias, Luis, 188
Ilha Formosa, 8. *See also* Formosa
imagined community, 78, 98
indictment ritual, 45–46
Indonesia, 127, 132, 231n.8; Indonesian domestic workers, 112, 123
informal economy, 146, 231n.9. *See also* underground economy
infotainment, 91, 96
International Gay and Lesbian Human Rights Commission, 82
Itô Hirobumi, 12

Jade Almanac, 53–54, 223n.16
Japan, 3, 7, 153; acquisition of Taiwan, 4, 12–13; baseball, 175, 176, 177–180, 182, 183, 186, 188, 189–190, 191, 196, 199, 200, 201, 203, 233nn.7, 16, 17, 235n.38; changing Taiwanese customs, 15, 17, 41; colonial rule of Taiwan, 1895–1945, 14–19, 37–41, 75–76, 133, 135, 177–180, 238; cultural influences on Taiwan, 22, 90, 131, 142, 180, 182, 186, 187, 196, 199, 204, 220n.12, 231n.6, 234n.27; *dôka* assimilation policy, 14, 15, 178–180; educational system, 14, 15; interest in Taiwan, late nineteenth century, 6, 11–13; language, 15, 17, 21, 22; modernization projects, 14–15, 16; Movement to Create Imperial Subjects, 17; war vs. China, 1894–95, 4, 12–13; war vs. China, 1937–45, 17–18, 180, 183. *See also* baseball teams, Nippon Professional Baseball; baseball teams, youth (Japanese era)
Jiang Taiquan, 200, 234n.33
Jiayi: as center of CPBL gambling scandal, 200, 234n.32; as home of Taiwanese baseball, 178, 184, 197–198, 199
Jiji (9/21) earthquake (1999), 99, 197
Jin Chengwu (Kaneshiro Takeshi), 80
Jin Ping Mei, 55–56
Jin Xiuli, 92–96
judicial ritual, 37, 39, 44
justice: quest for, 48–49; class, 116, 118; racial/ethnic, 116, 117

kamikaze dogs, 24
Kangxi Emperor, 9
Ke Fei, 81, 82, 225n.9
Ke Naiying, 78
Kelly, William, 190, 203, 235n.38
Kim Yong Woon, 195

King, Larry, 91, 93, 100
kinship, cultural norms of, 125–128, 211, 217, 230n.19, 235n.5
Kissinger, Henry, 26
KMT (Kuomintang, Guomindang, Chinese Nationalist Party), 4, 70, 99, 106, 133, 177, 179, 187, 198, 202, 221n.28, 228n.55, 230n.2, 237–239; and American support, 23–25, 238; arrival in Taiwan, 19–20, 76, 147, 148, 180; and baseball, 180–183, 185–186, 233n.16; carpetbagging in Taiwan, 20, 181–182; control of media, 94–95; as dominated by "mainlanders," 95, 103, 237, 239; education, 25; fighting communism in Taiwan, 21, 181; land reform, 24, 156; official history of Taiwan, 7; orthodox Chinese identity, 104, 144; rule of Taiwan (1945–2000), 19–28, 237–239; "soft authoritarianism," 24, 27; suppression of dissent, 89, 185–186; Taiwanization, 27, 99, 226n.24; and 228 Incident (February 28, 1947), 5, 21–23, 198, 237, 238, 239; ultra-nationalist secret societies, 26; work to retake Chinese motherland, 24, 90, 226n.22, 239
Kondō Hyōtarō, 178
Korea, 9, 132, 191
Korean War, 23, 182, 238
Kōshien High School Baseball Tournament, 178, 179, 233nn.5, 6
Kuomintang. *See* KMT

labor brokers, 114, 119, 121–124, 126, 230n.16
labor market, 111–112, 115, 154–156
Lai Zhengzhe, 82–83, 87
language: Aboriginal languages, 199, 228n.49; "Beijing language," 103; constructed dialogue, 101, 227n.39; "Formosan language," 103; Huayu, 103–104; Japanese, 15, 17, 21, 22; Mandarin, 25, 95, 103, 228n.48, 238; "national languages," 17, 95, 103; Taiwanese (Hokkien, Hoklo, Minnanyu), 17, 21, 25, 95, 29, 228n.48, 237, 238
Latin Americans: in baseball, 187–188, 196
laws: and cable TV, 95; and employment, 113, 117, 118–119, 229n.1; Law No. 63, 14, 16.
Lee, Ang, 206
Lee Teng-hui (Li Denghui), 25, 27, **42**, 99, 198, 221n.29, 226nn.23, 24, 237, 238
Lefevbre, Jim, 234n.25
Legislative Yuan, 41, 71, 85, 201, 227n.38
Lequeo Pequeno, 6
lesbian culture, 76–77, 86–87, 224n.1; T/*po* distinction, 224n.3. *See also* gay and lesbian commercial establishments
Li Ao, 226n.17
Li Hongzhang, 12
Li Juming, 201
Li Kunzhe, 184
Li Laifa, 199

Li Tao, 91–92, 96, 97, 101, 226n.16, 227nn.35, 37
Li Yajing, 197–198
Li Yingyuan, 103, 227n.44
Li Yuanzhen, 116
Lian Zhan, **42**, 200
Liao Tianding, **28**
Liberal International, 30–31
light industrial sector. *See* small-scale industries
Lin Guixing, 178, 181
Lin Yixiong, 26
Little League, 29, 182–186, 188, 202, 232n.1, 233nn.10, 16. *See also* baseball teams, Taiwan Little League
Liu, Henry, 26
Lu, Annette (Lü Xiulian), 99, 102
Luo Daohou, 233n.7

Ma Yingjiu, 71, 80, 83–84, 87, 225n.11
Macao, 200
Macgowan, John, 45–46
"mainlanders" *(waishengren)*, 5, 26, 28, 91–92, 97, 98, 101, 106–107, 144, 181, 185–186, 198, 228n.58, 237, 238, 239
Malaysia, 132, 229n.5
male fears of women, 205, 206, 207–208, 213–217
Manchu. *See* Qing Dynasty
Mandarin, 25, 95, 103, 228n.48, 238
Manzanillo, Ravelo, 188
Mao Zedong, 56
marriage, 38, 67; and filial piety, 67, 72, 73, 78; and gay men, 68, 70, 71, 72, 73, 78, 85; and ghosts, 56; and monogamy, 67, 72; polygyny, 72, 78
martial arts, 205–206, 236n.12
martial law, 5, 27, 69, 75, 80, 89, 94, 95, 176, 186, 238, 239
Martinez, Teddy, 195
mass media, 94–108, 145; development, 94–95; and politics, 95
Masuda Fukutaro, 37, 38, 40
Mazu, 41, **71**, 178
Meihua system (Amway), 158–159, 165, 166
Mejia, Cesar, 188
Metoyer, Tony, 188
migrant workers, 113–128, 135, 229n.1, 231n.8. *See also* "foreign laborers"; "foreign maids"
Milton, John, 224n.18
Ming Dynasty (1368–1644), 8, 10, 11
Mishima Yukio, 75
Moreno, Jose, 233n.19
mouse association, 153, 157, 160, 169
movies and documentaries, 204–217; audience, 204–205, 206, 210, 212, 223n.11, 235n.2; *The Bride with White Hair*, 236n.12; *A Chinese Ghost Story*, 56, 63, 204, 205–206, 208–217, 223n.12, 235n.1, 236n.12; *A Chinese Ghost Story 2*, 223n.12, 235n.8; *A Chinese Ghost Story 3*, 210, 212, 213, 235n.8, 236n.12; *A Chinese Odyssey Part I*, 236n.12; *A Chinese Odyssey Part*

II, 236n.12; *Crouching Tiger, Hidden Dragon*, 206, 236n.12; *The Demon's Baby*, 236n.12; *Field of Flowers Wedding Events*, 236n.12; *The Mad Monk*, 236n.12; *Maple Leaf Legend*, 203; *Mr. Vampire*, 236n.12; *The Reincarnation of Golden Lotus*, 55–56; *Royal Tramp*, 236n.12; *Trobriand Cricket*, 177; Westerns, as genre, 216. *See also* Hong Kong, movie industry
Mulian, 52
Murdoch, Rupert, 190
Musha (Wushe) Rebellion (1930), 16–17
Mytinger, Lee, 152

Naluwan Corporation, 195–196. *See also* Taiwan Major League
National Central University, 84
National Chenggong University, 69
National Games, China (Seventh, 1948), 181
National Taiwan University, 25, 70, 71, 80, 85, 181
nationalism, 25, 29, 177, 183, 186, 203
Nationalist Party. *See* KMT
nativization. *See* KMT, Taiwanization
New Park, 69, 75, 76, 78, 79–80, 82, 83, 87. *See also* 228 Park
New Party, 98, 99, 225n.3, 226nn.22, 24
night markets, 129–149; and capitalism, 133, 137, 145; compared to day markets, 137–138; contents, 129, 135–137, 138; defined, 131–132, and folk/local culture, 132, 133, 136, 142, 143, 147, 148–149; history, 132–133, 134–137, 140; and leisure, 132, 135, 137, 144; and modernization, 133, 136, 149; and nostalgia, 136, 147; social context, 129–131, 133, 138–140, 141–142, 145; and social mobility, 145–146; and state control, 133, 146, 149, 231nn.7, 10; and Taiwanese identity, 143–144, 147–148; and work ethic, 131, 145–147
Nitobe Inazō, 14, 219n.9
Nixon, Richard, 26, 221n.29
Nu Skin, 152, 154
Nutrilite Company, 152

oaths, 35, 37, 41, 43, 47; gambling on, 42–44
Olympic Games, 29, 190, 194, 199, 200, 220n.22
O'Malley, Peter, 194–195, 234n.24
open talk, 92, 108
opium, 14
opposition *(dangwai)*. *See* anti-KMT opposition movement
"Orphan of Asia," 6, 19, 24
Osuna, Al, 194
Owens, Jesse, 183
Ozaki Hotsuki, 18

Peng Ming-min, 22, 25, 179
People First Party (PFP), 99, 144, 226n.24
phallic imagery, 213–216
Philippines, 3, 7, 9, 111–112, 181, 182, 229n.1, 231n.8

political liberalization, 27–28, 30–31, 69–71, 82–88, 89, 94–95, 98, 108
Portuguese, 8
postindustrial economic structures, 154–156
Potsdam Declaration, 220n.18
PRC (People's Republic of China), 23, 72, 76, 85, 89–90, 113, 132, 148, 162, 177, 182, 183, 185, 206, 214, 221n.29, 228nn.48, 50, 235n.2; baseball in, 195, 200, 234n.33; diplomatic leverage against Taiwan, 29, 202–203, 239; "historical" claims to Taiwan, 29; Maoist era, 23, 24; "reunification" plans, 29–31, 90, 98, 176, 196, 221nn.30, 31, 226n.25, 238, 239; Taiwanese investments in and trade with, 1990s–, 30, 231n.2. *See also* baseball teams, PRC
Presbyterian Church, 70
presidential elections: 1996, 28, 238, 239; 2000, 28, 41, 42, 69, 176, 225n.3, 226n.20, 227n.29, 228n.55, 238
prostitution, 67, 209, 235n.4
Pu Songling, 56, 205, 208, 210, 213
public ritual, 38
Puyuma tribe, 203, 228n.50
pyramid schemes, 151–152, 158–159

Qing Dynasty (1644–1911), 4, 205, 217; cession of Taiwan (1895), 4, 12–13; reforms in Taiwan, 12, 14; rule of Taiwan (1683–1895), 4, 9–13, 18, 29
Qiu Fusheng, 195–196
Queer & Class, 82, 87
Queer Nation, 87

racial identity: Han-Chinese, 113; Han-Taiwanese, 112–113, 114, 126–128
racialization, 113
racism, 112–113, 192–194
radio, 22, 24, 81, 89, 95, 96, 179, 184
Rainbow Community, 71, 82, 83
reality TV, 91
religion: afterlife, 50–63; imagery, 56–58; and law, 35, 48–49, 50; processions, 58
"Retrocession" (1945), 19, 180–182, 220n.18. *See also* KMT, arrival in Taiwan; ROC
"reunification." *See* PRC, "reunification" plans
ritual violence, 47
Rivera, Elvin, 188
ROC (Republic of China), 4, 18, 90, 113, 184, 221n.28, 226n.25, 233n.13, 238, 239; expelled from United Nations, 26; legal claim to Taiwan, 18–19, 220n.18; national anthem, 104, 228nn.51, 53; "Retrocession" (1945), 19, 180, 220n.18; as trustee of Allied Powers for Taiwan, 18. *See also* Taiwan; KMT
Roman, Jose, 233n.19
Ruth, Babe, 179

Sakuma Samata, 178
"saliva wars," 92, 97, 225n.6
Sampo Electronics, 195
saunas, gay, 73, 74, 77–78, 79, 81–82
Senior Little League Championships (Gary, Indiana), 185–186
sex: and male depletion, 207–209, 213–214, 216, 219n.2, 235n.10; and marriage, 67. *See also* castration anxiety; Daoist bedchamber manuals; phallic imagery; saunas, gay
Shanghai Communiqué, 26
Shi Lang, 9–10
Shi Wenbin, 130–131, 148, 230n.1
Singapore, 47, 116, 132, 228n.48, 228n.50, 229n.5
Sino-Japanese War (1894–1895), 4, 12–13
Sinon Agrochemical Corporation, 194
Siraya tribe, 219n.4
small-scale industries, 25, 131–132, 136, 144, 230n.2
"sodomy" anti-gay laws, 73, 79
Song Dynasty (960–1279), 47, 48, 55, 56, 134–135, 137, 140
Song Meiling, 181
Soong, James, 41, **42,** 80, 226n.23
Southeast Asia, 115, 118, 127, 132
Soviet Union, 232n.2
Spanish colonists, 6, 8
Springer, Jerry, 93
Stalin, Joseph, 19
Stonewall, 79, 88
Stoole, Steve, 188
Strange Tales of Liaozhai, The (Liaozhai zhiyi), 205, 208
Sun Yat-sen, 239
superstition, 41

Tai-Jia. *See* Taiwan Family
Taiwan: and world economy, 9, 12, 31, 74–75, 111–112; contemporary reunification discourse, 90, 98, 226n.24, 228n.50; as different from "China," 143, 149, 176, 177, 186, 196, 206, 219n.2, 228n.47, 235n.37; as economic "miracle," 25, 130, 136, 146, 157; export strategy and trade surpluses, 24–25, 29; independence, 28, 90, 98, 99, 103, 185–186, 196, 226n.25, 228n.50, 238; industrial development (ROC), 24–25, 29; investments in and trade with PRC, 30, 231n.2; as island frontier, 10–11; Japanese era, 14–19; as multi-ethnic, multi-cultural nation, 28; national identity, 99, 100, 143–144, 147–149, 176, 177, 182–186, 190, 206, 214; national security, 102–103; Qing Dynasty era, 9–13; as "rice basket" for Japan, 16; ROC era, 19–31; sovereignty, 29, 31, 96, 98, 180; Zheng era, 8–9. *See also* ROC
Taiwan Family (Tai-Jia), 152–153, 169
Taiwan Major League (TML, 1997–2002), 176, 195–199, 201, 203, 233n.14, 234n.28;
"Aboriginal" influence, 196–197, 198–199, as authentically "Taiwanese," 196, 197–199; 234n.29; as globalized, 196, 234n.25, 234n.26; pro-Japanese orientation, 196; "territorial philosophy," 197; theft of CPBL players, 199, 234n.34; "228 Opening Game" tradition, 198. *See also* baseball teams, Taiwan Major League
Taiwan Provincial Games (First, 1946), 181
Taiwan Republic (1895), 13
Taiwan Solidarity Union (TSU), 99, 226n.24
Taiwan Straits. *See* cross-Straits relations
Taiwanese: *benshengren*, 91–92, 97, 98, 99, 101, 106–107, 185–186, 237–239; consciousness, 95; as language (Minnanyu, Hokkien), 17, 21, 25, 95, 219, 228n.49, 237, 238; representation in KMT and ROC, 21, 24, 26, 27; "spirit," 176, 202; views of "mainlanders," 20–22; "volunteers" for Japanese military service, 17–18, 220n.16; welcome given to KMT, 19
Taiwanese Communist Party, 16
Taiwanese political movements: Aboriginal, 220n.26; anti-KMT protests, 21–23, 25, 26; elite public societies, 15, 16; Independence activists, 19, 25, 27, 185–186; political activists, Japanese period, 16–17, 18. *See also* anti-KMT opposition movement *(dangwai)*
Taiwanization *(bentuhua)*, 91, 98; of KMT, 27
talk shows. *See* call-in shows; United States, talk show culture
Tang Dynasty (618–907), 134
Tang Jingsong, 12
Taroko tribe, 16–17
tea, 12, 14, 141
teahouses, 73, 98, 148
television programs, 89. *See also* call-in shows; United States, talk show culture
television stations: CTN (Dadi), 226n.14; ETTV (Dongsen), 97, 226n.14; FTV (Minshi), 226n.14; Global TV (Huanqiu), 226n.14; and KMT, 94–95; Star-TV, 190; TTV, 182–183; TVBS, 95, 96, 226nn.13, 14; TVIS, 190, 196, 199. *See also* underground media, cable television *(disitai)*
temples, 53, 55, 56, 60, 61, 63, 73, 98, 197, 209; Buddhist, 17, 41, 58; to City Gods, 38, 39, 40, 45, 46, 48, 58; Confucian, 9; Daoist, 57, 58; and judicial rites, 35–36, 37, 44–45, 48; and night markets, 129, 133, 135, 136, 137
terrorism, 24, 185, 220n.24
Thailand, 132, 231n.8
Tiburcio, Freddy, 188
TML. *See* Taiwan Major League
Tongguang Christian Church, 85
tongzhi (comrade), 70
transnationalism, 142, 177, 235
Treaty of Shimonoseki, 12–13, 18
tree witches, 209, 213–215
Tsao Chin-hui (Cao Jinhui), 201
Twain, Mark, 203

Index **277**

228 Incident (February 28, 1947), 5, 21–23, 106–107, 181, 237, 238, 239; commemoration, 79–80, 198, 237
228 Park: and gay culture, 79. *See also* New Park

underground economy, 133, 231n.9. *See also* informal economy
underground media: cable television *(disitai)*, 95; radio, 95
underworld deities/bureaucracy, 41, 48, 50–56, 222nn.1, 6, 9
United Nations: 1990s attempt to regain seat, 29–30; ROC withdrawal, 26, 183
United States, 152, 157–158, 202, 221n.29; baseball, 175, 177, 182, 183, 184–185, 186, 187–188, 194–195, 196, 200, 201, 203, 232nn.2, 3, 234n.25; cultural influences on Taiwan, 89, 90, 204, 216, 225n.2; homosexuality and gay movement in, 71, 73, 74, 79, 82–83, 85, 87, 88, 224nn.4, 5, 6, 225n.10; interest in Taiwan, late nineteenth century, 6, 11; recognition of PRC, 25–26; support of KMT, 23–25, 238; talk show culture, 91, 93–94, 95, 97, 100, 225nn.1, 8, 9, 10. *See also* baseball teams, Major League Baseball
"unsinkable aircraft carrier," 6, 23

Valdez, Rafael, 188
Van Andel, Jay, 157
Vasquez, Aguedo, 188
Vidor, Paul, 223n.16
Vietnam, 127

waishengren. See "mainlanders"
Wang Jinping, 201
Wang Junlang, 195
Wang Ping, 82, 84
Warner Village, 83–84
westerners, Taiwanese views of, 118, 127–128, 192–195, 229n.7
white terror, 23, 238, 239
Williams, Montel, 93
Williamsport, Pennsylvania: and Little League World Series, 183–185, 233n.10
Winfrey, Oprah, 93
World Health Organization, 30–31

World Trade Organization, 202
World War II, 17–18, 180, 183
Wu Bo (Kure Masayuki), 178–179, 233n.7
Wu Linlian, 200
Wu Shuzhen, 221n.32
wuxia films, 205–206

xenophobia, 112–113, 114, 115
Xi Shenglin, 91, 92–93
Xiao crime gang, 200, 234n.32
Xiao Juzhen, 203
Xie Dongmin, 220n.24
Xie Zhiwei, 104
Ximending, 75–76
Xu Shengming, 200
Xu Yousheng, 70, 82, 84, 87

Yamane Toshida, 192
Yan Qingbiao, 41, 43
Yang, C. K., 220n.22
Yanluo, 56, 223n.14
Ye Qitian, 230n.2
Ye Tiansong, 233n.7
yin/yang, 206–207, 209, 213, 216, 217, 235n.10
Yŏ Un-hyŏng, 233n.8
Yonamine, Wally, 190
Yu Fu, 96, 101–103, 226n.17, 227n.45
Yu Hongkai, 184
Yu Zhengxian, 176
Yung Wing, 12

Zeng Zhizhen, 189
Zhan Huosheng, 115, 229n.3
Zhang Huimei (Amei), 104, 228n.30
Zhang Xiaohong, 85
Zhang Zhengxian, 234n.31
Zhang Zhenyu, 201
Zhao Shiqiang, 197–198
Zhao Shoubo, 115
Zheng Baisheng, 234n.33
Zheng Chenggong (Koxinga), 8–9
Zheng Jing, 9
Zhou Enlai, 24
Zhou Jinsheng, 97
Zhu Weicheng, 85
Zhu Yigui, 11
Zhuo Kunyuan, 234n.31